Parents and Families of

STUDENTS *With*
SPECIAL NEEDS

I would like to dedicate this book to my immediate family, at the time of this writing, Jim, Nora, Tasha our dog, Fritzy our cat, and Cadbury our rescue bunny. To my extended family, who I am still trying to get to know through researching my family tree with Mom and Dad, parents whom I love and admire for their value of family. To all those families of children with disabilities whom I have worked with over the years and presently still work for today. To those families who have served as host mentor families for my students. I would also like to thank my EDA 503, Family Systems in Special Education course West Chester University students and acknowledge in particular Alyssa, Agavanimari, Michael, Ashley, Kristen, Sarah, Mary, Christine, Jennifer, and Julie for their careful reading.

Vicki McGinley

I would like to dedicate this book to my amazing family, Brett, Hannah, and Eli, my parents, Karma and Gordon, and of course to my sister Rebecca, one of the most dedicated special educators I know. I would also like to thank my amazing colleagues for being the example of collaborative professionals. In addition, I would like to thank all of the families of children with disabilities that I have had the pleasure of working with over the last quarter of a century. You all have taught me what it means to be an advocate for individuals with disabilities and have given me a better understanding of what individuals with disabilities can achieve.

Melina Alexander

Parents and Families of

STUDENTS *With*

SPECIAL NEEDS

Collaborating Across the Age Span

Vicki A. McGinley
West Chester University

Melina Alexander
Weber State University

Los Angeles | London | New Delhi
Singapore | Washington DC | Melbourne

FOR INFORMATION:

SAGE Publications, Inc.
2455 Teller Road
Thousand Oaks, California 91320
E-mail: order@sagepub.com

SAGE Publications Ltd.
1 Oliver's Yard
55 City Road
London EC1Y 1SP
United Kingdom

SAGE Publications India Pvt. Ltd.
B 1/I 1 Mohan Cooperative Industrial Area
Mathura Road, New Delhi 110 044
India

SAGE Publications Asia-Pacific Pte. Ltd.
3 Church Street
#10-04 Samsung Hub
Singapore 049483

Acquisitions Editor: Terri Accomazzo
Editorial Assistant: Erik Helton
Production Editor: Andrew Olson
Copy Editor: Kim Husband
Typesetter: Hurix Systems Pvt. Ltd.
Proofreader: Sue Irwin
Indexer: Robie Grant
Cover Designer: Michael Dubowe
Marketing Manager: Kara Kindstrom

Printed in the United States of America

Library of Congress Cataloging-in-Publication Data

Names: McGinley, Vicki A., editor. | Alexander, Melina, editor.

Title: Parents and families of students with special needs : collaborating across the age span / [edited by] Vicki A. McGinley, West Chester University; Melina Alexander, Weber State University.

Description: Thousand Oaks, California : SAGE, [2018] | Includes bibliographical references and index.

Identifiers: LCCN 2016039120 | ISBN 9781506316000 (pbk. : acid-free paper)

Subjects: LCSH: Children with disabilities—Education—United States. | Special education—Parent participation—United States. | Special education teachers—Professional relationships—United States. | Children with disabilities—Family relationships. | School-linked human services.

Classification: LCC LC4031 .P37 2018 | DDC 371.9—dc23 LC record available at https://lccn.loc.gov/2016039120

This book is printed on acid-free paper.

SUSTAINABLE FORESTRY INITIATIVE
Certified Chain of Custody
Promoting Sustainable Forestry
www.sfiprogram.org
SFI-01268
SFI label applies to text stock

17 18 19 20 21 10 9 8 7 6 5 4 3 2 1

BRIEF CONTENTS

DETAILED CONTENTS

SECTION II • WORKING WITH FAMILIES OF CHILDREN WITH DISABILITIES ACROSS THE LIFESPAN

Chapter 12: Postschool 246

Brian Freedman, Laura Eisenman, Cathy Cowin, Sean Roy

PREFACE

When we began to discuss our work for this text, we were both very excited about addressing working with families of children with disabilities throughout the lifespan. While there are many good texts related to working with families, we have found that in our own work as professionals (teachers, counselors, therapists, etc.) and as parents, there are different knowledge and skills needed when working with families of children with disabilities depending on the life stage of the child. Thus, for this text, we intentionally chose authors that are experts in their field of study, experts that are knowledgeable of the varying levels of child development, as well as parents of children with disabilities and parent professionals. Those voices are heard throughout this text. For many of us who are in higher education, preparing all types of teachers that work with families, we rely on the Council for Exceptional Children (CEC) Standards. CEC is the largest international professional organization that supports us and provides standards for working children with disabilities and their families. Although not repeated in this text, the skills and knowledge standards from CEC for collaborating with families in culturally responsive ways to address the needs of the family and the child are dominant throughout this text. It is imperative that all teachers working with children and their families have a fundamental grasp of the laws, screening and assessment, children at risk for disability and children with disability throughout their lifespan.

Having an opportunity to develop this valuable resource has been an honor and a privilege. Working with this diverse group of authors offers the reader an expert, comprehensive perspective for working with families of children with disabilities throughout the lifespan.

The first section of this book addresses the many formations of diverse families, family systems theory, those groups of children who are at risk for disability, foundations of the laws that impact families, the professionals who work with families, assessment throughout the child's lifespan, and a look at siblings. Chapter 1 gives an in-depth look at family living arrangements and types of families. Chapter 2 covers family systems theory with a look at family identity, the family life cycle, and models of family therapy. Chapter 3 provides a comprehensive look at families of children who are at risk for disability, delving closely into families that suffer risk as a result of sociological and biological variables. Chapter 4 covers the laws that support families of children with disabilities. Chapter 5 takes a look at all of those professionals that work with children with disabilities and their families and their specific roles. Chapter 6 covers the varying assessments used at different lifespan stages as well as some disability-specific assessments. Chapter 7 looks at the role of the sibling, an important family member.

This first section sets the reader up well for the remainder of the text, which covers the child's lifespan, as it is here that early intervention and the primary and secondary school years are addressed, ending with postschool.

Chapter 8 gives an overview of specific disabilities through the life span. Chapter 9 addresses the child and family through the early intervention years. Chapter 10 focuses on the needs in the primary school years, Chapter 11 the secondary school years, and Chapter 12 postschool.

We hope you find this book helpful and poignantly presented, providing knowledge and sensitivity about working with families with children with disabilities.

ACKNOWLEDGMENTS

Writing a textbook takes a lot of time, effort and person power. The goal is to provide an excellent book for the audiences that will benefit from it. Professional and parent experts were called upon to write, edit and review our textbook. As such, we owe a huge debt of gratitude to colleagues who spent many months researching, writing and rewriting their respective chapters. We want to publicly thank them for their dedication to this text. They are:

- Tara S. Guerriero for defining the family
- Sandra Sepulveda-Kozakowski for her work in family systems theory
- Barry Bullis, Samuel Zimmerman for addressing families of children at-risk for disability
- Shirley Dawson, Tracie McLaurghlan, Denise Adams for their research and writing on the laws that support families
- Natalie A. Williams, Kristin L. Nelson, Tori J. Lybert for addressing the professionals and their roles
- Ieva Margevica for her work in family assessment
- Amy F. Conner Love, Lorie Taylor, Lisa P. Turner, Richard Sabousky for supporting siblings of children with disabilities
- Mary A. Houser for her chapter on prominent disabilities across the life span
- Brenda Eaton for addressing children birth through age 5
- Melissa E. Hudson for addressing children in the primary school years
- Desna Bergold for addressing children and adults with disabilities in the secondary school years
- Brian Freedman, Laura Eisenman, Cathy Cowin, Sean Roy for addressing the post school years

We also would like to acknowledge the invaluable contributions from the reviewers of this textbook: M. Robert Aman, Emporia State University; Cynthia R. Chambers, East Tennessee State University; Hank McCallum, Chadron State College; Ariane K. Schratter, Ph.D., Maryville College; Jane E. Baker, PhD, Tennessee Technological University; Bernard J. Graney, Ph.D., Springfield College; René E. Hauser, St. Bonaventure University; Thomas Black, Middle Tennessee State University; Dr. Nicole Dobbins, University of North Carolina Greensboro; Elizabeth J. Erwin, Montclair State University; Georgia M. Kerns, University of New Hampshire; Myung-sook Koh, Eastern Michigan University; Esther E. Onaga, Michigan State University; Jim Siders, The University of Alabama; Leslie C. Soodak, Ph.D., Pace University; Melinda Swafford, Ph.D, Tennessee Technological University; and Donna E. Dugger Wadsworth, Ph.D., University of Louisiana at Lafayette.

We are extremely thankful to the talented team from SAGE Publications who supported our work from day one up to the final product, with the last couple of months being extremely challenging. We appreciate their patience, their professional excellence, and their persistence in supporting us to move along and bring this work to fruition and publication. Specifically, a great deal of thanks goes to Terri Accomazzo, Acquisitions Editor; Andrew Olson, Production Editor; Erik Helton, Editorial Assistant; David C. Felts, Senior Project Editor; and Kara Kindstrom, Senior Marketing Manager, whom we know has faith in us and our work.

One other group deserves acknowledgement: the many mentor families that we and our students have worked with over the years, and the many families we have had the pleasure of serving in schools and communities. Without their questions, striving for excellence for their child, advocacy, and love, this book would not have been possible.

ABOUT THE AUTHORS

Denise Adams is a special education teacher of secondary students with mild to severe disabilities in a suburban school and is also a licensed hairdresser. She has been married to her husband, Jeff, for 26 years and is the mother of two adult children. Her husband and children have disabilities. Her current goals are to learn more about autism to help her students and her family. She enjoys reading, music, arts and crafts, and collecting. In her spare time Denise plays the piano and organ.

Desna Bergold is the founder and owner/operator of DB Consulting and associates, LLC, a small firm specializing in technical writing, meeting organization and support, documentation, facilitation, and training. Before founding DB Consulting, Desna worked for the Utah Department of Transportation for 25 years in Materials and Construction. In the course of her work for UDOT, Desna developed materials acceptance programs and systems manuals, earning her special recognition from the Federal Highway Administration. While working for the UDOT, Desna was the Training Coordinator for the UDOT Transportation Technician Qualification Program (TTQP). In that capacity she developed training materials and trained all UDOT and consultant laboratory and materials inspection personnel in construction materials sampling and testing. Desna also is the parent of a child who was identified as needing special education services.

Barry Bullis, EdS, is an adjunct assistant professor in the special education, childhood, and adolescent departments at Pace University in New York City. Full-time, Barry has spent 23 years in K-12 education as special educator, instructional coach and administrator, and is currently a professional developer, focusing on literacy instruction, for the New York City Department of Education. His experiences have allowed him to work with children of every special education classification. Barry has presented on literacy and special education topics at numerous national and international education conferences.

Cathy L. Cowin, NCC, LPCMH, is the Transition Specialist in Christina School District in Delaware. She oversees transition programming for secondary students who have disabilities, working closely with school staff, families and the community. In her first year she was presented the Council for Exceptional Children (CEC) Division on Career Development and Transition (DCDT) Rookie Transition Specialist of the Year Award. Previous to her current job, she was a parent consultant with the Parent Information Center of Delaware and provided parents and professionals information about special education law. She earned her Master's Degree in Mental Health Counseling and is a Licensed Professional Counselor of Mental Health in the state of Delaware. She has been an adjunct professor at Wilmington University and taught a class about advocacy for counselors. In addition, she has worked with youth who have significant mental health issues and with youth in foster care. She has been appointed by the Governor to the Governor's Advisory Council for Exceptional Citizens and is the Chair of the Adult Transition Committee. She is also the parent of a young adult who has successfully transitioned into the workforce.

Shirley Ann Dawson, assistant professor at Weber State University, holds a Utah Level 3 Teaching Certificate in Elementary Education, Gifted Education, and Special Education. She taught in public schools for over 23 years and has been teaching undergraduate and graduate courses in higher education since 2010 in law, research, collaboration, and transition. Dr. Dawson's research interests include educator ethics and preparing effective teachers. Community involvement centers on advocating for children with disabilities and teacher preparation programs to serve those children.

Brenda Eaton has a Master's Degree from Temple University in Curriculum, Instruction and Technology in Education. She has worked at a Public Educational Agency in PA for 14 years. Ms. Eaton is a Board Certified Behavior Analyst, and is a Coach for neuro-diverse individuals. In addition, Ms. Eaton has developed programs such as the CATCH Team for early diagnosis and entry into Early Intervention. Brenda Eaton is also a parent of a daughter with LD and a son with neuro-diversity.

Laura T. Eisenman, Ph.D., is an associate professor in the University of Delaware's School of Education and affiliated with the University's Center for Disabilities Studies as faculty coordinator for the undergraduate disability studies minor. Her research interests include understanding the social and community experiences of young adults with intellectual and developmental disabilities, exploring the meaning of disability in educational contexts, and the integration of disability studies perspectives into interdisciplinary professional programs. She teaches undergraduate and graduate courses on secondary special education and transition to adult life. She is on the editorial boards of Career Development & Transition for Exceptional Individuals and Review of Disability Studies. She previously worked as a counselor and administrator in community programs for adults with disabilities.

Brian Freedman, Ph.D., is the associate director of the University of Delaware's Center for Disabilities Studies, co-Director for Delaware's Leadership Education in Neurodevelopmental Disabilities (LEND) program, and an assistant professor in the university's School of Education. He oversees a variety of community-based model demonstration programs, including inclusive higher education programs for students with learning disabilities, autism spectrum disorders and intellectual disabilities. He also teaches undergraduate coursework in Disabilities Studies. His research interests include postsecondary transition for students with disabilities, community involvement among adults with disabilities, and factors impacting the experience of raising a child with a disability. Brian has a background in clinical psychology and previously was the clinical director of an interdisciplinary autism clinic.

Mary A. Houser received a BFA in Related Arts from Kutztown University of Pennsylvania, an MAT in Special Education from The College of New Jersey, and an EdD in Educational Leadership from Fayetteville State University. She is currently an Assistant Professor of Special Education at West Chester University of Pennsylvania. She teaches both undergraduate and graduate courses in behavior management, autism spectrum disorders, and family systems. Dr. Houser has also taught graduate special education courses for Walden University where she served as a special education curriculum developer and assessor. In addition, she has taught graduate special education courses and supervised pre-service special education teachers for Campbell University (NC). Dr. Houser has worked as a learning disabilities specialist and has taught high school special education in both inclusive and self-contained settings. Her research interests include families and students with autism spectrum disorders and improving parent-teacher relationships for students with disabilities.

Melissa E. Hudson, assistant professor, is a faculty member at East Carolina University in the Department of Special Education, Foundations, and Research. Melissa has taught both undergraduate and graduate courses in special education, assessment, augmentative and alternative communication, inclusive practices in general education, and teaching learners with multiple and physical disabilities. Melissa's professional experience in special education spans nearly 30 years and includes 10 years of classroom teaching experience for students with moderate and severe disabilities. Melissa's research interests include general curriculum access, alternate assessment, transition, and evidence-based practices for students with moderate and severe intellectual disability and she has published several professional articles and book chapters with colleagues on these and related subjects.

Tara S. Guerriero is an associate professor in the Department of Special Education at West Chester University of Pennsylvania. She teaches at the graduate and undergraduate level in the areas of foundations, assessment, curriculum and instruction/methodology, and communication development and assistive technology. She previously attended Northwestern University where she received her Ph.D. in Learning Disabilities, with a concentration in Cognitive Neuroscience. Dr. Guerriero's research interests include assessment of learning disabilities, inclusive practices associated with special education, and both assessment and teaching within the areas of mathematics and reading in the field of learning disabilities.

Amy Conner Love, associate professor, is a faculty member at Clarion University of PA in the Special Education and Policy Disabilities Studies Department. She has taught both undergraduate and graduate courses in characteristics of exceptionalities, behavioral disorders, applied behavior analysis, teaching reading to individuals with exceptionalities, teaching writing to individuals with exceptionalities, and teaching math to individuals with exceptionalities as well as courses on methods of instruction. Presently, her teaching and service work focus on providing appropriate instruction to struggling learners and advocating for equal opportunities. Her publications reflect her teaching and have been in the areas of literacy and teacher preparation.

Tori Lybbert is a Special Education Teacher at DaVinci Academy in Ogden Utah. She is currently in her Masters of Education at Weber State University. Working with individuals with disabilities has been not only challenging but very rewarding. Tori wishes to continue her education and is always looking to become a better teacher.

Ieva Margeviča-Grinberga, leading researcher, docent, is a faculty member at University of Latvia, Faculty of Education, Psychology and Art in Teacher Education Department. She has taught both undergraduate and graduate courses in foundations of education, educational treatment of diversity, intercultural education, and second and foreign language acquisition. She is an author of international publications about plurilingual and intercultural competence, and about educational programs to tackle social exclusion. She collaborates with partners from Spain, Argentina, Brazil, and the USA on research related to teacher training, social inclusion, intercultural communication and education. She is also a member of RIAICES (Red Iberoamericana de Investigación sobre la Calidad de la Educación Superior) and CiCea (European Children's Identity and Citizenship). Her current interests are related to foreign and second language acquisition, inclusion of minorities in the education workforce in teacher education and educational treatment of diversity in high school.

Tracie McLaughlan is married and a mother of three children, two of which have Autism Spectrum Disorder. She has always loved teaching and helping children. She was an Elementary School Teacher for twelve years before she had her second child. After that, she chose to stay at home instead of teach, so she could meet the needs of her children and get them the help they needed to be successful in life. She has been very involved in her children's schools and has worked tirelessly as their advocate. Her children are now becoming young adults with the last one in his senior year.

Kristin Nelson is an Associate Professor of Practice at Simmons College in Boston, Massachusetts. She received her doctorate in education with a focus on reading/literacy from the University of Utah. She has worked both as a high school English teacher and an elementary school literacy coach. Her recent publications include "Vocabulary Instruction in K-3 Low Income Classrooms During a Reading Reform Project" (Reading Psychology, 2015) and "The Sustainability of a National Reading Reform in Two States" (Reading Research Quarterly, 2015). She is currently completing a study of secondary English teachers' vocabulary instructional practices.

Sean Roy is the Co-Director of PACER's National Parent Center on Transition and Employment housed within PACER in Minneapolis Minnesota. In this position he works to improve the success of youth with disabilities who are transitioning from school into life in the community. Roy is an experienced curriculum developer, writer, trainer and presenter, often speaking to professionals and families about issues of employment, accessing postsecondary education, and promoting family involvement in transition planning. Mr. Roy holds a Master's Degree in Human Service Planning and Administration, and draws from previous employment experience in education and juvenile corrections, as well as being a sibling of an adult with autism.

Richard Sabousky has served as the department chair in Special Education for 6 of the last 8 years at Clarion University. He was recognized with the Innovative Excellence in Teaching, Learning, and Technology award presented at the 21st International Conference on College Teaching and Learning held in Ponte Vedra Beach, Florida. He has made contributions in empirical based practices in reading and mathematics as a school consultant and has various publications and presentations in case management program effectiveness and using applied behavior analysis in vocational counseling.

Sandra Sepulveda-Kozakowski, Ph.D. is a licensed clinical psychologist. She is currently an adjunct professor at The College of New Jersey in Ewing, NJ. Sandra has taught a variety of undergraduate courses including abnormal psychology, child development, development across the lifespan, and the psychology of oppression, power and privilege. In addition, Sandra provides child, adult and family therapy in an outpatient private practice as well as individual therapy to elders in a nursing home in Pennsylvania. Her research and publications focus on the impact of foster care, adoption and maltreatment on children's healthy development.

Lorie K. Taylor, professor, is a faculty member at Clarion University of PA in the Special Education and Disability Policy Studies Department. She has taught both undergraduate and graduate courses in foundations, assistive technology, classroom administration, applied behavior analysis, methods, and differentiation.

Lisa Turner is a Professor in the Department of Special Education & Disability Policy Studies at Clarion University. Her primary areas of interest include: assessment, parent education, gifted education, and learning disabilities. She is a nationally certified Educational Diagnostician as well as a Special Education Supervisor.

Natalie Allen Williams is an associate professor at Weber State University in Ogden, Utah. She completed her undergraduate degree at Utah State University in Special Education. She received her Master of Science degree at The University of Utah, also in Special Education. She completed her doctoral degree in 2005 at The Ohio State University in 2005 in Applied Behavior Analysis and Special Education. She began her career in special education as a paraprofessional and has been in a special education classroom for over 20 years. Her research interests focus on Applied Behavior

Analysis and academic and behavioral strategies for supporting students with behavior disorders in the general education classroom. Dr. Williams has been married for 10 years, and has two daughters, ages six and eight.

Samuel J. Zimmerman is an adjunct lecturer in the Educational Leadership department at Endicott College in Beverly, Massachusetts and concurrently serves as the Deputy Superintendent of Student Services for the Public Schools of Brookline, Massachusetts. Prior to Endicott College, he taught graduate courses in behavioral disorders, action research, classroom management, and differentiated instruction for ten years at Pace University in New York City. Samuel is a past recipient of the Grand Portage Tribal Research award for research in community and family partnerships and descriptive processes of the whole child with a focus on inquiry based school reform in Brooklyn, New York where he served as an Administrator of Special Education. His research has been presented at national and international conferences focusing on expanding the partnership between school and community stakeholders around inclusion and school reform.

ABOUT THE EDITORS

Vicki A. McGinley, professor, is a faculty member at West Chester University of PA in the Special Education Department. She has taught both undergraduate and graduate courses in foundations, communication and behavioral disorders, action research, family systems, and legal issues. She has served in two states as a due process hearing officer and serves as a university fact finder as well as mediator. Presently, her teaching and service work focus on diversity issues, specifically, teaching in the urban environment and international education. She was recently awarded a research and teaching Fulbright Scholarship to work in Eastern Europe. Her publications reflect her teaching and have been in the areas of urban education, legal issues, best pedagogical practices, inclusive practices, and working with families.

Melina Alexander is an associate professor at Weber State University in the department of teacher education. She completed a PhD in Special Education and a Post Doctorate in Distance Education. Melina has over 25 years of experience working in special education including 9 years in K-12 education where she taught students with behavioral challenges. She currently teaches a variety of courses in teacher education including special education reading and math methods. She has published articles on online math methods and methods to improve pre-service teacher performance.

FOUNDATIONS, DEFINITION, AND ASSESSMENT

1

DEFINING THE FAMILY

TARA S. GUERRIERO
West Chester University of Pennsylvania

"What's in a name? That which we call a rose by any other name would smell as sweet."

—William Shakespeare (in *Romeo and Juliet*)

LEARNING OBJECTIVES

The purpose of this chapter is to better understand the complexities associated with family structures. After reading this chapter, you will be able to:

1. Identify and define childhood living arrangements as they relate to the caretaker/parent structure.
2. Identify and define the different types of families and understand the complexities associated with defining a family.
3. Identify unique familial circumstances that may influence education.

What defines a family? The concept of the family is important when trying to better understand children and their educational needs. The circumstances surrounding families are complex, and the first step to understanding the living arrangements of children and defining different types of families and family structures is to understand the terminology that is associated with the concept of "**family**," including **family**, **family household**, and **family group**. The United States Census Bureau (n.d.) defines family in part as "a group of two people or more (one of whom is the householder) related by birth, marriage, or adoption and residing together; all such people (including related subfamily members) are considered as members of one family."

While this may be a formal definition for the term "family," what does a family mean in reality, through the eyes of the child, or through the eyes of the school system? A family means something different to each person. Each child that enters the school system comes with a different experience surrounding family, and it is the responsibility of those who work with children to understand how those differences can influence the child. The role of the family in life, and more specifically in education, is complicated and looks different for every child.

To further appreciate the complexity surrounding the "family," it is necessary to fully understand what a child may view as his or her family. Would a child consider all members living in his or her household members of the family? The U.S. Census Bureau (n.d.) defines a family household in part as

> a household maintained by a householder who is in a family, and includes any unrelated people who may be residing there... the family household members include all people living in the household, whereas family members include only the householder and his/her relatives.

Would children understand the technical distinction between a family and a family household? Or would children consider any individual living in their house a member of their family? There is no simple answer to this question because it may be different for each child. To increase the complexity even further, the term "family group" is defined by the U.S. Census Bureau (n.d.) as any two or more people (not necessarily including a householder) residing together, and related by birth, marriage, or adoption. A household may be composed of one such group, more than one, or none at all. The count of family groups includes family households, related subfamilies, and unrelated subfamilies.

What is the distinction among a family, a family household, and a family group? Further, is it necessary for educators to understand the differences among the three terms? For the majority of families, there is no distinction; each term refers to the same group of people. However, for many children, the three terms diverge, and the concept of "**family**" becomes more complex. There are many different combinations that can exist in one household, and it may be important to consider how these three terms relate to one another. "Families and living arrangements in the United States have changed over time…it is difficult to talk about a single kind of family or one predominant living arrangement in the United States" (Vespa, Lewis, & Kreider, 2014, p. 1). In response, it is necessary for the school system to consider the different faces and attributes of "**family**" and relate to both children and the family accordingly.

In conjunction with understanding the structure of the family, it is necessary to be clear on who is deemed a "parent" according to both the Family Educational Rights and Privacy Act of 1974 (FERPA; U.S. Department of Education, n.d.), a law governing the privacy associated with the access and dissemination of educational records, as well as the Individuals with Disabilities Education Act (IDEA) 2004, a law governing special education, because these definitions determine who has access to a child's educational records and who can make educational decisions for a child. FERPA defines a parent as "a parent of a student and included a natural parent, a guardian, or an individual acting as a parent in the absence of a parent or a guardian" (34 CFR 99.3, Authority: 20 U.S.C.1232g). FERPA further states that

> An educational agency or institution shall give full rights under the Act to either parent, unless the agency or institution has been provided with evidence that there is a court order, state statute, or legally binding document relating to such matters as divorce, separation, or custody, that specifically revokes these rights. (34 CFR 99.4, Authority: 20 U.S.C.1232g)

According to IDEA (U.S. Department of Education, 2004), a "parent" means the following:

- A biological or adoptive parent of a child;
- A foster parent, unless state law, regulations, or contractual obligations with a state or local entity prohibit a foster parent from acting as a parent
- A guardian generally authorized to act as the child's parent, or authorized to make educational decisions for the child (but not the state if the child is a ward of the state);
- An individual acting in the place of a biological or adoptive parent (including a grandparent, stepparent, or other relative) with whom the child lives, or an individual who is legally responsible for the child's welfare; or
- A surrogate parent who has been appointed in accordance with Sec. 300.519 or section 639(a)(5) of the Act. (Section 300.30, a1–a5)

THE ROLE OF THE FAMILY IN A CHILD'S EDUCATION

Educators may find themselves wondering why it is so important to focus on a child's living arrangement or family when it is the child who is being educated in the school system. In reality, the familial experiences that children carry to school are often the cornerstones behind their approach to the world of education, either positively or negatively. It is often just as important for a family to be engaged in the educational process as it is for the child. This engagement is especially crucial for families of children with disabilities, as the family plays a vital role in the educational team that makes educational decisions for the child. The family's engagement and, subsequently, the child's education may be greatly enhanced if the family dynamics are adequately considered and addressed. It is the responsibility of the school system to ensure that each child has the opportunity to grow and thrive regardless of family structure or the family's desire or ability to be engaged in the child's education. Boberiene (2013) indicated the following:

> Studies of family engagement in education reveal large associations between family involvement and success for students in elementary and secondary school levels. Family engagement also improves classroom dynamics: It is associated with increased teacher expectations, better student–teacher relationships, and more cultural competence. When parents collaborate with teachers and make real-world connections to students' learning, students show improved motivation, increased achievement, and higher graduation rates. (p. 349)

The U.S. Department of Education (Noel, Stark, & Redford, 2015) conducted a survey that indicated the following statistics about the nature of parent participation and involvement with the school system:

- 87% percent of the parents participated in parent/teacher organizations or general school meetings.
- 76% percent of the students' parents reported that they regularly attended parent/teacher conferences.
- 74% of the students' parents reported that they had attended a school or class event.
- 58% of the students' parents reported that they had participated in some type of school fundraising effort.
- 42% of the students' parents reported that they had volunteered at the school or served on a committee.
- 33% of the students' parents reported that they had met with their child's guidance counselor.

The survey further provided information about school communication with parents and indicated the following:

- 87% of the students' parents indicated that they had received newsletters, memos, e-mail, or notices addressed to all parents from their child's school.
- 57% of the students' parents indicated that they had received written communication (notes or email) from the school that was specific to their child.
- 41% of the students' parents indicated that they had received communication by telephone.

Further, the National Longitudinal Transition Study 2 (Newman, 2005) examined family involvement in families of children with disabilities between the ages of 13 and 17 and indicated the following level of school participation (outside of involvement in IEP meetings):

- 77% of the students' parents indicated that they attended school meetings.
- 73% of the students' parents indicated that they attended parent–teacher conferences.
- 62% of the students' parents indicated that they attended school or class events.
- 23% of the students' parents indicated that they volunteered in some capacity at school.
- Overall, 93% of the students' parents indicated that they participated in at least one of these school-related activities.

Aside from taking into consideration the familial experiences of children, it is also imperative that teachers take into account the many ways in which family dynamics are woven into the curriculum or school culture. The following are just a few of the most typical examples: back-to-school night; parent/teacher conferences; parent/teacher organizations; parent volunteers within the classroom or on field trips; parent responsibility for signing assignment notebooks, tests, or report cards; and school projects or assignments that are born out of the family structure (such as the development of a family tree or the development of a Punnett Square that identifies eye color).

The role of the family becomes increasingly critical and more complex when working with children with disabilities. The family then becomes an instrumental part of the educational team that determines the direction of the child's education and the development of the **individualized education program (IEP)**. Among other means of participation, families will likely be involved in interviews and meetings in which they act as a resource in providing information about their child, the development of educational goals, and the determination of the best possible route for instruction. According to the **Individuals with Disabilities Education Act (IDEA)** 2004, it is legally mandated that "Each public agency must take steps to ensure that one or both of the parents of a child with a disability are present at each IEP team meeting or are afforded the opportunity to participate" (U.S. Department of Education, 2004, Section 300.322, a). If the role of the family and the nature of the family structure aren't taken into account by teachers or the school system in these and other instances, children may not be able to be successful in the school environment.

IDENTIFYING AND DEFINING CHILDREN AND THE FAMILY

The primary source of definitions and data for this chapter comes from the U.S. Census Bureau (see Appendix) because it provides the most comprehensive information surrounding childhood living arrangements, households, and families. The U.S. Census Bureau reports data from the perspective of the designated householder. A householder is

> the person (or one of the people) in whose name the housing unit is owned or rented (maintained) or, if there is no such person, any adult member, excluding roomers, boarders, or paid employees. If the house is owned or rented jointly by a married couple, the householder may be either the husband or the wife. The person designated as the householder is the "reference person" to whom the relationship of all other household members, if any, is recorded. (U.S. Census Bureau, n.d.)

While many households have more than one adult, there is only one designated householder. The relationships to children and others in the household are based on the designated householder. Similarly, in the examination of living arrangements, the information comes from the perspective of one reference parent. It is necessary to understand that the findings of the U.S. Census Bureau may be different depending on who is the designated householder or reference parent. As an example, if a married couple had three children, and two children were the father's biological children from a previous marriage, the identification of the children as stepchildren would depend on who was completing the survey. If the father was completing the survey as the designated householder, there would be three biological children in the family. Alternately, if the mother was the designated householder in this instance, the family would have two stepchildren and one biological child. The interpretation of data surrounding family structure is complex and must be understood as such.

It is necessary to be cognizant that the following discussions of living arrangements and/or family type do not take into consideration how a child functions or is treated within a family structure or type; it only conveys the definitions based on the relationship among household members. Similarly, it does not consider different cultures or languages that may exist in the family. The school system should not consider children the same simply as a function of their living arrangement or family type.

CHILDHOOD LIVING ARRANGEMENTS

The childhood living arrangement is based both on the relationship between parents and the relationship between the parent(s) and the child(ren). When considering childhood living arrangements, it is important to first define what is meant by the term "children." The U.S. Census Bureau (n.d.) defines children as "all persons under 18 years, excluding people who maintain households, families, or subfamilies as a reference person or spouse."

Children may have four different types of living arrangements (Laughlin, 2014, p. 4):

- Two Married Parents: The child lives with two married parents both of whom may be considered biological, step, or adoptive.
- Two Unmarried Parents: The child lives with two unmarried parents both of whom may be considered biological, step, or adoptive.
- One Parent: The child lives with one parent who may be considered biological, step, or adoptive.
- No Parent: The child lives with a guardian, in the absence of a biological, step, or adoptive parent.

Table 1.1 demonstrates the percentage of living arrangements as a whole and based on race and/or ethnicity (U.S. Census Bureau, 2014, Table C9).

The living arrangement helps identify the family or family structure, and while the number of children in a family is not taken into consideration when looking at living arrangements or family type, it is important for educators to consider the presence or absence of siblings or other children in the home (biological, step, half, adoptive, and/or unrelated). A child may be an only child, have one sibling, or have multiple siblings; further, the children in the family may be close in age or have a wide age range. Consider the following examples of possible sibling structures, and think about how the circumstances may impact the different children in the family:

- A family has two biological children and one adoptive child. The dynamics of that family structure may be very different for the two biological children than for the adoptive child. The adoptive child may be particularly sensitive to relationships between the siblings or may not have any difficulties with the sibling structure.
- A family has three biological children, one set of twins and a third child who is not a twin; the three siblings may have equal relationships with each other, or the child who is not a twin may feel more isolated from his/her siblings than the twins.
- A family has one biological female child and five biological male children. The male children may be particularly protective of their female sibling, and that may be evident in the way that they interact with other children in the classroom.
- A family has two children who are half siblings and who are separated in age by 13 years. They may be extremely close and think of each other as biological siblings, or they may not feel the same connection that they might if they were full biological siblings or closer in age.
- A family has four children, one of whom has a severe disability. The family may give more attention to the child with a disability because that child needs the additional attention. The other siblings may develop a greater empathy for children with disabilities, or they may feel resentment for the additional time that was given to the sibling with disabilities.

There are many different sibling structures that can exist in a family, and each different variation may be accompanied by a different set of circumstances for each child. Educators need to take

TABLE 1.1 ■ Living Arrangements					
Who Are Children Living With?	All Races	White Alone, Non-Hispanic	Black Alone	Asian Alone	Hispanic
Two Parents	68.7%	77.3%	39.0%	86.8%	64.9%
Two Married Parents	64.4%	74.5%	34.5%	84.6%	57.8%
Two Unmarried Parents	4.2%	2.8%	4.5%	2.2%	7.1%
Biological Mother and Father	62.0%	70.4%	33.2%	82.1%	58.5%
Biological Mother and Stepfather	3.9%	4.0%	3.5%	1.7%	4.3%
Biological Father and Stepmother	1.2%	1.4%	0.8%	0.7%	1.1%
Biological Mother and Adoptive Father	0.2%	1.3%	0.1%	0.2%	0.2%
Biological Father and Adoptive Mother	0.0%	0.0%	0.0%	0.0%	0.0%
Adoptive Mother and Father	0.9%	0.8%	0.8%	2.1%	0.6%
Other Combination	0.3%	0.3%	0.4%	0.0%	0.3%
One Parent	27.5%	19.8%	54.9%	11.2%	30.7%
Mother Only—Biological	23.1%	15.2%	49.8%	8.5%	27.0%
Mother Only—Nonbiological	0.5%	0.3%	1.0%	1.1%	0.5%
Father Only—Biological	3.7%	4.1%	4.0%	1.7%	2.9%
Father Only—Nonbiological	0.2%	0.2%	0.2%	0.0%	0.2%
No Parent	3.8%	3.0%	6.1%	2.0%	4.4%
Grandparents Only	2.2%	1.7%	3.7%	0.8%	2.2%
Other Relatives Only	0.9%	0.5%	1.7%	0.8%	1.2%
Nonrelatives only	0.6%	0.6%	0.6%	0.3%	0.7%
Other Arrangement	0.2%	0.1%	0.1%	0.1%	0.3%
Living Arrangement					
At Least One Biological Parent	94.3%	95.4%	91.6%	94.9%	94.0%
At Least One Stepparent	5.7%	5.9%	5.2%	2.5%	5.9%
At Least One Adoptive Parent	1.7%	1.5%	1.6%	3.3%	1.3%

Adapted from a set of tables from the following: U.S. Census Bureau. (2014). America's families and living arrangements: 2014: Children (C table series): Table C9 Children by presence and type of parent(s), race, and Hispanic origin: 2014. Retrieved from: www.census.gov/hhes/families/data/cps2014C.html

into consideration how those dynamics may impact the child and ultimately the child's education. An awareness of the sibling structure may allow educators to better understand the behavior of their students. Sibling relationships will not specifically be addressed in this chapter; however, it should be understood that the presence or absence of siblings or other children in the home may have a great impact on the role of the family and its interactions. This may be particularly true for children who have disabilities or for children who have siblings with disabilities.

TYPES OF FAMILIES

Consider a class of 30 children; then consider how many different family structures may be possible in that one classroom. How can educators ensure that they are properly addressing the concerns of each child when there are so many possibilities for family structures? The first step in better understanding the role of the "**family**" is to consider the different types of families that exist, define the different family structures, and acknowledge that children may not identify with just one family structure.

The following types of families will be discussed during the course of this chapter:

- a traditional nuclear family
- an **unmarried- (opposite-sex) couple** family
- an extended family
- a single-parent family
- a blended or step-family
- an adoptive family
- a subfamily
- a foster family
- a same-sex-parented family
- other family groupings (sibling groupings)

A Traditional Nuclear Family

A traditional nuclear family is a husband–wife or a married-couple household in which there is a biological father and a biological mother who are married. If there is more than one child in the nuclear family, the children are full siblings. In a nuclear family, no other individuals live in the household aside from the parents and the children (Fields, 2001). In a nuclear family, the family, the family household, and the family group are the same.

An Unmarried (Opposite-Sex) Couple Family

Children may also live in a household with two parents who are unmarried. This type of household is termed an unmarried-couple family or household. An **unmarried couple** is composed of "two unrelated adults of the opposite sex (one of whom is the householder) who share a housing unit with or without the presence of children under 15 years old. Unmarried couple households contain only two adults" (U.S. Census Bureau, n.d.).

In an **unmarried-couple family**, the relationship of the parents to the child(ren) may be biological, step, or adoptive. Although there are differences between the two, would these differences be evident to a child? If a child lives with both biological parents, but the parents are not married, is there a distinction for the child? In the eyes of a child, is that considered a nuclear family? In the eyes of the school system, there may not be a distinction between an unmarried-couple family and a traditional nuclear family unless both parents are not considered legal parents.

An Extended Family

An extended family is a household in which a child lives with at least one parent and at least one person outside of his/her family that is either related or unrelated (Fields, 2001). In many families, this may be grandparents, aunts, uncles, cousins, or unrelated individuals. Children living in extended families may come to school with different experiences than children not living in extended families. There may be a number of reasons a child lives in an extended family, two of which might be related to finances and health. It is important to note that children may form the same level of emotional attachments to other individuals living in the household as they do to their parent(s). When discussing subjects that include the family in a school setting, it may be necessary to acknowledge the importance of those relationships. **Multigenerational households**

are family households consisting of three or more generations. These households include (1) a householder, a parent or parent-in-law of the householder, and an own child of the householder, (2) a householder, an own child of the householder, and a grandchild of the householder, or (3) a householder, a parent or parent-in-law of the householder, an own child of the householder, and a grandchild of the householder (U.S. Census Bureau, 2013, p. 78).

Table 1.2 presents the demographics associated with multigenerational households.

A Single-Parent Family

A single-parent family is one in which there is only one parent in the home. That parent may be a biological, step, or adoptive parent. There are many different circumstances in which a child may have come to live in a single-parent family, including the following:

- The second biological parent may be unknown or, if known, there may have been no relationship between the parents.
- The child may have been conceived through surrogacy or a donor (anonymous or known).
- The second parent may have left the home voluntarily.
- The second parent may have left the home as a result of separation or divorce.
- The second parent may have left the home involuntarily (e.g., incarceration, hospitalization, etc.).
- There may have been a death of a parent.

A single-parent family may not be able to have the same level of involvement in a child's education because there may be physical constraints. Although every family is different and there may be little functional difference between a single-parent family and a two-parent family, there may be differences that should be considered by the school system. A single parent may have more time constraints that impinge on their opportunity to be involved in education. For example, if there are two children in

TABLE 1.2 ■ Multigenerational Households					
Multigenerational Households	**All Races**	**White Alone, Non-Hispanic**	**Black Alone**	**Asian Alone**	**Hispanic**
Multigenerational Households in Relation to All Households	4.6%	3.0%	8.3%	6.3%	8.4%
Multigenerational Households with Children Under 18	39.6%	29.4%	38.3%	59.9%	52.8%
Multigenerational Households					
Grandparent(s) Is Householder	64.1%	72.5%	68.1%	34.7%	55.6%
Parent(s) Is Householder	34.2%	25.9%	30.7%	62.6%	42.5%

Adapted from Vespa, J., Lewis, J., & Kreider, R. (2013). America's families and living arrangements: 2012. Current population reports, P20-570. Washington, DC: U.S. Census Bureau.

a home and both children need help with homework or reviewing for a test, a single parent may have less time to be able to dedicate to each child as compared to a two-parented household in which the parents may be able to divide their time. A single-parent family may also have financial constraints if there is one income. This may impact a child's ability to participate in extracurricular activities or school-based activities such as field trips. Additionally, depending on the reason the child is living in a single-parent family, the child may feel a sense of loss for a parent who is not present.

A Blended or Step-Family

A blended family is "formed when remarriages occur or when children living in a household share one or no parents. The presence of a step-parent, step-sibling, or half-sibling designates a family as blended" (Fields, 2001, p. 2).

"A step-family is a married-couple family household with at least one child under age 18 who is a stepchild (i.e., a son or daughter through marriage, but not by birth) of the householder..." (U.S. Census Bureau, n.d.).

> Traditionally, a stepchild was the biological child of an individual's spouse who was not also the individual's biological child. However, earlier data show that the usage of the term has shifted and adults who are not currently married, and in some cases have never been married, report living with stepchildren. Often, these adults have an unmarried partner in the household, who is presumably the child's biological parent. Since the English language does not have a more precise word to describe this kind of relationship, some respondents may decide to report their partner's child as their stepchild, even though they are not married to the child's biological parent. (Kreider & Lofquist, 2014, p. 3)

As was discussed in a previous example, it is important to bear in mind that the estimates surrounding the number of step-families may depend on who is the designated householder. Additionally, children may be members of more than one family. Consider the following:

> It is important to keep in mind that, as is the case for adopted children, estimates of stepchildren from decennial and American Community Survey data do not capture all children who are living with a step-parent. This is because these surveys only ask for the relationship to the householder. If the child has a second parent in the household, the type of relationship between that second parent and the child will not be captured in the data. In addition, many children may have step-parents who live in other households. Since U.S. Census Bureau surveys sample addresses, and then determine who lives in the housing unit at that address, the data do not reflect relationships that cross household boundaries. Similarly, there is some potential overlap between children who are reported as adopted and those reported as stepchildren, since stepchildren may be adopted by their step-parents. (Kreider & Lofquist, 2014, p. 3)

It is necessary for the school system to adhere to rules surrounding step-parents. As was previously stated, both **FERPA** and **IDEA** 2004 consider step-parents legal parents if they have obtained legal guardianship.

An Adoptive Family

An adoptive family is one in which one or more children have been adopted by one or both parents. The U.S. Census Bureau may consider various types of adoptions, including "adoption of biologically related and unrelated children, adoption of stepchildren, adoption through private and public agencies, domestic and international adoptions, and independent and informal adoptions" (Kreider & Lofquist, 2014, p. 2). Since information gathered by the Census Bureau is completed through self-reports, the extent to which the term adoption is used in reference to legal and informal adoptions is not clear (Kreider & Lofquist, 2014, p. 2).

In considering the educational needs of a child that is living in an adoptive family, it is important to consider whether the child knows or does not know his or her biological parent(s). In thinking about the previously described ways in which family is woven into the curriculum, particular assignments or projects such as the development of a Punnett Square based on the genetics associated with eye color or the development of a family tree could be very difficult and unsettling to a child who does not fully know his or her heritage. Sensitivity in these types of situations is of utmost importance. Case Study 1 illustrates an example of when these types of assignments may cause difficulties for a child.

CASE STUDY 1
A CHILD IN AN ADOPTIVE FAMILY

Joseph is a 14-year-old male who is currently in ninth grade. He was adopted by his adoptive mother and father at birth. He has always known that he was adopted and has the opportunity to talk openly about it with his family. His adoption was closed, one in which his adoptive parents were not given information about the identity of his biological parents.

Joseph also has a younger brother who is 8 years old and who is the biological son of his adoptive parents. Joseph has a very loving relationship with both his adoptive parents and his brother and has reported that he feels so lucky to have such a wonderful family.

During the past school year, however, Joseph has been showing signs of sadness and has been acting out during his biology class. Early in the year, each member of the class completed a family tree and presented it to the class. Joseph completed the assignment about his adoptive family and asked the teacher how he should include himself in the tree since he was adopted.

Most recently, the class has been completing a unit on genetics, and Joseph has become increasingly more withdrawn as this unit has progressed. The class is learning about dominant and recessive genes and their role in hair and eye color. They were learning about Punnett Squares and how to complete a Punnett Square based on eye color. The students have been asked to interview their family and try to figure out why they have the eye color that they have based on their family and extended family's eye color. Joseph has been refusing to go to class or participate in classroom activities, and he makes jokes about biology, saying that it shouldn't even be a required class because most people "don't even like it or learn from it."

As a teacher, what concerns would you have about Joseph and his situations? How could a teacher be sensitive to his situation and adapt the content or assignments for him?

A Subfamily

According to the U.S. Census Bureau (n.d.), a **subfamily** is a married couple with or without children, or a single parent with one or more own never-married children under 18 years old. A **subfamily** does not maintain their own household, but lives in the home of someone else."

Subfamilies can either be related or unrelated to the householder.

- "A related subfamily is a married couple with or without children, or one parent with one or more of their own never married children under 18 years old, living in a household and related to, but not including, the person or couple who maintains the household. One example of a related subfamily is a young married couple sharing the home of the husband's or wife's parents. The number of related subfamilies is not included in the count of families." (U.S. Census Bureau, n.d.)
- "An unrelated subfamily is a married couple with or without children, or a single parent with one or more of their own never-married children under 18 years old living in a household. Unrelated subfamily members are not related to the householder. An unrelated subfamily may include people such as guests, partners, roommates, or resident employees and their spouses and/or children. The number of unrelated subfamily members is included in the total number of household members, but is not included in the count of family members." (U.S. Census Bureau, n.d.)

Depending on the dynamics between the subfamily and the householder, children may feel completely comfortable in their home, and there may be no real impact of their living arrangement on their life or education. Alternatively, they may feel like visitors in their home, or they may feel that their home is not their own. The use of "sub" may have a negative connotation and suggest that the child's family is not of the same importance as the householder and his or her family. It may be important for educators to demonstrate sensitivity to the children who are in these types of situations, because possible insecurities related to the family structure may possibly extend to their academic performance.

A Foster Family

A foster family is one in which there is a foster child present in the household. A foster child

is a person under 21 years old, who is placed by the local government in a household to receive parental care. Foster children may be living in the household for just a brief period or for several years. Foster children are nonrelatives of the householder. If the foster child is also related to the householder, the child is classified as that specific relative (U.S. Census Bureau, 2013, p. 77).

Educators may need to pay particular attention to foster children, as they may have situations that impact their education. It is possible that a foster child may change households and school systems frequently, thus reducing continuity in education. There are a number of ways that a classroom teacher could assist the child. For example, the teacher could informally evaluate the child's academic skills or talk to the child about what he or she has been learning; the teacher could also facilitate social interactions with other children by helping develop a social network for the child. For students with disabilities, ensuring parent participation may be more difficult as changes in the child's living arrangements occur. For example, an IEP meeting may be scheduled with a foster parent, and then the child's living arrangement changes, thus necessitating a possible change in the time/date of the meeting to include a new foster parent.

A Same-Sex-Parented Family

A same-sex-parented family may be comprised of a same-sex spousal couple or a same-sex unmarried couple. Children of same-sex-parented families may be biological children of one of the parents (either from a previous relationship or from an anonymous or known donor). Children may also be stepchildren from a previous relationship or adopted by one or both parents.

In a same-sex-parented family, the child has two mothers or two fathers. It is important that the teacher make every effort to make that child feel comfortable when discussing or teaching about topics that refer to both a mother and a father as part of the familial structure. For example, if the teacher were to ask the children to draw a picture of their family, he or she should be careful not to ask the children to draw a picture of their mother and father. Further, if the teacher is planning to hang the pictures in the classroom, it needs to be done in an encouraging manner that allows for diversity among families. It is also necessary that educators be sensitive to and use terminology appropriately. The Child Welfare Information Gateway (2011) is a resource that discusses terminology and its correct usage.

Other Family Groupings

Other types of families may exist outside of the previously described family types. An example of one such type may be when a sibling is acting as the parent for another sibling. Many different types of structures might not clearly fit into a defined structure, and it is necessary to acknowledge the complexities of these families as well.

UNIQUE FAMILIAL CIRCUMSTANCES THAT MAY INFLUENCE EDUCATION

In addition to thinking about family structures, there are other unique circumstances that children may face with regards to their family life. These circumstances may be intertwined with the family structure as in the case of separation or divorce, or they may exist outside of the scope of the family structure and relate more to particular family circumstances. The following unique circumstances will be discussed:

- parental separation or divorce
- homelessness
- parents with disabilities
- teenage parents
- migrant families
- foreign-born or immigrant families
- military families

Parental Separation or Divorce

Many children have parents who have been legally separated or divorced. In those instances, children often find themselves becoming part of two different families (the two families may be any of the family types that have been previously discussed). When working with children who have separated or divorced parents, it is necessary to consider the following:

- Do not make an assumption that either the mother or the father is the primary parent. The court assigns two different types of custody: physical custody and legal custody.
  - Physical custody involves the physical location(s) where the child lives.
  - Legal custody relates to legal decisions that are made by the parents, including educational decisions.
- The types of custody that are often assigned are full custody, primary custody, shared custody, partial custody, or no custody. In any given family situation, these five levels of custody may be

different for physical and legal custody. Consider the following example: One parent has primary physical custody (while the other has partial physical custody); however, both parents have shared legal custody. In this instance, it is necessary that the school understand the legalities associated with shared legal custody and not assume that the parent that has physical custody is the only person who makes the educational decisions. Both FERPA and IDEA refer to both biological parents as legal parents unless they have legally lost parental rights.

• Parents may have different types of relationships. Parents may have an amicable relationship in which they have maintained good communication in relation to the child(ren). Alternately, parents may not have a good relationship and either may not communicate at all or may argue about situations involving the children. It is important as the educator to try to take into consideration the particular family structure and accommodate as appropriate. For example, if the parents request separate parent–teacher conferences, it would be beneficial for the teacher to comply. It is necessary in these situations that meetings with the parents focus on the needs of the children as opposed to the relationship of the parents or the disagreement that is occurring between the parents.

Consider Case Study 2 and think about how a teacher could help address the needs of this family and student.

CASE STUDY 2
A CHILD OF A DIVORCED FAMILY

Courtney is a 12-year-old female whose parents were divorced when she was 5 years old. Her parents did not have an amicable divorce, and they have very different parenting styles.

Her mother was remarried when Courtney was 8 years old, and Courtney has a half sister who is 2 years old from that remarriage. Her father was remarried when Courtney was 7 years old, and Courtney has twin half brothers who are 4 years old.

Her biological mother and father have shared physical and shared legal custody. Her physical arrangement consists of the following:

> She spends Monday and Tuesday nights and every other weekend with her biological mother and step-family. She spends Wednesday and Thursday nights and every other weekend with her biological father and step-family. She is a member of both step-families, and she considers both households her home. Both of her households are located in the same school district, and both are in the same neighborhood school area.

Consider the following circumstances and think about how the teacher may be a resource or advocate for Courtney:

• The school has a policy through which it only sends mailings home to one household, and they have chosen to send mailings to the mother's household. The father has repeatedly asked for mailings to be sent to his home; however, the school has indicated that it is the responsibility of the parents to share information. Although both parents have shared custody, the father is not being provided with the same information or access to Courtney's education.

• The parents do not want to attend parent/teacher conferences at the same time and have requested that they be able to have separate meetings with the teacher.

(Continued)

CASE STUDY 2 (Continued)

- The day before back-to-school night, the teacher asks the children in the classroom to write a letter to their parent(s) about their classroom. Courtney feels uncomfortable with this request and doesn't want to write a letter.

- At the beginning of the school year, the children are given textbooks and are asked to bring them home for the remainder of the year. Courtney indicates that she doesn't know what to do with the books, so she will just keep them in her locker.

- On Mother's Day, the children are asked to make cards for their mothers. Courtney becomes sad and says that she doesn't want to make a card.

Homelessness

A child may be a member of a homeless family, and it is important that the school system understand the influence that might have on a child's education. The following is a definition of homelessness that has been provided by the U.S. Department of Housing and Urban Development (2013):

- "An individual or family who lacks a fixed, regular, and adequate nighttime residence, meaning:
  - An individual or family with a primary nighttime residence that is a public or private place not designed for or ordinarily used as a regular sleeping accommodation for human beings, including a car, park, abandoned building, bus or train station, airport, or camping ground; or
  - An individual or family living in a supervised publicly or privately operated shelter designated to provide temporary living arrangements (including congregate shelters, transitional housing, and hotels and motels paid for by charitable organizations or by federal, state, or local government programs for low-income individuals); or
  - An individual who is exiting an institution where he or she resided for 90 days or less and who resided in an emergency shelter or place not meant for human habitation immediately before entering that institution;
- Any individual or family who:
  - Is fleeing, or is attempting to flee, domestic violence, dating violence, sexual assault, stalking, or other dangerous or life-threatening conditions that relate to violence against the individual or a family member, including a child, that has either taken place within the individual's or family's primary nighttime residence or has made the individual or family afraid to return to their primary nighttime residence; and
  - Has no other residence; and
  - Lacks the resources or support networks, e.g., family, friends, and faith-based or other social networks, to obtain other permanent housing." (pp. 2–3)

It is possible that a teacher may not know that a child is homeless unless he or she is told. However, there may be many implications that may have to be considered by the teacher, including, but not limited to the following: malnourishment or limited food intake, cleanliness, resources for completing homework, fatigue related to a lack of sleep, and emotional difficulties that result from the situation. The school system must make every effort to accommodate children as much as possible.

Parents With Disabilities

Many children live in situations in which one or more of their parents have a **disability**. Those disabilities may be of any nature, including, but not limited to medical, physical, intellectual, and emotional. Children may or may not know that a parent is living with a disability. As a school system, it is necessary to ensure that the parents are able to be included in their children's education regardless of the possible limitations that they may have. It is also necessary to understand that a child may worry about a parent with a disability, and that concern may impact the child, educationally.

Teenage Parents

Children are sometimes born to teenage parents. In some instances, teenage parents will raise their children in their own household; however, they may also raise their children as a subfamily in another's home. It is the responsibility of the school system to acknowledge the custodial parent(s) and remember that it is the custodial parent who takes responsibility for the child(ren). For example, consider a situation in which there is a teenage married couple who is raising a child but living in the household with one of the child's grandparents. However, the grandparents want to have a say in the child's education. It is necessary to determine who is considered the legal custodial parent(s). If it is the teenage parents, then the school is required by law to acknowledge that the child's parents are the legal decision makers for the child. That means that the school system has to maintain confidentiality with regard to the grandparents and proceed as the parent(s) wish.

Migrant Families

A migrant family is one that travels during one or more parts of the year for occupational work. Migrant families are frequently employed in agricultural positions that are seasonal. That often necessitates moving during different seasons depending on the nature of the particular agricultural crop. Migrant families have different types of living patterns; however, many return to the same locations yearly. Children in migrant families often change schools frequently, and it is important to consider the impact that different school systems may have on a child's learning. A child may relocate before a particular concept is solidified and move to a school where the concept has already been learned. Alternatively, a child may have already learned a concept and move to a school that has not yet learned it. Accommodations may need to be made for children to ensure that they are getting the best from their educational experiences.

Foreign-Born or Immigrant Families

"The foreign-born population includes anyone who was not a U.S. citizen or a U.S. national at birth. This includes respondents who indicated they were a U.S. citizen by naturalization or not a U.S. citizen" (U.S. Census Bureau, 2013, p. 69). Children who are foreign born or who have parents who are foreign born may have cultural or language differences that may need to be addressed within the school system. Further, the school needs to make every effort to ensure that the parents are able to be included in educational decisions regardless of a possible language barrier or cultural difference. For children either who are being evaluated for a disability or who are being reevaluated, it is necessary to ensure that the student is given a nondiscriminatory evaluation in whatever language is appropriate for the child. It is also necessary to ensure that parents understand their rights and what they are consenting to before an evaluation may commence. As members of the educational team, it is also necessary that the school communicate with families in a way that they can understand. Many foreign-born families may not have language or cultural barriers, but many do, and it is imperative that the school system acknowledge those differences for those families both with and without children with disabilities.

Military Families

Children of military families may have one or more parents who are in the military. The following should be considered for children of military families:

- The family may relocate frequently.
- One or more parent may be deployed for prolonged periods of time, and their child(ren) may be living with one parent or a guardian.
- Children may be afraid for the safety of their parents.

The school system should make efforts to ensure that they are sensitive to the possible emotional needs of children who are members of military families. Children who have family members who are deployed may have fears surrounding the safety of their family members. Similarly to the discussion surrounding foster children, it may be necessary for teachers to facilitate instruction and peer interaction for those children of military families who frequently relocate.

Families of Children With Disabilities

While it is necessary to consider the family structure for all children, it is imperative that the school system understand the dynamics of the family structure when working with families of students with disabilities. As was stated previously, the school system is legally required under IDEA 2004 to make every effort to ensure parental participation in the education of students with disabilities. In addition to participation on the IEP team, the following are some examples of ways in which the school system is required to involve parents according to IDEA (U.S. Department of Education, 2004):

- "The agency proposing to conduct an initial evaluation to determine if the child qualifies as a child with a disability shall obtain informed consent from the parent of such child before conducting the evaluation." (TITLE IB, 614, a1, D i, I)
- "The public agency must make reasonable efforts to obtain informed consent from the parent for the initial provision of special education and related services to the child." (Section 300.300, b2)

In these and other instances, it is necessary for the school system to obtain consent and request participation from legal parents/guardians, regardless of the family structure. The following should be considered by the school system:

- Adhere to FERPA laws and maintain confidentiality for the child with all other individuals who are not deemed legal parents/guardians. Among others, this may be particularly applicable to step-parents, extended family members (such as grandparents or older siblings), and same-sex parents who are not legal parents.
- Different types of family structures may have different opinions or approaches to education, and it is important for the school to be open to working with the family to ensure the best education for the child with a disability.
- Ensure that there is a clear understanding of who can legally make decisions for the child (if the information has been disclosed). If there are two legal parents that live in different households, make sure that communication, requests for participation, and requests for consent adhere to the special education guidelines.

- When completing an evaluation that requires an interview of the parents, take into consideration any familial circumstances that may have led to difficulties that are not as a result of a disability.

EDUCATING ALL CHILDREN

There are many different types of families and definitions associated with family, and those definitions are constantly changing. As the culture of the American society also changes, the types of families will likely continue to evolve. All families are different regardless of whether they conform to one of the previously described family structures. It is very difficult to view family types in isolation because the particular family type gives a limited view of how the family functions. Every child in a classroom will have unique family circumstances that will influence his or her approach to learning and that may require attention and understanding from the school system.

It is imperative that teachers understand how different living arrangements and family structures can influence education. It is necessary to ensure that every child is given the opportunity to succeed regardless of the family situation in which he or she is involved. Since the family construct for many children falls outside of the traditional nuclear family, the school system must make accommodations to how it relates to families from both legal and practical standpoints. What can the school system and teachers in particular do to help facilitate learning and engage families while being cognizant of the wide range of family types? The following are some examples of what educators can do to enhance the educational experience for families of different types:

- Ensure that the communication between the school and the family is legally appropriate based on the FERPA laws that relate to who can access school records and IDEA laws that involve students with disabilities and the requirement of parental consent and participation. If the child has more than one household or lives in a household with other adults that are not legal parents, it is necessary that educators adhere to the guidelines.

- The culture of the school system may need to evolve with the ever-changing family structures and unique circumstances. Many children are falling outside of the definition of the traditional nuclear family, and the teachers may need to change their approach to learning and the way in which they weave family into the curriculum. There may need to be alterations to the current practices and assignments to include more children that don't fit into the majority. For example, when completing a project that relates to family heritage, develop an alternative project that includes different family types that may not be based on biological relationships. Find an approach that allows the student to include nonbiological family members while at the same time maintaining the integrity of the instruction.

- Teachers can facilitate communication between the home and the school. At the beginning of the school year, consider doing some type of project that helps highlight the unique children that may be in the classroom. This could prove to be a source of information for the teacher about the different familial circumstances in the classroom, as well as assist the teacher in determining the best way to engage families in their children's education and facilitate interactions between the family and the school. It may also help children understand that every family is different and that they can freely talk about their own family structure.

- Consider all aspects of a child's life when evaluating their performance and behavior. If a teacher doesn't take the time to really think about why a child is demonstrating changes in behavior in class, it could really hinder future educational endeavors. Similarly, think about the sibling structure and whether that may have some impact on how children approach their education and relate to their peers.

• Try to find ways to facilitate communication with parents and ease the burden that living in two different households may place on a child. For example, send home a second set of books so that she may access her textbooks at both houses. When sending mail or email communication to the families in the classroom, be sure to include both families. While it is not legally required to allow for multiple conferences, be open to holding two separate parent–teacher conferences that will allow for each parent to discuss his or her child's progress. When developing schedules or letters for the parents in preparation for events like back-to-school night or open houses, include a separate set of documents for each parent.

• Don't discount the concerns that children show in relation to their families. It is very difficult for children to separate their family life from their school life. Find ways to enhance their education by including their unique circumstances in the curriculum.

Summary

While it is important for the school system to understand the existing family types, the ultimate importance associated with defining the family goes well beyond understanding family structures. The realization and understanding that the nature of the family may have a great impact on children and their education is of utmost importance. Family structures may change over time, but the importance of family engagement in the child's education will not change, and it is important that the school system make an effort to engage all families.

Additional Resources

Web-Based

United States Census Bureau: www.census.gov. The U.S. Census Bureau is a source for detailed definition and demographic information about American families. A discussion of the different surveys that involve children may be found at: http://www.census.gov/topics/population/children/surveys.html.

United States Department of Education: www.ed.gov. The U.S. Department of Education provides a wealth of information about educational laws and data.

Appendix: U.S. Census Bureau Surveys Related to Children and Families

The U.S. Census Bureau provides a wealth of demographic information on the American population. The U.S. Census Bureau provided the following description of the survey types and resources that are conducted and provided by the U.S. Census Bureau in relation to children (retrieved from http://www.census.gov/topics/population/children/surveys.html):

Data on children can be found from a variety of sources. These sources are listed in what follows with brief descriptions to help you decide which data source would best suit your needs. Availability of data by time and geography is highlighted in the sections below. The links will take you to the appropriate page for data on children by survey.

The American Community Survey (ACS)

The American Community Survey (ACS) is an annual national survey collected monthly that provides communities with reliable and timely demographic, housing, social, and economic data every year. Data about children are available for the U.S., states, metropolitan areas, and more specific geographic areas that meet minimum population sizes for the given survey year.

There are more than 1,000 detailed tables in American FactFinder (AFF). There are about 990 recurring tables with data about children. Data are available from 2000 to the present.

The Current Population Survey (CPS)

The Current Population Survey (CPS) is a monthly survey of about 50,000 households conducted by the Census Bureau for the Bureau of Labor Statistics. The survey has been conducted for more than 50 years. Data about children are collected annually as part of the Annual Social and Economic Supplement (ASEC).

Data about children are available for the U.S. from 1960 to the present.

The Survey of Income and Program Participation (SIPP)

The Survey of Income and Program Participation (SIPP) is a longitudinal survey of demographic information, income, labor force characteristics, and program participation in the United States. Supplemental topical modules are included on a rotating basis and include questions on topics such as child well-being, child care, and detailed household relationships.

Data about children are available for the U.S. for each panel starting in 1991.

The Decennial Census

The Decennial Census occurs every 10 years, in years ending in zero, to count the population and housing units for the entire United States. Its primary purpose is to provide the population counts that determine how seats in the U.S. House of Representatives are apportioned.

Data about children are available for the U.S., states, counties, and subcounty statistical areas (such as zip codes and block groups), from 1790 to the present.

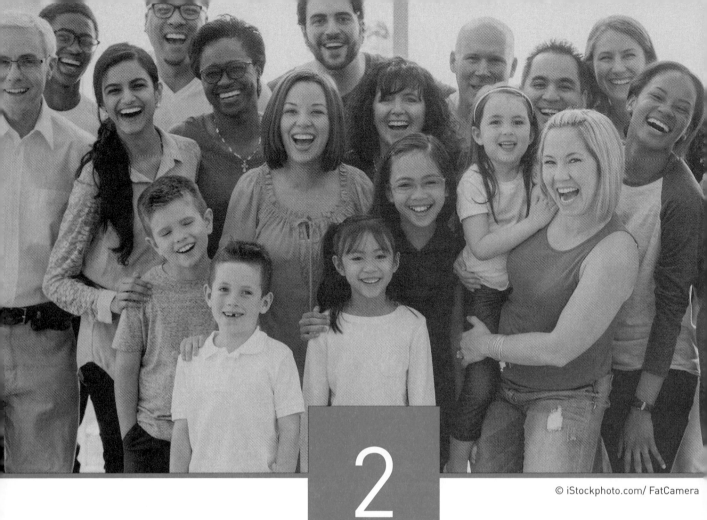

2

FAMILY SYSTEMS THEORY

SANDRA SEPULVEDA-KOZAKOWSKI
The College of New Jersey

"Man survives in groups... An infant's most basic need is for a
mother figure to feed, protect, and teach him."

—Minuchin (1974, p. 46)

After reading this chapter, you will be able to:

1. Define family systems theory
2. Define the major principles of family systems theory: subsystems, boundaries, communication, adaptability/flexibility, cohesion, and circular causality
3. Apply principles of family systems theory to working with children with disabilities
4. Discuss the role of culture in applying family systems theory

Given that human infants cannot survive alone, understanding the **family** is vital. Families, groups of people connected either by biology or emotion, have always existed in cultures all over the world. Whether an individual rejects or remains close to his or her family, one's health and wellbeing are influenced by family experiences. Family experiences are influenced by a variety of factors within and without the family. Family systems theory is a perspective that highlights the role of the family in understanding one's overall psychological functioning.

WHAT IS FAMILY SYSTEMS THEORY?

Family systems theory asserts that families are units in which members of the family impact one another in bidirectional ways, striving to maintain equilibrium (Karraker & Grochowski, 2012; Minuchin, 1974). If an event happens to one person in the family, the event will impact the other members of the family in a variety of ways, a concept known as interdependence. Having a child born with a disability or receiving the diagnosis of a disability for a child later in life is a lifechanging event for many families. Some families embrace the diagnosis with hope and empowerment, and other families experience feelings of loss, anger, frustration, and guilt over the diagnosis. The process of understanding and living with the disability of the child impacts the entire family. Understanding this process via the lens of family systems theory is the goal of this chapter.

THE FAMILY IDENTITY

Families are united by a variety of factors such as name, biology, and emotion, to mention a few. These factors support the identity development of a family. One family may identify as strong, another as athletic, another as religious and/or successful. It does not really matter what the label of the identity is; what matters is that the family members share this identity and subsequently feel like they belong to the family system. When an individual family member does not feel like he or she belongs to the family, then feelings of isolation, rejection, and alienation may ensue. Minuchin (1974) described the human identity as having two main components: a sense of separateness and a sense of belonging. Balancing the tension between these two concepts is challenging for many people. For example, sense of belongingness has been found to be particularly important for adolescents in stepfamilies (King, Boyd, & Thorsen, 2015). Differences, if not embraced, will offer natural opportunities for rejection, isolation, and despair. Families then need to choose how they will deal with differences in their members to promote closeness and cohesion rather than isolation and despair.

Having a disability in a family member or members forces families to decide if and how they are going to incorporate that disability into their identity. Some families need to reconceptualize how their future will be. What will birthday parties and school be like? Will changes need to be made? If so, what are those changes, and how will the family make those changes? What feelings arise because of these changes? How families react to these questions often reflects the interaction of subsystems within the greater family system.

FAMILY SUBSYSTEMS

When thinking about families via family systems theory, visualize baking a cake. First you mix all the ingredients together, and then you put the cake in the oven to bake. The final product, the cake, is more than the sum of the individual ingredients but represents a wonderful combination and symbolizes the family (Laszloffy, 2002). The different layers of the cake represent different generations within the family. Cutting the cake represents possible changes or stressors that upset the equilibrium of the family and need to be addressed to restore balance to the family, as the cake would fall apart without balance (Laszloffy, 2002).

According to family systems theory, subsystems exist within the family (Minuchin, 1974). Certain family members may form alliances or subsystems, which are often organized by different themes such as marriage, gender, disability, siblings, and so forth. Each subsystem has specific goals. The subsystems are interdependent, and each family member belongs to multiple subsystems. For example, the father is part of the parent subsystem with the mother while also part of the male subsystem with his sons. When the members of the subsystems have difficulty achieving their goals, maladaptive behaviors and/or crises develop. For example, in the Smith family, the mother, Tara, primarily takes her daughter, Violet, who has attention deficit/hyperactivity disorder, to her medical appointments. Unfortunately, Tara sometimes misses her other daughter, Margaret's, tennis matches while she is at the appointments with Violet. The father, Michael, primarily attends Margaret's tennis matches and misses Violet's medical appointments.

While this schedule allows each child to have a parent present for their respective activities, it may create a subsystem in which Violet and Tara are in alliance and Michael and Margaret are in an alliance. The potential for alienation and rejection exists for family members who are not part of a particular subsystem. Family systems theory asserts that it is imperative that the family members acknowledge these subsystems and alliances and discuss any feelings associated with them to support closeness and togetherness within the family unit. In addition, in order for a family system to function in a positive fashion, the system as a whole, as well as each subsystem, must find balance in boundaries, communication, cohesion, adaptability/flexibility, and climate.

BOUNDARIES

Boundaries are the rules delineating "who participates and how" (Minuchin, 1974, p. 53). Rules and boundaries exist to maintain equilibrium for the family unit. Boundaries exist within and without the family system along a continuum from rigid to enmeshed. Rigid and enmeshed boundaries are problematic, representing the extreme ends of a continuum, while the middle of the continuum represents clear and well-defined boundaries (Minuchin, 1974). Examples of the rigid pattern are shutting family members out, not sharing any highs or lows of life, and isolation. Examples of enmeshed boundaries include family members being involved in all aspects of individual members' day-to-day lives as well as little privacy or respect for independence. The middle of the continuum represents a balance of respect for individual privacy and autonomy along with closeness and trust. Families that are organized and can respond to change positively are considered "healthy" according to family systems theory (Minuchin, 1974).

Members of the family will experience changes throughout a lifetime, and these changes, while inevitable, represent threats to the equilibrium of the family unit if boundaries are not adjusted. The physical and psychological changes that accompany growth and maturation impact both children and adults in different ways. For example, parents may play a decisive role in choosing a young child's playmates; this represents a more rigid boundary structure. However, when a child goes through adolescence, these rigid boundaries may need to loosen to allow greater autonomy in friend selection. Navigating such developmental changes often presents unique and additional stressors for families with children with disabilities. Boundaries, which are often changed for a child without disabilities, may need to remain constant to support the child with a disability. For example, sleeping or bathing independently may not be a safe option for some children with disabilities. Successfully navigating developmental changes, stressors, and adjustment of boundaries is often related to how well a family communicates.

COMMUNICATION

Communication is paramount for the survival of the family system. If information is communicated clearly and positively, then homeostasis remains within the family system; if information is miscommunicated or a threat is perceived, then change occurs, and the family unit will work to achieve homeostasis again (Almagor & Ben-Porath, 2013). In some families, information flows easily from one member to the other, while in other families, communication is rigid, obstructing the flow of information. Regardless of how easily the information flows within a family, it is important to note that communication is circular. Circular communication means that one conversation often leads to another conversation within and without subsystems. Subsystems may control or monitor the flow of information from other subsystems.

COHESION

Feeling connected, bonded, and close to one another is known as cohesion and is a characteristic of healthy families according to family systems theory (Berg-Cross, 2000; Minuchin, 1974). Families vary in their degrees of closeness. Members of families with rigid boundaries may feel isolated, as they operate mostly independently and don't share their feelings with one another. Members of other families with more enmeshed boundaries may feel suffocated and lacking autonomy. Degrees of cohesiveness may also vary throughout a family's life cycle. During infancy, parents may feel very close and connected to their babies as they delight in the baby's first smiles, steps, and accomplishments. During adolescence, parents may feel disconnected from their teens as they begin to confide in their peers more than the parents. As adult children become parents, they may feel a renewed sense of closeness with their parents. The life cycle presents natural stressors and milestones for all families. How adaptable and how flexible a family is will also impact how well a family navigates these changes.

ADAPTABILITY/FLEXIBILITY

Adaptability or flexibility represents the extent to which a family can amend its organization, rules, and/or boundaries. Many parents have preconceived expectations and/or dreams for what their lives will look like with children. Some people spend lots of time planning, preparing, and discussing what their parental roles, attitudes, and philosophies will be prior to the arrival of their child or children. Other parents spend less or no time on these ideas. Some parents become parents suddenly and/or unexpectedly, such as in instances of death or foster care. Regardless of the route to parenthood experienced by a parent(s), once you are a parent, you are in the parenting business and this means you are responsible for the well being of another person(s). Once you are a parent, the ideas of adaptability and flexibility often become part of your day-to-day thinking. Deciding which decisions to be firm on and which decisions to bend on becomes a day-to-day or even hour-to-hour battle. Do you allow the child another cookie, 15 more minutes of video game time, or permission to drive the car after midnight?

For parents who are more anxious, embracing adaptability and flexible thinking strategies and behaviors is very overwhelming. For example, a parent of a child with a disability may be anxious about the child learning and may find it difficult to be flexible. Such parents often prefer consistency, as it helps them regulate their own anxiety. Adhering to rigid parenting patterns to regulate a parent's anxiety often has a negative impact on children. Children may consequently feel controlled and disrespected. On the other hand, children benefit from routines, as it helps them learn self-regulation.

Therefore, we return to the important family systems concept of balance. Embracing a moderate degree of **adaptability** and **flexibility** in which family members feel connected, respected, and supported is the goal of family systems work. Families with a moderate degree of **cohesion** and adaptability were posited to represent healthy psychological functioning among their members (Berg-Cross, 2000).

CLIMATE

Developing a context for understanding using concrete data is important because there are components of family functioning that are less concrete such as climate. Climate is the physical and emotional environment of the family. Emotional environment reflects feelings such as peace, anxiety, control, and spirituality. Familial climate changes with individuals' moods and behaviors. When a parent has been mistreated at work and returns home angry and/or exhausted, the parent may be short, critical, and/or hostile toward the children. The child may respond with negativity, sadness, and/or positivity depending on the child's mood and age. Families with children with disabilities may experience heightened levels of stress and anxiety which may permeate their family climate. For example, Margalit and Heiman (1986) found that families with sons with learning disabilities demonstrated more emphasis on control and less support of emotional expression than families with sons without learning disabilities. The climate of the family changes often, but the overall climate of the family is key as it relates to the family's identity.

THE FAMILY LIFE CYCLE

The formation of a family and how the family changes across time represents the life cycle (Minuchin, 1974). When a couple unites in either marriage or commitment they develop patterns of interactions defined as mutual accommodation according to Minuchin (1974). Household chores are divided, routines and rules are established. Partners learn to read each other's cues (e.g., a certain tone or facial expression can suggest a tough day at work) and alter their behaviors and routines to accommodate their new relationship. Loyalties are shifted from families of origin to the new family the couple is forming.

When a child enters a family through birth or adoption, the organization of the family is changed again. Parents establish new routines and rules to integrate the child into the family. The emotional and physical demands of raising children require the family to adapt and reorganize. Additional events such as disease, moves, changes to employment, or caring for grandparents (to name a few) are all components of the life cycle that require "continual accommodation" (Minuchin, 1974, p. 18).

Zilbach (2003) asserted there are three main lifecycle phases divided into different stages: *gestational or courtship phase (forming and nesting)*, which included coupling and arrival of the first dependent, which is usually a child but may be an elder relative or parent; *middle phase*, which includes family separation processes during which children go to school, leave home, become independent; *last phases*, which include adult children becoming fully independent and death of parents (Shovelar & Schwoeri, 2003). Families must master specific goals for each stage, although the stages do not always happen in linear progression. In some families, parents die while their children are young, which interrupts the nesting phase and brings families into the last phase. Therefore, it is important to remember that these phases represent theoretical frameworks of the life cycle, which when applied to real families may look different.

CASE STUDY 1
SANCHEZ FAMILY

The Sanchez family includes Theresa (mother), age 43, Alex (father), age 45, Matthew and Connor, 7 years old (twin boys), and Isabelle (3-year-old girl). Theresa's mother, Rita, recently moved in with them, as she is 80 years old and can no longer live independently. Theresa's father died 10 years ago. Theresa works part time as a nurse, and Alex works full time as a lawyer. Rita is from Puerto Rico. Theresa has three older brothers, one of whom lives nearby with his family. The other two brothers live in different states from the Sanchez family. Alex's parents are from Italy and live nearby. All grandparents help with child care for Matthew, Connor, and Isabelle, although Alex's parents (Leona and Joseph) are reluctant to care for their children in the home if Rita is there.

Matthew and Connor are in second grade and attend a public school. Isabelle attends preschool. Isabelle was diagnosed with autism approximately 1 year ago. She has multiple therapy appointments throughout the week. She has a behavioral therapist who works with her several hours a day. Theresa and Alex reported feeling very overwhelmed with caring for their children and Rita. They have been arguing more frequently and sleeping less. Theresa described her days as running from appointment to appointment, home, and work. Matthew and Connor play tennis and participate in the Boy Scouts. It has been difficult for them to attend their activities lately, as Theresa and Alex are struggling to take care of things. Matthew's teacher also reported that he has been sleepy in class lately and not completing his homework assignments on time. The Sanchezes identify as Roman Catholic and attend church weekly. It is difficult for Isabelle to sit quietly throughout church, which often results in Theresa missing Mass, which upsets her.

Using Zilbach's theory about the three life-cycle stages, assess the Sanchez family. Describe which stage/stages they are in and how any changes to the life cycle might contribute to their current functioning. Discuss how culture impacts the family's experiences navigating the life-cycle stages.

Individual family members respond to changes in the life cycle in their own unique ways, which also impacts the family unit. Some changes are sudden, and some are expected. Families that are more enmeshed or rigid have trouble mastering changes in life and may become stuck during certain stages. Zilbach (1989) argued that families may then carry over unresolved characteristics from the previous stage to the next stage (Goldenberg & Goldenberg, 2000). Conversely, positively addressing these changes will strengthen the family unit and help the family survive to endure future changes. In addressing balance through redefining boundaries, maintaining cohesion and flexibility, and ensuring a positive climate, families will persevere.

FACTORS IMPACTING FAMILY SYSTEMS

Circular Causality

In families, information flows in a circular pattern via the subsystems. For example, an event in one subsystem may directly lead to a subsequent event in another subsystem, which in turn leads to an increase in the occurrence of the event in the first subsystem. Ideas, feelings, and behaviors interact within the subsystems of the family, which often ignite changes. During different developmental stages, such as toddlerhood and adolescence, children assert their autonomy, which involves testing parental limits and authority. For example, a teen who feels like her parents are too strict and treating her like a "baby" with a 10:00 p.m. curfew may decide to test the curfew by returning home at midnight. The parents may respond with consequences for the teen such as an earlier curfew and/or restriction of privileges (e.g., no cell phone use for a certain period of time). The teen may reject the parent's new boundaries or rules and try to impose a new boundary, which may result in additional consequences and/or restrictions. This cycle will continue if uninterrupted and is known as circular causality according to family systems theory.

In situations like the one described, according to family systems theory, it would be "inaccurate to attribute fault to any one part of the system" (O'Gorman, 2012, p. 10). Assigning blame or determining the cause of the problem is not helpful because the events keep interacting in a way that makes it impossible to identify a clear cause. In fact, the process of investigating who "caused" the problem may lead to more negativity, hostility, and tension within the family. In the example of the teen breaking her curfew, she will likely blame her parents for being too strict and disrespecting her, while the parents will blame the daughter for disobeying them and disrespecting their rules. Often, in families of children with disabilities, these situations can be acute and cause tension within and across subsystems. Imagine the same scenario with a teenager with a disability. The parents may struggle to establish appropriate boundaries, wanting to protect their child. When the child rebels, parents may disagree on appropriate ways to address the situation. In addition, communication may be hindered due to misperceptions of the child's abilities. It is consequently more useful for families to understand that the individual members contributed to the problem (e.g., the daughter could have discussed her desire to have a later curfew and more freedom with her parents, and the parents could have included the daughter in their discussions about curfews) and shift their focus to establishing new rules and boundaries that appeal to all the involved parties. Focusing on generating solutions is an important characteristic of circular causality.

EXTERNAL SYSTEMS

Although it may seem that our modern, nuclear, Western family exists independently, our perception is incorrect. Families interact with other families, with work colleagues, with community members, and with multiple institutions that represent external systems. External systems influence families in bidirectional ways. Bronfenbrenner (1977) argued that these systems can be conceptualized as having four components: the microsystem, the mesosystem, the exosystem, and the macrosystem. The microsystem represents the connections people have in their immediate environments such as parents and siblings or primary caregivers (e.g., day-care workers, nannies). Bronfenbrenner defined a mesosystem as "a system of microsystems" (Bronfenbrenner, 1977, p. 515). Microsystems connect to represent the mesosystem, meaning that what happens in one system influences the other system (Kail, 2015). Events that do not directly happen to an individual but may impact the individual (e.g., neighborhood events, extended family changes, etc.) represent the exosystem. Cultural norms, mores, and practices represent the macrosystem (Bronfenbrenner, 1977; Kail, 2015). A fifth component, the chronosystem, was added as a dimensional perspective to represent the idea that systems continually change over time (Kail, 2015).

Understanding Bronfenbrenner's perspectives on systems helps us understand that families do not exist in vacuums but are alive and thriving. Some families may feel vulnerable, thinking that they are at the mercy of these powerful forces that are out of their control. Helping families think about how powerful they are and that their decisions and behaviors influence these external systems is the job of teachers, professionals on the multidisciplinary team (MDT).

COORDINATION OF CARE

External systems of support are helpful for all families. For families with a child with a disability, their survival may really depend on external systems such as medical personnel, social workers, educators, and inhome personnel. Transporting the child back and forth from home, school, and appointments/therapies may include bus drivers and/or use of public transportation. Successfully navigating these complicated systems is difficult. Families need support connecting to social workers and other support care providers to help them coordinate the care of their children.

CASE STUDY 2
THE CHANG-THOMPSON FAMILY

The Chang-Thompson family consists of Margo (mother), age 35, Lydia (mother), age 35, and two children, Sophia (10-year-old girl) and Lee (5-year-old boy). Sophia and Lee are biological siblings and were adopted from foster care by Margo and Lydia 3 years ago. Sophia has diabetes and Lee has cerebral palsy. Margo works part time as an art dealer, and Lydia works full time as a pediatrician. Sophia and Lee both attend a public school near their home. Lee has various medical and therapy appointments to attend weekly, whereas Sophia's appointments are not as frequent.

Margo has a history of depression and recently has been feeling more sad and overwhelmed. The family moved to a new city, away from their relatives and friends. The children are struggling to make new friends. Lydia has been working long hours because of her new job, which has left Margo with most of the child care responsibilities. Margo identifies as Chinese American, and Lydia was born in England but raised in the US since she was a teenager. The adjustment to the new school has been difficult for Lee. He was very close to his previous teachers and was sad to leave them.

Apply Bronfenbrenner's model of ecological systems to the Chang-Thompson family. Discuss how the meso-, micro-, exo-, macro-, and chronosystems relate to this family and their current state of functioning.

PARENTING RELATIONSHIPS

The relationships of the primary caregivers/parents influence the family unit. Some children are raised by heterosexual couples, samegender couples, single parents, grandparents, relatives, or foster parents. Regardless of the constellation of the caregiver relationship, the quality and level of happiness shared by their caregivers can be assessed via family systems theory. Much of the research conducted on caregiving relationships has included heterosexual married couples from Western cultures. Not surprisingly, Goldberg and Easterbrooks (1984) found that marital harmony was positively related to parenting attitudes for parents of toddlers; open communication and support for parenting decisions are also related to marital satisfaction (Kwok, Cheng, Chow, & Ling, 2015).

A concept known as the spillover hypothesis (De Luccie, 1995) has been investigated in the research to learn how difficulties in the marriage impact the parenting relationship and cause negative parent–child interactions (Kwok, Cheng, Chow, & Ling, 2015). For parents of children with developmental delays, they report significant levels of marital dissatisfaction and parenting stress (Robinson & Neece, 2015). Given the bidirectional nature of marriage and parenting, negative parent–child interactions may also negatively impact how parents treat each other in their marriage (Goldberg & Easterbrooks, 1984). Some parents may immerse themselves in their children to escape from the negativity of their marriage. This phenomenon is known as the compensatory hypothesis (Engfer, 1988). Parents seek the affection and satisfaction from their children that they are not receiving from their spouses according to the compensatory hypothesis (Kwok, Cheng, Chow, & Ling, 2015).

When working with caregivers/parents of children with disabilities, it is important to consider how stressors from caring for their children "spill over" into their caregiver relationship/ marriages. If one caregiver/parent does not feel supported by the other caregiver/parent, a host of negative emotions and behaviors may emerge. Feeling unsupported builds feelings of alienation and resentment toward one another. Similarly, it is also important to notice if boundaries change and certain alliances are formed between one parent and a child with a **disability**. Some parents/caregivers in these alliances may feel that it is necessary to immerse themselves in an alliance with their child because of the demands of the disability and not realize how their marriage/relationship has become strained. If they realize it, they may not know how to change it.

CULTURE, RACE, AND ETHNICITY

So far we have discussed the major tenets of family systems theory: subsystems, external systems, boundaries, communication, circular causality, adaptability/flexibility, and cohesion. These tenets are universal, yet the implementation of them directly relates to a family's culture, race, class, spirituality, and other identifying factors. Even within families, family members may differ on their identification and adherence to these identifying factors as well. Financial status may change within the family's life cycle, altering the family's economic class. Young children may adopt the same religious ideology and practices of their parents, while adolescent and/or adult children may not.

The communication styles and **behavior** patterns of families often reflect their culture (Santisteban, Muir-Malcolm, Mitrani, & Szapocznik, 2002). For example, families define closeness differently and may have certain expectations about which behaviors represent closeness as compared to another family. For example, the Hispanic culture values closeness, which often looks like parents and children talking frequently and participating in the decision-making process of all individuals in the family. Some may consider this degree of closeness "enmeshed" with respect to boundaries (Santisteban, Muir-Malcolm, Mitrani, & Szapocznik, 2002). Similarly, collectivism, which values the good of the group over the good of the individual, is often found in Asian cultures. These elements of closeness and collectivism often conflict with the American ideology of individualism. Individualism asserts the good of the individual and encourages parents to encourage their children to separate from them early on. This emphasis on individuation is seen during infancy, for example, by having babies sleep independently in cribs in separate rooms as opposed to cosleeping with their parents. Cosleeping with your child is a common practice around the world and supports the emotional attachment of parents and children. Yet it is not often embraced by many American middle class parents.

Language barriers also challenge the boundaries and hierarchy of the family. If some family members, especially parents, are not fluent in the dominant language, the other family members who are fluent in the dominant language will be in a position of power over the other family member (Santisteban, Muir-Malcolm, Mitrani, & Szapocznik, 2002). Such changes or threats to the organization of the family will threaten the homeostasis of the family unit. When working with any family, it is important to learn about their particular culture and its subsequent impact on their family.

External systems such as social and legal policies directly impact how supported a family is and feels. In 2015, the Supreme Court of the United States granted federal support to same-sex marriages, making it possible for same-sex parents to marry in every state in the United States. This historic legislation allows many families to be recognized in a way that they previously were not. Changes in medical insurance coverage for children also impacts parents—in particular, parents with a child with a disability. Paying for a multitude of medical services and procedures is stressful for many parents and would not be possible without external systems such as Medicare. For children in foster care, continuity of care is extremely difficult to maintain amid placement changes. This unfortunate reality poses life-threatening risks for children with disabilities in foster care.

SPOTLIGHT ON CHILDREN IN FOSTER CARE

Up until now, we have been discussing families and working from the assumption that we all have a family. And while this is true on some level, many children grow up without the *experience* of being part of a family; they are children in foster care. Many children in foster care experience disruptions in care, moving them from biological relatives to foster parents to adoptive parents or to reunification with biological parents. These disruptions in care cause much instability in a child's life and often negatively impact the child's development (Lewis, Dozier, Ackerman, & Sepulveda-Kozakowski, 2007). According to the Adoption and Foster Care Analysis Reporting System from 2012, there were 397,000 children in foster care in the United States (Children's Bureau, 2012). It is harder to find permanent homes for children with disabilities in foster care (Children's Bureau, 2012). Children with disabilities in foster care also have longer stays in foster care than children without disabilities (National Council on Disability, 2008). The National Council on Disability (2008) issued a report that addressed children with disabilities in foster care and issues unique to their experiences. Several points that emerged from that report were: insufficient funding at both the state and federal levels, difficulty coordinating with multiple systems of care, faulty education programs, deficient programs to ease transitions in placements as well out of the foster care system, and concerns about confidentiality and the sharing of information about the children's lives (National Council on Disability, 2008). Addressing these concerns and supporting the healthy development of children with disabilities in foster care is a shared responsibility. Unfortunately, the responsibility may not feel shared for the foster parent given the findings from the National Council on Disability (2008) report.

Often foster parents require additional training to care for a child with a disability which limits the number of families who can foster such children. At times, biological parents do not have the resources to care for their child with a disability. Some of those biological parents place their children in foster care with the hope that the child will receive those needed resources while in foster care. Professionals who work with children in foster care will need to understand that the child's family may include foster and biological members. Respecting the child's definition of family is fundamental to supporting the child. Because of the disruptions in care children in foster care experience, they may frequently mourn the loss of parents, caregivers, and siblings. Thus the definition and experience of family may be very complicated for children in foster care, so the principles of family systems theory need to be carefully applied to such families.

For more information on foster care and adoption as well as the Adoption and Foster Care Analysis Report, visit http://www.acf.hhs.gov/programs/cb/focus-areas/foster-care or the National Council on Disability Report at http://www.ncd.gov/publications/2008/02262008#_edn97.

Summary

This chapter discussed family systems theory, its major principles, and its special significance for families with children with disabilities. While all families would benefit from understanding the intricacies and details of their interdependence, families with children with disabilities often do not have a choice. The presence of a disability forces families to reevaluate their identities, values, and strategies for survival. Developing survival strategies can be achieved, often with the support of special education teachers and other special education professionals, including therapists.

As a child psychologist, I have worked with many different types of families over the years. These families have taught me that being part of a family has brought them their greatest moments of joy as well as sadness. Cherishing the loving moments and sharing the hardest moments have been sources of their greatest moments of achievement. Acknowledging our vulnerabilities and willingness to put another person's wellbeing first unites all parents. The value of the family is endless, and may this chapter inspire you in your work with families.

Additional Resources

Web-Based

For more information on family systems theory ideas and concepts: http://family.jrank.org/pages/597/Family-SystemsTheory-Basic-Concepts-Propositions.html.

For more information on the family environment scale: http://www.mindgarden.com/96-family-environment-scale.

For more information on children with disabilities in foster care, please refer to the National Council on Disability website: http://www.ncd.gov/publications/2008/02262008#_edn97.

3

FAMILIES OF CHILDREN AT RISK FOR DISABILITY

BARRY BULLIS
Pace University

SAMUEL ZIMMERMAN
Pace University

"Even though our journey as parents of a medically fragile child began with emotional turmoil, it has since become a purposeful odyssey that brings meaning and depth to our lives. This is the road we were born to travel."

—Charisse Montgomery, Home Care CEO
(A Parent's Guide to Managing in-home Pediatric Nursing, 2015)

This chapter is about the risk factors that are associated with developing or having **disabilities**. It is important to understand these risk factors and how they impact certain groups so that we can minimize the number of children needing intensive, long-term special education services and increase the number of students who experience school success. Specifically, after reading this chapter, you will be able to achieve the following:

1. Define risk, identify the need and benefits to studying risk, and name main categories of risk for children and families.

2. Understand the nature of risks and, for select groups, the challenges stemming from the risks and some professional interventions to begin alleviating these risks or challenges.

3. Experience two case studies that exemplify families' real-life processes.

WHY STUDY RISK?

Families are not microsystems created or sustained in their development within a closed environment. Environmental, cultural, and biological stressors exist outside this microsystem that may impact family structure and the persons who live together within a given family unit. Stresses on the family unit, specifically children, establish a foundation of risk for disability. Knowledge of environmental, cultural, and biological risk stressors and specific vulnerability of children allow families to identify pathways of support in addressing a child's needs. Early school years performance is an early indicator to a child's successful academic, behavioral, and social development during later stages of school and posteducational life stages. The identification of particular risk stressors at this early juncture allows families to identify the impact they may have on the child, possible symptomatic patterns, and, thus, identification and implementation of appropriate educational and/or medical interventions. The primary goal of risk identification is to intervene with children whose identified risk factors predispose them to disrupted learning (Huffman, Mehlinger, & Kerivan, 2000).

Studies discussing risk stressors with causal predictive relationships to a child being identified with disability upon school entry seek to identify frequency of stressors. The most frequently identified stressors are biological, socio-environmental, economic, and cultural in origin, and each possesses degrees of impact upon a child's development. Dominant biological stressors predictive for a child's disability identification are pre- and postnatal health, maternal substance abuse, and family genetics history. Socio-environmental stressors may also be used to predict a child's school performance outcome as well as to identify at-risk populations. Poverty, maternal/paternal education, quality of family parenting, access to quality medical care, family composition, and rural and urban settings are among these socio-environmental stressors identified with direct influence upon a child's educational/developmental progress. Finally, cultural stressors of language and immigrant status also play a role in predicting a child's risk for disability identification. Each of these stressors will be further explored in greater depth in this chapter.

A child's vulnerability for disability identification is established by the number of stressors, frequency of occurrence, and severity of the stressor upon the family and subsequently the children within. Depending on the origin of the stressor, families may have to partner with school teams or community agencies. For example, a dual-parent family in which one parent loses employment is certainly a stressor to the health of the family. However, when compared to the loss of employment within a single-parent household, the vulnerability stress upon the child intensifies.

BENEFITS OF IDENTIFYING RISK

When a family unit is exposed to stressors, the child may be considered at risk for disability. If the affected child begins to display symptomatic behaviors indicating vulnerability, this in turn may result in screening for eligibility for early intervention services to address skills and/or **developmental delays**. When is screening for educational impact necessary? Children displaying delays in social, emotional, language/communicative, cognitive, and movement/physical development may require specialized screening to identify the appropriate interventions and family support.

Since 2004, there has been a requirement in the education regulations, previously known as the **Individuals with Disabilities Act (IDEA)** and now known as the Every Student Succeeds Act, that school districts need to have a process in place to identify and evaluate all children from birth to 21 years of age suspected of having a disability (IDEA, 2004). This mandate is often called Child Find. The regulations were put into place to ensure that vulnerable children, namely those who are advancing in school but may need more support and migrant children were supported (Section 300). The regulation also helps ensure that children that are not in school or are in private schools by parent choice are also identified and evaluated if a disability is suspected. It should be noted that nothing in the regulations requires that a child be classified as having a disability if one is not determined to exist or labeled by their disability. Child Find for children from birth to age 3 is covered by early intervention.

Early intervention screening occurs from birth to 3 years old and identifies a child's skill deficit within normed developmental scales. Since 1986, the United States has offered early intervention services for infants and toddlers with or at risk for disabilities through the final regulations of Part C under IDEA, which will help improve services and outcomes for America's infants and toddlers with disabilities and their families. Early intervention is available for children who have "established conditions" that will likely lead to a delay, even if a delay is not yet evident. Thus, any child identified through newborn screening with such a condition would be eligible for Part C services. Part C includes a wide range of individualized educational, therapeutic, and family support services. Parents uniformly report a high degree of satisfaction with early intervention services. A recent study (Bailey, Skinner, & Warren, 2005) of a nationally representative sample of more than 3,000 families found that most were very positive about their child's entry into Part C programs, reporting relative ease in accessing services, positive impressions of professionals and services, and satisfaction with their involvement in decision making.

Screening is initiated after a child's parent, primary caregiver, teacher, or other stakeholder identifies a child's behavior or performance that is atypical to their age if the concern is severe enough to highlight a need for additional screening for disability. In a minority subset, teratogenic screening (lead blood levels, maternal substance abuse, fetal abnormalities) may also be identified when the child is in utero. Poor community health care services, toxin exposures partnered with poverty, and single-parent family structures all increase disability risks during pregnancy.

Screening focuses on one question: Does a potential problem exist that requires further attention? The screening process takes many forms, including the use of the following (Venn, 2004):

- formal screening tests
- informal screening checklists, scales, and inventories
- observations of behavior, speech, and language
- vision and hearing test results
- medical reports
- progress records
- intervention records
- educational history
- attendance history
- parent conferences
- child conferences

Early screening and identification allow for families to gain an understanding of the cause of their child's performance, support strategies including implementation of therapies and/or instruction, ongoing assessment, and expectations. However, parents often report they become overwhelmed during the early screening process for their child, not fully understanding who they should reach out to for guidance. Often parent concerns are met with "It is too early for your concerns" by either family members (including spouses), close friends, and, in many circumstances, their child's teachers and doctors.

In identifying, assessing, and designing treatments for at-risk children and families, various roles of stakeholders possess their own legal rights and participate in questioning or where additional help is needed for the child and family—often educational, medical, or social service agencies and behavioral therapists/specialists are all involved (Huffman, 2000).

IDEA identifies the local education agency (LEA), the school, as being the responsible party for providing services to students classified as disabled, and thus the prereferral supports to families are also legally mandated. Parents who are experiencing concerns during the prereferral process (a preventative approach to eliminate inappropriate referrals to special education) may reach out to their child's school district's special education office or review their state's governmental website, which will often list **special education support agencies**, including **advocacy** agencies to guide them through any concerns or questions that have not been addressed at the school or district level. There is a wide range of agencies that provide support to families that have identified developmental concerns for their child, are within the early intervention process, or have school-age children experiencing school difficulty.

Once the child is school age, having entered kindergarten, screening is done to identify performance areas of concern as well as prereferral supports. One such support is utilizing **response to intervention (RTI)**. RTI includes a multitier approach to the early identification and support of students who have been identified as at risk for academic and emotional delays as evidenced by their learning and behavioral needs. This multitier approach typically is aligned to three tiers, with each tier level providing increased levels and intensity of the identified support. When presented during the prereferral process, RTI strategies and tools enable educators to target instructional interventions to children's areas of specific need as soon as those needs become apparent (Individuals with Disabilities Education Act, 2004). RTI strategies differ within their implementation depending upon the severity of the identified performance gap. The planning of support and strategies requires collaboration between the family, school, and other identified stakeholders to ensure there is both an understanding of why particular strategies or support programs have been selected and the roles of each in implementing the agreed-upon support. It is clear (a) that family processes and practices are strongly related to students' academic, social, emotional, and behavioral outcomes while students are in school and beyond and (b) that when schools and families collaborate to support student learning, student outcomes are improved (Henderson & Mapp, 2002).

CASE STUDY 1
RAYMOND

Raymond is an extremely bubbly 4-year-old, small in stature for his age, who is receiving preschool special education services. He currently lives with his mother, Ellen, older sister, Lisa, and his maternal grandmother. He attends a special education pre-K program, where he is in a classroom with 15 students total and receives speech, occupational, and music therapy. After school, Raymond receives speech or occupational therapy or special education teacher services daily for an hour at home from his mother. The LEA provides some of these after-school services as a result of Ellen filing a due process complaint in which the LEA had not provided the mandated services identified during early intervention screening. The other after-school services are paid privately by Ellen. His screening indicated no limits with his cognitive functioning or his successful acquisition of adaptive skills but demonstrates current delays in toilet training.

In school, Raymond opts to play independently or plays with children 1 to 2 years younger than him. His mother attributes this to his peers not having either the patience to decipher his speech or that he cannot "keep up" with them. His speech is a concern for his mother, who reports that he speaks in two- to three-word sentences. When his after-school therapy is completed, his mother works with him on toilet training, which creates anxiety for Raymond. He cries and refuses to comply with directions. He is unable or unwilling to remove his pull-up training diapers independently.

The school has called for a transition-to-kindergarten meeting. The LEA and teachers feel that Raymond may be able to attend kindergarten in a general education classroom, and they recommend altering his service plan to a 504 plan. (A 504 plan, an alternative to an IEP, allows children with disabilities to receive accommodations that will ensure their academic success and access to the learning environment.) The team felt Raymond no longer requires the intense intervention supplied by the IEP. Although, according to his mother, he has made incredible progress and benefited from consistent early intervention services, identification of appropriate services, and additional behavioral therapies paid for by his parents, Ellen remains cautious in her optimism as she continues to navigate the bureaucracy of the LEA to ensure Raymond will continue to receive the appropriate services and accommodations as he enters kindergarten next year.

(1) Why would Raymond be considered at risk?

(2) How could you, as a representative of the school, assist Ellen in navigating the transition from preschool to kindergarten?

DEFINITION OF RISK

Risk factors are those characteristics that, when present in a disorder-free child, indicate a greater likelihood that the child will subsequently develop a disorder (Garmezy, 1994; Werner, 1992). In this chapter, when we use the term "at risk," we are using it to mean students who, for some environmental, biological, or genetic reason, are at greater risk for developing or being diagnosed with a disability. In studying children at risk for developing disabilities, we review the evidence of an association between risk factors and their relationship to specific disabilities. This definition differs from the common educational term for students who are considered *at risk*. The term "at-risk" is often used to describe students or groups of students, those with or without disabilities, who are considered to have a higher probability of failing academically or dropping out of school. However, there is a second subset of children who would also be considered at risk for disability classification, and this refers to those children who are exposed to the stressors outlined within this chapter. The term may be applied to students who face circumstances that could jeopardize their ability to complete school, such as homelessness, incarceration, teenage pregnancy, serious health issues, domestic violence, transiency, or other conditions, or it may refer to learning disabilities, low test scores, disciplinary problems, grade retentions, or other learning-related factors that could adversely affect the educational performance and attainment of some students (Hidden Curriculum Definition, 2013).

CATEGORIES OF RISK

Environmental

Environmental factors have a profound influence on a child's development (Brookover & Erickson, 1969; Morrow & Torres, 1995). Poverty, environmental toxins, crime levels, and access to quality health services are leading environmental factors impacting the health of the child as well as the family.

The effects of growing up in poverty, particularly for children raised in socially isolated, economically depressed urban areas, warrants greater concern (Carnoy, 1994). Poverty affects health on several levels: directly, through the psychological stress and social stigmatization that accompany living in poverty, and indirectly, through increased exposure to a wide range of environmental stressors such as pollution, crime, and lack of access to healthful food (Evans & Kantrowitz, 2001). Additionally, research shows poor children generally receive inferior services from schools and agencies that are located in the inner city. As such, poor children often have many unmet needs not being unique to geography, with both rural and urban children coming to school hungry, abused, and poorly dressed (Yeo, 1997), impacting healthy development, social behaviors, and long-term outcomes. Compounding lower socioeconomic status is the presence of different environmental toxins, thus leading to a higher risk of disability identification.

Factors that are considered in reviewing toxin exposure are degree of environmental and developmental intersection, health of the child prior to exposure, age of the child, duration and frequency of exposure, and intensity of exposure. Most common toxins can be found in cosmetics, medicines, alcohol, chemicals in cigarettes, and lead. For example, lead was found in commercial paint until 1978, when it was banned due to the fact that lead exposure may result in a variety of effects on neuropsychological functioning, including deficits in intellectual functioning, attention on tasks, organization of thinking and behavior, articulation, and language comprehension. Children are especially vulnerable to toxins compared to adults, as they pass through several delicate developmental stages and, pound for pound, they eat and breathe more environmental contaminants than adults (Rauch & Lanphear, 2012). The brain and lungs continue to develop postnatally, the brain through infancy and lungs through adolescence, during which toxin exposure may result in various disabilities as both organs are exposed to toxins during the noted developmental period. The number of children diagnosed with an activity limitation stemming from a chronic health condition rose from 1.8% in 1960 to 7.3% in 2006, while the prevalence of diagnosed developmental disabilities rose from 12.8% in 1997–1999 to 15% in 2006–2008 (Perrin, Bloom, & Gortmaker, 2011).

The lack of community health services in the form of prenatal clinics and child specialists impacts the ability of families in low-socioeconomic communities to protect the health of their children, thus preventing the development of disability. Possible consequences can be so debilitating that a child's life chances can literally be determined by a number of environmental and cultural factors such as the quality of prenatal care, quality of housing, and food available to the mothers that are simply beyond the control of an individual or even of concerted community action (Noguera, 2003). However, community-based interventions have demonstrated success in targeting early childhood health issues in areas absent of available healthcare resources. One such intervention is the practice of nurses' visits to low-income first-time mothers in their homes to promote care of healthy infants. One such program, the Nurse Family Partnership, which has been tested around the country and now operates in 32 states, shows evidence of reducing maltreatment of the child and subsequent decreases in behavioral problems and increases in cognitive performance in children (Olds et al., 2004).

CASE STUDY 2
SARAH

Sarah was placed and later adopted by her current parents when she was only 8 months old after being removed from her maternal grandmother's home. Child protective services reported that her biological mother did not receive any prenatal care, and Sarah was born testing positive for opiate exposure. Her parents noted no concerns regarding Sarah's developmental milestones. Concerns began with her when she approached language-acquisition milestones, as it sounded like "Sarah was speaking with marbles in her mouth"; her articulation was incomprehensible. She was found eligible for early intervention services and received supports with speech therapy. When she was ready to enter kindergarten, it was determined that she no longer required special education services, and she was placed in general education for kindergarten.

Sarah, now an 11-year-old fifth grader, is woken up by her dad Warren, who describes her as not a "morning person," requiring two to three wake-up alerts before she begins her morning routine. The bedroom she shares with her two younger sisters (a 5- and a 3-year-old) reflects each of the girls' interests. Sarah's space has her artwork hung up next to dance awards, with hair ribbons and colored pencils scattered on her dresser.

Sarah would prefer to have pancakes every morning for breakfast. She has been sitting at the breakfast table for 10 minutes staring down at her cereal bowl and spoon while her four siblings chat with each other or her dads. Her dad Warren reminds her to pick up the pace, as her bus for school will be arriving in 20 minutes. She looks back down at her cereal bowl, puts her spoon down, and argues with her oldest brother Mark, a 15-year-old, which results in another reminder from her dad to finish up breakfast.

Sarah has difficulty following directions. Her challenges in the completion of multistep directions remain a genesis of frustration for both Sarah and her parents, who have begun to collaborate with her teacher in developing an organized manner of providing her with an appropriate level of verbal and nonverbal prompts.

The curriculum became increasingly challenging for Sarah last year. Her father Brad reported to her teacher that homework tasks that would have typically taken a classmate 30 to 40 minutes took Sarah two hours to complete. She would become frustrated and anxious, especially in the area of mathematics. Sarah's fourth-grade teacher told her fathers that she could have reduced homework assignments, and her school year became more successful.

This year Sarah is again having difficulty in school. Her teacher this year is unwilling to make accommodations without some sort of documentation, stating, "It is not fair to provide special treatment to one student over the others." Sarah's fathers feel this instructional focus is simply on academic progress without considering their daughter's social and emotional needs.

(1) What factors place Sarah at risk?

(2) As a representative of the school, what would you suggest are the next steps for Sarah's family?

Biological

A multitude of biological factors may increase the risk of developmental disabilities in children with both short- and long-term consequences, such as gender, low birth weight, in-utero drug exposure impacting in-utero nutrition, and genetic abnormalities.

Male fetuses are more vulnerable to all kinds of prenatal problems (Boyd & Bee, 2006) and birth defects (Tanner, 1990) and have a higher likelihood of infections, jaundice, birth complications, and congenital conditions, but the biggest risk for males is due to preterm birth. For two babies born at the same degree of prematurity, a male will have a higher risk of death and disability compared to a female. Even in the womb, females mature more rapidly than males, which provides an advantage, because the lungs and other organs are more developed (Blencowe, Cousens, Chou, Oestergaard, Say, Moller, Kenney, & Lawn, 2012). In comparison, postnatally, auditory processing problems are most prominent in males, whereas females will demonstrate both auditory and visual cognitive impairments (Jacobsen, Slotkin, Mencl, Frost, & Pugh, 2007).

Being born with low birth weight is typically recognized if a baby is born under 5.5 lb (LBW, 2,500 grams). Low birth weight has been identified as a potential risk factor for certain disabilities (Calame et al., 1986), including intellectual disabilities, vision loss, and/or learning problems. Children with low birth weight, when compared to their normal-birth-weight peers, are at increased risk for many poor outcomes, including physical and cognitive delays (Hack et al., 1994), higher rates of academic problems (Grunau, 1986), lower scores on standardized tests of achievement/academic grades (Lagerstrom, Bremme, Eneroth, & Magnusson, 1991), and increased risk for learning disabilities and special educational services (Grunau, 1986). Lead causes of low birth weight are smoking, alcohol and drug use, poor nutrition, multiple fetuses, and early delivery from risk of preeclampsia (a dangerous pregnancy complication characterized by high blood pressure).

Behaviors of expectant mothers have been associated with children who are born at risk for developing disabilities. In-utero research studies focused on nicotine, alcohol, and opiate use during pregnancy have occurred continuously beginning in the 1960s as fetal medical treatment care technologies have improved.

Substance Abuse

Smoking during pregnancy can have profound effects on fetal development. Common physical and behavioral effects of prenatal exposure to nicotine have been observed, including low birth weight, enhanced locomotor activity, and cognitive impairment (Ernst, Moolchan, & Robinson, 2001). Additionally, damage from maternal smoking has a direct adverse effect on placental development, which decreases the transfer of nutrients and oxygen to the fetus and can result in premature delivery, fetal growth restriction, and smaller head size (Castles, Adams, Melvin, Kelsch, & Boulton, 1999).

Similar to tobacco use, expectant mothers within the United States have also received warnings regarding alcohol consumption from alcohol manufacturers since 1988 with the passage of the federal Alcoholic Beverage Labeling Act (ABLA) requiring all alcohol products to carry the warning, "(1) According to the Surgeon General, women should not drink alcoholic beverages during pregnancy because of the risk of birth defects." The most prevalent defect caused by prolonged alcohol consumption in alcoholic women is fetal alcohol syndrome (FAS), a pattern of anomalies occurring in children born to alcoholic women (Jones & Smith, 1973). The main features of this pattern are pre- and/or postnatal growth retardation, characteristic facial abnormalities, and central nervous system dysfunction, including mental retardation (Stratton, Howe, & Battaglia, 1996). Expectant mothers who drink alcohol but are not chronic consumers of alcohol still present a risk for fetal defect and disability. Drinking alcohol during pregnancy

TABLE 3.1 ■ Prenatal Drug Exposure: Potential Effects on Birth and Pregnancy Outcomes			
Tobacco	**Marijuana**	**Stimulants**	**Opiates**
Disturbed maternal–infant interaction Excitability Hypertonia Stress abstinence signs Conduct disorder Reduced IQ Aggression Antisocial behavior Impulsivity ADHD Tobacco use and dependence	Mild withdrawal symptoms Delayed state regulation Reading, spelling difficulty Executive function impairment Early tobacco and marijuana use	**Cocaine** *Neonatal/Infancy* Early neurobehavioral deficits: orientation, state regulation, autonomic stability, attention, sensory and motor asymmetry, jitteriness Poor clarity of infant cues during feeding interaction Delayed information processing General cognitive delay *Childhood* Lower nonverbal perceptual reasoning Lower weight for height Lower weight-curve trajectories Attention problems Disruptive behaviors by self-report and caregiver report	Neonatal abstinence syndrome Less rhythmic swallowing Strabismus Possible delay in general cognitive function Anxiety Aggression Feelings of rejection Disruptive/inattentive behavior
		Methamphetamine Poor movement quality (3rd-trimester exposure) Lower arousal Increased lethargy Increased physiological stress No mental or motor delay (infant/toddler)	

Source: Minnes, Lang, & Singer, 2011. Reprinted with permission (within public domain): http://www.ncbi.nlm.nih.gov/pmc/about/copyright/

can cause a range of lifelong physical, behavioral, and intellectual disabilities. These disabilities are known as fetal alcohol spectrum disorders (FASDs). Children with FASDs might have any or all of the following characteristics and behaviors (Riley & McGee, 2005):

- abnormal facial features, such as a smooth ridge between the nose and upper lip
- small head size
- shorter-than-average height
- low body weight

- poor coordination
- hyperactive behavior
- difficulty with attention
- poor memory
- difficulty in school (especially with math)
- learning disabilities
- speech and language delays
- intellectual disability or low IQ
- poor reasoning and judgment skills
- vision or hearing problems

Prenatal exposure to drugs can affect a child's development. With improved pain therapies utilizing opiates, oxycodone, and codeine, including an illicit use of illegal narcotics, the Centers for Disease Control has concerns of abuse, as opiate addiction rates have increased among women (Centers for Disease Control, 2012).

The placenta was once believed to protect the fetus against exposure to toxins and maternal substance use, but it is now known that metabolites of drugs, including cocaine, opiates, amphetamines, marijuana, and tobacco, enter the fetal bloodstream. Active metabolites can penetrate the fetal blood–brain barrier and interfere with early neuronal cell development or cause neuronal death (Lee et al., 2008). Maternal drug abuse also affects the fetus indirectly. For example, crack cocaine, heroin, tobacco, and marijuana cause vasoconstriction that restricts the fetal oxygen supply. Additionally, substance abuse often conflicts with healthy maternal practices—such as eating a nutrient-rich diet and accessing prenatal care—that reduce pregnancy complications such as diabetes, preeclampsia, and preterm labor (Minnes, Lang, & Singer, 2001). Nearly 2 million Americans living today were prenatally exposed to cocaine during the peak 1980s drug epidemic, many of whom are now adolescents or young adults. Currently, an estimated 50,000 infants are born in the United States each year having been prenatally exposed to cocaine (Minnes, 2011). Subtle negative effects involving perceptual reasoning, which refers to one's ability to envision solutions to nonverbal problems, such as the recreation of a spatial design with 3D colored blocks, has been associated with prenatal cocaine exposure in children 4 to 9 years of age (Singer et al., 2004). Perceptual reasoning impairments also impact a child's ability to recognize and use patterns, preventing the formation of mental pictures—all of these abilities are utilized in mathematical comprehension. Fetal exposure to illicit substances is contributing to a renewed focus on the social emotional development of school-aged children and possible long-term effects of exposure. Rule breaking, aggression, and other externalizing behaviors are associated and observed in school-age children with prenatal cocaine exposure and are attributed to a lack of self-regulation.

Ratings completed by teachers, experimenters, and caregivers indicate that being prenatally cocaine exposed, being male, and living in a high-risk environment are each independently predictive of aggressive behavior (Bendersky, Bennett, & Lewis, 2006).

Linares and colleagues (2006) reported that among prenatally cocaine-exposed 6-year-olds:

- 17% reported symptoms of oppositional defiant disorder, compared with 9% of unexposed agemates; and
- 12% reported clinically elevated levels of ADHD symptoms, compared with 7% of unexposed peers

However, there is hope if treatment is given. For example, treatment and parent success in addressing the needs of their children fetally exposed to drugs have been documented through early intervention services when they are provided to both mothers and infants over the course of 2 to 3 years following delivery and identification of positive drug exposure during pregnancy. As part of the Seattle Birth to 3 Program, paraprofessional advocates visited substance-abusing women and their children weekly for the first 6 weeks after birth, then at least biweekly, depending on need, for 3 years. The advocates worked to establish trusting relationships with the mothers and motivated them to identify and work toward personal goals. They made and monitored follow-up on community referrals for drug treatment and other services for mother and child and offered guidance and supervision to ensure that the child was in a safe environment either with or without their parent and received appropriate care. At 36 months postpartum, 69% of the children receiving the intervention service were in what the research team considered to be an appropriate and stable environment relative to their mother's current use of alcohol/drugs (i.e., with mother in recovery for at least 6 months or not with mother unable to maintain abstinence), compared with 29% of children in a control group (Ernst et al., 1999).

Genetic

Genetic history remains the unseen, dormant, and little-understood risk for disability. When we speak of nature impacting a child's development, parents' genetic histories directly increase the risk of disability in their offspring. The importance of genetic influences on disability has been recognized for a long time, but genetic analysis has only recently begun to yield insights into the genesis of disabling conditions. Currently, IDEA identifies thirteen categories of disability: autism, deaf and blindness, deafness, emotional disturbance, hearing impairment, intellectual disability (formerly mental retardation), multiple disabilities, orthopedic impairment, other health impairments, specific learning disability, speech or language impairment, acquired brain injury, and vision impairment—all of which can be caused by genetic abnormalities.

Genetic disorders may or may not be heritable, that is, passed down from the parents' genes. Genetic inheritance is classified as either dominant or recessive; dominant gene disease can occur in a child if only one parent has the gene, while recessive inheritance occurs only if both parents have the defective gene. In nonheritable genetic disorders, defects may be caused by new mutations or changes to the DNA. There are three forms of genetic disorders: single-gene disorders, chromosomal disorders, and complex genetic disorders. Single-gene disorders are typically rare, inherited by one parent, and directly related to the risk of a specific disease (sickle-cell anemia). Chromosomal disorders are those in which chromosomes are missing or mutated. The risk of chromosomal disorders increases as the age at which the mother becomes pregnant increases (Down syndrome). Complex genetic disorders are characterized by two or more mutations within genes and can be impacted by environment and lifestyle. Due to the wide range of genetic disorders that is known, diagnosis of a genetic disorder is dependent on the disorder. Most genetic disorders are diagnosed at birth or during early childhood.

The most common birth defect in the United States as reported by the Centers for Disease Control is the chromosomal disorder Down syndrome (Parker et al, 2010). It occurs in about 1 in 800 newborns. About 5,300 babies with Down syndrome are born in the United States each year, and an estimated 250,000 people in this country have the condition. Down syndrome is a chromosomal disorder resulting in intellectual disability and physical abnormalities such as weak muscle tone. All affected children experience mild to moderate cognitive delays.

Prenatal screening for Down syndrome began in the 1970s as medical technology improved. Until recently, prenatal diagnosis usually meant an amniocentesis, a second-trimester procedure routinely available for women over a certain age (usually 35 years in North America), for Down syndrome and other genetic anomalies (Lippman, 1991), in which a sample of amniotic fluid is taken from the amniotic sac (amnion) surrounding the unborn baby and its DNA is examined for genetic abnormalities. Recent advances in genetic screening for disability allow for diagnosis of disability to occur as early as 10 weeks into pregnancy using cell-free fetal DNA testing.

Community genetic services/screenings models vary in supporting families. Community genetics services include a number of activities for the diagnosis, care, and prevention of genetic diseases at community level (Alwan & Modell, 1997):

- diagnosis of congenital disorders and genetic diseases: clinical and laboratory (cytogenetics, biochemical assays, DNA testing, etc.)
- genetics counseling
- preconception care
- prenatal screening
- prenatal and preimplantation genetic diagnoses
- newborn screening
- carrier screening
- population genetic screening according to other established policies

Genetic screening presents both pros and cons for expectant parents. The benefit of knowing if a child is going to be born with Down syndrome, Tay-Sachs, Marfan syndrome, or other genetic disorders can help the family make preparations in advance should they decide to continue the pregnancy. There is also long-range planning to consider, such as physically preparing a home environment that is safe for a baby with special needs. If there are siblings at home, there might be a benefit in preparing them mentally and emotionally for a baby with a genetic disorder so that they can provide the care and attention that are necessary for this newborn (Garvey, 2012).

CHILDREN LIVING IN POVERTY

As mentioned earlier in the chapter, poverty is one of the largest and most pervasive environmental risk factors for families. According to the National Center for Children in Poverty (www.nccp.org), in 2010, 11.4 out of 24 million children under the age of 6 live in low-income or poor families (3 million living in extreme poverty). This is almost half of all children in this age group in the United States! Children living in poverty experience many of the risk factors identified earlier, but they may also experience one of seven other risk factors: households without English speakers, a large family (four or more children), low parental education, residential mobility, single parent, teen mother, and nonemployed parents. The largest risk factor associated with poverty is single-parent households, affecting 16% of children in poverty. Further, 20% (approximately 4.7 million) children are affected by three or more of these risk factors.

However, not all risk factors are experienced equally. Single-parent households share many of the other risk factors of poverty, including the parent being unemployed or underemployed, having the first child as a teenager, and having unstable living arrangements. Nearly 4 million children are living in single-parent households. In a large data analysis of Head Start families, Roy and Raver (2014) found that African-American families were more likely to fall in the deep poverty and single-parent category than other racial/ethnic groups, compared to Latino and White families that are in deep poverty and crowded conditions. Thus, the single-parent and poverty issue is affecting African American families more severely than other racial groups. They also discovered that those children coming from single-parent homes with stressors (such as low income, poor education, etc.) were more likely than any other group to have students with behavioral problems. Similarly, Beatty (1995) had previously reported on the long-lasting peer relations and self-image effects on children in single-parent households without fathers before the age of 5. In contrast, the crowded conditions of Latino and White families correlated with greater later academic delays. Single-parent households also have increased financial burdens when a child has additional medical or educational needs, often necessitating that the parent not work in order to ensure the child is served, truly a double bind and having ever-increasing downward cyclical effects (Parish, Rose, Swaine, Dababnah, & Mayra, 2012).

Other factors such as food insecurity and hunger, lack of material needs—clothing, school supplies, technology, etc.—and access to quality medical care also impact a child's preparation for education and may lead directly to lower cognitive ability. In fact, the consequences of food insecurity and hunger alone can cause a child to be fatigued, irritable, dizzy, have headaches, and have difficulty concentrating. Of course, this makes sense—just think of the last time you were so hungry that you couldn't concentrate.

The major effect of the risk factors and stressors of families living in poverty is that children come to school, even with access to early intervention, underprepared for school demands. In their now-seminal study of language and vocabulary growth, Hart and Risley (1995) found that children from homes with professional parents, by age 3, had double the number of vocabulary words than those from families in poverty (see Figure 3.1).

In this same study, it was observed that the amount of words heard by those in professional families was just over 2,000 words per hour versus about 600 in families in poverty. Extrapolating these numbers, that means that children living in poverty have heard 30 million fewer words by age 4 than those in upper-class families. This research has recently been extended and confirmed by a study by researchers at Stanford University showing that children at 24 months of age from lower-income families were tracking and identifying pictures at the same level as those children 18 months old from the higher socioeconomic group (Fernald, Marchman, & Weisleder, 2013). This under preparedness continues right into school age, mainly due to children spending very little time in their day in school. For students who possess limited vocabulary, their reading aptitude is also affected. Because reading is the major source of vocabulary growth, the limited reader is locked into a repeating cycle of failure and frustration (Nagy, 1989). Students living in poverty are also more likely to be retained, suspended and expelled and to drop out (Taylor & Adelman, 2000).

Education professionals should have a three-pronged approach when working with families living in poverty: (1) ensuring they are well versed in supporting families with community resources, (2) ensuring that families are fully integrated into their child's educational program, and (3) responding to the student's unique needs in the classroom. Peterson, Mayer, Summers, & Luze (2010) makes five recommendations for professionals in supporting families that align closely with the first prong: (1) monitor the children closely when families face multiple risks,

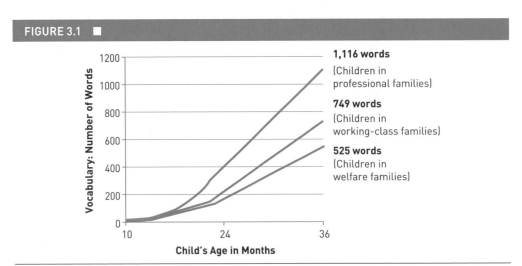

FIGURE 3.1 ■

Source: Hart & Risley, 1995, Brookes Publishing. Reprinted with permission

(2) develop clear procedures to determine when and how to refer families to services, (3) work collaboratively with community partners and health-care community to help identify possibility of disabilities, (4) focus on early intervention, and (5) provide services and supports to families.

To address the second prong, we must look to building trusting, productive partnerships with families. It begins with seeing the families as equal information sources, as well as equal in being problem solvers.

> It is time that we move from thinking about education in terms of each child, to thinking about education from a multiple life-cycles perspective. If we are serious about attaining long-lasting increases in student achievement, we should look to both the school and the home: early parenthood education should take its place alongside early childhood education as a primary means of getting education right from the start. (Sticht, 2012, p. 17)

The caveat, as just stated, is for educational/service providers to not be seen as the holder of all the answers, the only right approach, and so forth.

For the final prong, educational professionals must assess children's academic, behavioral, and social strengths and challenges at the very beginning of any relationship in order to understand how best to meet the child's needs and identify the strengths that can be used as a vehicle to meet those needs. In addition, teachers should include the cultural element of their student populations, increasing their cultural competence in language/literacy instruction so students can be bicultural and facile in their ability to move between school and home cultures (Ladson-Billings, 2002).

ENGLISH LEARNERS

In contrast to biological factors for risk, family culture may also play a role for disability risks. One such student subgroup is English learners (ELs), also commonly referred to as English language learners (ELLs), who are those whose native home language differs from English, many of which are first-generation participants in formal public education. Spanish-speaking families tend to have lower parental educational attainment and family incomes than Asian- or Pacific-language families (August & Hakuta, 1997). Although the majority of ELs in the United States are Hispanic and come from Spanish-speaking homes, students classified as EL speak more than 350 languages (Ethnologue, 2009). Half of the projected increase in the national school-age population will be children of immigrants, which poses strong concerns regarding educational equity, inclusion approaches, and a review of our screening practices for special education.

The individual families of these students might be equally diverse, and if we want them to become active and collaborative members of school communities regardless of language proficiency, we must get to know them personally. A present concern is the validity of screening for disability when families do not possess English proficiency. Non-Hispanic Whites currently are 67% of the population; by 2050, it is projected, they will be only 47% of the U.S. population. Within this same time span, the Hispanic population is expected to triple in size to 29% of the total, the Black population will increase slightly from 12.8 % to 13.4%, and the Asian subgroup will increase from 5% to 9% (Passel & Cohn, 2008).

We know less about possible barriers faced by non–English-speaking immigrant families with children with disabilities, many of whom have lower incomes, comprehensive understanding of special education due process guidelines, and access to appropriate educational and medical specialists. These families are equally diverse, and if we want them to become active and collaborative members of school communities regardless of language proficiency, we must get to know them personally. Gonzalez, Eades, & Supple (2014) shares additional risk factors for immigrant children: learning English, finding social support or networks, confronting racial labeling, acquiring new styles of learning, coping with posttraumatic stress, and understanding different cultural scripts. Historically, most immigrant groups are located in lower-socioeconomic communities, finding both residence and employment typically in impoverished urban or metropolitan areas. Frequently, immigrant families do not possess the financial or transportation resources to physically transport themselves to needed services; as relative newcomers, they may not know which services and providers are available; and because of cultural factors, they may be reluctant to seek outside service (Benjamin, Wallace, Villa, & McCarthy, 2000). Research findings indicate that health-care and community service providers encounter several challenges in providing care to immigrant families raising a child with a disability. Such challenges include the following: (1) lack of training in providing culturally sensitive care; (2) language and communication issues; (3) discrepancies in conceptualizations of disability between health-care providers and immigrant parents; (4) building rapport; and (5) helping parents advocate for themselves and their children (Lindsay, King, Klassen, Esses, & Stachel, 2012). While our knowledge about the sources and consequences of disability has grown with increased focus on different early intervention models implemented across diverse family structures, what we know about immigrant health and rate of disability has not kept pace.

Risks of disability classification increase, as immigrant families do not have access to early intervention services to address developmental obstacles displayed in their infants. Complicating this issue, early intervention, special education identification, placement, and instructional decisions for students who are English learners have been largely based on research and practices used with monolingual students with disabilities (Artiles & Ortiz, 2002). Variables relegating accessibility of assessments for students with disabilities and EL students may seriously hinder the academic performance of EL students. Furthermore, classification and **accommodation** for these students requires a more complex design than those for either ELs or students with disabilities. Regardless of monolingual screening practices, particular ethnic groups are over- and underidentified within the prevalence of disability. Minority groups remain higher than non-Hispanic white population. Native Americans have the highest rate of disability (21.9%), followed by Blacks (20.0%), Whites (19.7%), and Hispanics (15.3%). Asian-Pacific Islanders have the lowest rate (9.1.%; Bradsher, 1993) and remain consistent in 2015 according to U.S. census data. Proper identification of EL students is a challenge if their disability is masked by their limited English proficiency or vice versa. Improper identification may lead to inappropriate instruction, assessment, and accommodation for these students (Abedi, 2009).

For many ELs with disabilities, special education decisions may be problematic because they lack consideration of the linguistic demands and needs of students who are acquiring proficiency in English as well as another language (Vaughn, Mathes, Linan-Thompson, & Francis, 2005). **Response-to-intervention (RTI)** approaches should be implemented to support all students who are currently within general education settings and have not been identified for special education screening. RTI is a multi-tiered instructional and service-delivery model designed to improve student learning by providing high-quality instruction, intervening early with students at risk for academic difficulty, allocating instructional resources according to students' needs, and distinguishing between students whose reading difficulties stem from experiential and instructional deficits as opposed to a learning disability (Vaughn, 2005). However, RTI approaches cannot be embedded independently into pedagogical practices without also considering English-as-a-second-language instructional strategies. Both the RTI (Gersten et al., 2007) and EL (Gersten et al., 2008) practice guides from the Institute for Education Sciences indicate that screening and monitoring students' performance in English language phonological processing, letter knowledge, and word and text reading are helpful in planning instruction for ELs.

STUDENTS EXPERIENCING MARGINALIZATION

While many risk factors develop or appear at early ages and schooling, there is a category of youth that, due to their real or perceived lack of power and participation in the education process, are at high risk of not becoming successful learners. These students are *marginalized*, on the edge, in society and schools. Marginalized youth can be any adolescent facing challenges and risks to educational participation that may come from many stressors, including family related—no parent involvement, poverty, dysfunctional/abusive home life; community related—lack of community support for school, high crime, poor connection to the school; student related—low ability, pregnancy, drug abuse, negative friends, low self-efficacy; and school related—conflict between home and school, ineffective discipline and/or instruction, negative climate, and poor resources (Duttweiler, National Dropout Prevention Center, & National Educational Service, 1995).

African-American males, and now Hispanic males, especially those from low-income families or poverty, are of the most recognized marginalized groups, and the ones that have had very little change in this status over the years. (Richter, J., 2004 in Hughes, Newkirk, & Stenhjem, 2010), explains that there are four challenges in providing services to multicultural youth from high poverty: criminalization of youth, youth's pessimism toward society, youth's need for a sense of belonging, and adults' need to increase cultural competence. "Race, racism, and poverty conspire to affect teacher attitude, hiring practices, and social service delivery. This leads to alienation and disempowerment of youth, increasing their likelihood of acting out or dropping out" (p. 23). Further, African-American males often confront formidable challenges of developing a positive identity as self-directed individuals in the context of family, community, and a racist society while managing the turmoil of adolescence (Paster, 1985).

African-American and Hispanic students often enter school underprepared (see section on effects of poverty), and their school performance remains low throughout their school careers. Table 3.2 shows the percentage of students from various racial/ethnic backgrounds and their proficiency in reading and math on the National Assessment of Educational Progress, our nation's report card (www.nationsreportcard.com). Only 17 to 26% of African-American and Hispanic youth in grades 4 and 8 are being successful, compared to 45 to 54% of their White peers.

Considerable research data suggests that, for dominated minorities, the extent to which students' language and culture are incorporated into the school program constitutes a significant predictor of academic success (Campos & Keatinge, 1984; Cummins, J. 1983a; Rosier & Holm, 1980).

Another group that is greatly marginalized in schools is lesbian, gay, bisexual, transgender (LGBT), and questioning youth. The Gay Lesbian Straight Education Network (www.glsen.org)

TABLE 3.2 ■ Percentage of students at or above proficient				
National Assessment of Educational Progress—2013				
Race/Ethnicity	Reading		Math	
	4th	8th	4th	8th
All	35	36	42	35
White	46	46	54	45
Black	18	17	18	14
Hispanic	20	22	26	21

conducts surveys to report on the school experiences of this group. In their 2011 national school climate survey executive summary, they state: "Schools nationwide are hostile environments for a distressing number of LGBT students, the overwhelming majority of whom hear homophobic remarks and experience harassment or assault at school because of their sexual orientation or gender expression" (Gay, Lesbian, Straight Education Network, 2012, p. 5). Statistics reveal that:

- 84.9% of students heard "gay" used in a negative way, and 71.3% heard other homophobic remarks frequently or often
- 81.9%, 38.3%, 18.3% of respondents said they had been verbally harassed, physically harassed, or physically assaulted, respectively, because of their sexual orientation
- 55.2% of LGBT students had been cyberbullied in the past year
- Around 11% of LGBT students missed 4 or more days of school due to feeling unsafe or uncomfortable
- GPAs differed between those harassed more, 2.9, than harassed less, 3.2

Personal narratives collected from 31 youth and 19 school adults by Snapp and colleagues (2015) found LGBT students being punished more harshly for rule violations, such as public displays of affection and self-expression, and frequently blamed for their own victimization. Further, adults often perpetuated the name calling or failed to support students. This marginalization has a huge deleterious effect on LGBT youth. While LGBT and questioning youth represent approximately 5 to 7% of the youth population, they represent 13 to 15% of the juvenile justice population (Majd, Marksamer, & Reyes, 2009).

Children with disabilities and their LGBT and questioning peers are frequently the targets of discrimination and neglect and denied essential services such as basic health care, education, and other social welfare provisions. As a result of landmark court cases such as *PARC v. Pennsylvania* (1971), it was established that the 14th Amendment's equal protection clause required that students with disabilities have the same opportunity to receive a free and appropriate public education (FAPE) as students without disabilities and that, wherever possible, placement in a regular public school class should be the preference (Young, Ne'eman, & Geiser, 2011). Negative societal attitudes also expose children with disabilities to greater risk of violence (bullying), abuse, and exploitation (Media Centre, 2011). Marginalization of disabled students in the education system places them at a disadvantage when entering the employment market (Barnes, Mercer, & Shakespeare, 1999). and is a denial of the free and appropriate education as guaranteed under IDEA. In occurrences of bullying, it can be disability harassment if the bullying is on the basis of disability and/or targets people with disabilities. Disability harassment can be perpetrated by students and peers and even by school employees, such as teachers and administrators. To address the rate of discrimination, the federal government has the Office for Civil Rights (OCR) to eliminate discrimination on the basis of disability against students with disabilities. OCR receives numerous complaints and inquiries in the area of elementary and secondary education involving Section 504 of the Rehabilitation Act of 1973, as amended, 29 U.S.C. § 794 (Section 504; IDEA, 2004).

Yet another large subgroup of marginalized students is those who have been maltreated—neglect, physical abuse, emotional abuse, and/or sexual abuse—by their families or caregivers. According to the Children's Bureau of the Office of the Administration for Children & Families (U.S. Department of Health & Human Services, Administration for Children and Families, Administration on Children, Youth and Families, Children's Bureau, 2016), there were 3.6 million referrals to child protective services (CPS) in 46 states that involved approximately 6.6 million children in 2014. Of the 3.2 million children involved in CPS reports in all states, approximately 20% (640,000) were deemed to have substantiated abuse, with 75% being neglect and 17% being physical abuse. Children who experience some sort of maltreatment are generally known to be at risk for school difficulties and even disabilities. According to a review of literature conducted by Stone and Zibulsky in 2015, children in child welfare and juvenile justice systems exhibit poor school socialization and academic performance, and often the two are interrelated. Specifically, they show that these students are below grade-level expectations, are at increased risk of retention and dropping out, and have below to average IQs. Lower IQs of maltreated children were also found in a large study of foster care children by Viezel, Freer, Lowell, and Castillo (2015). Specifically, the children who suffered maltreatment (abuse or neglect) scored lowest on verbal comprehension and processing speeds, which in turn affected vocabulary and comprehension. In addition, Wilkerson, Johnson, and Johnson (2008) report that maltreatment may result in attachment and time-perception deficits. Pears, Kim, Fisher, and Yoerger, (2013) found that these and similar school and personal outcomes are a result of lower affective and cognitive engagement in school.

Fortunately, research studies (i.e., Ellis & Wolfe, 2009; Pears et al., 2013; Stone & Zibulsky, 2015; Wilkerson et al., 2008) show that the effects of maltreatment can often be overcome or partially alleviated by peer and school intervention. For example, Ellis and Wolfe discuss how peer-group control can exacerbate or buffer childhood experiences depending on early intervention and engagement. All the research studies reviewed suggest that there is an increased opportunity for the school social worker, guidance counselor, or psychologist, as well as for schools as organizations, to begin to encourage more coordinated efforts of all service providers. In addition, educators are encouraged to watch for the risk factors of maltreatment and act early.

To address marginalization of student groups, schools need to review and identify the appropriate pathways for changing school culture so that all marginalized youth can become better integrated and achieve success. However, many school programs, such as compensatory education, special education, safe and drug-free schools, dropout prevention, pregnancy prevention, and family resource centers are not coordinated (Taylor, 2000). Further, unless families and the youth are integral parts of the process, change will be minimal (Pinkerton & Dolan, 2007).

Following is a list of ways for school personnel to approach all students and the school environment to be modified so that marginalized youth will be full participants in the educational process (Rutstein in Richter, 2004; see also Miller, 2006; and Taylor & Adelman, 2000). School personnel need to:

1. believe that all human beings are fundamentally good
2. approach all students with high expectations
3. have a genuine desire to see students succeed
4. focus on discovering and developing student potential
5. focus on the oneness of humankind to reduce division of races
6. focus on the importance of serving others
7. develop an interdisciplinary approach to teaching and learning
8. value cooperation over competition
9. have classroom-focused approaches—reduce out-of-classroom referrals
10. provide student and family assistance—case management of services
11. provide crisis assistance and prevention
12. provide support for transitions—grade promotions and the like
13. encourage home involvement
14. facilitate community outreach—links to businesses, higher education, public and private agencies, faith organizations, and volunteer programs

Using community-based, participatory action research approaches (Yoshitaka, 2014; Yull, Blitz, Thompson, & Murray, 2014), narratives and autobiographies (Follesø & Hanssen, 2010), and service learning (Gosine & Islam, 2014) are all proven methods for gaining a greater understanding of marginalized youth and families' strengths and needs. The most important thread in all of these approaches is that these are ways to get to know the youth and families better, allow them to be efficacious with their voices, allow them to become leaders, and reduce the focus on the perpetual problems or the "fixing" of the youth and families. In addition, schools can also change their structure to incorporate more belonging, that is, by joining the "community" school movement, incorporating more peer-mediation programs (Duttweiler, National Dropout Prevention Center, & National Educational Service, 1995), and adding support groups, like gay–straight alliances (Toomey & Russell, 2013). Last, and certainly not least, teachers and school staff can increase their cultural competence through professional training and community experiences (Gonzalez, Eades, & Supple, 2014). Educational institutions need to once again be leaders in offering families and students the socialization training and social acceptance that students and families rely on.

GIFTED CHILDREN

Conventional wisdom states that educational professionals don't have to worry much about the risks associated with gifted populations, since they may be immune to such issues due to their high cognitive abilities. In reality, they have often been excluded in the research and discussions of risk based on these assumptions. Gifted students can and do differ as much from their peers as students with disabilities, and having these differences acknowledged, identified, served, and appreciated has been an ongoing struggle that both gifted educators and special educators share (Jolly & Hughes, 2015). People in the field believe that this population needs a closer look in addressing its specialized needs.

In 2015, Eklund and Stoll completed a study of 1,206 gifted and nongifted children on two behavioral measures—the Parent and Teacher Behavioral Assessment for Children and the Behavioral and Emotional Screening System. As with previous studies, and as expected, fewer gifted children than nongifted demonstrated emotional and behavioral risk. An interesting finding of this study, though, is that there was a difference in rating gifted children on internalizing behavior, such as anxiety, by parents and teachers, with teachers identifying fewer students. The implication for practitioners is that greater screening is needed to ensure that gifted children with emotional needs are being supported and, since there were differences of identification depending on who was reporting, to have multiple informants, especially parents.

Another area gaining attention in the gifted research is the issue of access to gifted programs by all students. To ensure more and diverse populations of students are being given access to more advanced courses, schools need to support excellence for all students. Despite the increasing percentages of ELLs in schools, they remain underrepresented in gifted programs (Pereira & Oliverira, 2015)—although states such as Arkansas, Colorado, Delaware, Georgia, Indiana, Kentucky, North Carolina, Tennessee, and Vermont have experienced more than 200% growth in the numbers of ELLs in their schools from 1997 to 2008 (National Clearinghouse on English Language Learners [NCELA], 2010). Schools may increase access by developing the talent of the students with greater programming (i.e., more AP and honors courses, rigorous language curricula sequences, multicultural core and elective courses), build a greater awareness about the diversity of high-ability learners (i.e., break stereotypes that certain ethnic groups are genetically predisposed to be more mathematical, creative, etc.), attend to the noncognitive factors that affect achievement (i.e., poverty, attendance), provide challenging and enriching curriculum, create deliberate support networks for students (i.e., after-school enrichment and support programs, like the Concerned Black Men National Saving Lives and Minds program), and create partnerships to equalize opportunities (i.e., grant and business support for low-income communities and schools (Henfield, Washington, & Byrd, 2014; Olszewski-Kubilius & Clarenbach, 2014). When students at the secondary level begin to *become disengaged*, school teams can design specific and targeted support structures, coupled with a rigorous commitment to providing scaffolding, both critical to the success of minority and low-income learners in Advanced Placement classes and International Baccalaureate programs (Kyburg, Hertberg-Davis, & Callahan, 2007).

Children of poverty are also underrepresented nationwide in gifted and talented programs. The underlying causes for underrepresentation lie in the processes and procedures most commonly used in the identification of gifted students, in issues of grouping, in the curriculum and instruction of gifted programs, and in the school programs that prepare children from minority groups and poverty during the early years of school (Castellano, 2004). The policies and procedures that guide selection of students from underserved populations must first parallel good practice in student nomination (referral), identification, and placement (services/interventions; Johnstone, 2009).

Yet another area of concern within the gifted community is to help those who show extraordinary talents in the younger grades continue performing at the same level in upper grades. Past research shows issues such as social asynchronosity (gifted children maturing faster than their peers), unchallenging middle school curriculums, and possible poor self-regulatory strategies may all be risk factors for gifted youth. One particular area noted is that female students begin to decline in math and science at the middle school years. Ritchotte, Rubenstein, and Murry (2015) suggest borrowing from the special education field and conducting a **functional behavioral assessment (FBA)**, for gifted children who stop performing in middle school. An FBA contains a series of activities and techniques that attempts to get to the purpose of a behavior (or in this case, a ceasing of previously positive behavior) that will lead to the creation of interventions to bring about positive behavioral changes. Of course, all of the suggestions listed for marginalized students seem to be quite appropriate for this population as well.

Yet one further concern within the gifted community is those students who may be or have been identified as twice exceptional. This term refers to those children who have a disability but also have characteristics or traits of giftedness. Many of these students are difficult to identify, since the giftedness may be concealed by a disability, or the giftedness may hide a disability (Baldwin, Omdal, & Pereles, 2015). The role of the parent or primary caregiver is extremely important in ensuring that the gifts of the twice-exceptional student get identified and nurtured. Neumeister, Yssel, and Burney (2013) investigated the experiences of 10 families and found that the parents were often the first to recognize the child's gifts and had to seek out evaluations and educational supports for their children. It was also the parents who assisted the students and educational professionals to have high expectations and taught the children to advocate for themselves. Besnoy and colleagues (2015) found the same advocacy issues with the parents in their study but also highlighted the parents' struggles in developing appropriate knowledge (i.e., professional vocabulary and regulations and policies) to be effective advocates.

Additionally, multiple studies (i.e., Baldwin, Omdal, & Pereles, 2015; Baum, Schader, & Hebert, 2014) call for schools to ensure that a strengths-based approach to education is used for these youngsters so that their gifts may be appropriately identified. It is important that twice-exceptional children's strengths and weaknesses are not viewed in sum, with either their gifts or challenges preventing the other from being addressed by the educational setting. This strengths-based approach should include, as it should with all gifted and talented youngsters as described, a program that develops the talents in a safe, nurturing, and problem-solving environment.

DEVELOPMENTAL FOLLOW-UP

Since 1986, the United States has offered early intervention services for infants and toddlers with or at risk for disabilities through Part C of the **Individuals with Disabilities Education Act**. Early intervention is available for children who have "established conditions" that will likely lead to a delay, even if a delay is not yet evident. Thus, any child identified through newborn screening with such a condition would be eligible for Part C services (Baldwin, Omdal, & Pereles, 2015). Also, many advancements have been made in the medical field, for example, in the field of genetic testing and early medical interventions for current and possible symptoms, allowing for an earlier establishment of therapeutic and treatment planning.

However, as seen by the varied types of risk factors and the multitude of affected populations explored in this chapter, recognizing, addressing, and intervening for risk factors and successful school experiences is an ongoing project and requires a systematic process. Here's an illustrative example, again from the literacy perspective. Among children with preschool speech or language impairments, it is not unusual for their early deficits to lessen considerably in severity or even to disappear entirely by the end of the preschool period (regardless of whether intervention was provided). Yet studies have shown that these same children continue to remain at risk for future reading disabilities in the older grades, with some children showing severe deficits in decoding skills after third grade. Scarborough and Dobritch (1990) coined the term "illusory recovery" for the seeming disappearance of language deficits when there seems to still be an underlying challenge. The same holds true for those children who experienced deep poverty in the early ages—as each risk factor is addressed developmentally, new demands cause new factors to arise.

Thus, education professionals should continue to work with families throughout the life span to ameliorate risk and ensure educational and personal fulfillment.

Summary

A multitude of factors may cause a child to become at-risk for a disability at various ages, which result in similar poor educational outcomes for students, requiring early identification with both short-term and long-term family supports. This identification and intervention must be done with a team approach, as all stakeholders have valuable information to influence a more positive outcome. In addition, education professionals should continually improve cultural competence and resourcefulness to directly minimize the effects of risk on students and families, as well as needing to believe in every student, have high expectations, and create experiences that include all students and families so that positive reinforcement, attention to self-image, the democratic learning process, sensitivity to cultural differences and nuances, and student talents are all valued and supported. Many students come to preschool/ school underprepared for the educational demands and, unfortunately, current systems are doing little to help students' catch up or attain grade-level success. The increasing reality that the risks and challenges of poverty are often compounding factors with all other categories of risk means that these factors should be remediated aggressively by schools and communities. Further, educational institutions need to once again be leaders in offering families and students the socialization and acceptance they need to succeed, an especially important factor for families of ELs and LGBTQ students. It is also imperative that educational institutions don't forget about but instead nurture the talents of gifted students. And finally, all persons need to remember that risk factors are not static, and the whole community needs to work to minimize the onset of risks and to minimize the educational and social impacts of risks.

Additional Resources

Print-Based

Embracing Risk in Urban Education: Curiosity, Creativity, and Courage in the Era of "No Excuses" and Relay Race Reform by Alice Ginsberg

Family-Centered Early Intervention: Supporting Infants and Toddlers in Natural Environments by Dana Childress and Sharon Raver

Parents as Partners in Education: Families and Schools Working Together by Eugenia Berger and Mari Riojas-Cortez

The Everything Parent's Guide to Special Education: A Complete Step-by-Step Guide to Advocating for Your Child with Special Needs by Amanda Morin

Web-Based

Early Childhood Technical Assistance Center (ECTA Center): http://ectacenter.org/. Parent support and guidance regarding the Early Intervention Program for Infants and Toddlers with Disabilities (Part C of IDEA)

Special Education Guide for Families: http://www.specialeducationguide.com/. Resource for parents and educators who want to better understand special education terminology, procedures, and best practices in special education.

CLAS, the Early Childhood Research Institute on Culturally and Linguistically Appropriate Services: www.clas.uiuc.edu. CLAS Institute identifies, evaluates, and promotes effective and appropriate early intervention practices and preschool practices that are sensitive and respectful to children and families from culturally and linguistically diverse backgrounds.

Early Intervention Family Alliance: http://www.eifamilyalliance.org/. The Early Intervention Family Alliance (EIFA) is a national organization of family members and supporters dedicated to improving the national early intervention program for eligible infants and toddlers and their families.

Center for Parent Information and Resources: http://www.parentcenterhub.org/repository/. Information and products from the community of Parent Training Information (PTI) Centers and the Community Parent Resource Centers (CPRCs) so that they can focus their efforts on serving families of children with disabilities.

United States Department of Education: http://www2 .ed.gov/parents/needs/speced/edpicks.jhtml. The Department of ED's mission is to promote student achievement and preparation for global competitiveness by fostering educational excellence and ensuring equal access. Comprehensive source on different agencies to assist those with disability.

National Center for Learning Disability: http://www .ncld.org/. Organization that provides leadership, public awareness, and grants to support research and innovative practices in learning disabilities. Parent and educator support website around learning disabilities and advocacy.

Family Voices: http://www.familyvoices.org. Family Voices aims to support the achievement of family-centered care for all children and youth with special health care needs and/or disabilities by providing families with resources and support to make informed decisions, advocate for improved public and private policies, and build partnerships among families and professionals.

Centers for Disease Control and Prevention/ Developmental Disabilities: http://www.cdc.gov/ncbddd/ developmentaldisabilities/facts.html. Government reference and clearinghouse on developmental disabilities with a focus on basic screening, forms of developmental disabilities, research, and multimedia resources.

Gay, Lesbian, & Straight Education Network: http://www .glsen.org. The Gay, Lesbian and Straight Education Network (GLSEN) is an organization in the United States that seeks to end discrimination, harassment, and bullying based on sexual orientation, gender identity, and gender expression in K–12 schools.

4

LAWS THAT SUPPORT FAMILIES

SHIRLEY DAWSON
Weber State University

TRACIE MCLAUGHLAN

DENISE ADAMS

"The first IEP meeting is the worst. The acronyms and the words are so new you
have to trust someone to explain it to you and then you have to accept what they
tell you. You never know if someone is telling you the full truth, if something is
being held back or they are just telling what they want to tell you. The pamphlet
is thrown at you and you want to ask if you should get a lawyer to explain it to you.
When dealing with the struggles with your child, there is not a lot left over to deal
with the legal side. Your mind shuts down, because you can't take it all in."

—Anonymous Parent

"There is no more powerful advocate than a parent armed with information and options."

—Rod Paige, Secretary of Education

LEARNING OBJECTIVES

The purpose of this chapter is to provide a clear beginning understanding of the major laws supporting the education of students with disabilities in schools.

After reading this chapter, students will be able to:

1. Name the major laws that shape special education and support general education for students with disabilities.

2. Identify the five processes in special education and the six provisions under IDEA, explain the differences and similarities among IDEA, Section 504, and the Americans with Disabilities Act and its Amendments (ADAAA).

3. Describe the role of families in the laws for children with disabilities.

INTRODUCTION

The avalanche of information and terminology for special education can overwhelm even the most experienced parents. Given that it was **families** who started the push to include children with disabilities in public schools, it is sad and ironic that families are at risk for being pushed aside due to lack of understanding of the laws that support families of children with **disabilities**. The impetus for special education law was a Supreme Court case in 1954 (Huefner, 2006). In giving the opinion for the unanimous decision that segregating students by race was a violation of equal protection, Justice Earl Warren wrote:

> Today, education is perhaps the most important function of state and local governments. Compulsory school attendance laws and the great expenditures for education both demonstrate our recognition of the importance of education to our democratic society. It is required in the performance of our most basic public responsibilities, even service in the armed forces. It is the very foundation of good citizenship. Today it is a principal instrument in awakening the child to cultural values, in preparing him for later professional training, and in helping him to adjust normally to his environment. In these days, it is doubtful that any child may reasonably be expected to succeed in life if he is denied the opportunity of an education. Such an opportunity, where the state has undertaken to provide it, is a right which must be made available to all on equal terms. (*Brown v. Board of Education*, 1954)

This decision was printed in its entirety in major newspapers throughout the country, and the nation read it over the breakfast table and after work. Parents of children with disabilities read the decision that education was for *all* children and asked, "Then why is my child excluded from school?" Spurred by the ruling in *Brown v. Board of Education* that ALL children were deserving of an education, families began raising awareness of the limited or nonexistent educational opportunities for their children. Grassroots meetings led to the creation of the Association for Retarded Citizens (ARC) of the United States, the Council for Exceptional Children (CEC), and other organizations that united families in advocating and demanding public education for all children. Such advocating coalesced with the civil rights movement of the 1960s, paving the way for a federal inclusive education policy based on the equal protection and due process clauses of the 5th and 14th Amendments (Hardman & Dawson, 2008). As education is the sovereign right of the states, the 14th Amendment is often cited in education matters. Section 1 of this Amendment states that no government "shall deprive any person of life, liberty of property without due process of law; nor deny to any person within its jurisdiction the equal protection of the laws" (U.S. Constitution, Amendment V, 1791; U.S. Constitution, Amendment XIV, 1868). Section 5 states that Congress shall have power to enforce, by appropriate legislation, the provisions of the amendment. The **Individuals with Disabilities Education Act (IDEA)**, the **Americans with Disabilities Act (ADA)**, and Section 504 of the Vocational Rehabilitation Act (504) and their state regulations are appropriate legislation to enforce equal protection and guarantee due process for children with disabilities.

HISTORY

"My cousin Barney lived in the back bedroom of Aunt Donna's house. He never left the bedroom. Barney had severe cognitive and physical disabilities. Back in those days, parents had two options: send their children to a state facility or take care of their children alone. There was no such thing as special education, accommodations, family outings, or events to raise funds—let alone awareness. Aunt Donna couldn't bear the thought of sending Barney away, so she cared for him his entire life, lying on clean white sheets in the back bedroom."

—Anonymous

Pushed by parents and advocates, the IDEA for school for children with disabilities was first realized in 1975 when the Education for Handicapped Children Act (EHA) was passed. Prior to this time, there was no nationally recognized special education program. Children with disabilities did not get appropriate education services, were partially or entirely excluded from peers in educational settings, had undiagnosed disabilities preventing them from participating in school, and lacked access to public resources (IDEA, 20 U.S.C. 1400 §601).

The 1970s saw a flurry of judicial and legislative laws as understanding, awareness, and acceptance of people with disabilities expanded. The 1954 *Brown* ruling was followed by two landmark federal district cases in 1972: *Pennsylvania Association for Retarded Citizen (PARC) v. Pennsylvania Board of Education* and *Mills v. District of Columbia Board of Education*. These two court rulings marked the first time children with disabilities were specifically given the right to attend public school. Both *PARC* and *Mills* involved the removal of children from public schooling without due process or parental consent and the denial of educational equal protection. These cases, happening right on the doorstep of the national congress, were instrumental in the passing of the Education for All Handicapped Children Act (EAHCA) Public Law 94-142 (PL 94-142) in 1972, the forerunner to our present law, the IDEA. Rather than wait for individual states and district courts to pass uneven laws, it was time for a unified and enforceable national standard (Yell, 2012). Children with disabilities who were protected under this law were those who were seen as academically educable. The EAHCA included the basic rights iterated in *Brown*, *PARC*, and *Mills* while offering further protections to parents and children and defining disability. Specifically, the law required that children with disabilities have the right to a free and appropriate public education (FAPE) in the least restrictive environment (LRE) guided by an individual education plan (IEP) as determined by a comprehensive evaluation. Procedural rights were delineated to ensure parental involvement. The inclusion of all children (zero reject) underscored the *Brown* statement that education is the fundamental source of success in society.

Amendments in 1986 to EHA and EAHCA extended school to include preschool, added recovery awards for families who prevailed in court, and expanded education to include more than just academics. Four years later, the hope of families and advocates for children with disabilities was more fully realized with the passage of the IDEA.

INDIVIDUALS WITH DISABILITIES EDUCATION ACT (IDEA)

Disability is a natural part of the human experience and in no way diminishes the right of individuals to participate in or contribute to society. Improving educational results for children with disabilities is an essential element of our national policy of ensuring equality of opportunity, full participation, independent living, and economic self-sufficiency for individuals with disabilities. (IDEA, 20 U.S.C. 1400 §601)

The kingpin of special education law, the IDEA, was initially passed in 1990. Families played an essential role in this law. The term "handicap" was replaced with "disability" as a result of advocates and families working to put "people first" in discussions, outcomes, and society (Huefner & Herr, 2012). The number of disabilities covered was increased from 9 to 13 and parental rights elaborated. Some of these rights specified include holding states more accountable, seeking FAPE outside of the school district, and requiring resolution sessions when disagreements arise. The act requires reauthorization every 7 years. In each revision, additional and critical changes have been made to the law. The 2004 changes included a revision in name to the Individuals with Disabilities Education Improvement Act (IDEIA), but the law continues to be commonly known by its first acronym, IDEA. Requiring reauthorization every 7 years meant new regulations were due in 2011. Changes to the 2004 version based on current understanding of disabilities, pedagogies, and society were pushed by families, advocates, and educators but never occurred during the change in presidential power. It is anticipated that the earliest a reauthorization of IDEA could occur is 2016 (Ziegler, 2015).

IDEA provides regulations on the purposes, processes, and provisions for educating children with disabilities. The overarching purpose of IDEA is to "ensure that all children with disabilities have available to them a free appropriate public education that [*sic*] emphasizes special education and related services designed to meet their unique needs and prepares them for further education, employment, and independent living" (IDEA, 20 U.S.C. 1400 §601). Other major purposes include protection of parental rights in the education of their children, provision of necessary resources (such as technology development, training, or research) to educators and parents, and assessment of education efforts.

The processes of special education are not complicated but can be time consuming and lengthy. The rules state that the procedures must be followed to determine whether a child has a disability under the IDEA, the nature, and the extent of special education and related services needed by the child (20 U.S.C. 1400 §601).

Before the steps in this process are given, it is helpful for parents and others to understand how IDEA defines disability. Under the IDEA, a person with a disability is first a child, second, has one of the 13 eligible conditions, and third, needs special education and related services (20 U.S.C. 1400 §602). All three criteria require evaluation and satisfaction.

The first prong is age criteria. Children must be between the ages of 3 and 21 to be considered. Changes in the EAHCA expanded age span to include infants and toddlers. Children from birth to age 3 are covered under Part C of IDEA, and children aged 3 to 21 are covered under Part B. The child is eligible for services through age 21, but on the 22nd birthday services cease because the child is no longer a child and thus no longer eligible. Other laws (i.e., Section 504 and ADA) do not have an age criterion. It can be discouraging for many parents to learn that their child "ages" out of the IDEA services. But families can take heart, realizing that other laws exist to support families and the child while prohibiting discrimination based on disability. IDEA is meant to cover the child in public education, not the person throughout his or her life.

The second prong is category criteria. IDEA requires the child to have one of 13 eligible disabilities. These 13 categories are intellectual disabilities, hearing impairments, deafness, speech or language impairments, visual impairments (including blindness), deaf-blindness, serious emotional disturbance, multiple disabilities, orthopedic impairments, autism, traumatic brain injury, other health impairments, or specific learning disabilities. If states elect to do so, an additional category, developmental delay, may be used to include young children. While there are many more disabilities, these are the only categories recognized as disabilities under IDEA. Other laws (Section 504 and ADA) have a much broader definition of disability and thus encompass many more disabilities.

The final prong is education criteria. The child must require special education and related services to be considered as having a disability. If the child is of the right age and has one of the eligible disabilities but does not need special education, then the child is not covered under IDEA (Osborne & Russo, 2014). All three criteria must be met through the process delineated in IDEA.

Processes

The procedural steps in the IDEA in determining if a disability exists and if special education is required are known as Child Find, Referral, Evaluation, Determination, and Re-evaluation (see Figure 4.1). The many steps and the timeframe for each step can loom lengthy and arduous for families. Remembering that children were denied access to public education prior to these processes can help make the procedure less intimidating and more palatable to families.

Child Find

The IDEA specifically mandates that states ensure children are identified, located, and evaluated to see if they have a disability. This process is called Child Find, and the agency responsible is determined by each state. In some states, the Department of Health is charged with finding children who may have disabilities, and in other states it is the Department of Education. For many families, a medical or health provider is the first professional seen. Requiring health departments to actively provide notice, make recommendations, or explore possibilities is therefore a natural first step in identifying children who may have disabilities. For other children, it may not be until school age

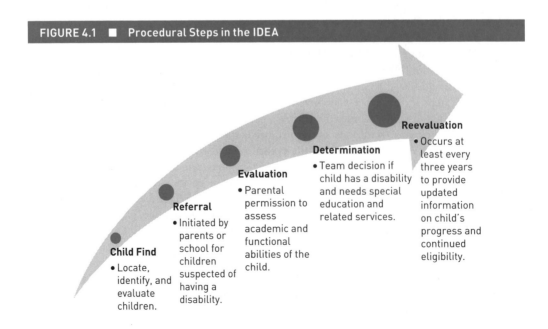

FIGURE 4.1 ■ Procedural Steps in the IDEA

Reevaluation
- Occurs at least every three years to provide updated information on child's progress and continued eligibility.

Determination
- Team decision if child has a disability and needs special education and related services.

Evaluation
- Parental permission to assess academic and functional abilities of the child.

Referral
- Initiated by parents or school for children suspected of having a disability.

Child Find
- Locate, identify, and evaluate children.

that the disability becomes apparent. No matter the responsible agency, the law is clear: states and local school districts must actively seek to find children in public or private schools who may have a disability. Families in flux are not forgotten in Child Find. The charge is explicitly extended to children who are homeless, migrant, or wards of the state (20 U.S.C. §1412).

Referral

A referral is simply a written request to determine if the child has a disability. It can be thought of as the starting point in special education (Pierangelo & Giuliani, 2007a). Only the state agency (schools are state agencies) or parents (including legal guardians) may initiate a request for an initial referral. The referral includes the child's name and the reasons parents or state personnel suspect the child may have a disability. If parents initiate the referral, the school may agree with the suspicion and then seek permission from the parent to evaluate the child. If the school does not agree, it must provide, in writing, rationale for disagreement to the parents. Conversely, if the school initiates the referral, the school provides reasons to the family, and the parent may agree or disagree with the school's reasons. If the parents agree with the school's decision, they then must provide consent to begin an evaluation. If parents disagree, they can refuse to give permission, and the school may not evaluate the child unless further action is taken. Consent in the IDEA means written and informed. Verbal permission is not sufficient. Informed consent implies that both the parents and school know what evaluations will be given and for what purpose. Parents have the right to withhold or give consent at any time and are not obligated to their initial response. If parents refuse to give consent, schools are not obligated to provide special education to the child (20 U.S.C. §1441).

Evaluation

After parents give consent, schools have 60 days to complete a comprehensive, formal evaluation. The time limitation does not apply if parents refuse to send the child to school for the evaluation, if the child enrolls in a different school during the timeframe, or if despite good efforts, additional information is needed and both parties agree to a different specific date. The evaluation must be conducted by a multidisciplinary team (MDT) that includes qualified personnel and the parents and include assessments that address all areas of concern listed in the referral, whether academic, functional, developmental, or social. Parental input is to be sought and used. It was parents who helped determine that a single test or criterion is insufficient to determine the child's needs, strengths, limitations, or abilities (*PASE v. Hannon*, 1980). Assessments selected must be valid, reliable, unbiased, and administered by those trained to perform the evaluation. IDEA provides detailed criteria for assessment and evaluation within each of the 13 disability categories and what factors may incorrectly manifest as a disability when in reality there is none (20 U.S.C. §1441).

The IDEA allows for targeted early support for students who are not achieving in general education. Early intervening services (EIS) are coordinated services "for students in kindergarten through grade 12…who are not currently identified as needing special education or related services, but who need additional academic and behavior support to succeed in a general education environment" (CFR 34 § 300.226(a)). Response to intervention (RTI) is one scientific research–based EIS strategy that is allowed under the IDEA. RTI is a technique wherein educators use specific tools to track a child's progress or lack of progress despite targeted and increasingly more intensive instruction. Schools may elect to use RTI, traditional assessments, or a combination to determine the existence of a specific learning disability (SLD) (34 CFR 300.8(c)(10)). EIS and RTI are only allowable in determining SLD, but these tools may be used to support any child in general education settings, whether or not that child has an SLD or any disability.

Determination

When the evaluation is completed, a determination must be made as to whether the child has a disability and thus is eligible for special education and related services. This determination is made by the MDT. It should be rigorously stressed that parents are qualified, are to be specifically included, and must be present on all the teams regarding their child. Qualified personnel are those persons who have the expertise and specialized knowledge about the child or the suspected area(s) of disability. Qualified personnel or relevant IEP members may also include family who are not legal guardians or parents of the child. All assessment results, including outside results that families share with the school, must be considered in making eligibility determination. The role of the MDT is to make the determination; team consensus is not required. A member of the team (the IDEA does not specify who; it can be the parent or any other team member, but usually the psychologist or special education liaison) writes the determination report, including all assessment results, family input, and any other data that was considered to make the decision. If the team determines the child is eligible and needs special education and related services, then an IEP must be written within 30 days and implemented as soon as possible. If the team determines the child is not eligible, then other resources can be investigated.

Reevaluation

Reevaluation of the child's continued eligibility for special education under IDEA is to occur at least every 3 years (20 U.S.C. §1441). For families, this triannual evaluation is helpful to provide input on their child, get updated information from formal evaluations, and make changes to the education program (Pierangelo & Giuliani, 2007b).

PROVISIONS

The provisions or principles within IDEA serve to make sure the major purposes of IDEA are to provide FAPE through special education, to protect parental and child rights, to assess education, and to provide necessary resources (IDEA, 20 U.S.C. 1400 §601). The provisions are: zero reject, due process, procedural safeguards, least restrictive environment (LRE) and placement, individual education program (IEP), and free appropriate public education (FAPE).

The purpose of the IDEA is to provide an education for children with disabilities. This overall purpose is achieved through implementation of the provisions. Because these provisions are the hallmark legacy of IDEA and undergird special education in America, it is important families understand what they mean. Each of these provisions is vital in ensuring that the purposes of IDEA are made a reality for families and children with disabilities (see Figure 4.2).

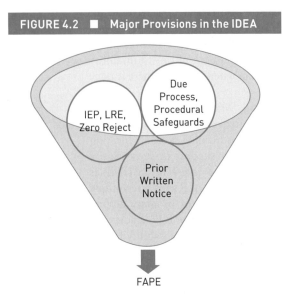

FIGURE 4.2 ■ Major Provisions in the IDEA

Zero Reject

The concept of zero reject has its roots in the *PARC* (1975) and *Mills* (1972) cases, in which families advocated for children who were excluded from public school. Zero reject means that no child can be excluded from school despite severity of the disability or necessary accommodations

(*Timothy W. v. Rochester*, 1989). Before IDEA, families with children like Barney in the earlier quote were turned away from schools. Under the principle of zero reject, families do not have to be concerned about their child being denied entrance or participation in public education. Zero reject is not to be confused with zero tolerance, in which gun or weapon violations bring about immediate removal from the school.

Due Process

The principle of due process is one of fundamental fairness. The IDEA ensures that fair procedures are used (Huefner & Herr, 2012). Prior to EHA families had no recourse when they disagreed with the school's decisions. Parents in *PARC*, *Mills*, or *PASE* (1980) felt they were treated unfairly because they were not given the opportunity to provide input or disagree with decisions the schools made unilaterally for their children. From these and other parental concerns about their involvement in education evolved the provision of due process in IDEA. The basic elements of due process are threefold: right to receive notice, right to respond and be heard, and right to fair decision if families and schools cannot reach agreement. As discussed before in the 5th and 14th Amendments, life, liberty, or property cannot be deprived or restricted without the right to due process. Special education does not seek to deprive life, but liberty and property can be viewed as denied in that special education results in a different property or a restricted liberty. The child now has a different education (special education not general education) in a different place (special room or teacher). The provision of due process means that families have the right to receive notice concerning the education of their child (i.e., referral, evaluation, determination), the right to respond (i.e., consent, agree, disagree, withhold consent), and the right to seek a decision from an outside impartial party if families and schools disagree (Latham, Latham, & Mandlawitz, 2008).

Procedural Safeguards

Due process rights are given to parents to exercise on behalf of their children. Due process undergirds the procedural safeguards in the IDEA to make sure schools do not act unilaterally in making education decisions (Yell, 2012) and that parents are full partners in creating an appropriate education for children with disabilities (Osborne & Russo, 2014). Families are provided with specific procedural safeguards, and written notice of those safeguards must be given to parents or family legal guardians at specific times (Bartlett, Etscheidt, & Weisenstein, 2007). The IDEA requires that parental participation be optimized; procedural safeguards honor this commitment and the concept of due process. The safeguards are: consent, parental participation, prior written notice, independent educational evaluation, access to education records, and mediation (34 CFR §300.501–504). These safeguards expound on the elements of notice by adding procedures to establish the proper balance of fairness to parents and schools. Parents must be given notice of their safeguards at least once a year and upon initial referral for evaluation, upon the first state or due process complaint, when the child is moved for discipline, or whenever the parent requests a copy (Wright & Wright, 2012). Families can also readily access procedural safeguards via the Internet at http://idea.ed.gov/.

Consent

Parental consent must be obtained when the school is proposing to evaluate, reevaluate, or change the placement of the child. Families are given the utmost protection during these times. By law, without informed written consent from parents or legal family guardians, the school may not evaluate the child for special education or change the child's educational placement. If the family refuses consent to evaluate or reevaluate the child or to approve initial special education services, the school may not proceed or override the parent without a legal hearing.

Participation

Parental participation in all aspects of their child's special education is of paramount importance in the IDEA. Parents must be given the opportunity to participate in meetings and provide input about the identification, evaluation, and placement of their child, as well as in meetings and input regarding FAPE and the IEP. Alternative methods of participation must be allowed if the parent(s) cannot be present in person. Families should see this requirement as participation and not a hindrance but as a boon to ensuring that their child's interest remains tantamount in all discussions.

Prior Written Notice

Without notice of meetings, it would be hard for families to participate in meetings. For participation to occur, families must be given notice of these meetings in the language they can understand, and their input is sought. Information in these notices must include a description of what the school is proposing or refusing, why it wants to do so, what else was considered or rejected, and when the school proposes to act. Schools are required to notify families at these times to make sure parents are coequal partners (20 U.S.C. §1415).

Independent Education Evaluation

In circumstances in which parents do not agree with the evaluation completed by the school, the IDEA allows families to obtain an independent education evaluation (IEE) by someone outside of the school agency at no cost to the parent. Only one IEE can be obtained for each contested, completed school evaluation, and the district or state may have rules regarding who may perform the IEE. An IEE is one form of an impartial decision in case of disagreement between parents and schools (20 U.S.C. §1415).

Access to Education Records

For full and meaningful participation to occur, parents must be accorded access to the same records and information schools have. This means parents have the right to look at, inspect, and review all education records that pertain to the identification, evaluation, placement, or provision of FAPE for the child (34 CFR §300.501). No fee may be charged to *look* at the records, but schools may charge a nominal fee to *copy* records.

Conflict Resolution

It may seem strange to families that given the historical confrontation due to unilateral decision making by schools, the original EHA did not contain any reference to conflict resolution. The founders of PL 94:142 did not conceive of the possibility that families and schools would disagree if everyone had the child's best interest in mind. Through the revisions of the IDEA, resolution procedures have been expanded and detailed to ensure fairness in decision making. Newer regulations require mediation offered when there is a dispute on any matter and a resolution session when there is a due-process complaint (34 CFR §300.506). However, parents may waive the right to either a mediation or resolution session and go directly to a formal due process hearing. Mediation and resolution sessions offer several benefits to families. First, families are not required to pay for either mediation or resolution proceedings. Second, the methods of dealing with conflict are less adversarial in that the goal is to find a common goal and workable solution rather than assign blame. Third, attorneys are not required, sparing money, time, energy, and resources. Fourth, the home/school relationship can be strengthened by both parties working together instead of in opposition. Fifth, there is no winner and hence no loser. It is a win-win solution, agreed upon through shared participation by both parents and educators. Last, the proceeding is not closed, so that families and schools may revisit the situation over time. In formal due process and litigation hearings, attorneys are present, costs and time are increased, an adversarial nature is present in that one side "wins," and the decision is made by an impartial outside due process hearing officer or a judge. The decision is legally binding and cannot be revisited except in another formal proceeding (McLaughlin, 2009; Osborne & Russo, 2014; Yell, 2012). Because families must often continue to work with the same educators they formally charged, the home/school relationship can be negatively charged following civil action complaint procedures. For many families, the mediation or resolution proceedings offer better results at a much lower emotional and monetary cost.

Individualized Education Program (IEP)

The individualized education program (IEP) is defined as a "written statement" (20 U.S.C. §1414 (d) (A)(i)), but the purpose and importance of the IEP is far greater than those two words convey. Many educators and families alike refer to the IEP as a plan, but the law itself identifies it as a program. However, whether it is called a plan or a program, the IEP is often referred to as the "heart" (Boyle & Weishaar, 2001) or the "keystone" (Yell, 2012) of special education under IDEA in guaranteeing the child receives FAPE. The IEP is the important piece of IDEA, not only as a compliance tool to ensure that FAPE is provided but also as a communication and collaboration tool between families and schools, the chief instrument for committing resources and individualized services for the child, a key method in ensuring parental participation and resolving misunderstandings, and an evaluation tool for education effectiveness (Huefner & Herr, 2012). To accomplish these important and multiple purposes of an IEP, there are of course multiple requirements for the IEP to be considered complete, legal, and workable. The checklist in Table 4.1 may be useful to families in determining if all the required components are included in their child's IEP.

Of more significance may be an understanding of how the IEP is written and what families can do to support the implementation of their child's IEP. A meeting to write an IEP must be conducted within 30 days of an eligibility determination and implemented "as soon as possible" thereafter (20 U.S.C. §1441). Parents are considered equal partners in writing the IEP and should

TABLE 4.1 ■ Required Elements in an IEP
• A description of the child's present levels of academic achievement and functional performance
• A statement of measurable annual goals
• A description of how the child's progress toward meeting the annual goals will be measured and when periodic reports on that progress will be provided
• A statement of the specific special education and related service and program modification to help the child achieve goals
• Make progress in general curriculum
• Participate in extracurricular and other nonacademic activities
• Participate with children without disabilities.
• An explanation of the extent to which the child will not be participating in the regular class and nonacademic activities with children who do not have disabilities
• Appropriate accommodations necessary to measure the academic achievement and functional performance of the child on state- and districtwide assessments
• The anticipated frequency, duration, and location of services and modifications is stated.
• Transition statement in place for students who are 16 of appropriate measurable goals, based on age-appropriate transition assessments, and transition services needed

feel valued in giving input as to their child's needs, strengths, and goals. More is not necessarily better when creating IEP goals or including accommodations and modifications.

Remember, families are partners in not only the creation but also the implementation of the IEP. Many families will ask what they can do specifically to support the IEP, offer input, and keep samples of work that was sent home to share with the MDT. They may be able to expand or enlarge their child's progress by working on goals at home and in the community and be active in the school community and special education meetings (Pierangelo & Giuliani, 2007a).

Least Restrictive Environment (LRE) and Placement

"When it comes to LRE, I know my child has rights to be in the classroom. The goal is to have your child as normal as possible, to feel part of the classroom. You need to be in the classroom to feel like part of the environment. Sometimes kids are pulled out of the classroom so much that they don't feel they belong. They hate to be pulled out because they may miss out on something, and that just causes more anxiety."

—Tracie McLaughlan, parent

The description of LRE has not changed substantially over the years. The IDEA statute gives us this charge regarding LRE:

Each public agency shall ensure that to the maximum extent appropriate, children with disabilities, including children in public or private institutions or other care facilities, are educated with children who are not disabled, and special classes, separate schooling, or removal of children with disabilities from the regular educational environment occurs only when the nature or severity of the disability is such that the education in regular classes with the use of supplementary aids and services cannot be achieved satisfactorily (20 USC §1412(A)(5)). The regulations give more guidance to how LRE is to be determined (CFR §300.114) but it was parents, through court channels, who garnered the greatest clarification on what is the "maximum extent appropriate" (*Daniel R. R.*, 1989; *Rachel H.*, 1994; *Roncker*, 1983). From the courts we get these four factors to be considered in LRE: benefits, sufficiency, effect, and cost. The following questions can help families and schools when determining LRE:

1. What are the benefits of the general and special education classrooms? Both academic and nonacademic benefits must be weighed as well as benefits of full- or part-time placement in special education environments.
2. Has the school provided sufficient supplementary aids and accommodations in the general classroom? Attempts to accommodate the child by providing aids, services, interventions, and modifications and their effectiveness must be measured.
3. What is the effect of the child on other children and the teacher in the general classroom? Not only the ameliorated effects but also any negative or disruptive effects in the learning of other children or on the quality of services received in the classroom are to be assessed.
4. Does the cost of providing education in the general classroom negatively impact other children? The reduction of money for the education of children with and without disabilities is a determining factor as well.

The IDEA regulations on LRE provide greater detail in how LRE is to be determined in implementing a child's IEP. A continuum of alternative placements is required. Schools may not offer a single type or place for special education. All options must be considered and the best one selected from those options. Supplementary aids services (i.e., resource room) can be provided in conjunction with general education (CFR §300.115). The LRE decision "is made by a group of knowledgeable persons" which includes families (CFR §300.116). In conformity with LRE provisions of the IDEA, the placement decision must be determined annually, based on the student's IEP, and, unless otherwise needed or indicated in the IEP, as close as possible to student's home and in the neighborhood school that he or she would attend if nondisabled. Removal from education in age-appropriate regular classrooms is not solely because of needed modifications in the general education curriculum (CFR §300.116).

It is usually surprising to families to discover that cost is a legal consideration in determining LRE because so much attention is given to FAPE and its declaration of "free." Although special education is free to families, it does not necessarily mean that cost is not a factor for schools. Terms such as "inclusion," "mainstreaming," and "neighborhood schools" are often used by parents and educators, but the law does not use these terms in describing LRE. This does not mean that the IDEA does not value the concept of inclusion. Instead, the regulations go to great lengths to ensure that each child is indeed educated to the maximum extent appropriate with peers. Families are encouraged to carefully consider the four factors in determining which placement options are most aligned with the intent of inclusion for their child and to remember that special education is a service, not a place (CFR §300.39).

Free Appropriate Public Education (FAPE)

The aforementioned procedures and provisions all come together to support the concept of FAPE (refer to Figure 4.2). However, the provision of FAPE, free appropriate public education, can be confusing to parents. Understanding each word in the acronym is the first step to clearing the meaning of this provision. "Free" means there is no charge for special education. Schools may charge fees for books, activities, and such. What cannot be assessed is a fee for special education. Students with disabilities pay the same fees as other students but do not pay extra fees for special education. We will come back to the word "appropriate." Next, "public" refers to schools that are not private or parochial. The last word, "education," includes academic and functional skill development and attainment (Osborne & Russo, 2014). Functional skills include social, physical, emotional, and independent living skills.

The word that often creates confusion is "appropriate." What is appropriate and who decides what is appropriate can cause contention between families and service providers. The law itself provides some direction on what "appropriate" means. IDEA defines FAPE as having four parts (20 U.S.C. §1401). The first part requires special education and related services are provided without charge (the "free" part). Another part is that FAPE must be provided in conformity with the child's IEP (the "appropriate" part). Two parts are combined: FAPE must meet state standards and include secondary, elementary, and preschool (the "public" and "education" parts). The definition of "appropriate" in the law itself is still confusing to most families and professionals. It was families who again pushed to have more clarity of what an "appropriate" education means. From family persistence, the courts have provided greater understanding of "appropriate." The landmark FAPE definition in the *Rowley* Supreme Court case is helpful to many parents and educators in determining if a child is indeed receiving FAPE. *Rowley* defined "appropriate" as an education that meets all the legal procedures in IDEA and is "sufficient to confer some education benefit" (*Rowley*, 1982 p. 200). Therefore, an appropriate education is one in which the IEP that has been written in accordance with IDEA has been reasonably calculated to confer some meaningful level of education (McLaughlin, 2009). This modest right to "some educational benefit" was seen as less than appropriate to parents and advocates who were looking at "appropriate" as meaning maximizing the child's potential (Latham et al., 2008).

SECTION 504

"It is so scary when your child turns 22 and you think, 'Now what?' Is there life after an IEP? How do we get the help needed? Just when you are starting to get the hang of special ed [sic] it is all over and you feel like you start new again trying to understand what to do."

—Tracie McLaughlan, parent

In 1973 Congress passed The Rehabilitation Act of 1973, which included Section 504 to prohibit discrimination toward individuals with disabilities. Originally viewed as a law to specifically help returning war veterans in employment realms (Osborne & Russo, 2014), it was largely ignored in education until 1977, when subsequent regulations were applied to public school children. "No otherwise qualified individual with a disability...shall, solely by reason of her or his disability, be excluded from participation in, be denied the benefits of, or be subjected to discrimination under any program or activity receiving federal financial assistance" (29 U.S.C. §794 (a)). As all public schools (including colleges and universities) receive some sort of financial assistance, all are under the mandate that prohibits discrimination against people with disabilities.

It is important to remember that the basic nature of 504 is widely different than that of the IDEA. Section 504 is *not* a special education law. It is a civil rights law. The purposes of 504 are prohibition of discrimination against persons with disabilities in employment (Latham et al., 2008) and to ensure that persons with disabilities have equal opportunities when assessing federally funded public services and programs (Wright & Wright, 2012). As such, 504 does not have the same entitlements (i.e., IEP) as the IDEA, but it also does not have the same restrictions (i.e., age, disability, and specificity) that the IDEA does either. Remembering that these two laws are not written for the same purposes can help families understand the differences and similarities.

Differences

Major differences for families to know are age applicability, disability types, and implementation specificity. In 504, nondiscrimination requirements apply from birth to death. The individual never "ages out" under 504, either in employment or education realms. Section 504 nondiscrimination requirements apply in the areas of employment, health and social services, pre-K–12 education, transportation, higher education, and facilities and program access. Families, teachers, and children are all protected from discrimination if they are "otherwise qualified."

Second, the types of disability covered are far broader than the limited 13 categories in the IDEA. Disabilities in statute are defined as physical or mental impairments (you can see just how broadly and differently disability is defined; 29 U.S.C. 705). The regulations, while providing more wording, only serve to broaden the definition all the more because the list is just an example and not a complete listing of all disabilities. Disabilities include

...any physiological disorder or condition, cosmetic disfigurement, or anatomical loss affecting one or more of the following body systems: neurological, musculoskeletal, special sense organs, respiratory, including speech organs; cardiovascular; reproductive, digestive, genitourinary; hemic and lymphatic; skin; and endocrine; or any mental or psychological disorder such as intellectual disability, organic brain syndrome, emotional or mental illness, and specific learning disorders. (34 CFR §104.3).

Last, there are several important differences in implementation of Section 504 for families to understand and know. Section 504 is a civil rights statute. No funding is attached to this law to help ensure compliance with the nondiscrimination requirements. If an agency accepts federal funds under any other statute, it is prohibited from discriminating on the basis of disability, but it does not get more money to carry out compliance. The IDEA is a funding statute. Federal funds are appropriated to help carry out its requirements. Section 504 is not an entitlement program but an access law. Individuals with disabilities are not to be discriminated against in accessing public programs (i.e., employment, education, transportation, and communications), but funding is not available to gain access. Section 504 is less specific than IDEA in terms of educational programming. Students receive a plan sometimes called a service plan or a 504 plan (the law does not specify that the writers of this must include parents), and the school, usually general education, is responsible for implementing it. Discrimination in school is failure to provide reasonable accommodations or the failure to provide equal opportunity to participate in or benefit from educational services. Courts have left the determination of what is reasonable for evaluating, planning, implementing, and determining largely to the schools as long as those processes are indeed reasonable (Yell, 2012).

Similarities

Like the IDEA, 504 determines which individuals have disabilities, provides FAPE, and offers some procedural safeguards. As discussed previously, the definition of disability is much broader under 504, but it also comes with a determination for eligibility, as does the IDEA. The determination for eligibility protection under 504 has three major parts:

1. a person who has a physical or mental impairment, which substantially limits one or more major life activities; or
2. has a record of such an impairment; or
3. is regarded as having an impairment (29 U.S.C. § 706[7]).

These determining factors narrow the pool of all people who have a disability to those whose impairment substantially limits one or more major life activities. These activities include walking, seeing, using one's hands, working, learning, breathing, talking, taking care of oneself, or hearing (34 CFR §104.3). The term "substantially limiting" is not defined in the law, and the Office of Civil rights has been reluctant to define this term; instead, guidance is given that substantially limiting is to be determined on a case-by-case basis and it is more than a minor limitation (Huefner & Herr, 2012). If the person was identified as having a disability under the IDEA before aging out, that person would be deemed as having a record of impairment and could then be considered as having an impairment under Section 504. The eligibility determination for Section 504 can be determined solely by the school or employers, but wise professionals include families in the process, and wise families seek to be included.

A second similarity between Section 504 and the IDEA is the concept of FAPE. Both laws provide a free and appropriate public education to eligible students with disabilities. But whether Section 504 FAPE offers more or less benefit than the IDEA is debated (Yell, 2012). Whereas the IDEA standard of FAPE is one of some measure of educational benefit, the standard of FAPE in 504 is a comparison standard. Under 504, FAPE is accorded when education (including regular education) and services are designed to meet individual educational needs as adequately as the needs of nondisabled students are met. This means that appropriate education for the child with impairment is compared to the same access to benefit from education that other children have.

FAPE under IDEA is looking at the individual child's needs, while 504 FAPE is looking at making sure the child is not discriminated against when compared to other students' education (Huefner & Herr, 2012).

A third important similarity is the requirement of procedural safeguards for families. Under Section 504, procedural safeguards are not as numerous but do include access to educational records, notice, consent (neither notice nor consent is as detailed as the IDEA), and hearing and complaint procedures. Parental rights are not as strong under 504. While legal wording mandates that qualified professionals must be part of teams when making decisions, the law does not require parents or the person with the disability to be part of those teams.

AMERICANS WITH DISABILITIES ACT AMENDMENTS ACT

"No one tells you anything after your child leaves IDEA. Even though you think your child still needs help because obviously they are still struggling and will be struggling, you are not told of other options. I wish I would have known that there were more options available to help my child."

—Denise Adams, parent

In 1990, the antidiscrimination protection of 504 was extended to the private sector with the Americans with Disabilities Act (ADA; Osborne & Russo, 2014). The ADA mandates that even those private enterprises that do not receive federal funds cannot discriminate against individuals who have disabilities. Families with children who are leaving educational settings and moving to private employment will find the ADA is most applicable to them. The protection for individuals with disabilities was further expanded in 2008 with subsequent changes that broaden the definition and determination of disability (42 U.S.C. §12101). These changes are known as the Americans with Disabilities Act Amendments Act (ADAAA). Congress believed that too many individuals and families were being denied protection because of narrow interpretation of the ADA (EEOC Fact Sheet, n.d.). The definition of major life activity was revised to

include, but are not limited to, caring for oneself, performing manual tasks, seeing, hearing, eating, sleeping, walking, standing, lifting, bending, speaking, breathing, learning, reading, concentrating, thinking, communicating, and working…also includes the operation of a major bodily function, including but not limited to, functions of the immune system, normal cell growth, digestive, bowel, bladder, neurological, brain, respiratory, circulatory, endocrine, and reproductive functions. (42 USCA §12101.4)

Furthermore, "an impairment does not need to prevent or severely or significantly restrict a major life activity to be considered 'substantially limiting.' Nonetheless, not every impairment will constitute a disability. The term 'substantially limits' is to be construed broadly in favor of expansive coverage" (EEOC Fact Sheet, n.d.).

The new definition of disability under Americans with Disabilities Act Amendment Act (ADAAA) 2008 is broader and more far reaching and comes with the change that determination of disability should not require extensive analysis to establish the disability. ADAAA retains the mandate for individualized assessment but does not negate the ameliorative effects of mitigating measures individuals take on their own behalf (42 USCA §12101). For families, these changes shift the burden from proving disability to prohibiting discrimination.

ELEMENTARY AND SECONDARY EDUCATION ACT (ESEA)

Although educational discussions touted the No Child Left Behind (NCLB) Act as a new federal law, it was an iteration of legislation that existed since 1965. The Elementary and Secondary Education Act (ESEA) was first created in 1965 under President Johnson. Since then, it has undergone many revisions and name changes. In 2001, the ESEA was amended to include an emphasis on standards based assessment, and this reformed change came to be commonly known as NCLB. This was the first time children with disabilities were specifically called out to be included in required assessments to measure student academic proficiency (Bartlett et al., 2007). For families of children with disabilities, this targeted inclusion of children with disabilities could be seen as a two-edged sword. On one hand, it reiterated the concept of inclusion and the principle of zero reject. All students, including those with disabilities, were expected to have high achievement through access to the general curriculum and research-based instruction (Hardman & Dawson, 2007). However, the focus on holding schools accountable for student learning in standards-based curricula engendered many concerns among parents and educators, such as overlooking the individualized nature of special education (Reichman, Corman, & Noonan, 2008) or not expanding assessments to incorporate accommodations needed by students with disabilities (Yell, Katsiyannas, & Shriner, 2006). Since 2001, the ESEA amendments have seen names changes such as Race to the Top and Student Success Act (Ziegler, 2015). The latest amendments reauthorized the original 50-year-old law with a new name change to Every Student Success Act (Elementary and Secondary Education Act as Amended Through P.L. 114-95, Enacted December 10, 2015). The full text is available at http://legcounsel.house.gov/Comps/Elementary%20And%20Secondary%20Education%20Act%20Of%201965.pdf.

FAMILY EDUCATIONAL RIGHTS AND PRIVACY ACT OF 1974

The Family Education Rights and Privacy Act (FERPA; also known as the Buckley Amendment) is another federal law to help families. The parental push to access school records incubated in special education, where information was plentiful and used to make educational decisions without parental consent or knowledge. This push carried over to general education because school practices gave information to outsiders but not to parents or students. The requirement in FERPA guarantees parents have access to their child's records, limits release of those records, and allows for information to be corrected or rebutted (20 U.S.C. §1232g). Five main elements of the act apply to all public and private schools or other educational agencies that receive federal education funds. First, FERPA requires school districts to inform parents of their rights under the act each year. Families are typically informed of their rights under this law at the beginning of each school year (Cambron-McCabe, McCarthy, & Thomas, 2007). Second, parents are guaranteed the right to inspect and review the educational records of their children. This right ensures families can not only have awareness of information but also assess the accuracy of that information. Next, the law establishes procedures for parents to challenge accuracy of student records and protects confidentiality of student records by preventing disclosure to outsiders. Historically, school records were available to government inspectors, employers, and others but not to parents. Last, parents are entitled to file complaints for alleged failures to comply with this Act (20 U.S.C. §1232g).

CASE STUDY 1
LISA AND BRENDA

STUDENT: Third-grade, age 9, girl named Lisa

SETTING: Lisa and her mother, Brenda, are attending the yearly IEP meeting with the special education case manager, class teacher, and vice principal. During the IEP, the special educator tells mom and daughter that Lisa's IQ is very low and that there is nothing that can be done to raise her IQ level. Brenda interprets this to mean that her daughter would not do well educationally and thus not be very successful in her life. Brenda was given no suggestions or anywhere she could go to get a second opinion (in fact, she did not really know she could get a second opinion) even though she has always been given the safeguards at each IEP. Brenda is feeling helpless and hopeless. Brenda left the IEP in tears, while Lisa really does not know why her mom is upset.

What education law can this be referred to?

Where can Brenda turn for help now?

Is there anything that the special education case manager should or could have done differently?

Summary

Families and parents have always played integral roles in advocating and creating changes for their children with disabilities. The familial role might not be readily apparent in special education law, but families were at the beginning in creating special education laws. Families now can take advantage of laws to more fully interact with public schools, agencies, and other organizations to be involved in their child's education and life goals. The major law for special education in the United States is the IDEA. It provides protections, rights, and provisions to ensure that all children with disabilities are provided a free and appropriate education with nondisabled peers to the maximum extent appropriate within an individualized education program. Other laws, such as Section 504 and the ADA, provide discriminatory protection and access to programs for children who may or may not be covered under the IDEA. These two laws have broader definitions and extend protections beyond school. Families and parents need to understand and be fully informed about the difference between Section 504 and IDEA and what protections and helps they can expect to get for their children with disabilities. Other laws, such as NCLB and ESEA, are not laws exclusively for children with disabilities but include students with disabilities in their requirements. Awareness and understanding of the legal tools available to families and children can help families continue to meet the needs of their children in schools and in society.

Additional Resources

Print

Eason, A. L., & Whitbread, K. (2006). *IEP and inclusion tips*. United States: Attainment Publication.

This book was written by an attorney and a professor to help parents prepare for IEP meetings, track progress, and handle disagreements. Provides over 100 tips for parents, teachers, and administrators in creating legal IEPs and developing relationships.

Siegel, L. (2009). *The complete IEP guide: How to advocate for your special ed child*. Berkeley, CA: Nolo.

A book setting up the nuts and bolts of special education from first problem to graduation. Guidebook is especially useful for first-time parents, with a listing of 125 advocacy groups.

Web-Based

Building the Legacy: IDEA 2004, U.S. Department of Education: http://idea.ed.gov/. This site was created to be a "one-stop shop" for resources related to IDEA and its regulations.

Center for Parent Information and Resources, NICHY Legacy Resources: http://www.parentcenterhub.org/resources/. Offering resources for parents in both general and special education with links to specific state parent centers.

Elementary and Secondary Education Act, U.S. Department of Education: http://www.ed.gov/esea. Information on the latest news and resources on the ESEA.

Laws and Guidance, U.S. Department of Education: www.ed.gov/policy/. Legislations, regulations, guidance, and other policy documents and information on all federal laws.

National Center for Learning Disabilities, Learn the Law: http://www.ncld.org/action-center/learn-the-law/. Online resources to help parents learn the laws governing education for students with disabilities.

Section 504, U.S. Department of Education, Office for Civil Rights: http://www2.ed.gov/about/offices/list/ocr/504faq.html#introduction. Provides information and frequently asked questions and answers about Section 504 and the education of students with disabilities.

Understanding the Americans with Disabilities Amendments Act Amendments Act: https://www.disability.gov/resource/understanding-the-americans-with-disabilities-act-amendments-act-adaaa-section-504-of-the-rehabilitation-act/. Provides information for parents regarding changes to the ADAAA and how they apply to Section 504 in schools.

Wrights Law: http://www.wrightslaw.com/. Resources for parents, educators, administrators, and attorneys who seek reliable information about the laws for educating students with disabilities.

5

THE PROFESSIONALS AND THEIR ROLES

NATALIE A. WILLIAMS
Weber State University

KRISTIN L. NELSON
Simmons College

TORI J. LYBBERT
DaVinci Academy

"I've learned that people will forget what you said, people will forget what you did, but they will never forget how they made you feel."

—Maya Angelou

LEARNING OBJECTIVES

After reading this chapter, you will be able to:

- Identify and describe the roles of each member of the multidisciplinary team (MDT)
- Implement strategies for communicating effectively with members of the MDT
- Describe an effective process for resolving conflict

As the old African proverb tells us, "It takes a village to raise a child." As a member of that village, you play a critical role in bringing together all the members of the multidisciplinary team (MDT). You, families, the parents, school administrators, and all the related personnel must function as partners working toward a common goal of ensuring the child thrives in the school setting. In this chapter, we will start by introducing you to the roles typically played by members of the MDT to ensure that everyone works together harmoniously and productively. Then we will discuss partnerships in the school setting with families and professionals. Finally, we will describe the communication skills necessary to establish and maintain these partnerships and provide approaches for resolving conflicts that may arise.

PROFESSIONALS OF THE MULTIDISCIPLINARY TEAM

For students with special needs to receive appropriate services, it takes the cooperation and expertise of many professionals in the student's village. When a child qualifies for services, an Individualized Education Program **IEP** team is formed to design an education plan. In addition to the child's parents, the IEP team must include at least one of the child's regular education teachers, a special education teacher, someone who can interpret the educational implications of the child's evaluation, such as a school psychologist, any related service personnel deemed appropriate or necessary, such as a social worker or an occupational therapist, and a representative of the local education agency (LEA) who has adequate knowledge of the availability of services available and the authority to commit those services on behalf of the child (Heward, 2013). This team then collaborates to write an IEP for the individual child that will be a guide toward providing a free, appropriate public education.

In this section, we describe the roles that various professionals in a child's "village" may play before, during, and after the IEP. These professionals are generally those related service personnel and may include the speech pathologist, the school psychologist, the school nurse, the behavior analyst, the social worker, the occupational therapist, and a doctor.

General Educator

There are many people who serve on a child's MDT; however, the teacher is a critically important member, as he/she is the professional who often spends the most time with the child at school and, therefore, brings the most expertise about the child's educational programs and classroom environment. The general educator also is usually the first and the main person of contact with a student's family and must be able to communicate effectively with everyone involved. The general education teacher is the content expert and will have a great depth of knowledge concerning the general education curriculum. This professional knows how a student with **disabilities** performs academically, interacts with peers, and behaves with adults. In addition, the teacher knows which approaches have previously been tried with the child to improve his or her learning or behavior (Menlove, Hudson, & Suter, 2001). Often, the general educator is the person who has identified what supports the child might need to achieve at school and is usually the professional who has referred the child for an assessment to receive services if needed (Gartin & Murdick, 2005).

Special Educator

Another important professional on a child's team is the special educator, because this person is responsible for overseeing the implementation of the IEP and/or actual implementation of many of the goals and objectives of the IEP. This professional will work collaboratively with all team members including families and the general education teacher to generate strategies and accommodations to the general education curriculum so the child with a disability will have access to that curriculum. Along with the psychologist, the special educator also will interpret educational test results, make recommendations about instruction, and help develop a list of goals and objectives for the child.

Depending on the child's LRE, special educators might push into the child's regular classroom to provide intervention or pull the child out for services elsewhere in the school. They are responsible for maintaining records to track a child's progress with intervention and adjusting the instruction as needed.

Local Education Agency Representative

It is important that every team has an individual representing the school system, and that is usually a director of special education or administrator. This person should have an understanding about special education services and educating children with disabilities in general. In addition, this professional can provide information about the necessary school resources. Moreover, this professional has the authority to commit resources and be able to ensure that whatever services are set out in the IEP are provided in the least restrictive environment.

Speech Language Pathologist

Speech language impairments (SLI) are the second-most-common disabilities affecting children (U.S. Department of Education, 2013). Services for these students are generally provided by a speech language pathologist (SLP), also known as a speech therapist. SLPs specialize in the evaluation and treatment of communication and swallowing disorders. Examples of areas of concern for them include speech-sound and language delays and disorders as well as fluency disorders such as stuttering. These professionals evaluate whether students have a disorder and to determine whether it has an "adverse educational effect" that would qualify them for services (Heward, 2013). If a child is deemed eligible for speech services, the SLP would identify goals and provide services to the child. These services could include working with families to prevent, eliminate, or modify a student's delays or disorders. They might work with students by pushing into their classrooms or by pulling the child out for periods of time. They would document their work with students and keep families and all the members of the IEP informed about a student's progress (American Speech-Language-Hearing Association, 2007).

School Psychologist

One of the principles of IDEA is that children have the right to a nondiscriminatory, multifactored evaluation. Often such evaluations are conducted by the school psychologist, who is a clinician trained to assist educators and parents in meeting the behavioral and learning needs of the student. After written parental consent is given, the psychologist can assess a student's overall academic, intellectual, and psychological functioning through various means including standardized tests, rating scales, observations, and interviews (Watkins, Crosby, & Pearson, 2001). Some common examples of tests they might give include the Wechsler Intelligence Scale for Children (WISC) and the Woodcock Johnson Psycho-Educational Battery (see Chapter 6).

It is important to understand that school psychologists conduct evaluations and serve on a child's IEP as interpreters of the results. They generally do not identify, select, or evaluate curriculum or instruction or any other service a student might receive.

School Nurse

The school nurse is a trained professional who plays several important roles on a child's MDT. Children such as those with an Other Health Impairment (OHI) may have multiple issues including health needs that, without intervention and treatment, could prevent them from success in school. The nurse has health expertise that can assist members serving on the MDT as they develop their plans. School nurses provide health care services and inform the IEP team about the effects of the medical conditions on students' educational programming (Heward, 2013).

Behavior Analyst

As any teacher can describe, all children are not well behaved all the time in school. Teachers must have procedures, rules, and consequences in place for managing their students and their classrooms. In some cases, however, behavior issues for students involve more than a one-time outburst or meltdown. Children that may have more significant behavioral needs can include those with attention deficit/hyperactivity disorder (ADHD) and autism, whose behavior can be an obstacle for their success in school. It is important to know that under IDEA, educators are required to provide behavior support services to children in need. The use of positive behavioral interventions and supports must be considered in the case of a child whose behavior impedes his or her learning or that of others.

Behavior analysts are mental health professionals who can work with the MDT to evaluate the child's behaviors through observation and interviews with parents and teachers. The IEP team could use the information to develop annual goals and specific services to help children learn appropriate behaviors (Sugai et al., 2000). Additionally, they can work with the child on meeting behavior goals and expectations through a positive behavioral intervention plan that may be used at school and at home. The IEP team could use the information to develop annual goals and specific services to help children learn appropriate behaviors (Sugai et al., 2000).

Social Worker

Children in our schools come from diverse backgrounds and have had a variety of experiences that can impact their abilities to succeed in school. Social workers can play an important role in the child's village by helping act as the bridge between their homes and communities to their schools. In some cases, they serve as advocates for children when family members are unable. They also can provide mental health intervention, crisis management, and other forms of nonacademic support to students. As members of the MDT, to help students succeed, social workers have expertise in navigating social services and making connections to outside resources (National Association of Social Workers, 2010).

Occupational Therapist

To succeed in school and at home, children must be able to participate fully in the activities and perform the tasks associated with them. For some children, their disabilities make it challenging to play a musical instrument, swallow or eat without difficulty, or even hold a pencil. Occupational therapists (OT) are the professionals whose main focus is to support the child's success with functional skills, specifically those skills that involve fine motor skills. An OT would complete assessments and work with other members of the team to help determine what services are necessary for the student to be successful in the child's LRE (Reeder, Arnold, Jeffries, & McEwen, 2011). The OT works with the IEP team to develop modifications to the environment and put into place supports that would allow students to access a school's spaces, equipment and resources. In addition, the OT can work with families to develop similar strategies to use at home.

Physical Therapist

Physical therapy is another related service under IDEA and is provided to support students who have physical disabilities (Reeder et al., 2011) and/or challenges with activities involving movement. The physical therapist (PT) is the member of the MDT whose main responsibility is the gross motor development of the student, particularly related to neuromuscular and musculoskeletal systems. Their main responsibility is to promote gross motor development and increase the student's ability to participate in everyday routines and activities that are part of the educational programming. The PT will focus on safe, functional mobility of the child with a disability and can assist families with these issues as well (Herr & Crandall, n.d.).

Physician

Finally, as any parent of a student with a disability knows, the child's doctor is an important member of the MDT. It is in the visit to the physician that parents often first receive information about their children's health and well-being. Under IDEA, children with disabilities need to have what is referred to as a "medical home," such as the physician's office, which can serve as the home-base for their medical records and plans for care. Physicians would provide counsel and advice to parents about referring their children for services in their schools. They also could be involved in the child's assessment, diagnosis, and determination of eligibility of services (Ziring et al., 1999).

BENEFITS OF PARTNERSHIPS

There are many benefits to families, children, teachers, and all the members of the MDT working together cohesively and professionally. Parental involvement was a key component in the original writing of the Education of the Handicapped Children Act (PL 94-142). Each reauthorization of the law has continued to emphasize the importance of parent and family participation. Under IDEA (2004), children have the right to several protections including the development of an individualized education program (IEP) or individual family service plan (IFSP). The program must be designed to meet the unique educational needs of that child in the least restrictive environment (LRE) appropriate to the needs of that child. Parent and student participation and shared decision making is a process also mandated by IDEA (http://idea. ed.gov/). Although there are many reasons increased collaboration is critical to the success of the child, there are three main elements that are clear: parents want to be involved; better educational outcomes result when parents are involved; and federal law requires collaboration (Heward, 2013).

Parental involvement is a powerful tool in increasing academic achievement and decreasing truancy and dropout rates (McNeal, 1999; Sui-Chu & Williams, 1996) of school-age students. Collaborative partnerships with parents also will result in

- more meaningful IEP goals
- greater consistency across the two most important environments (i.e., home and school)
- increased opportunities for learning
- access to broader resources and services (Heward, 2013)

Smaller schools and/or classes may be associated with a safer, more inviting environment, where parents are more likely to become engaged in their child's education and develop more personal relationships with teachers and staff. Teachers are able to spend more time during IEP meetings taking parents' input into consideration, demonstrating respect, and therefore conveying to the parents their involvement is important to the IEP team (Rodriguez & Elbaum, 2014).

FAMILY–STAFF RELATIONSHIPS

Families are a powerful influence in the lives of children, with and without disabilities. Unfortunately, there have been occasions when parents are viewed by educators as an inconvenience or a burden. Teachers have been well prepared to work with children with disabilities but often have received little instruction in how to work collaboratively with adults and families of children with disabilities (Simmons, 2002). As families have changed and the profession has grown, good working relationships between the families of students with disabilities and the professionals that work with them are a critical element in the educational success of the child (Sui-Chu & Williams, 1996). There is increasing recognition that collaborative relationships with families lead to early dispute resolution and prevention of more costly actions (e.g., mediation, due process hearings; Feinberg, Beyer, & Moses, 2002).

Epstein (2001) proposes a model in which family, school, and community are intertwined and overlap with one another to develop a strong partnership. In a partnership, educators, families, and community members work together to share information, mentor students, solve problems, and celebrate the individual success of the child. The structure put forth by Epstein consists of overlapping and nonoverlapping spheres that represent the school, family, and community. The amount of overlap is determined by three forces: time, experiences in families, and experiences in school. Due to the nature of children with disabilities, the amount of overlap between schools and families tends to begin earlier (e.g., early intervention) and last longer (e.g., postschool transition) than those without disabilities.

Worthwhile relationships between school and home do not occur automatically and will require work. Fortunately, when schools and families are willing to invest in the process, much can be accomplished. Three basic assumptions set forth by Howe and Simmons (1993) can assist in that process:

1. Assume Goodwill
   When discussing the progress of a child, parents and teachers need to assume they both share a personal interest in the success of the child and they have a desire to see the child flourish both inside and outside the classroom. It is essential that professionals welcome the concept that parents genuinely care about their child.

2. Assume Competence
   Parents and professionals often see situations quite differently, but when they work collaboratively to identify what is best for the child, they will find suitable solutions. Although the child's best interest may be interpreted differently by each professional, their perspectives are typically a reflection of differences in understanding and experience, not a result of indifference (Howe & Simmons, 2000). Parents know more about their child than anyone else and should be given ample opportunities to share information that will allow the school to better meet the needs of the individual. When parents feel their input is welcomed and valued, they are more likely to support school expectations at home (Orlich, Harder, Callahan, & Gibson, 1998).

3. Assume a Shared Responsibility
   All team members must assume ownership in solving problems and developing good working relationships between home and school. To determine what is best for the child, everyone needs to cooperate and actively participate in mapping out plans for the child, both for now and in the future. Everyone must work together to achieve a common goal; there should be no passive observers. Positive parent–school communications benefit parents. The manner in which schools communicate and interact with parents affects the extent and quality of parents' home involvement with their children's learning.

Table 5.1 contains text from interviews conducted with three separate parents of children with disabilities. These comments provide some good insight into how we can better communicate with families.

TABLE 5.1 ■ What Are Parents Saying?	
What have been some very successful school meetings that you have had with your child and his school?	Meeting with the principal to create an all-day program for kindergarten for Steve. His last IEP meeting was great. During the meeting, I feel that each member of "the team" is invested in helping Brad succeed. They come to meetings prepared. Notes are taken during the meeting and reviewed at the end. Parent/teacher conferences & IEP
What do you suppose made that particular meeting "successful"?	His teachers (aides and special ed teacher) being fully engaged and willing to help in anyway to help Steve progress. The teachers (aides and special ed teacher) being excited about helping him to succeed.
What have been some unsuccessful or frustrating meetings that you have had with your son's school?	I have often felt like a meeting was successful only to be later frustrated that there was little to no follow-through. However, I feel like I have to babysit...the team to check on if things are being followed up on as discussed. After some difficulty Brad had in kindergarten, ...the teacher came in to the meeting and would not make eye contact with me and basically sulked during the entire meeting. I attended the meeting with the attitude of resolving the problem. Although the teacher agreed to some changes, she did not implement those changes. Another frustrating thing that happened recently was that a member of the team agreed to conduct some testing. He conducted the testing and promptly reported back to the team with a statement to the effect of "This is something the team needs to be aware of and make accommodations where needed." I replied to ask if he could suggest specific accommodations. As of now, he hasn't replied. We think he needs more care and assessment than he is currently receiving. Sometimes it's been hard to really push what you want without being an overbearing parent. Parents know their children best.
What were the components of that meeting that you have deemed "unsuccessful"?	The IEP meeting was great and successful with the aides, but his actual kindergarten teacher seemed to deflect most responsibilities off to the aides. Trying to engage his actual kindergarten teacher in asking her for homework on Sam's level that he could be successful with and more appropriate for his level. It was kind of like...if you want some[thing] more geared to Sam's level, the special ed teacher and aides need to supply that. I had just had a baby when we had the meeting, so I felt I didn't get to say all I needed to say and I wasn't as prepared as I normally would have been as a parent. I felt rushed during the meeting.
What have been the most beneficial forms of communication?	Email. Email and text. Email, phone calls, blog.
What have been the least beneficial forms or even roadblocks to successful communication with your child's school?	Communication journal. Hard to write at the end of the day with all the kids wanting to go home and needing to get all their stuff together. If I drop Brad off with one teacher and there's something that needs to be communicated with his aide, I basically have to hope the message gets passed on. His aide works 9:45–1:45, so I never see her. He also spends his day with four different teachers (general ed, math resource, reading resource, and special ed) and works with three different therapists (OT, PT, and adapted physical education). When homework has been sent home by one teacher, I've sent it back only to have it stay in his backpack for days at a time. Not getting a response from sending an email or a phone call.

Excerpts from interviews conducted with three different parents of children with disabilities. Personal communication, Dingman, Kuculyn, & Van Leeuwen. **All names are pseudonyms.

PEER RELATIONSHIPS

There are many benefits to you if you develop strong partnerships with the other members of the MDT. Each member of the MDT brings to the table a specific area of expertise, and each member should be able to rely on each other for help. For example, if you have a student who is having difficulty with particular writing tasks, you can turn to the occupational therapist (OT) for expertise in this area. He or she could offer strategies to support the student within the classroom and, if necessary, determine whether an OT evaluation would be necessary to test for fine motor delays.

Similarly, a speech therapist might collaborate with the social worker if, during a one-on-one speech session, the child mentions a family-related situation that the social worker could address. If necessary, the social worker could then follow up with a home visit with the family. In some cases, the LEA may be able to offer suggestions for district resources that would result in better services for the students in your classroom. It will only benefit you to turn to others in a spirit of trust and cooperation.

Another advantage of the MDT is the opportunity and ability to solve problems as a group. When using a cooperative group structure, members of the MDT can complement each other's strengths and weaknesses. For example, one person may have strong organizing skills, and another person might be a good writer or have an idea for how to approach a parent with a question. Additionally, they may work interdependently to scaffold ideas. You may have the beginning of a plan, and another person could build on it given his or her experience and level of expertise. Cooperative group problem solving helps strengthen the ability of the group to address concerns raised by each member of the team. When the team takes time to brainstorm strategies, provide accommodations, and create a meaningful IEP, the outcome for the student will be greater, as all members of the MDT have contributed to the educational plan for the student.

Sometimes one member of a team will have a better working relationship with the family than other members. Capitalizing on this relationship is a great way to strengthen the connection to the family while allowing other members of the team to focus on other areas. For example, a student has recently transferred into your classroom from another school in the district and has received services at the previous school with the same speech therapist that serves your classroom. It would make sense for the speech therapist to make the initial contact because of the existing relationship he or she has with both the student and family.

Another benefit to working in a strong, cohesive team is that you can avoid duplicating what other team members are already doing. In most cases, the special educator will be the case manager, but occasionally other members of the team may take on this responsibility. When this happens, it will be important to clarify who is responsible for what task so that there is little confusion. For example, when a student who is classified as speech language impaired only receives service from the SLP, it would make sense that the SLP would serve as the case manager and should take on those roles and responsibilities.

BUILDING AND SUSTAINING PARTNERSHIPS

Believing in the importance of partnerships is one thing, but creating and sustaining them is more difficult than we might imagine in an educational setting. Schools are complex organizations with many stated and unstated rules and ways of operating. There are those who have formal positions of power, and there are others who have pockets of informal control and power. In addition, educators work in increasingly diverse settings with people from various backgrounds with a range of experiences with and expectations of the roles of school personnel, families, and the community. In some cultures, for example, educators are viewed as authority figures, and parents are less likely to ask questions of them. Educators need to be knowledgeable about the norms and practices of the settings and the communities in which they work.

In general, experts believe that for a partnership to be effective, there must be positive communication practices, collaborative planning, and the pursuit of common goals (Kelley, 1996; Lumsden, 2005). Aguilar (2011) suggests these ten tips for developing positive relationships with families:

Smile when you see families

Learn their names

Communicate often and in various forms

Make a positive phone call home and lead with good news

Ask questions about the child

Keep it clean (i.e., do not talk about the child in front of the child)

Be very specific (i.e., provide ideas for families to support their children at home)

Be a broker of resources (i.e., if you share a concern with a family, be prepared to provide suggestions for addressing those concerns

Thank the family for their time

Share every success

Others have stated that participants in any partnership should have clearly articulated roles and responsibilities and an understanding of and respect for the roles of other professionals with whom they work (King et al., 2009; Lumsden, 2005). How much time should each participant put into the partnership? Who is the manager? These are issues that need to be worked out together.

One suggestion for creating partnerships comes from the Northwest Regional Education Lab (Ellis & Hughes, 2002). In their report called *Partnerships by Design: Cultivating Effective and Meaningful School Family Partnerships*, they created a protocol for establishing various types of partnerships for improving schools in general as follows:

- Define the goals and outcomes for this effort, including both immediate and future directions.
- Describe the means you will use to attain those goals.
- Outline the details of the roles each partner will play in helping reach the overall educational goals.
- Anticipate potential barriers along the way and formulate responses to them.
- Identify strategies to evaluate the success of the partnerships in meeting the planned goals, and formulate a process to advertise findings and regularly revise the plan. (Adapted from Ellis & Hughes, 2002)

INTERPERSONAL COMMUNICATION FOR PARTNERSHIPS

Experts tell us that interpersonal communication also is a complex process that involves, at a minimum, the words we choose to express our messages as well as our body language. One approach to ensuring that our messages are well received is to be "mindful" as we attempt to communicate. Mindfulness is when you are conscious of your reason for thinking or behaving, a self-focused attention and awareness of your behavior (Bishop et al., 2004; Bodner & Langer, 2001; Brown & Ryan, 2003). It is important to be mindful of the specific situation in which you are trying to communicate, the options available to you for communicating, and the rationale for why one option might be better (Burgoon, Berger & Waldron, 2000; Elmes & Gemmill, 1990). Langer (1989) offers some suggestions for how to improve your mindfulness, including "being open to new information and points of view," "being aware of relying too heavily on first impressions," and to "think before you act."

When considering the options, it can be useful to know that communication forms can be described as "one way" or "two way." One-way communication involves one person sending messages in a method, such as through writing, that doesn't allow for interaction with the receiver of the message. Examples of one-way communication are newsletters to parents and websites that describe homework assignments (Graham-Clay, 2005). Two-way communication, then, involves a dialogue between two people who act as both senders and receivers of messages. Examples of methods for two-way communication are conferences, phone calls, texts, and emails (Graham-Clay, 2005). All of these choices can be effective but they also can all create **barriers to effective communication** if they are not well executed. For example, it would not be fair to rely strictly on email for communication if all the receivers do not have reliable access to technology. Or it would not be fair to schedule an IEP meeting when a parent could not attend because of a work schedule. Regardless of the type of communication employed, it is important that exchanges reflect "a thoughtful, planned approach" (Graham-Clay, 2005).

THE REALITY OF CRITICISM

It is impossible to go through life without receiving criticism. Whether you are giving or receiving criticism, you should expect this to be a part of both your professional and personal lives. Due to the nature of your job, you will have opportunities to deliver and receive criticism, but what matters is how we respond to that challenge. Provided in what follows are some useful guidelines for both giving and receiving criticism (adapted from Deering, 1993).

Giving Criticism

We often avoid giving criticism because it tends to provoke defensiveness and arguments. When it is necessary to deliver criticism, consider the following:

- Choose an appropriate time and place.
    o Let time pass so anger can subside.
    o Address the individual alone; there should be no other team members or parents present.
    o Criticism should be about behavioral change, not public embarrassment.
- Phrase the criticism in terms of what *should* happen rather than what *has* happened.
    o Say "I would like every member of the MDT to arrive on time," rather than "You're late to every meeting we have."
- Avoid blanket statements.
    o Be sure to make specific comments about an event rather than about the person.
    o Remember that criticism is based on perception.
    o There are two sides to every story.
    o Use terms like, "From my perspective" or "As I see it."

Receiving Criticism

How professionals handle criticism is an indicator of whether they will grow in their roles or alienate themselves from the other members of the team. The most natural response to hearing criticism is to become defensive; however, if you do, you may miss an opportunity for growth. Two effective ways to respond to criticism are to ask for more information and to agree with the critic. When you ask for more information, it allows the person to provide specifics and for you to paraphrase the criticism. When you take the opportunity to agree with the critic, the following may result:

- You acknowledge that the feedback is valid.
    o There is nothing more admirable and professional than to admit when you have made a mistake.
    o The criticism has been acknowledged, and this allows both parties to focus on the problem and clear up any misconceptions.

- It disarms the critic.
  - ○ Doing so may defuse any potential argument. It is impossible to argue with someone who agrees with you.
  - ○ Agreement will allow the team member to focus on supportive communication and on how to prevent similar problems from arising in the future.

As you work with families and other professionals in the field of special education, it is imperative that you view criticism as an opportunity to focus on the problem rather than stir up feelings of humiliation and defensiveness. The important point to remember is whether the criticism is true. Adopting a positive and assertive approach allows you to cope with it constructively. Criticism is necessary to help us evaluate the quality of our work and, if appropriate, will prevent problems from growing to the point that relationships are affected. It is true that criticism is unpleasant, so carefully consider if and when to criticize. If you are criticized, turn the experience into an opportunity for self-reflection and professional growth. If you are delivering the criticism, do not forget to compliment your team members and families when they are doing well (Deering, 1993). Positive or negative criticism is more effective than ignoring the issue and/or ostracizing someone. Neglecting an issue is more difficult than giving negative criticism. Therefore, criticism is a necessary part of producing a successful relationship (Clarocco, Sommer, & Baumeister, 2001).

CASE STUDY 1
CRITICISM

You have been the special education teacher at Freedom Elementary school for the last 5 years. Prior to that, you had worked as a paraeducator in the same district for 10 years. You have worked quite closely with your team over the last 5 years and have known many of the team members even prior to becoming the classroom teacher at Freedom. Beginning in the fall, a new psychologist was assigned to your school. He recently graduated with his master's degree in school psychology, and this is his first assigned school.

Paul is a sixth grader who receives special education services as an emotionally disturbed student. He is an extremely likeable student who was diagnosed with pediatric bipolar disorder just over 4 years ago. Paul's academic success and emotional stability are often unpredictable. His moods swing from feelings of hopelessness and depression to goal-directed and even a grandiose level of ability. Paul sees a psychiatrist to manage his medication and meets weekly with the social worker at the school for group social skills instruction. Paul's medications have stabilized his behavior, but they often leave him fatigued, and as a result he has been sleeping more often in his morning classes. While in history class yesterday, Paul fell asleep. His teacher woke him, and Paul was quite enraged. He immediately became physically aggressive and, in fact, threw the teacher's laptop out the window. He was immediately suspended from school.

A meeting to determine whether this behavior was a manifestation of his disability has just ended. The school psychologist shared evidence with the team that you had not followed the student's behavior intervention plan appropriately; Paul had not been attending group social skills instruction with the social worker. Following the departure of the parents, the school psychologist turns to you and says, "We may be going to a due process hearing because you didn't do your job!" You are furious with the psychologist because of his comment, and you say, "You are brand new to this school, and you have no idea what you are talking about! You don't have a clue what even happened!" You then storm out of the classroom.

After you leave, the speech therapist informs the school psychologist that the social worker has been on maternity leave and you have been delivering the social skills instruction in your classroom. The school psychologist realizes that he has misunderstood the details of the situation but does not apologize for shouting at you during the meeting.

Questions

Considering the appropriate way to receive criticism, how might you have responded to the comment by the psychologist?

Considering the appropriate way to deliver criticism, how might the psychologist have spoken to you?

ASSERTIVENESS VERSUS AGGRESSIVE COMMUNICATION

There are appropriate and inappropriate ways to respond to both parents and professionals. There are three basic styles of communication: passive, aggressive, and assertive. Table 5.2 contains examples of each type of interaction. Communication is most effective when delivered assertively; individuals who respond passively rarely get their needs met because they alienate people with whom they are interacting. Individuals who respond with aggression get their needs met using power, language, or coercion to have their needs met (Anderson & Martin, 1995). Aggressive communication ignores or disrespects the rights of others, and this is obviously never a good choice when working with parents and professionals.

Assertive communication is productive in that it allows team members to get their needs met in a positive manner. Assertive communicators are able to express their thoughts and communicate their needs while respecting the rights of others (Kolb & Griffith, 2009). Those who are assertive communicators acknowledge the differing viewpoints of other members of the team and realize that results come through conscious decision making and speaking logically.

Not every individual is innately an assertive communicator, but there are skills that anyone can develop to become better. Those skills may include rehearsal, compromise, and proactiveness. Rehearsal includes role-playing with other team members or a significant other. For example, you could prepare for an upcoming conversation by rehearsing the language with a nonbiased party

TABLE 5.2 ■ Basic Styles of Communication		
What Would You Say?		
Aggressive Response	**Passive Response**	**Assertive Response**
That is the most ridiculous idea I have ever heard!	I don't think this goal is appropriate for this student, but it's better than nothing.	We need to rework this goal so that it will really address the needs of this student.
I cannot stand working with this parent! She drives me absolutely crazy. It's no wonder her child has been in three schools this year.	I am just going to not return her call. She is just too demanding, and I don't want to have an argument.	Would you mind meeting with me and Ms. Jones next week? You have known her longer, and you seem to have developed a nice working relationship with her.

TABLE 5.3

Assertive Communication Strategies

- Respond calmly and directly immediately after the offense.
- Focus on the specific behavior displayed by the team member by using "I" statements.
- Share what feelings you experienced as a result of the identified behavior.
- Describe your preferred outcome and how it might be different in the future.

Adapted from Kolb & Griffith (2009)

and then receiving explicit feedback as to how to phrase your ideas more assertively (Elliott & Gresham, 1993; Kolb & Griffith, 2009).

Working together as a team to solve a problem will often require a compromise. Finding a solution to a conflict so that all parties can save face or avoid undesirable circumstances can be difficult. A preferred approach is to compromise and choose a solution that is both appealing and appropriate. When a palatable compromise is reached, you are more likely to get support from team members and families.

The final skill that may need developing is "proactiveness." Sometimes it is possible to anticipate in advance problems that may occur in a meeting. If so, it is a good idea to prepare for the possibility that you will have to take charge of the discussion and assert a plan for how to address the problem. Thinking about potential situations and forming strategies ahead of time as to how you might respond will increase the likelihood that the desired outcome, one that best meets the needs of the child with disabilities, will occur (Kolb & Griffith, 1993). Developing and practicing assertive communication skills will benefit you and the members of the MDT.

RESOLVING CONFLICTS

Unclear communication contributes to interpersonal conflict. Ineffective communication between people leads to unclear limits and vague leadership. The lack of or unclear communication can also create an absence of mutual decision making with regard to issues that affect all members of the team. The pressure one may feel to avoid any type of conflict can lead to one or all parties becoming disengaged and never fully resolving the conflict.

Misconceptions and misjudgments also are contributing factors to interpersonal conflict. Misconceptions can occur because of limited ability to understand another point of view (place oneself in the other's shoes). When engaged in conflict, most people maintain their own beliefs and views and are less likely to entertain the conflicting party's beliefs and views. For example, the teacher may believe a student's inappropriate behavior is an attempt to gain peer attention, but the family may disagree with the teacher's hypothesis and therefore refuse to entertain any suggestions proposed by the teacher.

Many years ago, Johnson (1974) claimed, "In order for a conflict to be managed constructively, there must be effective and continued communication among the individual parties" (p. 64). This concept holds true today, as communication between school and family is a precondition for a partnership. Two-way communication between parent and teacher efficiently supports the development of the child (Palts & Harro-Loit, 2015). Team members can use communication to resolve differences, provide information concerning their intentions and position, express feelings, and eventually develop an understanding. Appropriate communication is critical in the conflict-resolution process.

Filley (1975) offers a set of beliefs that would be productive to conflict problem solving:

1. Belief in the availability of a mutually acceptable solution that will achieve every team member's goals
2. Belief in cooperating rather than competing
3. Belief that everyone is of equal value
4. Belief that opinions expressed by others are respected
5. Belief that differences of opinion are helpful
6. Belief in trusting all other team members
7. Belief that the other team members can compete but choose to cooperate

Establishing open and mutual trust is critical for conflict resolution and for maintaining a positive relationship. Creating a trusting atmosphere encourages individuals to take the risk of opening up and trusting another. For example, suppose a new student transfers into your classroom, and you have very little background information on this student. It is important in the initial meeting with the student and family that they know they can trust you and that you have the student's best interest in mind. You might begin the meeting with asking questions about the old school and what brought them to the area. You also may ask the student what hobbies he/she has or what extracurricular activities in which he/she participates. It is important to remember trust is demonstrated through verbal and nonverbal communication. One way to quickly establish trust in a relationship is to suggest that the family member come into the classroom and observe, volunteer, or participate in some other way in the child's life at school. When school personnel value the significant place of families in the educational process, they will feel more committed to the families with whom they work and devoted to the children they teach.

Academic success also is linked to trust, accountability, and responsibility among families, school, and community. School and family awareness of the power and significance each of these entities has on students' academic success will encourage all those involved to understand and value the importance of family, school, and community.

Unfortunately, there may be times when conflict between families and MDT team members occurs (Wherry, 2005). Here are eight suggestions to help teachers resolve these conflicts:

- Make personal contact with the family of each student.
  - This can be accomplished in a number of ways (e.g., telephone, email, or in person). Aim to begin communication early in the school year. Initial contact should take place when the child is doing well. This approach sets up teamwork in the event difficulties or issues arise.
- Contact the family immediately when potentially serious problems occur with their child.
  - Do not let concerns grow too big to be corrected.
- Call at least two family members per week with good news.
  - A proactive and trust-building opportunity is to contact families with good news. It is likely to boost both the child's and family members' ego. It may also result in increased parent involvement.
- Send quick notes home to acknowledge something special.
  - Quick notes may be in the form of an email or written note in a student's folder. These quick notes are an easy and effective way to show the family their involvement is noticed and appreciated.

- Put the greatest strength of parents to work for you.
  - o Families know their child best. Ask family members questions about their child, and listen to their responses.
- Learn how to deal with angry families.
  - o React calmly. Rephrase what the family members say. This strategy gives you and the family time to think. Emphasize what both parties have in common: "We both want your child to do well."
- Do not make quick judgments about family members' level of interest.
  - o Studies have found that no matter the economic or educational background, families love their children and want what is best for them.
- Let families contact you after school.
  - o It is important to accommodate families' difficult schedules by allowing them to contact you before and after school hours. Allowing after-school contact will increase communication and decrease both stress and conflict between all parties. (Adapted from Wherry, 2005)

Developing collaborative relationships between families and other members of the MDT is critical to the child's academic success. Unfortunately, there are barriers that impact the development of a truly collaborative relationship between home and school. Such barriers include:

- Logistical problems
  - o Families may have substantial logistical problems such as arranging for transportation, babysitting, or taking time away from work to attend conferences or IEP meetings. These are serious problems that, if recognized, schools can help families overcome. For example, instead of always meeting at the school, the school personnel can plan to meet at the family's home or a neutral location near the parent's workplace.
- Misconception of apathy
  - o Educators must control their own biases and not use the stereotype of parental apathy. In many cases, family members do not know *how* to become involved. It would be appropriate for the teacher to provide a list of ideas for how they could contribute to the classroom. The list should include opportunities for volunteering both inside and outside of the classroom. Additionally, the teacher should include activities that could be completed during the daytime or evening hours so all types of families could participate.

As we work to develop partnerships and resolve conflict, remember: (a) the family is the basic unit of our society, (b) families are diverse, (c) cohesion and adaptability significantly can impact the parent–teacher relationship (cohesion is the links within the family, and adaptability is how the family adjusts and responds to outside conflicts and pressure), and (d) communicate openly and often with families (Johnson, Pugach, & Hawkins 2004). Understanding school and home dynamics will encourage a productive and well-functioning MDT and can decrease the conflict among all team members.

CASE STUDY 2
IEP MEETING

Principal Jones had been an elementary principal at Washington Elementary for more than a decade. The school was in an affluent school district outside of a major city in the Northeast, where most children had two professional parents who worked long hours. He was assigned to act as the LEA for a newly identified student by the director of special education and, although he had attended many IEP meetings, this was the first time he had scheduled, planned, and chaired an IEP meeting for a student with a disability. The student was a second-grade boy who had recently been diagnosed as having a specific learning disability in reading, a problem with executive functioning, and ADHD.

In the past, Principal Jones had always left IEP meetings, thinking they were too long and disorganized, so he thought instead he would run a tight meeting. He scheduled it at a convenient time for him: 3:30 on the day before Thanksgiving. He knew that some people might not be able to attend, but he was sure that the most essential professionals and at least one of the parents would attend the meeting. He sent out an email to the student's teacher and the student's parents. He assumed that the teacher would invite anyone else who she thought should be present at the meeting.

After sending out the email, he received a confirmation from the teacher that she would be there but that she could only stay about 20 minutes because she had to catch a train home for the holiday. He also received a rather curt response from the student's parents indicating that it was an inconvenient time for them and that they might be late to the meeting.

At the scheduled time, the student's teacher rushed into the meeting with all her bags packed and wearing her coat. Principal Jones asked who else they could expect besides the parents who, by the way, would be running late. The teacher said she did not know and asked him who else he had invited to the meeting. When they realized their miscommunication, the teacher ran down the hall to find the reading specialist.

By the time everyone was at the table, the teacher could only stay another few minutes. As a result, Principal Jones kept the meeting short and allowed no time "for emotions to become adversarial." He kept the discussion to a minimum and discouraged the questioning of the professionals. After all, he thought, the teachers were experts in their areas of service provision, and their recommendations should not be second-guessed by him or the parents. After the teacher and the reading specialist had spoken, Principal Jones declared the meeting over, believing it was a success. He was proud that he had accomplished a productive individualized educational program (IEP) meeting. He asked the parents to sign off on the IEP, but instead, they appeared upset. They said they would not sign anything at that point, and they left, saying they would be in touch after the holiday.

After the meeting, Principal Jones was sure that all had gone well with the meeting, because it appeared that he had headed off any serious disagreement in the meeting. After all, it was Thanksgiving.

Questions

1. What false assumptions did Principal Jones make as he prepared the meeting?
2. Did the meeting satisfy both the letter and the spirit of IDEA?
3. What could you expect the parents to do after the meeting?
4. What would you do differently if you were in charge of this meeting?

Summary

A productive home/school relationship requires a collaborative team effort from both the family of the child with the disability and the professionals that work with that family. Adults who share a mutual respect and have the child's successful education and best interest at heart will result in good outcomes, both educationally and socially, for the child. Good relationships require hard work, and the onus of developing that relationship lies with the teacher. Once parents believe that the teacher and other professionals are concerned about their child and are willing to work hard to meet the needs of that child, very few problems are beyond resolution, and their cooperation can result in impressive outcomes in the lives of children with disabilities.

Additional Resources

Print

Johnson, L. J., Pugach, M. C., & Hawkins, A. (2004). School–family collaboration: A partnership. Focus on Exceptional Children, 36(5), 1.

Lytle, R. K., & Bordin, J. (2001). Enhancing the IEP team: Strategies for parents and professionals. Teaching Exceptional Children, 33(5), 40–44.

Virginia Department of Education, Office of Student Services, Offices of Special Education (2002). Collaborative family-school relationships for children's learning: Beliefs and practices. Retrieved from http://www.doe.virginia.gov/support/student_family/family-school_relationships/collaborative_family-school_relationships.pdf

Web-Based

Council for Exceptional Children (CEC): https://www.cec.sped.org. The Council for Exceptional Children (CEC) works to improve the educational success of children and youth with disabilities and/or gifts and talents.

National Association of Special Education Teachers (NASET): https://www.naset.org. NASET is a national membership organization dedicated to rendering all possible support and assistance to those preparing for or teaching in the field of special education. NASET is dedicated to ensuring that all children and adolescents with special needs receive the best education possible.

National Center for Learning Disabilities: http://www.ncld.org. The mission of NCLD is to improve the lives of the one in five children and adults nationwide with learning and attention issues—by empowering parents and young adults, transforming schools, and advocating for equal rights and opportunities.

The Individuals with Disabilities Education Act (IDEA): http://idea.ed.gov. The Individuals with Disabilities Education Act (IDEA) is a law ensuring services to children with disabilities throughout the nation. IDEA governs how states and public agencies provide early intervention, special education, and related services to more than 6.5 million eligible infants, toddlers, children, and youth with disabilities.

The Iris Center: http://iris.peabody.vanderbilt.edu. An organization dedicated to educational faculty and independent learners. The research-based tutorials, web tours, and webinars offer tips for students, parents, and teachers.

Special Education Guide: http://www.specialeducationguide.com. Special Education Guide is an online resource for parents and educators who want to master the terminology, procedures, and best practices in special education.

U.S. Department of Education: http://www.ed.gov. A government organization dedicated to all involved in the public education system.

What Works in Education: George Lucas Educational Foundation: http://www.edutopia.org. The George Lucas Educational Foundation is dedicated to transforming kindergarten-through-12th-grade (K–12) education so all students can acquire and effectively apply the knowledge, attitudes, and skills necessary to thrive in their studies, careers, and adult lives. The U.S. Department of Education provides a wealth of information about educational laws and data.

6

ASSESSMENT TO RESEARCH-BASED INTERVENTION: PROVIDING FAMILIES SUPPORT

VICKI A. MCGINLEY
West Chester University

IEVA MARGEVICA
University of Latvia

"Development, it turns out, occurs through this process of progressively more complex exchange between a child and somebody else."

—**Urie Bronfenbrenner**

LEARNING OBJECTIVES

After reading this chapter, you will be able to:

1. Identify assessment points throughout the child's lifespan and the role the family and you as a professional have in assessing the child.

2. Understand the different types of assessments specific to lifespan transition points and those specific to disability and behavior.

3. Identify the needed content and knowledge related to assessment so as to best communicate and collaborate with families based on their level of need, as well as the barriers to effective communication and collaboration with families around assessment.

4. Understand the decision making process for intervention—the assessment-to-intervention process and the role the family plays in that process.

OVERVIEW

Perhaps you are looking at the title of this chapter and saying to yourself, "Not another reading on assessment!" It seems that testing (used synonymously with assessment) is all we do. Yet the reason for this, we know, is because assessment is important. It is linked to the child's program of study from the initial screening and potential evaluation for diagnosis to follow-up assessments, evaluation reports, and intervention.

As such, assessment must be done thoroughly and reliably so that the child's program of study, the individualized family service plan (IFSP) and/or the individualized education plan (IEP), can produce the needed interventions and results.

A main goal of this chapter is not to replicate the many resources that describe the assessment process and the assessments we use. However, some description of processes, assessment types and actual assessments is needed. The focus will be on the needs of the family and your role as a professional in working with the family as a member of the multidisciplinary team (MDT, covered in depth in Chapter 4). In Chapter 3, we covered the law around nondiscriminatory evaluation, and in various other chapters you've read about critical lifespan points. So the focus of this chapter is on the family's contributions and needs around assessment at different points in their child's life—specifically, what the family needs to know and how they contribute to the assessment process to make it successful and, finally, what we as professionals need to do to collaborate with and support families.

ASSESSMENT HISTORY AND FAMILY INVOLVEMENT

There is a long history of assessing children in our schools. Family involvement in the assessment process for children with disabilities evolved parallel to the family advocacy movement throughout the 1950s up through the 1970s with the passage of the major special education law, the Education for all Handicapped Children Act of 1975 (EHA), now known as the IDEIA (Individuals with Disabilities

Education Improvement Act, or IDEA 2004). Prior to this act, children with disabilities may have been excluded from education, thus assessment altogether, and, if assessed, discriminatory practices prevailed. Within this special education law, it was affirmed that families participate in their child's education and, thus, assessment and decisions related to intervention, such as the development of goals. Families' participation is affirmed within IDEA through its procedural safeguards, including the rights of families to provide consent for the initial evaluation that will determine eligibility for early intervention and special education services thereafter (Lloyd, Landrum, Cook, & Tankersley, 2013). If a child is denied eligibility, it could be considered the denial of a free and appropriate public education for the child (FAPE; Bateman, 2011).

The positive benefits of including families in a child's education has been researched (Davies, 1993; Turnbull, 1995), and when families are included throughout the special education process, from assessment to intervention, it has numerous benefits, such as increased success with the child meeting his/her goals and objectives (Childre & Chambers, 2005; Turnbull & Ruef, 1996) and better communication between the MDT and the home, specifically with the teacher understanding the child's home environment (Meyer & Mann, 2006).

So, if there are positive benefits to families participating in assessment, what are the barriers to such participation? A number of studies (Harry, 1992; Hughes & Ruhl, 1987) have indicated what we know as professionals: that special education is filled with jargon, thus sometimes creating a knowledge and communication barrier between families and professionals. Jargon may be especially difficult for families from diverse linguistic backgrounds. Issues of cultural diversity and parent participation have been studied (Kalyanpur & Harry, 1999; Sileo, Sileo, & Prater, 1996) and help us better understand characteristics of families that may result in more passive participation and/or differing views of disability (Harry, 2008). This knowledge supports us in understanding why reaching agreement on goals, objectives, and placement for the child may be challenging. Additionally, knowing the technical aspects of assessment adds difficulty for families. This, along with not understanding their rights concerning the assessment process, may work to exclude parental participation.

All professionals of the MDT have standards that guide their work with children. Additionally, teacher educator standards for working with children with disabilities are provided by the Council for Exceptional Children (CEC). CEC is the largest international professional organization for preparation on working with children with disabilities and provides standards for assessment. It is with consideration of these standards that this chapter is written.

WORKING WITH FAMILIES TO UNDERSTAND ASSESSMENT

There is much more that a family needs to know when it comes to assessment of their child—for example, the terminology of assessment, how to interpret testing results, what the results mean in terms of identification and eligibility, as well as how to make the best intervention decisions based on the results of assessment. Like special education jargon, testing terminology may be difficult to understand.

For all assessment lifespan points of the child, similar types of assessment are used. Additionally, all children will be screened and/or assessed using multiple measures and multiple types of assessments when decisions for eligibility and/or intervention are the goal. As such, during early childhood, the primary school years, middle and high school, and transition to postsecondary school and/or work, the MDT will use standardized measures—both norm- and criterion-referenced tests, as well as classroom-based measures that have strict protocols to produce valid and reliable results. However, more informal measures will also be used as well, such as observations, interviews, and alternative assessment measures, such as portfolio assessment. As part of the MDT, it is critical that you have knowledge of the types of assessment and understand all of the assessment technical terminology that goes along with these measures.

TECHNICAL ASSESSMENT TERMINOLOGY

Initially, families will need to understand the screening process, what it entails, and what outcomes it may produce. Families will need to understand that if a concern is noted in any area (e.g., developmental, sensory, motor, communication, etc.), with the families' permission, a formal evaluation may take place. This evaluation is conducted by a specialized professional from the MDT with more extensive, specific assessment tools. The evaluation outcome may result in the development of an IFSP or IEP. The screening process is outlined in Figure 6.1.

Throughout this initial screening process, families will want to understand the types of assessments being performed, what these assessments will entail in terms of time, location, level of involvement, and potential outcomes. Prior to the assessment, throughout the screening process, and certainly once the results are interpreted and reported, family members may need a lot of support with testing specific terminology, such as developmental age, chronological age, ceiling score, and so on. Appendix A lists assessment terminology families will encounter along the way with a brief definition of each term. Each family will be different and come to the

FIGURE 6.1 ■ The Screening and Assessment Process

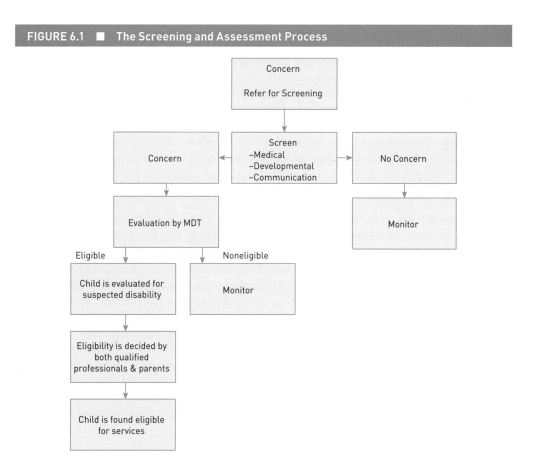

assessment process with different levels of knowledge as well as knowledge they wish to receive. It is important to assume that families will want as much information as possible, but it is also extremely important to take the cues from the family and respect what level, type, and mode of communication they desire. For example, some families may not be in the position to have a primer on assessment type and technical terminology due to working outside of the home and home responsibilities, or they may believe that assessment is the sole responsibility of the professional. However, the family will bring a lot of input and will be the most important member of the team, specifically for initial screening when all developmental history is extremely important. Also, families will share critical observations of skills they observe their child doing in the home.

You, as the professional, will need to know and understand the assessment process, types of assessments, the protocols for implementation, and how to interpret and explain results—essentially, the meaning of all of the terminology! For example, do you know how to explain descriptive statistics, what a grade equivalent score means, and the concepts of reliability and validity? The good news is that there are many quality texts that will help you with terminology, and the actual application through training and practice with the test will cement that knowledge.

In the next sections, we discuss some of the types of assessments done at critical life points of the child.

LIFESPAN ASSESSMENT

Early Childhood Assessment and the Family

Chapter 9 covers birth through age 5 and gives you a lot of information on this lifespan point. Therefore, the goal of this section is to focus on the types of assessment used with the young child and the family's involvement in this process. Since IDEA 2004, all states must have extensive Child Find services in place for locating and screening infants, toddlers and young children who may be at risk (LeDosquet, 2015) for disability. Therefore, the first thing we need to think about as professionals when working with the early childhood population is that families with children within this age range (as defined in Part C of the Act for children ages 0–2 and Part B for children ages 3–5) will be new to special education. Some of them will know their child has a disability at birth (some perhaps even within the prenatal period). Others will be going through the process of screening for identification and evaluation for possible further assessment within this time period, such as our families of children with autism that typically find out within the child's first two to three years of life that their child has a disability. Each family will be different in its coping, functioning, and support system (see Chapter 2 for family systems theory) and will bring to the team many strengths and challenges. However, being new to the screening and assessment process and then, potentially, early intervention special education, each family most assuredly will need some level of support, as they will have many questions about testing, prognosis, intervention, and present and future outcomes. We will need to support families throughout the screening, evaluation, assessment, and possible diagnosis and, if diagnosis is the outcome, with the understanding that for some young children (younger than school age), a categorical label such as "learning disabled" is avoided, as the MDT is focusing on any at-risk measures for delay and/or a developmental delay (Hall, 2008) with the possibility that specially designed instruction (SDI) and thus special education may not be necessary. At this point, for some families, we may need to help them to understand the difference between screening for possible delays and a follow-up in-depth assessment, which will pinpoint difficulties in any of the affected domains (i.e., cognitive, communication, motor, sensory, social-emotional). Therefore, we need to be clear on the differences. According to the Early Childhood Technical Assistance Center (2016),

> Screening, evaluation and assessment are distinct processes with different purposes under the provisions of Part C and Part B. Screening includes activities to identify children who may need further evaluation in order to determine the existence of a delay in development or a particular disability. Evaluation is used to determine the existence of a delay or disability, to identify the child's strengths and needs in all areas of development. Assessment is used to determine the individual child's present level of performance and early intervention or educational needs.

Families will need to understand that assessment of the young child is done via an ecological approach (Pierangelo & Guiuliani, 2012), including evaluation in all settings of the child's life (the natural, least restrictive environment as mandated in legislation) so that professionals will be working within the family's home. As such, they will be important team members. Also, assessment will include all domains (motor, cognitive, communication, social, etc.), administered by members of the MDT.

Considerations With Assessment of the Young Child

Professionals need to expect differences in testing due to cultural, linguistic, and other diverse variables to include socioeconomic status and parenting styles. Variability of assessment performance due to these variables is important to consider. Thus, an ecological approach to assessment, which supports the team in better understanding the home and community from which the child comes, will help all to better interpret assessment results and to help make best decisions on interventions with the family for the child. For example, for some families, providing bilingual professionals in the home and school will be needed. However, before we even get to intervention, the team may need to consider assessment being implemented with a professional from the same cultural and linguistic background of the family—again, to produce valid and reliable results and, thus, sound interventions (Basterra, Trumbull, & Solano-Flores, 2011).

In order to ensure that the assessment process procedures are done with a family-centered approach, Hanson and Lynch (1995a) have developed a list of questions that the team should address:

1. Are diagnostic or eligibility assessment procedures clearly identified?
2. Are assessment procedures linked to intervention?
3. Are professionals conducting assessments trained to implement the assessment?
4. Are the assessment instruments used valid and reliable instruments?
5. Are all MDT members involved in the assessment?
6. Is there adequate time to plan and complete the assessment with the family?
7. Are assessments conducted in familiar settings with family members present?
8. Is the assessment conducted in a variety of ways (observation, interview, etc.)?
9. Are the child's strengths and needs considered?
10. Are family members' concerns, priorities, resources, and diversity considered?

These questions need to be answered in the affirmative for best results for the family and the child.

Implementing Assessment: What and How We Assess in Early Childhood

For early childhood, since we are viewing the child's functioning within the context of the family, in addition to the child's strengths and areas of need, we are assessing the family's strengths and needs (Hall, 2008). This is not judgment of the family; this is assessment of what the family will need to support the child in agreed-upon goals and objectives on the child's IFSP or IEP. When the child reaches preschool-age services, school readiness will become most important and will include early literacy skills, writing, and mathematics. Appendix B describes some of the more common structured assessments performed with young children both in the 0-to-2 range as well as the preschool 3-to-5 age range. However, below is a general description of the types/ areas of assessments performed with young children.

DEVELOPMENTAL ASSESSMENTS Making sure developmental milestones are met and good health is maintained are of primary importance and will be the responsibility of health-care professionals and other members of the MDT, specifically family members. It will be important for the MDT to have health screening information for case review. In addition, an infant/toddler may need to be assessed for such things as sleep disturbances, excessive crying, eating difficulties, unusual self-stimulatory behaviors, failure to discriminate caregivers, and/or lack of interest in socialization and objects (Mayes, 1991). Early childhood educators will certainly be involved in assessing developmental areas, such as cognitive, motor, and communication development and may use such assessments as the Bayley Scales of Infant and Toddler Development—the Brigance, among others.

However, as indicated, informal measures will be used at all lifespan levels, such as interviews and observations.

INTERVIEWS Interviews in the home are needed to complete a thorough assessment and can be a bit anxiety provoking to the new professional, specifically when entering a home environment that is vastly different from what we are accustomed to (different from our socioeconomic status, race, and culture). It is important to keep in mind that the family members may be feeling the same way. Thus, as professionals, we must be prepared, sensitive, and knowledgeable of any cultural differences. Although we are all busy, it is important to block off a lot of time. Be prepared to spend time in "small talk," essentially building rapport, before the assessment begins. Families may need to talk about a lot of things related to their child before the actual assessment questioning starts. It is important to note that a lot of information can be gained from this initial dialogue as well.

Some suggestions for conducting sound interviews (Hanson & Lynch, 1995b) are provided:

1. Understand the cultural rules in the home. For example, in one home, a parent of a certain gender may defer to the other in answering questions, or someone from an older generation may be deferred to in answering questions.
2. Be professional in your dress and communication and, if working with other team members, such as an interpreter, give all team members time to warm up to the family.
3. If you are taking assessment materials to the home, make sure you may leave something (i.e., coloring books and crayons), and if the child has siblings, they must be considered also as this will be important for intervention.

Assessment in the child's natural setting is critical, as well as all other environments in which the child spends time. The formal term for this type of assessment is ecological assessment.

ECOLOGICAL ASSESSMENT   Since the child's development is assessed within the context of the family's home and culture, ecological assessment is necessary. Ecological assessment is a formal way to conduct observations in the child's natural environment, with comparisons made to skills shown and skills needed for independence. Thus, ecological assessment requires observation in the home but may also require observation in other settings (i.e., grandparent's home, daycare, etc.). McCormick and Noonan (2002) describe a process for ecological assessment:

1. Document the child's routines and activities within the setting.
2. Document skills exhibited and skills needed to perform the behaviors in the daily setting, comparing present skills to skills needed to function.
3. Determine what skills are needed to be included in the child's plan.

During ecological assessment the MDT should certainly see the child engaged in play, as it is through play that children learn. As such, it is an important tool that we use for assessment referred to as play-based assessment.

PLAY-BASED ASSESSMENT/ARENA ASSESSMENT   As children learn through play, one of the best ways to assess is through observing, and play-based assessment is standard practice when assessing young children. The MDT will set up the environment to evoke skills through play. Certain skills such as object permanence and/or language/communication skills will then be recorded as no evidence, present, or emerging. However, there are also a number of standardized tools that help assess young children and do this through having the child look at and/or play with a certain object. The Transdisciplinary Play Based Assessment (TBPA; Linder, 1990) is a more structured tool that is widely used by the MDT to assess cognitive, social-emotional, communication, and sensorimotor skills of infants through preschool age children and then helps the team in addressing the information they receive from this assessment in intervention.

In arena assessment for preschool-age children, all members of the MDT, to include the family, are involved. One member facilitates while other members record their observations. Skills via play may be evoked during this type of assessment as well.

SPECIFIC STRUCTURED ASSESSMENT MEASURES   As all needed domains must be assessed, many professionals from a variety of disciplines may be involved (e.g., speech-language pathologists, occupational therapists, audiologists, etc.; see Chapter 5 for the description of the professional team), and each will use domain-specific assessment tools and measures. As such, it is not the goal of this chapter to cover all of the most commonly used assessments by the various team members; however, it is important for all team members to understand the results of these assessments. Some of the assessments are norm-referenced tests, which are designed to compare the child in relation to other children within the same age range, and others are criterion-referenced tests, which are designed to measure the child's performance in a domain against a predetermined fixed developmental criterion or learning standard; for example, in preschool, a child's knowledge of colors and the skills assessed will build on one another through the child's first years. However, it is during the transition from Part C to Part B services that the focus of the assessment will change.

TRANSITION FROM PART C TO PART B

As children transition from Part C, early intervention services, to Part B, school-based services, it is important for all educators to understand the assessment approaches used in early childhood, as well as what it means to transition from an IFSP to an IEP. There will be another important transition to a school-based program when the child enters kindergarten. However, the family should be familiar with the IEP by that point, alleviating a bit of stress. Many professional educators are familiar with the IEP but not the IFSP. However, it is important to be familiar with both specifically, due to the fact that transition from home-based to school-based services may be a stressful lifespan point for families. As indicated in Chapter 9, one of the main differences is that the IFSP focuses on needed resources and supports for the family as determined via the assessment, and the IEP focuses on school-based services. Families may now have to become used to being a vital member within a school-based setting as well as, if a school setting is determined to be the child's least restrictive environment (LRE), getting used to their child being out of the home for extended periods of time. For some families, this will be a very challenging transition, but others may welcome their child learning in a preschool setting around other children as a time of growth. However, the IEP will be the mechanism of intervention and, as such, the IEP will be the focus from here on and is certainly the focus of the primary school years. It is this lifespan point that is covered in the next section.

PRIMARY SCHOOL YEARS

Another critical transition point for families is the move from kindergarten, where the child may have spent only a half a day at school, to first grade and the primary school years. Although certain school readiness skills including some academic skills have been addressed prior to first grade, whether the child is in a segregated classroom setting or has been included with typically developing children up to this point, the thought now moves to full-time schooling for many years to come. Most children with disabilities will be included in the general education setting, and with that comes an increase in the skills needed to be academically successful (e.g., spelling, writing, reading, mathematical, problem-solving, and organization and study skills). Children must now meet their state-specific standards and/or the national Common Core Standards, which address what all children should know to show evidence of learning the prescribed curriculum. It is within these first couple of primary school years that some children may be initially diagnosed with a disability. For some children, that will result in the development and implementation of a Section 504 plan or an IEP, either continued and reviewed annually and/or first developed. As such, the focus of this section will be on what parents need to know and contribute about assessment in the content-area subjects, as well as, for some children, what it means to be assessed via alternative assessments.

Increased testing has become part of our school culture with the passing of the No Child Left Behind Act of 2004 and the parallel provisions in IDEA 2004 indicating that all children must be assessed, and although there has recently been criticism concerning the amount and type of testing taking place in our schools, all children with disabilities will continue to need to be assessed for the development of goals and objectives. As such, every child will be assessed using standardized assessments (See Appendix B) for commonly used content-area achievement tests). However, there are many classroom-based assessments that the teacher will use to ascertain the student's progress in meeting the curriculum and subsequently his/her IEP goals.

STANDARDIZED ASSESSMENTS When a test is standardized, it means that the conditions under which the professional will implement the test are the same across all students as specified in the testing protocol. Professionals cannot vary in the way they implement standardized norm-referenced tests, as the child's results are compared to a norm group. Standardized assessments give testing procedures. Professionals follow these procedures to ensure that the results are valid. This strict assessment implementation is important so the MDT can obtain results that will show if the child is divergent from other children and if progress is being made and, if so, to what capacity. If the child has not moved along the correct path in terms of goals and objectives that are indicated on the child's IEP, the team will need to know this so that the appropriate intervention can take place. Standardized tests are one type of assessment that helps the MDT make sound intervention decisions for the child. For school-age children, content-area skills are an important part of assessments in areas such as math and literacy and will be of particular importance in the early primary school years. For example, if standards indicate children should be fluent readers by the end of grade three and assessment results indicate that a child is performing below grade level in fluency, the MDT may determine that the child should receive additional or alternative types of instruction.

Family members will be involved throughout the standardized testing process. They will want to know when the testing will take place to assure the child has had a good night's sleep and is healthy. In addition, families may want to remind their child of the testing procedures and expectations before the day of the test. They also may be choosing to work with the child on some of his/her goals in the home. If the standardized assessment allows, there may be MDT agreed-upon accommodations to testing implementation as specified in the child's Section 504 plan and/or IEP. If this is the case, family members may need to be reassured that their child will be tested with the identified accommodations in place (i.e., increased time, testing location, etc.).

Once the testing is completed, families will want to know how their child fared on the day(s) of testing (i.e., did he/she cooperate, what was the stress level, etc.). They will also want, and are entitled to, the testing results, as these will become part of the evaluation report (ER). At this time, your professional technical knowledge is necessary, as you will need to be able to best describe what the various scores mean and all testing results.

Overall, standardized tests measure aptitude, intelligence, and achievement, essentially the underlying ability and learning of the child. Achievement tests are standardized tests that usually cover a number of grades and have one version that includes a wide range of items arranged in order of difficulty (McLoughlin & Lewis, 2008). **Standardized achievement tests** may be given across skill and academic discipline areas such as written instruction, reading, mathematics, and spelling. Examples of the more common achievement tests used are the Peabody Individual Achievement Test, the Woodcock-Johnson III, and the Wechsler Individual Achievement Test.

Classroom- and Curriculum-Based Assessments

In addition to achievement tests, teachers collect data on children in their classrooms every day through observation, assignments, homework, and so on. Thus they are assessing students all the time. In fact, it is through classroom-based assessment that professionals feel the most critical information is obtained, as this type of assessment demonstrates where the child is on a daily basis, and with these, the teacher has firm knowledge of the student's present levels of performance in all areas (McLoughlin & Lewis, 2008), and it is this type of assessment in which parents have sometimes almost daily involvement. Teachers also use more structured classroom assessments, referred to as **curriculum-based assessments (CBA)**, in which **curriculum-based measurement (CBM)** probes are collected. This type of assessment occurs across multiple areas and disciplines such as mathematics, reading, spelling, and writing. In CBA, observation is used as well as inventories, tests, and quizzes to include criterion-referenced tests (CRT), diagnostic probes, and error analysis. When a teacher is using observation in the academic areas, he/she may be observing and recording such things as how long it takes the child to complete five math problems, as we know that fluency in math is important, or how much time it takes the child to read a 100-word paragraph with number of errors recorded. Both scenarios impact performance in academic areas, and both are important goals to work on. When using error analysis within CBA, a teacher is studying a child's errors, looking for patterns such as in writing, where a child may consistently confuse "p" and "d," and in math difficulties with carrying and double-digit addition. Error analysis can be performed in all subject areas and helps the teacher focus on the correct type of support the child needs. In using diagnostic probes (also used in the CBA) brief, timed, easily administered quizzes that measure skill acquisition, fluency, and maintenance of a specific skill (Spinelli, 2012) are implemented. During this time, teachers record the number of correct and incorrect responses. All of this data is used in intervention decisions, and as it is classroom based, it gives the MDT the most accurate, up-to-date levels of student performance. Usually teachers will be communicating with family members on almost a daily basis via papers being sent home, a communication log, quizzes and tests, and the like. Parents may need support with helping their child with the actual work, how to support study skills, and so forth. An effective way to communicate will need to be established and maintained. Some parents will appreciate technology, such as a classroom learning management system setup, or email communication, while others will like a telephone call or the standard written communication log.

For some children, for example those with significant intellectual disabilities, their evaluation reports will dictate areas needed to be assessed. So although these children may follow Common Core standards, an alternative form of evaluation and assessment is needed. These types of assessment are described later in this chapter.

In any event, following the primary school years, there will be a major transition for the family as the child reaches adolescence and enters the middle, high school, and post–high school years with different types of assessments encountered.

SECONDARY SCHOOL YEARS: TRANSITION ASSESSMENT

The focus of this section is on assessment during secondary school years and the family's involvement in the process. For information on establishing goals, see Chapters 11 and 12, which cover the middle, high school, and postschool years.

As a professional working in middle school and/or high school, you will definitely be involved in transition assessment and intervention. However, transitioning to life after school starts from day one of the child's schooling. That may sound a bit strange to some. Why would we be thinking about life after school when a child is 5 years old? For families with children with disabilities, the adult years of their child may be something they think about on a daily basis. Questions they may be asking themselves and others include: Will my child be independent in his/her living and work? If my child needs ongoing supports throughout his/her life, who will provide that support, and will my child be supported in the manner he/she should be? What if my child cannot make decisions for him/herself—what will happen? This lifespan transition will be stressful for all families, but adding in disability involves a whole different set of stressors that families of more typically developing children may not encounter. As such, for every child, we must plan for postsecondary outcomes from day one—work and/or additional schooling and independent living.

As covered in Chapters 11 and 12, the federal law guarantees that each state begin the postsecondary transition process before their 16th birthday with coursework in the child's IEP, and by age 16, a more thorough individualized transition plan (ITP) is completed, in which statements must focus on needs, services required, and needed school subjects included. Outside state and community agencies that families may not have ever heard of before must now be included (Kritikos, 2010).

So what is involved in transition assessment? What will families want and need to know? First, it is important that families understand their rights as they relate to transition assessment. The most recent reauthorization of IDEA 2004 dealt directly with transition and specifically with assessment (Spinelli, 2012). Specifically, related to transition are the role of families and the child directly in the transition process, the transfer of rights (for decisions) to the child related to age of majority (18 in most states), and the inclusion of a general educator as part of the ITP team. Assessment-related changes in the act that also impact transition are inclusion of students in statewide testing (either standardized or alternative). Schools must provide evidence that students participate in the transition process. In relation to intervention, IDEA 2004 added an exit provision that requires that all students have a summary of performance (SOP). The SOP summarizes the child's academic and functional performance, the student's postsecondary goals from the IEP, and how to reach those goals at graduation from high school. Family members will have contributed to this document along the way through participation in the assessment and IEP. However, this lifespan point will be challenging, and a smooth transition with all professionals working together to ensure that the SOP will be met will help. Additionally, family members will want to know their rights as they pertain to work and postsecondary education (Section 504 and the Americans with Disabilities Act; see Chapter 5) so that if accommodations are needed, they are provided.

Family members must realize the transition assessment is based on the child's skills, as well as preferences and interests, so child-centered choice is what drives the process, as well as strengths and areas of need. As such, at this time in the family's and child's life, in addition to assessment types already discussed, other types of assessments, with different team members involved in the assessment process, will be implemented. Also, different skill areas of the child will become critical for consideration at this time. Things such as self-advocacy skills and self-awareness of disability may be assessed.

In addition to all of the assessments that the child has been involved in throughout his/her schooling (i.e., developmental, achievement, etc.), specific areas that will be assessed and additional types of assessments include situational assessments, career track, work sample analysis, self-determination, checklist and rating scales, portfolios, performance assessments, and curriculum-based vocational assessments. Some of these types of assessments have already been described in this chapter, and some will be described in depth a bit later. However, some may be new to you as a professional and may also be unfamiliar to the family.

Sitlington, Neubert, and LeConte (1997) propose that transition assessment must involve three components:

1. Student assessment to identify strengths, interests, preferences, and needs.
2. Environmental analysis to identify potential living, work, and educational settings. Environmental demands and needed supports and accommodations must be part of this analysis.
3. The match between student strengths, preferences, and needs to his/her environment. (adapted, in McLoughlin & Lewis, 2008).

Following is a description of some of the assessments used at this lifespan stage of the child.

Vocational/Aptitude/Ability Testing

General and more specific job skills assessments may include assessment in such areas as motor skills, communication, physical endurance, work habits, attitude toward work, ability to follow direction, and tolerance for stress. Additionally, in these areas, job-readiness skills such as interviewing as well as punctuality and response to supervision are important. Job analysis, which is systematic observation of the skills needed and of the performance on the job, is also required assessment. This is sometimes referred to as **situational assessment**. Work samples and simulations are also part of some assessments and may help reveal adaptive behaviors and social skills.

Self-Determination Assessment

According to Wehman (2006), self-determination assessment involves assessing whether the student can act autonomously, the behaviors(s) are self-regulated, and the student is empowered. Thus, assessment in this area focuses on whether the student believes he/she can control outcomes, is effective, knows strengths/weaknesses, has a positive self-concept and self-esteem, exhibits problem solving, decision-making and choice-making skills based on interests and preferences, and can set goals and self-advocate (Brolin & Loyd, 2004).

Overall, many checklists, rating scales, and interest inventories will be used in transition assessment to address performance, future planning, and self-determination (ECTACenter.org, 2016). The next section deals with disability-related areas that will cross all age ranges.

SPECIALIZED ASSESSMENT AND DISABILITY-RELATED ASSESSMENTS

Due to the nature of the child's disability across his/her early intervention and school-age years, specific areas of need may be assessed due to the nature of the disability. So what are those specific disabilities that may require a different assessment process and perhaps different assessments than what we have covered so far in this chapter? Following are descriptions of the process for those children that fall into those categories.

Children With Challenging Behaviors

Some families may be experiencing children with challenging behaviors and/or children who are at risk for behavioral problems due to their disability. For example, children with learning difficulties, intellectual disabilities, children within the autism spectrum, and those experiencing mental health issues sometimes exhibit challenging behaviors. These are the children in the top portions of the Positive Behavior Support Pyramid (see Figure 6.2), which means they have difficulties following appropriate rules and thus need more specific interventions.

Usually, families are experiencing behavior challenges at home, and for some children, the placement in a category requires the behavior to be occurring across settings (i.e., emotional disturbance). However, for other children, behaviors may be exhibited under different contexts, such as only in certain academic classes.

Specific assessment for behaviors will include children exhibiting both internalized and externalized behaviors. Internalized behaviors may sometimes be overlooked, as usually the child exhibiting these types of behaviors is quiet, withdrawn, depressed, and thus not a "problem" in the classroom or at home. It is more the aggressive, assaultive, externalizing behaviors that are noted and assessed. However, both internalizing and externalizing behaviors may cause serious life problems and stressors for the child and the family.

Considerations of Behavioral Assessment

Since there may be beliefs and perceptions around behaviors related to "poor parenting," as there is a long history of such (e.g., mothers of children with autism being described as "cold"), family members may feel that they are being judged and limit the behaviors they report seeing

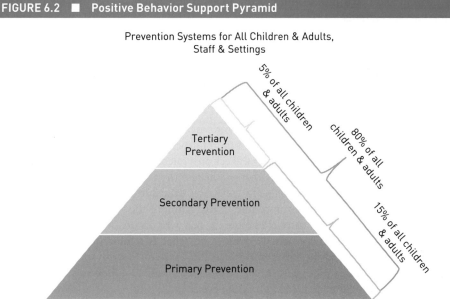

FIGURE 6.2 ■ Positive Behavior Support Pyramid

Prevention Systems for All Children & Adults, Staff & Settings

5% of all children & adults

80% of all children & adults

15% of all children & adults

Tertiary Prevention

Secondary Prevention

Primary Prevention

their child exhibit. In addition, professionals may observe behaviors in the school that family members do not see at home; this discrepancy may produce tension within the team and lack of trust on the part of families. It is important to remember that there are many causes of behavior, such as student's abilities, classroom instruction, peer interactions, and so forth; and behavioral assessments should therefore encompass many dimensions. As such, a thorough assessment will take place in the school, but may also include the home and community environment.

Data Collection

One of the first tasks of the team will be to collect data on the behaviors of concern. Many teachers and other school personnel, as well as family members, will be asked to provide information so that the behavior is assessed across settings.

Interviews

To obtain information on behavior, both structured and unstructured interviews are used. Formal interview protocols, those that have a specific set of questions, may be used to gain a more comprehensive view. Behavioral challenges occur for a variety of reasons. Therefore, it is necessary to receive information from numerous sources, including families, health professionals, and educational professionals. MDT personnel may want to not only conduct live interviews but also review the child's records.

Observations

Observations will be extremely important and in some instances mandatory, such as when a functional behavior assessment is required. Observations provide an in-depth look at behaviors. Whether required or not, observations are necessary, as rating scales and record reviews may only provide indirect information. The information gathered from a direct observation may include both descriptions of the behavior and data on the behavior including duration, frequency, or latency. Observations should also be conducted in different settings and at different times of the day. McLoughlin and Lewis (2008) and Pierangelo and Giuliani (2012) provide the procedures for conducting observations:

1. Define the target behavior so that all team members are observing the same behavior.
2. Select and develop the measurement (data collection) system that is appropriate to the behavior being measured such as anecdotal, event, latency, or duration recording.
3. Carry out the observation

In some instances, the MDT will develop a tool for parents to collect observational data in the home. This may be similar to the school's protocol and/or may have to be simplified due to the many responsibilities in the home (i.e., such as placing a check on a calendar). In any event, family members may need support in how best to collect data that will help in the assessment process.

One technique widely used in schools for collecting data during observations is the ABC or antecedent-behavior-consequence procedure. This requires the observer to record what specifically is happening in the environment before the behavior occurs (what are the antecedents to the behavior), how the behavior actually looks, and what is reinforcing the behavior (the consequence). Another type is the observation recording system (Ysseldyke, 1998), in which observers go into the observation with a set number of times to observe, set times, and a predetermined measurement system (i.e., duration, event, etc.).

Behavior Rating Scales

For rating scales, members of the team rate the child on such things as the extent to which the behavior occurs (Salvia, Ysseldyke, & Bolt, 2010). There are several types of rating scales that are useful in providing preliminary or basic information about the child in relation to their social-emotional and behavioral functioning. Although they provide a tool and structure for data collection, these rating scales measure the rater's perception of the child's behaviors, so it should not be a surprise if there are differences in ratings across persons completing the rating scale. For example, getting out of a seat may be considered excessive and problematic in some academic classrooms but not so much in others.

Some of the most common behavioral assessments used are described in Appendix B and include the Behavior Rating Profile, Behavioral Assessment System for Children (BASC-2), the Attention Deficit Disorders Evaluation Scale: Secondary-Age Students (ADDES-S), and the Connors Rating Scales-Revised (CRS-R).

Functional Behavioral Assessment

Required in IDEA for certain students, a functional behavior assessment (FBA) includes many of the techniques already described such as interviewing and observation. However, emphasis is placed on the factors that influence the behavior and their role in the subsequent development of a positive behavior support plan. The two main procedures for an FBA are observation and interview. This should not be confused with functional behavioral analysis, which would include the third step of formation and testing of a hypothesis to explain behaviors. Most classroom teachers and families can come up with hypotheses as to why the behaviors are occurring as a result of quality interviews and data but will not be in a position to test hypotheses, which involves manipulating the environment in some way to evoke the behavior. However, once the FBA is completed, according to O'Neill and colleagues (1997), outcomes that support positive interventions for the child are the following: a clear description of the behavior (how often, when, and where it occurs); the antecedents (situations that predict when the behavior will occur) are identified, and thus the MDT also knows when the behavior will not occur; consequences (also called reinforcers, or situations that follow the behavior that continue to evoke the behavior) are identified, and thus, what consequences will not evoke the behaviors are also discovered. Sound statements and/or hypotheses of when the behaviors may occur and the reinforcers that maintain the behaviors may be developed so that the MDT may develop intervention addressing environmental situations that are more likely to maintain the behaviors. For example, it may be discovered that a young child has difficulties with transitions; so positive programming or a change in the environment such as the child walking with a peer may be built in at those times. An adolescent may need a "safe out," and this may have to be discussed with the team as to how to implement it successfully.

An area that definitely impacts a child's behavior is their social-emotional competence. According to Bryan (1997), domains that need to be considered when assessing children in this area are the child's affective status (emotional state and ability to regulate emotion), beliefs and attributes (the child's locus of control or what he or she believes is responsible for outcomes), friendship and peer relations, social skills, and maladaptive behaviors.

DISABILITY-SPECIFIC ASSESSMENTS

For children with specific disabilities, certain required screenings and assessments will be necessary. For example, it should make sense to you that children with visual and hearing impairments will need health screenings in their area of sensory deficit, and children with other health impairments will need ongoing assessment and support from health-care professionals. However, for some children, the law defines very specifically what types of assessments are required and which particular MDT professional member must be involved in the *implementation* of the assessment (i.e., a doctor's diagnosis for ADHD; a school psychologist for conducting IQ testing with children with intellectual disabilities and learning disabilities; occupational and/or physical therapists if the child is deemed as needing those services as part of their intervention plan, etc.). These same members of the MDT will be involved in interpreting and explaining assessment results and, as such, working with family members.

Children With Intellectual Disabilities

Like all other disability categories, children with intellectual disabilities will fall within a continuum of level of disability. The DSM-5 defines intellectual disability as a disorder with onset during the developmental period that includes both intellectual and adaptive functioning deficits in conceptual, social, and practical domains (American Psychiatric Association, 2013). According to the American Association on Intellectual and Developmental Disabilities (AAIDD, 2015), to diagnose and assess children with intellectual disabilities, there are three major criteria used: significant limitations in intellectual functioning, significant limitations in adaptive behavior, and onset before the age of 18 (American Association on Intellectual and Developmental Disabilities, 2013). Therefore, essentially two types of assessments will be used with children with intellectual disabilities—an intelligence quotient (IQ) test and measures of adaptive functioning. The school psychologist is the only member that is trained to implement an IQ test. However, multiple team members will be involved in measures of adaptive functioning.

Intelligence Tests

An IQ test is an assessment that measures *intellectual functioning* such as the Stanford-Binet Intelligence Scales (see Appendix C). To meet diagnostic criteria for intellectual disability, the deficits in adaptive functioning must be directly related to the level of tested intellectual impairment (mild = IQ 55–70; moderate = IQ 40–55; severe = IQ 25–40; profound = IQ < 25; American Psychiatric Association, 2013). However, since the reliability of IQ tests on children with intellectual disabilities has been severely criticized, parents may really wonder why these tests are used, and it may be as simple an explanation as that they are still needed to maintain the child's category and special education services. However, more important measures, particularly when it comes to intervention, are the adaptive behavior scales.

Adaptive Behavior Scales

According to AAIDD (2015), adaptive behavior scales cover three types of skills:

- Conceptual skills—language and literacy; money, time, and number concepts; and self-direction
- Social skills—interpersonal skills, social responsibility, self-esteem, gullibility, naïveté (i.e., wariness), social problem solving, and the ability to follow rules, obey laws, and avoid being victimized
- Practical skills—activities of daily living (personal care), occupational skills, health care, travel/transportation, schedules/routines, safety, use of money, use of the telephone

It is when at least *one* domain of adaptive functioning—conceptual, social, or practical—is sufficiently impaired that ongoing support is needed. Adaptive functioning is assessed using standardized evaluations with knowledgeable informants (e.g., parent or other family member, teacher, counselor, care provider) and the child to the extent possible. Deficits in adaptive functioning may result in failure to meet developmental and sociocultural standards for independence and social responsibility. Without ongoing support, the adaptive deficits limit functioning in one or more activities of daily life, such as communication, social participation, and independent living, and across multiple environments, such as home, schoolwork and school, work, and recreation (American Association on Intellectual and Developmental Disabilities, 2013).

Having a child with intellectual disabilities may mean that the child will need lifelong support. Family members need to have quality MDTs working with them. Each transition point may be a time of joy but also a time of grief and stress as they see their child not driving or participating on a school sports team. Families may need support with resources that are available in their communities.

Children With Learning Disabilities

For families, having a child with a learning disability (or suspected learning disability) means that they will discover this when the child is in his/her early primary school years. To diagnose a child with learning disabilities, the child must either have a significant discrepancy between his/her scores on a test of general intelligence (e.g., an IQ test such as those described earlier) and scores obtained on an achievement test (e.g., the Woodcock Johnson Achievement Test) or not respond to a more commonly used assessment approach for diagnosis, response to intervention. The IQ achievement-discrepancy model, the approach traditionally used to identify children with learning disabilities, is determined by the child's score on the IQ test being at least two standard deviations (30 points) higher than his/her scores on an achievement test. If this occurs, the child is described as having a significant discrepancy between IQ and achievement. As indicated, however, more schools and districts are using a response to intervention (RTI) for diagnoses of learning disabilities. It is when RTI does not work that the child is diagnosed with a learning disability and provided with special education services. RTI involves monitoring all students' progress closely to identify possible learning problems, providing a child showing evidence of difficulties with help on different levels, or tiers, and moving that child through the tiers as appropriate while increasing support if he/she does not show progress and only referring to special education after RTI has failed and an IEP is needed for specially designed instruction and/or related services.

Essentially, though, the requirements for eligibility may be summed up as the following. First, the child must show a performance problem in a school subject. Second, the child must either show poor progress in school even when provided with high-quality interventions, or there must be a pattern of strengths and weaknesses. Third, the child's school performance problem must not be due primarily to another disability (e.g., hearing or intellectual disability), cultural or language factors, or environmental or economic disadvantage (Education.com, n.d.; National Institute of Health, 2014).

The MDT will look at both current functioning levels in academics as well as the child's attention span, perceptual-motor skills, memory, organization, strategies for learning, and study skills. It should be of note here, however, that the National Joint Committee on Learning Disabilities (1994) has placed emphasis on performance problems in basic skills ("significant difficulties in the acquisition and use of listening, speaking, reading, writing, reasoning, or mathematical abilities"), and thus would focus assessment and intervention in these areas of need. Achievement tests would certainly be implemented, such as the WISC-4, the Detroit Test of Learning Aptitude, and the Woodcock-Johnson. However, for some children with learning disabilities, just like other specific disabilities, an alternative assessment or authentic assessment may be used.

For children with learning disabilities, family members may have ongoing questions about such things as reading and math levels. Any frustration or learned helplessness the child may be exhibiting due to his/her learning disability may need to be addressed both at home and at school, as well as any social competence and skills areas. As the child ages, peer pressure and life goals will become increasingly important.

Children With Autism

For children with characteristics most prominent in children along the autism spectrum (i.e., behavior, communication, sensory), there are a number of very specific assessments used. Following are some of the more frequently used assessments:

The Childhood Autism Rating Scale-2 (CARS-2) is designed to be completed after direct observation of a child. There are two forms. The CARS-2 assessment (n.d.) is directed toward children under age 6, or over age 6 but with an estimated IQ of 79 or lower or notable communication impairment. The CARS-HF is directed at children age 6 or older, with an estimated IQ of 80 or higher and fluent communication. This assessment must be performed by professionals who have had parent questionnaire with this assessment (Schopler, Reichler, & Renner, 2010).

The Autism Diagnostic Interview-Revised is a standardized, semistructured parent interview that is administered by a trained professional. It includes 93 items focusing on early development, language/communication, reciprocal social interactions, and restricted, repetitive behaviors and interests. Most items are rated separately for current behavior as well as the period between the individual's fourth and fifth birthdays, or the point in the individual's lifetime at which the behavior in question was regarded as most atypical. Results yield a classification of "autism" or "non-autism" (Lord, Rutter, & Le Couteur, 1994).

The Autism Behavior Checklist (ABC, n.d.) is a checklist of nonadaptive behaviors capable of indicating how an individual compares to others. This checklist reflects an individual's challenges to respond appropriately to daily life situations and addresses sensory behaviors, relation behavior, body and object use behaviors, and language (Miranda-Linné & Melin, 2002).

Finally, the Autism Diagnostic Observation Schedule (ADOS) is an instrument for diagnosing and assessing autism. This assessment consists of a series of structured and semistructured tasks that involve social interaction between the professional and the child. The professional observes and identifies segments of the child's behavior. This assessment generally takes from 30 to 60 minutes to administer, with the professional providing opportunities for the child to show social and communication behaviors relevant to the diagnosis of autism (Lord, Rutter, DiLavore, Risi, Gotham & Bishop, 2002; Lord, Luyster, Gotham, & Guthrie, 2012).

ALTERNATIVE ASSESSMENTS/AUTHENTIC ASSESSMENTS FOR CHILDREN WITH DISABILITIES

For many children with intellectual disabilities and those with more severe levels of a variety of disabilities (learning disabilities, autism, etc.), alternative assessment (sometimes referred to as authentic assessment) is best used. Due to the severity of the disability, rather than standardized measures, alternative assessments yield the best results for the child. This type of assessment differs from standardized assessment, as it is aligned with the child's curriculum and IEP goals (Goh, 2004). Alternative assessment is simply assessment that shows us what a child can do. It is not standardized; however, there may be a protocol from your state and/or district on how to implement a certain alternative assessments, and in fact this type of assessment may be part of the state or district wide assessment program. Authentic assessment, performance assessment, and portfolio assessment are all types of assessments that are considered to be **alternative assessments** (Bintz & Harste, 1994). Much of what is involved in alternative assessment teachers already use, such as observation, oral assessment, compiling and analysis of student work samples, as well as assessment of hands-on skills. So a main feature of alternative assessment is that it is based on direct assessment of student performance and allows the student to show his/her competency in skill areas in a nontraditional, nonstandardized way. There are a number of types of alternative assessments. The most common described in the literature and used in the classroom are performance assessment, authentic assessment, and portfolio.

In **performance assessment**, the child must actually "perform, demonstrate, construct, and develop, a product or a solution under defined conditions and standards" (Khattri & Sweet, 1996, p. 3). The task will involve a behavior or activity to be performed and may result in a tangible object. An example of performance assessment is the use of task analysis to assess a child with intellectual disabilities' performance on hand washing. The evacuations of the performance are based on established criteria (i.e., a goal of 80% independence in hand washing).

"Authentic assessment" and "performance assessment" are sometimes used interchangeably. However, the literature points to a subtle but important difference, which is that for authentic assessments, skills should be demonstrated in real-world experience—for example, reading street signs throughout your community and following the appropriate action rather than just showing evidence of word recognition of street signs in the classroom. Additionally, abstract concepts are best learned when the intervention is related to how we will be assessing the student, such as when we are going to test the child on weather and the child can identify and demonstrate appropriate outer wear.

In **portfolio assessment**, the teacher is evaluating a compilation of the students' work. However, the work collected is done so with a plan in mind, such as to show progression in a subject area, students' writing skills across the curriculum, and/or skills and knowledge across all IEP goals. According to Moya and O'Malley (1994), a model portfolio assessment procedure must include the following six elements: (1) the purpose and focus of the portfolio; (2) design of portfolio (e.g., contents, data collection procedures, and evaluation criteria); (3) collection and analysis of portfolio content; (4) use of content for educational decisions; (5) use of results for intervention and educational decisions; and (6) assurance of reliability and validity of procedure.

Once all assessment data for all children is complete, the results will be interpreted and the evaluation report (ER) will be written. The ER will include the reason for referral, background history, behavioral observations, tests and procedures administered, test results, and conclusions.

When the child has an IEP, all assessments will result in an evaluation report.

THE ASSESSMENT REPORT/ THE EVALUATION REPORT

The assessment has been completed, the results have been interpreted, and it now is time to write the report. Many members of the MDT may have had input into the assessment process and may be providing, first, written results that will go into the evaluation report, but also the verbal communication of the results to the family perhaps before, but definitely at the MDT meeting. The communication of the assessment results will be most critical for family members and will need to be clear and concise and explained in terminology that the family can understand. The contents of the report will include all demographic and identifying information, the reason for the report (e.g., referral or reevaluation), and any necessary background information and relevant developmental, academic, and social history, the parents' perceptions of strengths and areas of need, behavioral observations, tests and procedures administered, and testing results. Finally, there will be conclusions and recommendations (see Sample Evaluation Report in Appendix C). An evaluation report can be quite lengthy, filled with important information that includes a lot of jargon and test results, and may be very overwhelming to families. Careful plans must be made for time to discuss all of the results, answering all questions, and, most importantly, ensuring comprehension so that appropriate decisions can be made concerning intervention and placement.

MAKING INSTRUCTIONAL DECISIONS FOR INTERVENTION

So what does all this mean for decision making? Sound decisions are based on quality data that the MDT has collected as a result of assessment. According to Brigham and Crockett (2013), "Actions that are independent of thought and data are unlikely to result in actual benefits for the individuals with disabilities they are intended to help" (p. 70). There are two levels of decisions consistently made on behalf of children with disabilities. One is program and the other is placement. There has been a lot written on both areas, as one pertains to the IEP provisions and the other to the least restrictive environment provisions of the law. It is understood within special education that the MDT decides on the program, the IEP, prior to the placement, the child's FAPE in his/her LRE. This is to ensure that educational goals are not governed with a specific placement in mind but are the result of sound assessment in all areas of need. After the IEP is developed, the MDT will then, as a result of a sound decision-making process, decide where the program will be implemented along the continuum of placements to best meet the child's needs for growth in all areas.

Actually, many decisions will need to be made throughout the screening-evaluation-assessment process, such as Should a referral be made to the MDT for testing evaluation following a screening?

What types of assessments (data) are needed? Which team members need to be involved? And so on. However, once the child is determined eligible for special education services, the process of goal setting occurs. As a result of assessment, an evaluation report will be written and will serve as the road map for IEP development. However, it is only a road map, and goals will be finalized with all MDT members at the IEP meeting. The components of the IEP are governed by IDEA and will contain the child's current educational levels of all assessed areas, as well as specific measurable annual academic and functional goals, to include behavioral goals and the incorporation of a positive behavior support plan if needed. Also, the child's age will determine selection of goals, since if the child is 14, career-related goals would be considered, with the formation of the ITP as part of the IEP by age 16. Since the IEP must state how progress toward meeting those goals will be measured as well as identification of specially designed instruction and related services, intervention decisions will be made.

Schools are held accountable to the students they serve. IDEA, paralleling NCLB, has requested that all states test all students and hold schools accountable for student learning and progress. As such, whatever goals and standards (the latter set as a result from the same standards as all other students or modified standards determined by a number of factors but usually a result of severity of disability), the MDT decides as a result of the assessments given to the student, all MDT members will be held accountable for student progress. Thus we end the chapter, where we began: with the importance of the assessment-to-intervention loop!

CASE STUDY 1
ASSESSMENT FOR JOSE, AGE 13

Jose lives with his parents, whose primary language is Spanish spoken in the home. He was referred for testing after his teachers raised concerns about his classroom performance. Specifically, he does not complete class work or homework assignments, nor does he participate in class.

Initial assessments revealed that when compared to others of his age, his cognitive abilities are in the below-average range, and his language development standard score is within the low to low-average range for his age. His word knowledge and comprehension are limited. Jose's academic achievement is in the below-average range, and his overall ability to express himself in writing is limited. In Math, Jose is 3 to 4 years below grade level. Jose's oral language standard score is within the very low to low-average range. His oral language skills are limited.

Questions for Critical Thinking

1. What other assessments would you recommend?
2. What types of assessment?
3. What additional information would help the team make recommendations for Jose?

CASE STUDY 2
SECONDARY LEVEL: INGRIDA

Ingrida is a 16-year-old student with moderate intellectual disabilities. Intelligence test results indicate significant deficits in written and verbal communication and memory. Additionally, she displays immature behavior at school, at home, and in the community. Ingrida works part time in the evenings bagging groceries and is currently enrolled in a community work experience part time during the school hours, where she works in a day-care center as an aide. She has indicated that she would like to do that in the future. Ingrida is transported to her work site from school. The rest of the day, she is in a self-contained special education classroom.

Ingrida will continue to live with her parents when school is completed and has expressed no desire to live elsewhere. However, as she is an only child, her parents are concerned about independent living skills and would like to see her in a supported living arrangement while they are still living. They do not understand how to make this happen given that Ingrida is resistant and additionally lacks skills such as cooking, using money, and any independent travel. However, Ingrida does participate in her many community-based recreational programs, so even if Ingrida does not always live with her parents, the family has expressed their wish that she remain in the community she has resided in her whole life.

Questions for Critical Thinking

1. What are the domain areas that should be incorporated in Ingrida's individualized transition plan as she nears school completion/graduation?

2. From what types of community agency supports might Ingrida benefit?

Summary

Throughout this chapter, you were given an overview of assessment at critical lifespan points. With each assessment, families play a critical role for their child and the team. Professionals need to be able to work well within many different types of families, as indicated in Chapters 1 and 2, and to be effective at the assessment process with each family. As such, following are some closing words on working with families during the assessment process:

Throughout this text, you will be presented with a number of strategies for working with parents. In conclusion, those same strategies apply to assessment and include:

1. Effective communication that is clear, frequent, open, positive, and encourages participation

2. Demystifying testing and special education jargon

3. Sensitivity and knowledge of cultural diversity issues and how they may impact assessment partnerships with families

4. Being a committed professional to the partnership by being responsible, consistent, flexible, encouraging, and positive

5. Being committed to equality and respect in the teaming process, developing and keeping trust

6. Knowing (having the skills) all we need to know about assessment and conveying that knowledge to families when necessary. Sharing all information.

Additional Resources

Web-Based

http://www.progressmonitoring.org. Produced by OSEP, Research Institute on Progress Monitoring. Provides the research from 5 years of study on progress monitoring.

http://www.teach-nology.com/web_tools/rubrics/. Technology provides rubrics for most all subject areas and also allows the teacher to make his or her own for assessment purposes.

Reschly, A. Schools, Families, and Response to Intervention: http://www.rtinetwork.org/essential/family/schools-familes-and-rti.

http://www.rti4success.org/resources/family-resources Family Resources for RTI.

The Role of Parents/Family in Response to Intervention. (2015, January 1): http://ldaamerica.org/the-role-of-parentsfamily-in-response-to-intervention/.

A Family Guide to Response to Intervention (RtI). (2010, January 1): http://education.nh.gov/nhresponds/documents/fam_guide.pdf.

FBAs

Behavior Assessment, Plans, and Positive Supports. (2014, May 1). http://www.parentcenterhub.org/repository/behavassess/

Jordan, D. (n.d.). *Functional behavioral assessment and positive interventions: What parents need to know.* Retrieved April 28, 2015, from http://www.wrightslaw.com/info/discipl.fba.jordan.pdf

http://archives.gadoe.org/DMGetDocument.aspx/FBA_and_BIP_Fact_Sheet_6-11.pdf?p=6CC6799
F8C1371F68A7E0B0548DA1B3FA1AB7A11E6C2
FB27498EA199A303A21F

Assessment and Consideration

Lepi, K. (2013, July 22). The 6 types of assessments (and how they're changing). http://www.edudemic.com/the-6-types-of-assessments-and-how-theyre-changing/

Luke, S., & Schwartz, A. (2010, October 1). Assessment and accommodations. http://www.parentcenterhub.org/repository/assessment-accommodations/

Makofsky, S. (2013, January 1). The assessment process—special education guide. http://www.specialeducationguide.com/pre-k-12/what-is-special-education/the-importance-of-the-assessment-process/

Common Core

Fulton, D., & Kastner, P. (2010, January 1). Implementing the Common Core: Considerations for elementary special educators. http://www.pattan.net/Videos/Browse/Single/?code_name=what_every_educator_should_know_about

Parents' Guides to Student Success. (n.d.). Retrieved April 28, 2015, from http://www.pta.org/parents/content.cfm?ItemNumber=2583

Walker, T. (2013, October 16). 10 things you should know about the Common Core—NEA today. Retrieved April 28, 2015, from http://neatoday.org/2013/10/16/10-things-you-should-know-about-the-common-core/

Culturally Responsive Interventions

http://www.nccrest.org/professional/culturally_responsive_response_to_intervention.html (Culturally Responsive Response to Intervention)

Ray, J., Pewitt-Kinder, J., & George, S. (2009, September 1). *Partnering with families of children.* Retrieved April 28, 2015, from http://www.naeyc.org/files/yc/file/200909/FamiliesOfChildrenWithSpecialNeeds0909.pdf

APPENDIX A: ASSESSMENT TYPES/TECHNICAL TERMINOLOGY DEFINED

Assessment Type/ Technical Qualities	Description/Definition
Achievement Tests	Achievement tests are designed to measure the knowledge and skills students learned in school or to determine the academic progress they have made over a period of time. Achievement tests are "backward looking" in that they measure how well students have learned what they were expected to learn. http://edglossary.org/standardized-test/
Adaptive Behavior Scales (ABSs)	According to the American Association on Intellectual and Developmental Disabilities (AAIDD, 2015). ABSs provide precise diagnostic information around the cutoff point where an individual is deemed to have "significant limitations" in adaptive behavior. The presence of such limitations is one of the measures of intellectual disability. Parents, teachers, and other caregivers who know the behaviors of the child or adolescent being rated typically complete adaptive behavior scales, such as semi-structured interview forms and rating scales. Such informant-based adaptive behavior scales offer a number of benefits to users, including providing summaries of observations of behaviors across varied settings, such as homes, schools, and community settings. http://aaidd.org/intellectual-disability/diagnostic-adaptive-behavior-scale#.VUsTE_BQ3QI
Age Score/Chronological Age	The number of years a person has lived, used especially in psychometrics as a standard against which certain variables, such as behavior and intelligence, are measured. Age equivalent scores are almost always given in years and months. http://www.thefreedictionary.com/chronological+age
Alternate Assessment	Alternate assessment is a generic term for a family of methods used to assess the academic performance of students with significant disabilities or limited proficiency with English. Alternate assessments are an important component of each state's assessment system and, as such, are required to meet the federal regulations outlined in Title I of the Elementary and Secondary Education Act. Orelove, F. P., Sobsey, D., & Silberman, R. K. (2004). *Educating children with multiple disabilities: A collaborative approach*. Brookes Publishing Company.
Basal	Denoting a standard or reference state of a function, as a basis for comparison. A basal is the "starting point." It represents the level of mastery of a task below which the student would correctly answer all items on a test. All of the items prior to the basal are not given to the student. These items are considered already correct. For example, on an IQ test, the examiner may start with Question 14 because of the age of the child. That is the basal.

Assessment Type/ Technical Qualities	Description/Definition
Behavior Rating Scales	Assessment instruments designed to obtain the perceptions or judgments of a subject's behavior in a standardized format. Raters may be the subject (self-rating) or others with the opportunity to observe and describe aspects of the subject's behavior (i.e., parents, teachers, etc.).
	Behavior rating scales are often used as screening devices to obtain information on and help identify individuals who may benefit from a more detailed assessment or who may be at risk for developing more serious problems and who may benefit from early interventions. Behavior rating scales are also used to monitor progress in treatment programs. Behavior rating scales should never be utilized as the sole source of information for the purposes of diagnosis or classification of a specific educational or psychological problem.
	Goldstein, S., & Naglieri, J. A. (Eds.). (2011). *Encyclopedia of child behavior and development* (p. 228)
Ceiling	The ceiling is the "ending point." It represents the level of mastery of a task above which the student would incorrectly answer all future items on a test. A ceiling is a testing term referring to the highest level of items a person can answer correctly before reaching the test's discontinuation criteria.
	http://learningdisabilities.about.com/od/C/g/Ceiling-What-Is-A-Ceiling.htm
Confidence Interval	A statistical approach that creates a band of acceptable passing rates based on size of the group tested, average test scores, and the range of scores, among other factors. Confidence intervals constitute a range of statistical values within which a result is expected to fall with a specific probability.
	http://eddataexpress.ed.gov/definitions.cfm
Continuous Recording	Continuous recording is required for direct measurement of the basic dimensions of behaviors.
	Mudford, O. C., Taylor, S. A., & Martin, N. T. (2009). Continuous recording and interobserver agreement algorithms reported in the *Journal of Applied Behavior Analysis* (1995–2005). Journal of Applied Behavior Analysis, 42,165–169.
Correlation	The state or relation of being correlated; specifically: a relation existing between phenomena or things or between mathematical or statistical variables which tend to vary, be associated, or occur together in a way not expected on the basis of chance alone. Degree and type of relationship between any two or more quantities (variables) in which they vary together over a period; for example, variation in the level of expenditure or savings with variation in the level of income. A positive correlation exists when the high values of one variable are associated with the high values of the other variable(s). A "negative correlation" means association of high values of one with the low values of the other(s). Correlation can vary from +1 to –1. Values close to +1 indicate a high degree of positive correlation, and values close to –1 indicate a high degree of negative correlation. Values close to zero indicate poor correlation of either kind, and 0 indicates no correlation at all. While correlation is useful in discovering possible connections between variables, it does not prove or disprove any cause-and-effect (causal) relationships between them.
	http://www.businessdictionary.com/definition/correlation.html#ixzz 3ZRs89yZc

Assessment Type/ Technical Qualities	Description/Definition
Criterion-Referenced Test	Criterion-referenced tests are designed to measure student performance against a fixed set of predetermined criteria or learning standards—that is, concise, written descriptions of what students are expected to know and be able to do at a specific stage of their education. In elementary and secondary education, criterion-referenced tests are used to evaluate whether students have learned a specific body of knowledge or acquired a specific skill set; for example, the curriculum taught in a course, academic program, or content area. http://edglossary.org/criterion-referenced-test/
Curriculum-Based Assessment	Curriculum-based measurement (CBM). A method to measure student progress in academic areas including math, reading, writing, and spelling. The child is tested briefly (1 to 5 minutes) each week. Scores are recorded on a graph and compared to the expected performance on the content for that year. The graph allows the teacher and parents to see quickly how the child's performance compares to expectations. http://www.studentprogress.org/library/monitoring_student_progress_in_individualized_educational_programs_using_cbm.pdf CBM encompasses an assessment methodology that can be used to develop goals, benchmarks, or short-term objectives for individualized educational programs for students with disabilities. Teachers also use curriculum-based measurement as a means for monitoring student progress across the year. CBM is a reliable and valid assessment system for monitoring student progress in basic academic skill areas, such as reading, writing, spelling, and mathematics. CBM is an alternative assessment system that also borrows some features from standardized, norm-referenced assessment. The CBM procedures, including test administration, scoring, and interpretation, are standardized; that is, tests are given and scored in the same way each time. The content of the CBM tests may be drawn from a specific curriculum or may represent generalized outcomes for a student at that grade level.
Diagnostic Test	Diagnostic assessments fall into two categories: standardized and informal. A combination of both types is often used to determine a student's eligibility for specialized programming such as special education or English as a second language programs. In the formal or standardized assessments, a student is given a battery of tests that have several subtests that measure a variety of skills and abilities. These tests must only be given by qualified staff and will reflect scores that are based on norms researched to be specific to the test given. Once stored, these tests provide a profile of abilities and skills. This type of assessment generally takes a significant amount of time to give. Interpretation of the profile must be delegated to specific staff members who are highly skilled in deriving conclusions from testing data. Educational decisions are then made for eligibility to specialized instruction such as special education or English as a second language programs (Fletcher, Coulter, Reschly, & Vaughn, 2004). Informal types of assessment can also review a student's subskills. These assessments can be as common as spelling tests, decoding surveys, or math calculation tests. They are very inexpensive, easy to give, and can be administered by a certified teacher with very little training.

Assessment Type/ Technical Qualities	Description/Definition
Diagnostic Test *(continued)*	The results of these assessments will break down a student's skill deficit area into its component parts on a hierarchy in order to plan instruction. The norms associated with the screening tests and probes can be used alongside the informal diagnostic tests and surveys to generate a profile of abilities and skills. Interpretation of these profiles is very easy and clear as to what the student needs for instruction in deficit areas. Educational decision using this type of assessment places students into appropriate instructional groups to remediate skill area deficits that will affect progress in state-required curricula. The advantage of using these types of diagnostic tests is that a student is able to get the appropriate instruction from Tier 2 interventions that are available in the general curriculum without the need to be "placed" into special education (Fuchs & Deshler, 2007; Fuchs & Fuchs, 2006). http://www.projectidealonline.org/v/definition-type-assessment
Ecological Assessment	An ecological assessment is a comprehensive process in which data is collected about how a child functions in different environments or settings. Sometimes, students eligible for special education perform or behave well in some environments but have difficulty in others. For example, at school, a student may be calm during class time but always upset in the cafeteria. Other children even have school phobia, which is an irrational, persistent fear of going to school. These children seem fine at home but consistently become anxious, depressed, or scared every time they have to go to school. Salvia, J., Ysseldyke, J. E., & Bolt, S. (2007). *Assessment in special and inclusive education*. Wadsworth.
Error Analysis	Error analysis involves the analysis of error patterns to identify difficulties that students may have with facts, concepts, strategies, and procedures. Identifying the type of error allows the teacher to address learner needs more efficiently. http://k6.boardofstudies.nsw.edu.au/wps/portal/go/mathematics/support-students-special-needs/assessment/error-analysis
Functional Behavioral Assessment	Functional behavioral assessment (FBA) is a variation on procedures originally developed to ascertain the purpose or reason for behaviors displayed by individuals with severe cognitive or communication disabilities (e.g., individuals with intellectual disabilities or autism). Because these individuals were unable to fully explain why they were displaying certain inappropriate behaviors, methods were developed to determine why they demonstrated such actions. These investigatory procedures were derived primarily from the orientation and methods of applied behavior analysis. http://www.behavioradvisor.com/FBA.html The term "functional behavioral assessment" comes from what is called a "functional assessment" or "functional analysis" in the field of applied behavior analysis. This is the process of determining the cause (or "function") of behavior before developing an intervention.
Grade Score	If the purpose is to compare the student's scores with those of peers in the same grade, grade-based scores should be used.

Assessment Type/ Technical Qualities	Description/Definition
Intelligence Testing	Intelligence tests are psychological tests that are designed to measure a variety of mental functions, such as reasoning, comprehension, and judgment.
	The goal of intelligence tests is to obtain an idea of the person's intellectual potential. The tests center around a set of stimuli designed to yield a score based on the test maker's model of what makes up intelligence. Intelligence tests are often given as part of a battery of tests. There are many different types of intelligence tests, and they all do not measure the same abilities. Although the tests often have aspects that are related with each other, one should not expect that scores from one intelligence test that measures a single factor will be similar to scores on another intelligence test that measures a variety of factors. Also, when determining whether to use an intelligence test, a person should make sure that the test has been adequately developed and has solid research to show its reliability and validity. Additionally, psychometric testing requires a clinically trained examiner. Therefore, the test should only be administered and interpreted by a trained professional.
	When taking an intelligence test, a person can expect to do a variety of tasks. These tasks may include having to answer questions that are asked verbally, doing mathematical problems, and doing a variety of tasks that require eye–hand coordination. Some tasks may be timed and require the person to work as quickly as possible. Typically, most questions and tasks start out easy and progressively get more difficult. It is unusual for anyone to know the answer to all of the questions or be able to complete all of the tasks. If a person is unsure of an answer, guessing is usually allowed.
	http://www.minddisorders.com/Flu-Inv/Intelligence-tests.html#ixzz 3ZSDFKd7N
Interval	The standard survey rating scale is an interval scale.
	When you are asked to rate your satisfaction with a piece of software on a 7-point scale, from Dissatisfied to Satisfied, you are using an interval scale.
	It is an interval scale because it is assumed to have equidistant points between each of the scale elements. This means that we can interpret differences in the distance along the scale. We contrast this to an ordinal scale, with which we can only talk about differences in order, not differences in the degree of order.
	Interval scales are also scales that are defined by metrics such as logarithms. In these cases, the distances are not equal, but they are strictly definable based on the metric used. Interval-scale data would use parametric statistical techniques.
Mean	Average score; sum of individual scores divided by the total number of scores.
Measures of Central Tendency	A measure of central tendency is a single value that attempts to describe a set of data by identifying the central position within that set of data. As such, measures of central tendency are sometimes called measures of central location. They are also classed as summary statistics. The mean (often called the average) is most likely the measure of central tendency that you are most familiar with, but there are others, such as the median and the mode.

Assessment Type/ Technical Qualities	Description/Definition
Measures of Central Tendency *(continued)*	The mean, median, and mode are all valid measures of central tendency, but under different conditions, some measures of central tendency become more appropriate to use than others.
	https://statistics.laerd.com/statistical-guides/measures-central-tendency-mean-mode-median.php
Measures of Variability	A mathematical determination of how much the performance of the group as a whole deviates from the mean or median. The most frequently used measure of variability is the standard deviation.
	http://www.alleydog.com/glossary/definition.php?term=Measures%20Of%20Variability#ixzz3ZSKEqnkF
	Measures of variability are statistics that describe the amount of difference and spread in a data set. These measures include variance, standard deviation, and standard error of the mean. If the numbers corresponding to these statistics are high, it means that the scores or values in our data set are widely spread out and not tightly centered on the mean.
	http://www.alleydog.com/glossary/definition.php?term=Measures%20Of%20Variability#ixzz3ZSKEqnkF
Median	The middle score in a distribution or set of ranked scores; the point (score) that divides a group into two equal parts; the 50th percentile. Half the scores are below the median, and half are above it.
Mode	The score or value that occurs most often in a distribution.
Nominal	Value is named; naming category (i.e., male, female). The lowest measurement level you can use, from a statistical point of view, is a nominal scale.
	A nominal scale, as the name implies, is simply some placing of data into categories without any order or structure.
	A physical example of a nominal scale is the terms we use for colors. The underlying spectrum is ordered, but the names are nominal.
	In research activities, a YES/NO scale is nominal. It has no order, and there is no distance between YES and NO.
	The statistics that can be used with nominal scales are in the nonparametric group. The most likely ones would be:
	• mode
	• cross-tabulation—with chi-square
	There are also highly sophisticated modeling techniques available for nominal data.
	http://www.csse.monash.edu.au/~smarkham/resources/scaling.htm
Norm-Referenced Test	Standardized tests designed to compare the scores of children to scores achieved by children the same age who have taken the same test. Most standardized achievement tests are norm referenced.
	http://www.wrightslaw.com/links/glossary.assessment.htm#sthash.272njqzm.dpuf
Normal Curve Equivalent	The normal curve equivalent, or NCE, is a way of measuring where a student falls along the normal curve. The numbers on the NCE line run from 0 to 100, similar to percentile ranks, which indicate an individual

Assessment Type/ Technical Qualities	Description/Definition
Normal Curve Equivalent *(continued)*	student's rank, or how many students out of 100 had a lower score. NCE scores have a major advantage over percentile rank scores in that they can be averaged. That is an important characteristic when studying overall school performance and, in particular, in measuring schoolwide gains and losses in student achievement. https://www.aea267.k12.ia.us/system/assets/uploads/files/1739/nce_score.pdf
Normal Distribution of Scores	Normal distribution, also known as the bell-shaped curve because of its distinctive appearance in that scores are distributed symmetrically about the middle, such that there are an equal number of scores above as below the mean, with more scores concentrated near the middle than at the extremes. The normal distribution is a theoretical distribution defined by specific mathematical properties that many human traits and psychological characteristics appear to closely approximate (e.g., height, weight, intelligence, etc.). See also: Distribution, Arithmetic Mean, Median, Mode, and Standard Deviation. Some features of the normal distribution are: 1. The mean, median, and mode are identical in value. 2. The scores are distributed symmetrically about the mean (50.0% above the mean and 50.0% below the mean). 3. 68.26% of the scores are within 1 standard deviation of the mean (34.13% above the mean and 34.13% below the mean). 4. 95.44% of the scores are within 2 standard deviations of the mean (47.72% above the mean and 47.72% below the mean). 5. 99.72% of the scores are within 3 standard deviations of the mean (49.86% above the mean and 49.86% below the mean). http://oms.umn.edu/mstp/tests_and_services/glossary.php
Ordinal	The simplest ordinal scale is a ranking. When a market researcher asks you to rank 5 types of beer from most flavorful to least flavorful, he/she is asking you to create an ordinal scale of preference. There is no objective distance between any two points on your subjective scale. For you, the top beer may be far superior to the second preferred beer but, to another respondent with the same top and second beers, the distance may be subjectively small. An ordinal scale only lets you interpret gross order and not the relative positional distances. Ordinal data would use nonparametric statistics. These would include: • median and mode • rank order correlation • nonparametric analysis of variance • modeling techniques can also be used with ordinal data. http://www.csse.monash.edu.au/~smarkham/resources/scaling.htm
Portfolio	Portfolio assessment is an evaluation tool used to document student learning through a series of student-developed artifacts. Considered a form of authentic assessment, it offers an alternative or an addition to traditional methods of grading and high-stakes exams. Portfolio assessment gives both teachers and students a controlled space to

Assessment Type/ Technical Qualities	Description/Definition
Portfolio *(continued)*	document, review, and analyze content learning. In short, portfolios are a collection of student work that allows assessment by providing evidence of effort and accomplishments in relation to specific instructional goals (Jardine, 1996). At its best, portfolio assessment demands the following: clarity of goals, explicit criteria for evaluation, work samples tied to those goals, student participation in selection of entries, teacher and student involvement in the assessment process, and self-reflections that demonstrate students' metacognitive ability, that is, their understanding of what worked for them in the learning process, what did not, and why. These elements enhance the learning experience and the self-understanding of the student as learner.
	There are a variety of portfolio types, each designed to help assess either the process or the products of learning: showcase portfolios, process portfolios, evaluation portfolios, online or e-portfolios.
	http://www.education.com/reference/article/portfolio-assessment/
Range	The range is the simplest measure of variability to calculate, and one you have probably encountered many times in your life. The range is simply the highest score minus the lowest score. Example: What is the range of the following group of numbers: 10, 2, 5, 6, 7, 3, 4? The highest number is 10, and the lowest number is 2, so 10 –‰ 2 = 8. The range is 8.
	http://onlinestatbook.com/2/summarizing_distributions/variability.html
Ratio	A ratio scale is the top level of measurement and is not often available in social research.
	The factor that clearly defines a ratio scale is that it has a true zero point.
	The simplest example of a ratio scale is the measurement of length (disregarding any philosophical points about defining how we can identify zero length).
	The best way to contrast interval and ratio scales is to look at temperature. The Centigrade scale has a zero point, but it is an arbitrary one. The Fahrenheit scale has its equivalent point at –32°.
	http://www.csse.monash.edu.au/~smarkham/resources/scaling.htm
Raw Score	The first unadjusted score obtained in scoring a test. A raw score is usually determined by tallying the number of questions answered correctly or by the sum or combination of the item scores (i.e., points). However, a raw score could also refer to any number directly obtained by the test administration (e.g., raw score derived by formula scoring, amount of time required to perform a task, the number of errors, etc.). In individually administered tests, raw scores could also include points credited for items below the basal. Raw scores typically have little meaning by themselves. Interpretation of raw scores requires additional information such as the number of items on the test, the difficulty of the test items, norm-referenced information (e.g., percentile ranks, grade equivalents, stanines, etc.), and/or criterion-referenced information (e.g., cut-scores).
	http://oms.umn.edu/mstp/tests_and_services/glossary.php
Reliability	Reliability is the consistency of a measure. In educational testing, reliability refers to the confidence that the test score will be the same across repeated administrations of the test. There is a close relation between the construct of reliability and the construct of validity.

Assessment Type/ Technical Qualities	Description/Definition
Reliability *(continued)*	Many sources discuss how a test can have reliability without validity and that a test cannot have validity without reliability. In the theoretical sense, these statements are true, but not in any practical sense. A test is designed to be reliable and valid, consistent, and accurate. Practical conceptualizations of reliability cannot be discussed separately from examples with validity. http://www.education.com/reference/article/reliability/
Response to Intervention	Response to intervention (RTI) is a multitier approach to the early identification and support of students with learning and behavior needs. The RTI process begins with high-quality instruction and universal screening of all children in the general education classroom. Struggling learners are provided with interventions at increasing levels of intensity to accelerate their rate of learning. These services may be provided by a variety of personnel, including general education teachers, special educators, and specialists. Progress is closely monitored to assess both the learning rate and level of performance of individual students. Educational decisions about the intensity and duration of interventions are based on individual student response to instruction. RTI is designed for use when making decisions in both general education and special education, creating a well-integrated system of instruction and intervention guided by child outcome data. http://www.rtinetwork.org/learn/what/whatisrti
Rubric	A rubric is a scoring tool used to evaluate and assess a set list of criteria and objectives. Rubrics are often used as a way to evaluate work that is subject to the evaluator's personal feelings, prejudices, or interpretations. Rubrics are typically displayed as a grid. The left-hand column of the grid lists the objectives that are being evaluated. The cells in each row describe, in a few phrases, specific criteria for receiving a low, medium, or high score. When given a copy of the rubric prior to an evaluation, the person whose work is being evaluated is able to see exactly what criteria the evaluator will be using to award the highest possible score. http://whatis.techtarget.com/definition/rubric
Standard Deviation	A measure of the variability of a distribution of scores. The more the scores cluster around the mean, the smaller the standard deviation. In a normal distribution, 68% of the scores fall within 1 standard deviation above and 1 standard deviation below the mean. http://www.wrightslaw.com/links/glossary.assessment.htm#sthash.272njqzm.dpuf
Standard Error of Measurement	Is associated with the test scores for a specified group of test takers. The standard error of measurement (SEM) is the standard deviation of errors of measurement that are associated with test scores from a particular group of examinees. When used to calculate confidence bands around obtained test scores, it can be helpful expressing the unreliability of individual test scores in an understandable way. Score bands can also be used to interpret intraindividual and interindividual score differences. Interpreters should be wary of overinterpretation when using approximations for correctly calculated score bands. It is recommended that SEMs at various score levels be used calculating score bands rather than a single SEM value. http://ncme.org/linkservid/6606715E-1320-5CAE-6E9DDC581EE47F88/showMeta/0/

Assessment Type/ Technical Qualities	Description/Definition
Standard Score	A standard score is a score that has been transformed to fit a normal curve, with a mean and standard deviation that remain the same across ages. Standard scores have a mean of 100 and a standard deviation of 15.
Stanine	Stanines are bands of standard scores that have a mean of 5 and a standard deviation of 2. Stanines range from 1 to 9. Despite their relative ease of interpretation, stanines have several disadvantages. A change in just a few raw score points can move a student from one stanine to another. Also, because stanines are a general way of interpreting test performance, caution is necessary when making classification and placement decisions. http://www.education.com/reference/article/types-scores-assessment/
Task Analysis	When most of us have a job to complete, we break it down into smaller steps. This is known as task analysis and can be used in the special education setting to help students gain independence. Task analysis is the process of breaking a skill into smaller, more manageable steps in order to teach the skill. As the smaller steps are mastered, the learner becomes increasingly independent in his or her ability to perform the larger skill. Task analysis is an effective way to plan the teaching of skills that require several steps to be performed in a certain order (chained behaviors) such as telling time, tying shoes, or doing long division, as well as larger, more complex tasks (e.g., preparing and serving a meal or cleaning a cafeteria). Task analysis can often be used to take a much larger group of skills and break them down into phases. The phases can be taught as smaller sections helping assist in mastering of the larger task. For example, one might teach a vocational task of cleaning the cafeteria by teaching someone to first prepare materials (phase 1), then clean the cafeteria (phase 2), and last, put away the materials (phase 3).
Validity	The practice of task analysis can be used to effectively plan for the teaching of academics and life and vocational skills. Task analysis can be used with children and youth across the autism spectrum. https://www.gvsu.edu/cms3/assets/.../task_analysis.docx The extent to which a test measures the skills it sets out to measure and the extent to which inferences and actions made on the basis of test scores are appropriate and accurate. http://www.wrightslaw.com/links/glossary.assessment.htm#sthash.272njqzm.dpuf Validity refers to the degree to which evidence and theory support the interpretations of test scores entailed by proposed uses of tests. Although classical models divided the concept into various "validities" (such as content validity, criterion validity, and construct validity), the currently dominant view is that validity is a single unitary construct. Validity is generally considered the most important issue in psychological and educational testing because it concerns the meaning placed on test results. These models can be categorized into two primary groups: classical models, which include several types of validity, and modern models, which present validity as a single construct. The modern models reorganize classical "validities" into either "aspects" of validity or types of validity-supporting evidence.

Assessment Type/ Technical Qualities	Description/Definition
Validity *(continued)*	American Educational Research Association, American Psychological Association, & National Council on Measurement in Education. (1999). Standards for educational and psychological testing. Washington, DC: American Educational Research Association.
	Messick, S. (1995). Validity of psychological assessment: Validation of inferences from persons' responses and performances as scientific inquiry into score meaning. American Psychologist, 50, 741–749.
	Nitko, J. J., & Brookhart, S. M. (2004). Educational assessment of students. Upper Saddle River, NJ: Merrill-Prentice Hall.
Vocational Interest Inventories	A career tool for self-assessment that aids in career planning to assesses the likes of particular objects, activities, and personalities using the theory that individuals with the same career tend to have the same interests.
	http://www.businessdictionary.com/definition/interest-inventory .html#ixzz3ZSY3jygq
	An interest inventory is a testing instrument designed for the purpose of measuring and evaluating the level of an individual's interest in or preference for a variety of activities; also known as interest tests. Testing methods include direct observation of behavior, ability tests, and self-reporting inventories of interest in educational, social, recreational, and vocational activities. The activities usually represented in interest inventories are variously related to occupational areas, and these instruments and their results are often used in vocational guidance.
	http://psychology.jrank.org/pages/343/Interest-Inventory.html#ixzz 3ZSYIXMm2
Work Sample Assessments	The Work Sampling System, an authentic performance assessment, is based on teachers' observations of children at work in the classroom learning, solving problems, interacting, and creating products. Designed for students in preschool through fifth grade, the Work Sampling System includes three interrelated elements:
	• developmental guidelines and checklists
	• portfolios
	• summary reports
	The system is based on seven domains or categories, each with performance indicators: Personal and Social Development (focusing on self-identity, the self as a learner, and social development); Language and Literacy (based on the theory that students learn to read and write the way they learn to speak, naturally and slowly); Mathematical Thinking (focusing on children's approaches to mathematical thinking and problem solving); Scientific Thinking (emphasizing the processes of scientific investigation, because process skills are embedded in and fundamental to all science instruction and content); Social Studies (understanding from personal experience and by learning about the experiences of others); the Arts (focusing on how using and appreciating the arts enables children to demonstrate what they know and to expand their thinking); and, Physical Development (developing fine and gross motor skills and a growing competence to understand and manage personal health and safety).

Assessment Type/ Technical Qualities	Description/Definition
Work Sample Assessments *(continued)*	The Work Sampling System is a continuous-assessment format, which helps teachers, families and students gain perspective on the student's development and skills over an 8-year period, from ages 3 to 11. It allows schools to create mixed-age groupings in classrooms if desired, and allows for longitudinal study over time to examine how a child has developed. The continuous use also allows parents and families to become extremely familiar with the assessment system and its benefits. http://www.fairtest.org/work-sampling-system

APPENDIX B: COMMONLY USED ASSESSMENTS

Assessment	Age Range	Contents	Publisher
Achievement Tests			
Brigance Comprehensive Inventory of Basic Skills	Grade 6–Adult	Criterion-referenced test	
Kaufman Test of Educational Achievement, 2nd Ed.	1–12	A norm-referenced test w/ subtests in reading decoding and comprehension, mathematics application and computation, spelling	Pearson
Peabody Individual Achievement Test-Revised-Normative Update	K–12	A norm-referenced test w/ subtests in mathematics, reading recognition, comprehension, spelling general information and written expression	Pearson
Terra Nova, 2nd Ed.	K–12	A norm-referenced test w/ subtests in reading, language, math, science and social studies	CTB/McGraw-Hill
Wide Range Achievement Test-4	Ages 5–75	Word reading, sentence comprehension, spelling, math computation	Pro-Ed
Behavior			
Attention Deficit Disorders Evaluation Scale, 3rd Ed. (ADDES)	Ages 4–18	Used to evaluate and diagnose ADHD; available in school and home versions; subscales Inattentive and Hyperactive-Impulsive	
Behavior Assessment System for Children (BASC)	Ages 2.6–18		
Behavior Evaluation Scale (BES-2)	Ages 4–19		

Assessment	Age Range	Contents	Publisher
Connors Rating Scale, 3rd Ed. (CTRS)	Ages 6–18	Assessment of ADHD w/ comorbid disorders of oppositional defiant disorder and conduct disorder. There is a parent, teacher, and self-report form	
Cognitive			
Kaufman Assessment Battery for Children, 2nd Ed.	3–18	Norm-referenced test Triangles, face recognition, pattern reasoning, block counting, story completion, conceptual thinking, rover, gestalt, closure, word order, number recall, hand movements, atlantic, atlantis-delayed, rebus, rebus-delayed, riddles, expressive vocabulary, verbal knowledge	Pearson
Stanford-Binet Intelligence Scale, 5th Ed.	Ages 2–85+	Object series/matrices, early reasoning, verbal and picture absurdities, verbal analogies, procedural knowledge, vocabulary, quantitative reasoning, form board and patterns, position and direction, delayed response, block span, memory for sentences, last word	Riverside
Wechsler Intelligence Scale for Children-IV (WISC-IV)	Ages 6–16.11	Similarities, vocabulary, comprehension, information, word reasoning, block design, picture concepts, matrix reasoning, picture completion, digit span, letter-number sequencing, arithmetic, coding, symbol search, cancellation	Pearson
Woodcock-Johnson Psycho-Educational Battery–III Tests of Cognitive Abilities	Ages 2–9+	Norm-referenced tests for verbal comprehension, auditory learning, visual-auditory learning-delayed, spatial relations, sound blending, incomplete words, concept formation, visual matching, numbers reversed, auditory working memory, general information, retrieval fluency, picture recognition, planning, auditory attention, analysis-synthesis, planning, decision speed, rapid picture naming, pair cancellation, memory for words	Riverside
Communication			
Boehm Test of Basic Concepts, 3rd Ed. (BTBC-3)	PreK–K	Measures 50 basic concepts: size, direction, quantity, time, classification, and general	

Assessment	Age Range	Contents	Publisher
Goldman-Fristoe Woodcock Test of Auditory Discrimination Test of Language	Ages 2.0–21.11 years	A norm-referenced test for sounds in words, sounds in sentences, and stimulability	Pearson
Peabody Picture Vocabulary Test, IV	Ages 2.6–90+	Norm-referenced test w/ no subtests	Pearson
Receptive and Expressive One-Word Picture Vocabulary Tests, 2nd Ed.	Ages 4.0–89.11	Receptive and expressive vocabulary	Pro-Ed
Test of Language Development, Primary and Intermediate, 4th ed.	Ages 4.0–8.11 and 8.0–17.11	Norm-referenced tests In Primary: picture, relational and oral vocabulary, syntactic understanding, sentence imitation, morphological completion, word discrimination, analysis and articulation In Intermediate: sentence combining, picture vocabulary, word ordering, relational vocabulary, morphological comprehension, multiple meanings	Pro-Ed
Early Childhood			
Battelle Developmental Inventory, 2nd Ed. (BDI-2)	Birth–Age 7	Use for screening, diagnosis, and evaluation of early development. Subtests include personal social, adaptive, motor, communication, and cognitive domains.	Riverside
Bayley Scales of Infant Development, 2nd Ed.	0–42 months	Norm-referenced test, all developmental domains	The Psychological Corporation
Carolina Curriculum for Infants and Toddlers w/ Special Needs	24–60 months	Curriculum-referenced test, all developmental domains	Brookes
Hawaii Early Learning Profile (HELP)	0–60 months	Curriculum-referenced test, all developmental domains	VORT Corporation
Peabody Picture Vocabulary Test, IV (PPVT-IV)	2.5–Adult	Receptive language	American Guidance Service
Preschool Language Scale (PLS-3)	Birth–6	Measures receptive and expressive language; birth to age 3 measures targeting interaction, attention, vocal and gestural behaviors; two separate scales: auditory and expressive communications scales measures vocabulary, concepts of quality and quantity, space and time, morphology, syntax and integrative thinking skills	

Assessment	Age Range	Contents	Publisher
Receptive-Expressive Emergent Language (REEL-3)	1–36 months	Norm-referenced test, prelinguistic skills	Pro-ED
Transdisciplinary Play Based Assessment	Infancy–6 years	Curriculum-referenced test for cognition, language, social-emotional and sensorimotor	Brookes
Test of Nonverbal Intelligence			
Test of Nonverbal Intelligence, 3rd Ed.	Ages 6–18.11	Pictorial and geometric analogies, pictorial and geometric categories, pictorial and geometric sequences	Pro-Ed
Math			
Comprehensive Mathematical Abilities Test	Grades 3–12	Norm-referenced test	
KeyMath-3	K–9	Norm-referenced test of student's understanding and application of mathematic concepts and skills. Subtests on numerations, rational numbers, computations, geometry, mental computation, measurement, time and money, estimation, interpreting data, problem solving	Pearson
Stanford Diagnostic Mathematics, 4th Ed. (SDMT)	Grade 1–12	Norm-referenced test for concepts and applications, computation	Harcourt
Test of Mathematical Abilities-2	8.0–18.11	Norm-referenced test assesses individual mathematical aptitude and student's attitudes toward math	
Measures of Adaptive Behaviors			
AAMR Adaptive Behavior Scales	School: ages 3–19 Residential ages 18–adult	Measures personal independence and coping skills for independent functioning, physical development, economic activity, language development, socialization, numbers and item, prevocation/vocational activity, self-direction, responsibility, social behavioral conformity, trustworthiness, self-abusive behavior, social engagement, disturbing interpersonal behavior and stereotypes and hyperactive behaviors.	

Assessment	Age Range	Contents	Publisher
Adaptive Behavior Evaluation Scale (ABES-R)	K–12	Assesses communication, self-care, health and safety, home living, functional academics, social skills, leisure, community use work skills	
Vineland Adaptive Behavior Scales, 2nd Ed. (VABS-2)	Ages 3–21	Parent and teacher rating forms that aid in diagnosis of intellectual disabilities and other disorders. assessment, communication, daily living and socializations. offers motor skills domain and maladaptive behavior index.	
Reading			
Test of Reading Comprehension, 4th Ed. (TORC-4)	Ages 7.0–17.11	Norm-referenced test that identifies strengths and weaknesses in silent reading comprehension skills and knowledge of word meanings	Pro-ED
Written Expression			
Test of Written Language (TOWL-4)	Ages 9–17	Vocabulary, spelling, punctuation, logical sentences, sentence combining, contextual conventions, story composition	Pro-ED
Test of Written Spelling, 4th Ed. (TWS-4)	Ages 6.0–18.11	Norm-referenced test with no separate subtests	Pro-Ed

7

SIBLINGS OF CHILDREN WITH DISABILITIES

AMY F. CONNER LOVE

LORIE TAYLOR

LISA P. TURNER

RICHARD SABOUSKY
Clarion University of Pennsylvania

"Sibling relationships—and 80% of Americans have at least one—outlast marriages, survive the death of parents, resurface after quarrels that would sink any friendship. They flourish in a thousand incarnations of closeness and distance, warmth, loyalty and distrust."

—**Erica E. Goode,** "The Secret World of Siblings," *U.S. News & World Report*, 1/10/94

LEARNING OBJECTIVES

This chapter outlines the special relationship that exists and may be cultivated between siblings of individuals with disabilities and the brother or sister with a disability, sibling effects on the individual with disabilities, and strategies to help or support siblings. Specifically, after reading this chapter, you will be able to:

1. Identify policy and legislation impacting the ability of siblings to care for one another.

2. Describe how a sibling with a disability has a changing and evolving relationship with members of his/her family.

3. Indicate how the severity of a disability can impact sibling relationships.

4. Explain some of the tactics to facilitate relationships between siblings with and without disabilities.

Sibling relationships prove to be among the longest-lasting relationships throughout the lifespan. As a result, for individuals with **disabilities**, the sibling's impact and relationship role can take on much more than just a sharing of genetics and experiences; it often becomes one of support and advocacy. According to the most recent census, approximately 56.7 million people had some kind of disability, with about 38.3 million people having a severe disability (U.S. Census Bureau, 2012). A vast majority of individuals with a disability have a sibling, and, more often than not, this sibling becomes the eventual caregiver of the brother or sister with a disability. In fact, it estimated that more than 72% of individuals with a disability receive support from family caregivers (Tanis, Rizzolo, Hemp, & Braddock, 2013). As a result, there must be more understanding of the various factors that impact siblings of individuals with disabilities. Specifically, sibling needs throughout their lifespan should be given much more attention.

SPECIAL RELATIONSHIP

Relationships of siblings can be varied and complex depending on various factors in any family. The variability and complexities may become, and often are, much more exaggerated in a family with a child who has a disability. Therefore, the relationship of siblings in a family that has a member who has a disability has more significance in today's society, as more and more siblings of individuals with disabilities become eventual caretakers and advocates.

IMPORTANCE OF SIBLINGS AND SIGNIFICANCE IN TODAY'S SOCIETY

Siblings often play powerful roles in the physical, psychological, cognitive, and social development of each other in any family. The relationship between siblings becomes even more important when one or more of the siblings have a disability. Particularly in families that have a child with a disability, siblings do more than just share genetic material, parents, and a history; in childhood and adolescence, siblings are instrumental in the development of their other siblings, often providing the first real introduction to social interaction. As such, siblings provide much of the modeling of appropriate and inappropriate behaviors in regard to verbal and nonverbal language, mobility through fine- and gross-motor play, and using play situations to teach socialization, navigation, and discovery into what is socially acceptable and what is unacceptable, as well as mediation and compromise. Siblings often learn the nuances of social skills through both vicarious and direct learning experiences. As such, siblings can often be considered first teachers and even behavior change agents for their sibling(s) who have disabilities by providing "real-world experiences" daily. This assumed "teacher role" as a child and/or adolescent often develops over the years and leads the adult sibling to take on more of a parental, caretaker, or advocate role, often replacing their own parent as their parent(s) become aged or deceased. The relationship and experiences developed during childhood and/or adolescence shape the trajectory of the individual with a disability's future as siblings approach and reach adulthood.

CASE STUDY 1

Betty is 18 years old and has two siblings. She is a senior in high school, and her sisters are 13 and 14 years old. Her sister Chrissy has Down syndrome and is in eighth grade at the junior high.

Betty says that having a sister with a disability is different because someone always has to be with her. She can't be left at home by herself, and Betty has a lot of responsibilities at home and even outside of the house. Betty has helped the family by taking Chrissy places like the movies and the bowling alley so that Chrissy could experience meeting other people and having a "social life." At first this was something that Betty's mother paid her to do, but as Betty got older, she realized that she enjoyed "teaching" Chrissy about how to act around others. Betty says she really feels like her sister has a better life due to following her around and participating in the same things as Betty. When asked if she regrets having to spend so much time with her sister, Betty adamantly says "No!" She goes on to say that she feels like she is a better person than she might have been because she learned to be outgoing, and taking Chrissy places has helped her meet many different people in life. Betty says that she thinks Chrissy actually helped improve her social life. "Everyone always wants to talk about how Chrissy is and wants to spend time with her, so I have never been scared to meet new people and have been able to make friends with people that I never would have otherwise."

Questions for Critical Thinking

1. How do you feel about the fact that Betty's mom paid her to take Chrissy places?
2. Would this be different if Chrissy didn't have a disability?

CASE STUDY 2

This case includes excerpts from an interview with Jacob, a 16-year-old who has a 14-year-old brother with autism, John.

"At home I am responsible for a number of things. Our dad left when John was born, so I have always felt like I had to take on the role of man of the house. Outside of school, I have a job so I can contribute to the finances of the house so we can get John the therapy he needs. I do a lot of cleaning the house and do different things that my mom asks me to do. I cook supper and do the dishes. I also have to help John with a lot of things like making sure he is ready for school and keeping him entertained when there is no one else around. He can't be at home by himself, so I have to be there when I am not working and mom is at her second job. I think having a brother with a disability has improved how I live because I have to care about him and I have more responsibilities. I feel like I have matured a lot faster than a lot of my friends. I want to go to college, but I worry about what will happen to John if I leave. Who will do all of the work that I am doing now? I also get anxious when I think about what will happen to John when he is done with school. My mom and I don't talk about this. She doesn't like to think about it, but I know it will need to be dealt with sooner than later. I just wish we could talk about it."

Question for Critical Thinking

1. What could be done to help John and his mom deal with John's anxiety?

Adult siblings take on an even more important role as they are no longer necessarily shaping their brother's or sister's development and socialization skills but are now expected to provide care and support of their siblings with disabilities in adulthood, including orchestrating employment, support services, and community engagement. This increased responsibility and resulting importance of the adult sibling is reflected in the sheer number of individuals with disabilities who receive family support in adulthood. As medical advances and access to quality health care increase the life expectancy of the general population as well as for many individuals with disabilities, they are simply outliving their parents more often, requiring siblings to take over the caretaker role parents had. This phenomenon has led to legislation and attempts for federal legislation changes and/or reform that allow or would allow for additional support for siblings to adequately care for their brother or sister as they age. Legislation is vital for siblings involved in the caretaking of their brother or sister who has a disability, as it serves to protect as well as provide fundamental decision-making guidelines. However, there are few policies that exist that are specific to the needs of siblings of individuals with disabilities, and those that exist are often underfunded or not funded at all. Much of the legislation or legislation efforts that have been put into place are due in part to the advocacy of siblings who often provide the majority of support or the orchestration of supports for the brother or sister with a disability. We will attempt to summarize these efforts.

The Family Medical Leave Act of 1993

Currently, **the Family Medical Leave Act** of 1993 (FMLA, 2006), while allowing individuals to take unpaid, job-protected leave to care for family members, disallows siblings the same job protections to care for their sibling(s) with a disability; the FMLA (2006) currently only indicates:

an eligible employee shall be entitled to a total of 12 workweeks of leave during any 12-month period for one or more of the following:

(A) Because of the birth of a son or daughter of the employee and in order to care for such son or daughter.
(B) Because of the placement of a son or daughter with the employee for adoption or foster care.
(C) In order to care for the spouse, or a son, daughter, or parent, of the employee, if such spouse, son, daughter, or parent has a serious health condition (Title I, Sec. 102).

Despite the use of the word "family members" in the legislation, not once is the word "sibling," "brother," or "sister" indicated in FMLA (2006) as part of the definition of "family members" despite the fact that for many, siblings are and will be the primary caregivers for the aging brother or sister with a disability.

Recognizing that for many families, siblings are or will be the primary caregivers for individuals with disabilities, the Family Medical Leave Inclusion Act was introduced in 2013. This amendment would not only expand the definition of "family" to include siblings but would allow siblings to take unpaid, job-protected leave to care for their brother or sister with a disability. This amendment has yet to be passed into law.

The Older Americans Act of 1965

This **legislation**, first enacted in 1965 and most recently reauthorized in 2016, supports both older Americans and individuals with disabilities with services that include caregiver support. The National Family Caregiver Support Program was established in 1990 under this act and allows siblings to receive caregiver services and supports. Specifically, under this program,

States shall provide five types of services: information to caregivers about available services, assistance to caregivers in gaining access to the services, individual counseling, organization of support groups, and caregiver training, respite care, and supplemental services, on a limited basis (U.S. Department of Health and Human Services, 2015).

With the 2006 Reauthorization of the Older Americans Act, the following specific family caregiver criteria must be met in order to receive services:

• Adult family members or other informal caregivers age 18 and older providing care to individuals 60 years of age and older;
• Adult family members or other informal caregivers age 18 and older providing care to individuals of any age with Alzheimer's disease and related disorders;
• Grandparents and other relatives (not parents) 55 years of age and older providing care to children under the age of 18; and
• Grandparents and other relatives (not parents) 55 years of age and older providing care to adults age 18–59 with disabilities (U.S. Department of Health and Human Services, 2015).

With the **Older Americans Act Reauthorization Act** of 2016 (P.L. 114-144), in addition to funding, stronger justice and legal support provisions, opportunities for shared sites (National Council on Aging, 2016), improvements and greater clarification to the organization and delivery of services to older Americans and their caregivers are provided. For instance, "the reauthorized law now provides more specificity on who ADRCs [Aging and Disability Resource Centers] serve by adding, 'for older individuals and individuals with disabilities… and the caregivers of older individuals and individuals with disabilities'" (U.S. Department of Health and Human Services, 2016).

The Lifespan Respite Care Act of 2006 (P.L. 109-442)

Recognizing that caregivers of individuals with disabilities, regardless of age, are often siblings who experience various stresses in finding and affording support services and respite care, this legislation was created to increase the availability of affordable and high-quality respite care services through the authorization of Congress to spend up to $53.3 million. However, the Lifespan Respite Care Act has not yet received any funding (American Psychological Association [APA], 2015).

Developmental Disabilities Assistance and Bill of Rights Act of 2000 (DD Act, P.L. 106-402)

This legislation allows for families to participate in designing services and supports for individuals with disabilities at the state level through the establishment of a set of programs: State councils on developmental disabilities, protection and advocacy agencies, university centers for excellence in development disabilities, family support programs, and projects of national and regional significance. Many of these programs are grossly underfunded and therefore inadequate.

The Achieving a Better Life Experience (ABLE) Act of 2013

Signed into law by President Barack Obama in December 2014, this act, in recognizing the financial burden of supporting individuals with disabilities, allows for the establishment of tax-free savings accounts to cover a variety of expenditures that an individual with a disability may incur, including medical and dental care, education and/or employment training, assistive technology, housing, and transportation for those siblings who will be supporting their brother or sister with a disability (National Down Syndrome Society, 2012). Currently, however, not all states have passed this legislation (to see an updated list of states with **ABLE** legislation passed or pending, go to http://www.thearc.org/what-we-do/public-policy/policy-issues/able-legislation-by-state).

LIFELONG RELATIONSHIP

Due to the aging of parents and the fact that most offspring, including individuals with disabilities, outlive their parents, the sibling relationship is the longest familial relationship. As a result, siblings become more likely to assume a greater role in planning for the future of an individual with a disability and often become caretakers.

INTERACTIONAL DYNAMICS AND RELATIONSHIP PATTERNS

All sibling relationships tend to change over time; they ebb and flow. The relationship between a sibling with a disability and a sibling without a disability is not different. However, the relationship patterns, durability, quality, and strength seem to be more sensitive and are often overly dependent on such dynamics as birth order, age difference between siblings, gender, socioeconomic status (SES), parental stress, parental communication levels, parenting styles, the sibling's understanding of the disability, and services and supports available to the family.

Sibling relationships are especially sensitive to the family structure and the impact the structure may have. It is particularly difficult for siblings when there is only a single parent raising them. This type of family structure often impacts and conflates financial burden and tends to orchestrate the need for increased sibling responsibility that includes added levels of household chores or caretaking so that the single parent may work. Even when the family unit has two parents, often the needs of the individual with a disability compromise the ability for both parents to be fully employed. This can cause increased financial stresses, as often the medical, educational, and other needs of the individual with the disability can be costly. In an already stressful environment, this additional element of financial stress simply may serve as additional fuel for family conflict.

Other dynamics impacting sibling relationships and the longevity of a high-quality relationship include the type and severity of the disability. Research indicates that the more severe or behaviorally charged the sibling with a disability, the more they will impact their siblings' **demeanor**, treatment, and plans for future caregiving (Aksoy & Yildirim, 2008; Heller & Arnold, 2010; Roper, Allred, Mandleco, Freeborn, & Dyches, 2014; Tozer, Atkin, & Wenham, 2013). Siblings of individuals with an autism spectrum disorder (ASD) indicate having lower quality of relationships with their brother or sister because individuals with ASD often have significant social and communication deficits (Pollard, Barry, Freedman, & Kotchick, 2013). The tendency for individuals with ASD to display more aggressive behavior often cause more sibling anxiety, as they must deal with the unexpected all the time (Aksoy & Yildirim, 2008), resulting in the siblings spending less time together. In order for siblings of brothers or sisters with ASD to have a higher-quality relationship, it would require much more effort, intervention, and maximum support in relationship building for proper social interaction between siblings. On the other hand, siblings of individuals with Down syndrome, while having many of the same characteristics as ASD, indicate having a higher quality of relationship with their brother or sister. This is most likely due to the fact that most individuals with Down syndrome tend to be more social, with increased levels of intimacy and nurturance (Pollard et al., 2013). Therefore there is an increased social support system between the sibling(s) and the individual with Down syndrome. As a result, the sibling(s) appears more socially competent, has fewer behavior problems, is more kind, and, therefore, has a heightened perception of relationship quality.

CHILDREN AND ADOLESCENT SIBLINGS

According to research, children and adolescent siblings have both positive and negative experiences with a brother or sister with a disability. According to Hames (2008), the age and developmental level of the sibling impacts the level of understanding of their brother's or sister's disability as well as the behaviors exhibited toward the brother or sister with the disability. Many siblings need to mature faster in order to take on more caregiving-type roles than siblings of individuals without disabilities. Maturity level of the sibling, which is based on both age and development stage, impacts roles and responsibilities as well as parental expectations (Saxena & Adamsons, 2013). In many instances, siblings who take on earlier responsibilities often develop closer relationships with the sibling with a disability later in life (Tozer, Atkin, & Wenham, 2013) and influence sibling plans for future caregiving (Hames, 2008). On the other hand, this early caregiving could also lead to anxiety, less time for the siblings' own friends (Sibling Leadership Network, 2013b), and feelings of resentment, causing distancing of relationships. Large age differences between the siblings can also impact the relationship dynamics—both positively and negatively. This is consistent with most families in which the siblings are separated by large age differences, regardless of the presence of a disability. Developmentally, siblings are often at different stages when there are relatively larger age gaps. The caretaking and emotional supports involved in infants/babies and toddlers/preschoolers are much different than those needed for school-age children and adolescents/teens. And, developmentally, the interests and priorities of children change as they develop. This may set the case for not only parental expectations for enhanced roles and responsibilities of the older sibling or earlier maturation of the younger sibling but also for a relationship distancing between the sibling and the individual with disabilities based purely on interests and emotional maturity.

In early childhood, toddlers model parents and will often exhibit caretaking behaviors they have witnessed their parents doing. According to Hames (2008), the more obvious the disability, the earlier the siblings exhibited such caretaking behaviors. As siblings begin to get older and have increased involvement in the community and/or school, social awareness may do one of two things—either increase embarrassment or increase the tolerances of the brother or sister with a disability (Hames, 2008). In adolescence, due to better understanding of the brother's or sister's disability, the sibling begins to show concerns over the future of the brother or sister (Hames, 2008).

In respect to gender, females have a tendency to provide more support and possess more understanding for their sibling with a disability than do males, and thereby there are increased expectations of both parents and the individual with a disability regarding the female sibling's role in the relationship and future caregiving (Heller & Arnold, 2010; Saxena & Adamsons, 2013).

In childhood, relationships between siblings and their brother or sister with a disability, for the most part, tend to be close and warm. This is not to say these relationships are perfect. There are, as in any family structure, bound to be conflicts between siblings. When it comes to conflict between siblings, studies seem to be equivocal, as some indicate a higher level of conflict between siblings, while others indicate no differences in levels of conflict when comparing siblings who have a sibling with a disability and siblings who do not have a sibling with a disability. This difference in levels of conflict can possibly be directly attributable to family dynamics explored earlier in this chapter.

ADULT SIBLINGS

As with children and adolescent siblings of individuals with disabilities, adult siblings have both positive and negative experiences. However, many adult siblings indicate gleaning positive benefits from their relationships with their sibling with a disability (Sibling Leadership Network, 2013a). Further, many adult siblings indicate that they consider the needs of their brother or sister with a disability when making life choices for themselves, including career decisions. Interestingly, despite the sibling's consideration for the individual with the disability in their own future planning, many siblings are not included in planning for the individual with a disability (Sibling Leadership Network, 2013a). It is also interesting to note that many adult experiences, both positive and negative, are closely related to their experiences with the individual with the disability throughout childhood and adolescence. The experiences tend to mirror one another—if they were positive in childhood and adolescence, this seems to carry over into adulthood. These experiences are overly sensitive to the dynamics surrounding home life.

Despite poor experiences in childhood and adolescence, Burbidge and Minnes (2014) explored the quality of relationships between adult siblings with and without disabilities and found that while participants reported less-close relationships in childhood and adolescence, there was evidence indicating that both siblings with and without disabilities desire a higher quality of relationship that extends beyond mere instrumental support in adulthood.

TEMPERAMENT

Siblings of individuals with disabilities experience increased stress, although the intensity, frequency, and resiliency varies (Hannon, 2012) and, once again, seems to be dependent on the dynamics surrounding the sibling, individual with a disability, and home life. Despite the challenges and stresses an individual with a disability brings to a family, most families are resilient.

CASE STUDY 3

My name is Bob. I am 28 years old and just finished up graduate school, earning my MBA. I live in the town I grew up in, near my mother and my 20-year-old brother, Peter. My parents were divorced when I was 9, and my dad has not been involved in our lives since then. Peter has an intellectual disability and is still in high school in a special education class to learn life skills. It was when we were younger and both in school and when Peter was with other children that, from an early age, I became attuned to his differences. I remember standing beside him when he was being teased and knowing that I had to be there to protect him. We got along, and I hung out with him some but also kept busy with my own social life. My mother has always taken care of the things that Peter needs, and selfishly I really didn't want to know the details about his disability. Since I left home to go to the local college, I haven't had much time to keep up with what is going on in Peter's life.

I always knew that Peter would need extra help in life and probably could never live alone, but I never thought much more about it. Never, that is, until we found out a month ago that our mother has cancer and is not expected to live more than one more year. I don't know what to do. I am dealing with the grief of finding out my mom may not win her battle with cancer, but I am also panicking about what will happen to Peter. I have talked with some people at Peter's school, and they suggest we come up with a life plan for Peter, which would include information about Peter's school and medical history, what services might be available and best for him, what will happen when he transitions from high school, information about health care, where he might live, and also financial planning. That is a lot to take in. I don't even know where to start. I worry about Peter and what will happen to him, but I also worry about my life. Can I even still have a life?

Questions for Critical Thinking

1. What are some things that could have been done earlier in Bob and Peter's life to prepare Bob for what is happening?

2. What do you see as the five most important things Bob needs to consider about Peter as the family starts to make plans for Peter's future?

SIBLING EFFECTS

The effects siblings and the individual(s) with a disability have on each other are transactional, which is to say that all parties have an impact on the quality of the relationship. In addition to the various dynamics that surround the sibling, the individual with a disability, and home life, parental attitudes and expectations and the characteristics of the sibling impact the effect they have on the brother or sister with a disability. In addition, two things to always consider are the type of disability and the severity of the disability.

Parental Attitudes and Expectations

Having a child with a disability brings many obstacles and is a life-altering event with ever-changing variables. When families have more than one child, it is overwhelming. When one of these children has a disability, this overwhelming feeling becomes multiplied and, needless to say, stressful. Parents impact the relationships between the sibling and the individual with a disability through their own management of stress, communication efforts, attitudes, and acceptance levels of the child with a disability and expectations placed on the siblings who do not have a disability. Parental stress and resulting depression compromises use of effective parenting strategies for helping the sibling(s) cope with the individual with the disability. And, again, the type and severity of the disability will often determine the level of stress encountered.

Simultaneously Meeting the Needs of the Family

In balancing life with children with and without disabilities, parents apply various strategies in attempts to meet the needs of all of their children. One such strategy stems around the concept of simultaneously meeting all the needs. This stems from the desire for increased whole-family activity, as the more activities families are able to engage in, the better the sibling(s)' adjustment to an ever-changing world a child with a disability brings (Giallo & Gavidia-Payne, 2006). Shared leisure activities give the opportunity to enjoy each other, improving the adjustment of siblings (Kramer, Hall, & Heller, 2013). According to a study conducted by Koch and Mayes (2012), this idea of simultaneous meeting of needs is one that most families attempt or intend to do; however, parents are unable to maintain consistency in using this style of parenting and resort to often interacting with siblings and the child with a disability individually. It seems that it is impractical to expect this idea of simultaneously meeting the needs of every family member all the time, as the needs of a "typically developing" child may be much different than those of a child who has a disability, particularly if the disability is more severe. Often the extensive caregiving required by parents inevitably alters family time.

Differential parenting seems to be the recourse for most family units with parents and families "prioritizing the needs of their [child] with disabilities" (Koch & Mayes, 2012, p. 470), resulting in the sibling(s) without disabilities receiving less parental attention (Hannon, 2012). This is particularly true if the disability is more severe or requires more attentive action. However, at times, seemingly, and often admittedly out of guilt, parents deliberately prioritized the siblings' needs ahead of the brother or sister with a disability (Koch & Mayes, 2012). The impact of parental differential treatment on the sibling, whether prioritizing the needs of the individual with the disability or the sibling's needs, is heavily dependent on the sibling's own understanding of the individual with a disability and the resulting need for differential parenting as it is given. It seems that siblings have higher levels of acceptance for the individual with the disability and increased personal social growth if they have a firm understanding of their brother's or sister's disability. This increased understanding of the disability and the needs of the individual with the disability are heavily dependent on communication. Hence, these siblings who have a firmer understanding of the disability, and therefore for the individual with the disability themselves, view differential parenting as being more acceptable than those siblings whose families lacked communication and resultant misunderstanding of the disability (Saxena & Adamsons, 2013). In some families, siblings indicate a high level of favoritism toward the brother or sister with a disability (Granat, Nordgren, Rein, & Sonnander, 2012) and experience a sense of isolation, that is, feeling ignored and even an unimportant part of the family. However, this feeling of isolation, particularly when periodic in nature, often can lead to more self-reliance as a result of differential parenting (Tozer, Atkin, & Wenham, 2013).

EXPECTATIONS

Research indicates a heightened expectation of sibling assistance by parents in caring for the individual with a disability or household chores from an earlier age (Saxena & Adamsons, 2013).

This heightened expectation often leads to the need for earlier maturation of this sibling. While some siblings, as mentioned earlier in this chapter, seem to thrive in this early maturation, others may view the sibling with a disability as a "chore," leading to animosity and avoidance. Despite heightened expectations, parents do not often include siblings—in childhood, adolescence, or adulthood—in planning for the immediate and distant future of the individual with a disability, if they even have a plan.

Open communication is a "must have" according to many parents (Koch & Mayes, 2012) as well as their own positive reactions to and actions with the child with a disability and their careful, thoughtful handling of differential parenting (Tsao, Davenport, & Schmiege, 2012). The more emotional stress exhibited by parents of a child with disabilities, the less communication occurred in families (Mazaheri et al., 2013). Careful attention to communication efforts, positive interactions and reactions to the child with a disability, and a sense of fair differential parenting lead to bettering the siblings' ability to adjust to the changing variables a child with a disability brings (Giallo & Gavidia-Payne, 2006). The lack of inclusion in conversations about the individual with a disability seems to perpetuate lack of sibling support, and many adult siblings admit to seeking out counseling for past "issues" (Tozer, Atkin, & Wenham, 2013). The level at which a sibling can understand and/or relate to the individual with a disability is a determining factor in relationship strength—the more they understand and relate, the more positive the impact on the relationship (Aksoy & Yildirim, 2008).

CHARACTERISTICS OF SIBLING WITHOUT DISABILITY

Siblings have both positive and negative experiences with their siblings who have a disability. Specific characteristics of siblings without a disability seem to be ultimately dependent on family variables (e.g., socioeconomic status, stress of parents, resources available to family). Characteristics displayed also tend to be linked to developmental stages, and, much like the relationship, change over time.

Some studies indicate positive characteristics of siblings of individuals with a disability. These include increased maturity (Saxena & Adamsons, 2013), empathy and understanding for the individual with a disability (Sibling Leadership Network, 2013a, 2013b), and higher levels of acceptance and social adjustment (Tsao, Davenport, & Schmiege, 2012).

Other studies indicate more negative characteristics such as anxiety, depression (Cuzzocrea, Larcan, Costa, & Gazzano, 2014), anger, sadness, fears of the future of the brother or sister with the disability, fears of their own future (Mazaheri et al., 2013), behavior and attention problems (Cuzzocrea et al., 2014; Giallo, Gavidia-Payne, Minett, & Kapoor, 2012). Other negative characteristics may include adjustment difficulty, guilt, low self-esteem, and fears of the disability. Many of these characteristics are correlated with heightened levels of parents' emotional stress (Cuzzocrea et al., 2014), decreased communication with parent(s), increased family conflict (Giallo & Gavidia-Payne, 2006; Mazaheri et al., 2013), as well as type and severity of disability their sibling has (Aksoy & Yildirim, 2008; Heller & Arnold, 2010; Roper et al., 2014; Tozer, Atkin, & Wenham, 2013). Anxiety of siblings may be tied to the challenging behaviors of siblings with a disability (Pollard et al., 2013; Saxena & Adamsons, 2013). Anger, worry, and a general sense of unease are also common characteristics that compromise relationships, as siblings often have more concern and anxiety over the future of their sibling with a disability and the impact this will have on their own future (Hannon, 2012).

SIBLING INTERACTIONS

Sibling relationships should be derived from the sense of comfort they provide one another in addition to being emotionally supporting. The closeness of the relationship and positive interactions of siblings is a predictor of later emotional well-being. Based upon understanding of their sibling's disability, many siblings often will over- or underestimate their sister's or brother's abilities, impacting interaction levels (Steel, Vandevelde, Poppe, & Moyson, 2013). Further, the level of cognitive and/ or social deficits of the individual with disabilities impacts the ability for siblings to demonstrate reciprocal support (Pollard et al., 2013). As with exploring interactional dynamics and relationship patterns, sibling interactions not only change over time but also are dependent on many variables that include ages of the siblings, age differences of the siblings, gender of the siblings, psychosocial behavior of the siblings, and parental factors. In addition, societal views of the sibling with a disability can impact sibling interactions and relationship (Hannon, 2012; Saxena & Adamsons, 2013), with many times the sibling taking on the role of protector (Hannon, 2012).

Expectations in the home often alter sibling interactions. Many times the sibling takes on a parental role (Hannon, 2012), which means they often take on the stresses, anxieties, and worries that often plague parents. How siblings handle this additional stress, anxiety, and worry is often dependent on how it was modeled by the parent(s) themselves.

COPING AND STRESS STYLES

The ability for a sibling of an individual with a disability to cope is highly dependent on the stress level of the parent(s) (Giallo et al., 2012), level of communication, SES, understanding of the disability itself, number of life areas affected, ages and developmental stages of the sibling(s) and the individual with a disability, and resources and support services available to the family. Common coping strategies used by siblings include emotional regulation, wishful thinking, social withdrawal, distraction, problem solving, social support, resignation, cognitive restructuring, blaming others, and self-criticism, with most siblings using more than one coping strategy at a time (Ross & Cuskelly, 2006). While coping strategy choice does not appear to be problem specific among siblings, emotional regulation appears to be the most popular coping strategy used, particularly by female siblings (Orsmond & Seltzer, 2007; Ross & Cuskelly, 2006). However, emotional regulation as a coping strategy is also identified as the least effective (Orsmond & Seltzer, 2007), particularly when used as a lone strategy. Because coping strategies impact relationship quality, siblings should be introduced to a plethora of effective coping strategies. Such strategies are discussed in the next section of this chapter.

Sibling Outcomes

Little research exists on sibling outcomes in regards to adjustment, empathy, and the impact on professional aspirations. While there is scant evidence of hindrances on the broader social relationships of adult siblings of individuals with disabilities (Howlin, Moss, Savage, Bolton, & Rutter, 2015), there is credible evidence that adult siblings of individuals with disabilities do often struggle with depression and anxiety (Hodepp & Urbano, 2007; Howlin et al., 2015; O'Neill & Murray, 2016). The level of depression and anxiety seems to be directly related not only to the severity of the disability but also to the amount of available support and services for both themselves as a caretaker and for the brother or sister with a disability (Coyle, Kramer, & Mutchlert, 2014; Taylor & Hodepp, 2012).

While one study suggests that siblings of brothers or sisters who have a mental illness are twice as likely to be unemployed (Wolfe, Song, Greenberg, & Mailick, 2014), there is little evidence of disadvantages on employment of adult siblings of individuals with other disabilities (Howlin et al., 2015). Interestingly, siblings of individuals with disabilities often enter a disability-related career and/or engage in volunteerism related to disabilities (Taylor & Shivers, 2011). In a study conducted with college-age siblings, nearly 40% indicated that having a brother or sister with a disability influenced their choice of major (Burton & Parks, 1994), with many choosing to study special education or a closely related field because they either want to know more about or make sense of their sibling's disability or they want to improve the conditions surrounding individuals with disabilities (Chambers, 2007; Marks, Matson, & Barraza, 2005). Others find themselves in an unintentional career path in the field of disabilities due to experiences and opportunities they have encountered as part of their own caretaking responsibilities, with negative experiences (i.e., struggles with securing and accessing services and appropriate educational programming) having a direct impact on their decision to enter the field of disabilities (Chambers, 2007; Marks, Matson, & Barraza, 2005). Siblings often feel that they have much to offer the field of disabilities with their own practical insight and empathy while, at the same time, gathering for themselves and their brother or sister with a disability additional information and skill sets for caretaking (Chambers, 2007). A sibling's decision to enter a disability-related field—whether through purposeful planning or unintentional consequences—as well as involvement in volunteerism related to disabilities may be attributed to the dynamics and characteristics that surround and have surrounded the sibling relationship. Siblings who have closer, more positive relationships with their brother or sister with a disability tend to be more inclined toward entering a disability-related field and/or active volunteerism (Taylor & Shivers, 2011).

STRATEGIES TO HELP SIBLINGS

Open Communication

Communication is crucial to a sibling's well-being. Day-to-day family interactions often do not provide an outlet for siblings to talk about their feelings. Parents must make time to ask about feelings related to having a sibling with a disability. Permit siblings to express their anxiety and concerns about the situation, listening and validating their concerns.

Acknowledge Guilt and Anger

It is possible for a sibling to experience guilt about not having a disability. They may feel pressure to achieve and excel in academics or athletics in order to "make up" for a sibling's disability. Parents must be sure to emphasize that there is no blame involved regarding the disability. The sibling with a disability should be viewed as a person with similarities and differences. The nondisabled sibling should be assisted in coming to terms with his/her sibling's disability by the parents or someone outside the family.

Recognize Embarrassments

Even without having a sibling without a disability, it may be difficult to fit in socially. In order to avoid embarrassment, the nondisabled sibling may avoid contact with a sibling with a disability or not invite friends to their home. It may help to talk over how to explain to friends about the sibling's disability. Help siblings realize that other family members may be embarrassing to them also, especially parents. Find social situations in which the sibling with a disability is accepted to set a good example for the nondisabled sibling.

Limit Isolation

For siblings, isolation may occur when typical activities are impacted due to the ramifications of the sibling's disability. These feelings of isolation may also result from feeling as if no one else understands or has the same situation. In order to discourage these feelings, family outings and social activities should be continued. Encourage the nondisabled sibling to have friends over, making sure that they feel welcome and that the environment is as comfortable as possible. Other adults may be available to accompany the sibling to activities to keep them feeling involved.

SIBLINGS AS TEACHERS

Siblings may serve as teachers for their brother or sister with a disability in practical ways. Older siblings may be able to assist with homework or academic tutoring. Siblings of any age provide supportive roles model in teaching social and interpersonal skills. Siblings can model appropriate social, language, behavior, and other skills. Because these skills occur in a natural environment, it may result in the sibling with a disability becoming more socially adept outside of the home.

Advantages and Disadvantages

Having a sibling as a teacher may provide advantages for both the nondisabled sibling and the sibling with a disability. For the nondisabled sibling, results may include greater levels of tolerance and appreciation, increased empathy, and patience. For the sibling with a disability, results may include improved social and interpersonal skills, improved academic achievement, and increased self-confidence.

Disadvantages for the nondisabled sibling may include negative feelings, such as resentment for having to take extra time to tutor their sibling with a disability, higher stress levels due to the increased responsibility, self-doubt regarding their own academic and/or social skills, or contributing to "learned helplessness" by doing too much for their sibling with a disability.

Why Use Siblings as Teachers?

The home provides a natural environment for social and interpersonal skills to be taught in authentic situations. Skills can be taught in a relaxed atmosphere on a daily basis, reducing stress levels of the sibling with a disability.

WAYS TO ESTABLISH SIBLING TEACHING PROGRAM

Guidance and support must be provided for a sibling to become an appropriate teacher. Appropriate behavior and social skills must be taught and established in nondisabled siblings in order for them to provide an appropriate role model for their sibling with a disability. The nondisabled sibling must have adequate academic skills prior to becoming a teacher for their sibling with a disability. Providing directions and structure for teaching situations is essential for successful interaction between the nondisabled sibling and their sibling with a disability.

SOCIAL INTERACTIONS

Importance

The interaction between siblings with and without disabilities may be as important as the parent–child relationship. The sibling relationship may last longer than the parent–child relationship. Interaction between siblings can provide roles such as teacher, learner, and friend. Sibling interaction may result in learning self-control, listening, fair play, sharing, empathy, insight, tolerance, and self-confidence.

Encouraging Social Interactions

Social interactions between siblings can be encouraged by having the nondisabled sibling assist with self-help skills such as simple food preparation and daily living skills.

Informal and casual play provides opportunities for social conversation, as well as the teaching of rules and acceptable behavior. Teaching and/or tutoring sessions between siblings provide means to develop appropriate in-school behaviors and self-advocacy. Involvement in early intervention and preschool programs encourages siblings to interact with one another in a social setting outside the home.

Limiting Jealousy

Parents are the key factor in limiting feelings of jealousy in the nondisabled child.

Parents should be available for support, guidance, and encouragement. They should make available time to spend exclusively with the nondisabled child so that the child with the disability is not seen as monopolizing all of the parents' time. The nondisabled child should be included in all family activities. Having the nondisabled child attend school meetings regarding their sibling enables them to gain more information about their sibling, as well as ask questions and provide information. Open communication should be encouraged to provide information to the nondisabled child about their sibling.

Handling Fighting

In any family, conflict will arise. Nondisabled siblings may have feelings of jealousy and resentment toward the sibling with a disability, leading to anger and fighting. Parents should be fair in their reaction to the situation and not place all of the blame on the nondisabled child. There should be a behavior management plan in place that is understood by all family members and implemented consistently. Feelings of jealousy and resentment can be minimized by following the suggestions mentioned earlier.

COUNSELING SIBLINGS

In order to assist the nondisabled sibling in coping and adjusting to the sibling with a disability, counseling may be beneficial. There are a variety of ways of providing counseling to nondisabled siblings to promote positive feelings and acceptance.

What Is Counseling?

Counseling is a means to provide therapy and support to individuals experiencing a variety of problems in their lives. For both nondisabled siblings and siblings with disabilities, counseling may provide a way to discuss their feelings openly in an accepting and nonjudgmental environment.

The Process of Counseling

Counseling may involve different types of therapists, from a school counselor to a child psychologist or psychiatrist. Depending upon the type of therapist, different types of therapies may be utilized. In any case, the process of counseling involves the sharing of feelings, gaining an understanding of their feelings, determining reasons the feelings are occurring, developing skills that assist them in dealing with problems, and building better relationships with their siblings with disabilities.

Group Counseling

Siblings will sometimes experience so much difficulty adjusting that families should be encouraged to seek counseling. Group counseling for siblings may provide a means for them to air their feelings in a therapeutic environment with others who are experiencing the same feelings. This may help resolve feelings of isolation and introduce other ways of coping and adjusting.

Additionally, provision of information about disability for nondisabled siblings can be very beneficial for them in gaining an understanding about their sibling's disabilities. It can also be helpful for them to learn about feelings and how to adjust to their sibling's place in the family.

Innovative Approaches

Sibling support groups are often sponsored by agencies serving children with disabilities and are facilitated by professional service providers. These types of groups typically meet on an ongoing basis. Sibling support groups meet to provide socialization for siblings in similar situations. The groups can also cover issues such as sharing information about their families; sharing information about their sibling's disability; learning about other types of disabilities; sharing their positive and negative feelings; and learning ways to cope and adjust to their sibling's disability. The sharing of experiences and resources may also help improve the sibling's self-confidence.

Sibling support groups can offer a variety of activities to encourage socialization, sharing of feelings, and providing information. These types of activities could include games, videos about disabilities or with characters with disabilities, group discussions, reading books about disabilities or with characters with disabilities, lunch and snack conversations, drawing activities, newsletters, and so forth.

Workshops

Workshops may be sponsored by the school or professional agencies. Workshops tend to focus on one area or issue at a time. They also tend to be provided periodically or on an as-needed basis. For example, a workshop may be held on providing information about disabilities, strategies for coping and adjusting to a sibling with a disability, problem-solving strategies, conflict resolution strategies, and the like.

Summary

In this chapter we explored siblings in a family with a person having a disability. We discussed the different roles from peers who do not have a brother or sister with a disability, such as caretaker, protector, teacher. We explored the positive as well as negative feelings associated with interrelationships between siblings with and without disabilities and looked at what impacts these relationships, such as the severity and type of a sibling's disability, which influences the quality of interactions and relationships between siblings and parents, and noted that typical sibling conflicts may be exaggerated by one brother or sister having a disability or the appearance of parental favoritism. We looked at the many pieces of legislation that exist to support families and pointed out the fact that much more work is needed to be done in this area. There are positive as well as negative feelings associated with interrelationships between siblings with and without disabilities, but there are interventions that may help, which we covered at the end of this chapter, such as support groups and counseling.

Additional Resources

Print

Johnson, J., & Rensselaer, A. V. (Eds.). (2010). *Siblings: The autism spectrum through our eyes.* London and Philadelphia: Jessica Kingsley Publishers.

Meyer, D. J. (1997). *Views from our shoes: Growing up with a brother or sister with special needs.* Bethesda, MD: Woodbine House, Inc.

Meyer, D. J. (2005). *The sibling slam book: What it's really like to have a brother or sister with special needs.* Bethesda, MD: Woodbine House, Inc.

Meyer, D. J. (2009). *Thicker than water: Essays by adult siblings of people with disabilities.* Bethesda, MD: Woodbine House, Inc.

Meyer, D. J., & Holl, E. (2014). *The sibling survival guide: Indispensable information for brothers and sisters of adults with disabilities.* Bethesda, MD: Woodbine House, Inc.

Web-Based

The Arc: https://www.thearc.org/siblings. In addition to providing resources and services to individuals with disabilities, this largest national community-based organization provides advocacy for both individuals and family members as well as updates to policies pertaining to individuals with disabilities.

Autism Society of America: http://www.autism-society.org/living-with-autism/family-issues/siblings/. This society provides information specific to individuals who have autism and includes resources specific to siblings and other family members.

Autism Speaks: https://www.autismspeaks.org/family-services/resource-library/websites-families. This organization provides updated information on available services and gives additional information via links.

Center for Parent Information and Resources: http://www.parentcenterhub.org/repository/siblings/ http://frcd.org/tag/siblings-of-individuals-with-disabilities/. This site is National Dissemination Center for Children with Disabilities (NICHCY)'s new home and provides resources to parents including parent training.

Psychology Today: https://www.psychologytoday.com. This site provides information on various topics including coping strategies, as well as information on such characteristics as anxiety, depression, and stress, which are common in siblings.

Sibling and Leadership Network: http://siblingleadership.org/. Provides information specific to siblings regarding advocacy.

Sibling Support Project: https://www.siblingsupport.org/. This project is dedicated to siblings of individuals with special needs. Information regarding sibling workshop offerings are included.

WORKING WITH FAMILIES OF CHILDREN WITH DISABILITIES ACROSS THE LIFESPAN

8

SPECIFIC DISABILITIES ACROSS THE LIFESPAN

MARY A. HOUSER
West Chester University of Pennsylvania

"There is in every child at every stage a new miracle of vigorous unfolding."

—Erik Erikson

LEARNING OBJECTIVES

After reading this chapter, you will be able to:

1. Understand parenting issues as they relate to specific disabilities across the lifespan

2. Gain a better understanding of child-rearing experiences of parents with children with special needs.

3. Identify key characteristics of disabilities served under the **Individuals with Disabilities Education Act (IDEA)**

Imagine how life would be different if someone in your family had a disability. Think about the additional parental skills needed to effectively parent this child and how they would be different from those of parenting a typical child. Consider how this disability might affect siblings, create challenges that the family could face, and obstacles they would be required to overcome. Each disability presents its own unique characteristics that impact and shape the exceptional family members. More importantly, these demands and challenges will develop and change across the exceptional person's lifespan.

DISABILITY RELATED TO BIRTH THROUGH AGE 5

Parenting a child with a disability is a new experience for most parents. For many, it will be the first time they encounter a disability of any kind. It will require parents to be knowledgeable about parenting skills and informed about their child's disability. They will need to perform both the typical parenting duties such as feeding and caring for their child's basic needs and those duties in direct relationship to a child's disability. Depending on the disability, this can mean anything from learning American Sign Language to addressing behavioral issues such as tantrums or aggressive behavior that can occur at home, at school, and in the community. As the child progresses through his life cycle, parenting roles will change and evolve to meet their child's needs.

As they begin their parenting journey, parents may experience several obstacles and stressors related to raising their child with special needs. These challenges apply to disabilities in general as well as to disability-specific populations. Parents who have a child with special needs have reported experiencing the following during the birth-to-pre-K stage:

- Discovering and coming to terms with exceptionality
- Obtaining an accurate diagnosis
- Informing siblings and relatives
- Locating early intervention services
- Participating in IFSP (individual family service plan) meetings
- Seeking to find meaning in the exceptionality
- Clarifying an ideology to guide decisions
- Addressing issues of stigma

- Identifying positive contributions of exceptionality
- Setting great expectations

(Heward, 2013, p. 99)

Alternately, increasingly more research indicates that parents are expressing positive outcomes from parenting a child with a disability (Taunt & Hastings, 2002). Examples of positive outcomes from raising a special-needs child include a changed perspective on life, increased tolerance of others, sensitivity to others, experiencing more family time, and opportunities to learn more about disability, to name a few.

DISABILITY RELATED TO PRIMARY YEARS

Primary years are defined as the first 8 years of a child's formal education (excluding preschool). During the primary years, children with disabilities will be entering school. As a result of their child entering this new setting, parents will be taking on additional duties. This can be a time of excitement and anticipation about how their child will perform in this new setting. Parents of children with special needs might experience some of the following issues during the primary years:

- Establishing routines to carry out family functions
- Adjusting emotionally to educational implications
- Clarifying issues of mainstreaming versus special class placement
- Advocating for inclusive experiences
- Participating in **individual education plan (IEP)** experiences
- Locating community resources
- Arranging for extracurricular activities
- Developing a vision for the future

(Heward, 2013, p. 99)

DISABILITY RELATED TO SECONDARY SCHOOL YEARS

Perhaps one of the most researched and talked-about stages in any child's development are the adolescent years. It is known as a time of growth and change, and parents of children with special needs will experience transitions as their child becomes older and prepares for postsecondary life and adulthood. Families of children with special needs have reported the following experiences during the adolescent years:

- Adjusting emotionally to possible chronicity of exceptionality
- Identifying issues of emerging sexuality
- Dealing with physical and emotional changes of puberty
- Addressing possible peer isolation and rejection
- Planning for career/vocational development
- Arranging for leisure activities
- Expanding the child's self-determination

(Heward, 2013, p. 100)

DISCOVERING THE PRESENCE OF A DISABILITY

Families of children with special needs may discover the presence of a disability at different times in their child's life. This realization may occur before their child is born, at the time of birth, or as the child develops throughout his childhood years. Families might receive notice while pregnant that their unborn child has Down syndrome or receive a diagnosis shortly after birth that their child has classic autism. Some families will not discover their child has a **disability** until after he enters school, as typically seen in children with learning disabilities. Disabilities are considered either congenital disorders or developmental delays.

Congenital Disorders

The term "**congenital**" means present from birth. Therefore, congenital disorders are conditions that are present at or before birth. Congenital disorders may also be called birth defects, congenital anomalies, or congenital malformations. They occur during fetal development or as a result of genetics. Examples of congenital disorders include: fetal alcohol syndrome, autism spectrum disorders, intellectual disabilities, and sensory disabilities, to name a few. Approximately 3% to 4% of children are born with a congenital disorder. There are five categories of congenital disorders: chromosome abnormalities, single-gene abnormalities, conditions during pregnancy that affect the baby, combination of genetic and environmental problems, and unknown causes (American Academy of Pediatrics, 2014, para. 2). Trisomy 21 is a congenital disorder that occurs when a child is born with an extra copy of chromosome 21. It is the most common form of Down syndrome. Phenylketonuria and Huntington's disease are examples of single-gene abnormalities. Spina bifida and heart defects are conditions that develop during pregnancy that can negatively affect a developing fetus. Environmental problems such as alcohol consumption and smoking during pregnancy have been linked to negative outcomes in children.

Developmental Delays

Developmental delays are defined as conditions that occur in a child aged three though nine (or any subset of that age, including ages 3 through 5) whose development is delayed in one or more of the following areas: physical development, cognitive development, communication development, social development, or adaptive development; and who, because of the developmental delays requires special education and related services (National Dissemination Center for Children with Disabilities, 2012). Most developmental delays occur during the prenatal developmental period; however, some may occur in the postnatal period due to injury or infection. Examples of developmental delays include problems with gross motor development, fine motor development, speech and language development, cognitive/intellectual development, and social and emotional development. Approximately 15% of children ages 3 to 17 have a developmental disability (Centers for Disease Control, 2015b). Developmental delays make children eligible for early intervention services.

SELECTED DISABILITIES AND THEIR IMPACT ON FAMILIES

Fetal Alcohol Syndrome

Fetal alcohol syndrome (FAS) is one of the leading causes of intellectual disabilities (Heward, 2013). It is caused by the mother's excessive alcohol use during pregnancy and is a completely preventable syndrome. Alcohol can cause damage to the developing fetus at any time during the prenatal period.

FAS can result in aggression, conduct problems, sleep disturbances, and hyperirritability. Physical characteristics of this disorder include nervous system abnormalities, growth problems, and facial abnormalities such as wide-set and narrow eyes (Centers for Disease Control and Prevention, 2014). Unlike other special-needs populations, many children with FAS are placed in foster care from birth as the result of suboptimal home conditions. This is problematic because as many as 75% of children in the foster care system have at least one parent with a mental illness. Research suggests that it is not uncommon for families to unknowingly adopt a child with FAS and become aware of their condition only after problems emerge as the child develops. This places unique challenges on the adoptive parent(s) and has sometimes resulted in unsuccessful adoptions (Whitehurst, 2012).

Autism Spectrum Disorders

Autism is one of the 13 disability categories identified in the Individuals with Disabilities Education Act (IDEA). According to IDEA,

(i)   *Autism* means a developmental disability affecting verbal and nonverbal communication and social interaction, generally evident before age three, that adversely affects a child's educational performance. Other characteristics often associated with autism are engagement in repetitive activities and stereotyped movements, resistance to environmental change or change in daily routines, and unusual responses to sensory stimuli.

(ii) Autism does not apply if a child's educational performance is adversely affected primarily because the child has a serious emotional disturbance as defined in paragraph (9c) (4) of this section.

(iii) A child who manifests the characteristics of autism after age three could be identified as having autism if the criteria in paragraph (c) (1) (i) of this section are satisfied. (34 *CFR*, Part 300 300.8[c][1][i–iii] [August 14, 2006])

Autism is a spectrum disorder. Its symptoms can range from very mild to severe. ASDs are typically diagnosed by the age of 3. Asperger's syndrome (AS), a milder autism spectrum disorder, may not be determined until a child reaches school age or older. Current statistics indicate that 1 in 68 children have been identified with an ASD, and this incidence continues to rise. (Autism Speaks, 2015) Students with ASDs have difficulties developing age-appropriate peer relationships, a delay in or total lack of development of language, inappropriate play, walking on tiptoes, and attachment to unusual objects. Causes of ASDs are largely unknown, yet some studies have indicated that environment and genetics play significant roles (Boutot & Myles, 2011). Food allergies and deficiencies in certain vitamins may also be contributing factors (Croen, Grether, Yoshida, Oduouli, & Van de Waterm, 2005).

Families might recognize a variety of distinct characteristics in their child with an ASD. These characteristics are related to communication, social skills, and unusual interests and behaviors. Table 8.1 lists a few examples.

TABLE 8.1 ■ Examples of characteristics of ASDs		
Communication	**Social Skills**	**Unusual Interests and Behaviors**
Delayed speech and language skills	Avoids eye contact	Lines up toys or objects
Repeats words and phrases over and over (echolalia)	Prefers to play alone	Gets upset with minor changes
Uses few or no gestures	Does not share interests with others	Obsessive interests

Source: Centers for Disease Control and Prevention, 2015

Due to the rise in children being diagnosed with ASDs in recent years, there has also been an increase in the number of individuals parenting children with ASDs. Parenting children with ASDs has proven to be a daunting task for many. Research indicates that higher levels of parental stress have been found in families of young children with autism than with other disabilities (Estes et al., 2009). Stressors that families may experience are related to behavioral, physical, and core symptoms of this disorder (Johnson, Giannotti, & Cortesi, 2009; Phetrasuwan & Miles, 2009). Examples of parental strain include a child with chronically disturbed sleep, tantrums at home and at school, and self-injurious behavior. In fact, parenting stress of students with ASDs has been reported as being much as four times higher than with other developmental disabilities. The financial burden of raising a child with autism has also been reported by families. Many children with autism require a range of medical and therapeutic services. Examples of these include early intervention and intensive treatments, which can be very costly (Thomas, Morrissey, & McLaurin, 2007). Until recently, many child behavioral health care plans have excluded autism altogether (Newacheck & Kim, 2005; Peele, Lave, & Kelleher, 2002). Once a child is diagnosed with autism, families might have a difficult time coping with the diagnosis. Some begin the grieving process, in which they experience denial, anger, bargaining, depression, and acceptance in reaction to their child's diagnosis (Boutot & Myles, 2011).

Children with ASDs will often receive early intervention during the birth-to-5 period. These interventions may occur at a designated school, clinic, hospital, or in a child's home. Programs range from a few hours a week to more intensive programs lasting up to 40 hours a week. Examples of evidenced-based interventions for children on the autism spectrum include applied behavior analysis (ABA), social skills training, and cognitive behavior therapy. Early intervention is a highly regarded practice for young children with ASDs. Such programming can be expensive and often requires a high degree of parental commitment.

Families of children with ASDs may be introduced to the school system for the first time when their child reaches school age. For many families, this is unchartered territory and can be a confusing and overwhelming experience. Families will be participating in IEP meetings and helping make educational and behavioral decisions that will guide their child's school day. They will be encouraged to learn special education jargon and special education laws and develop an understanding of their parental rights. They will help the IEP team determine the educational setting for their child, whether it be in an inclusive classroom, self-contained classroom, day treatment program, or residential setting. Families of children with ASDs have reported feeling nervous and unsure about their child entering school for the first time. These families have also reported an increased need for quality communication with school personnel during the elementary school years and beyond (Houser, 2014).

Families and caregivers of students with ASDs sometimes experience a significant transition from the primary school years to the secondary school years. According to Hume (2014), high school is among the most complex settings for serving students with ASDs. This is due to several challenges such as increased social demands, higher expectations related to independence, changing needs of students and families, and a shift in programming related to postsecondary life. Much is still unknown about students with ASDs' success with respect to academic achievement. Limited research exists about how adolescents with ASDs learn core academic subjects in both regular education and special education settings (Dunlap, Kern, & Worcester, 2001). Few studies on instructional strategies for achieving academic content exist, and students with ASDs may be denied access to academic skills because of their perceived lack of cognitive abilities or readiness skills (Mirenda, 2003).

According to Humphrey and Symes (2010), students with ASDs often have difficulties in the areas of social communication and social interaction that put them at risk for social isolation and bullying. Families report social challenges as a major impediment to the educational achievement of students with ASDs in high school (Camarena & Sarigiani, 2009). These students also struggle with noise and confusion that embody a typical high school environment

(Humphrey & Lewis, 2008). They also may struggle with executive function problems such as following multistep directions and self-initiation, both of which are considered critical for high school academic success.

CASE STUDY 1
MATT, A CHILD WITH AUTISM SPECTRUM DISORDER (ASD)

Matt's parents first became concerned with his development when he was around 18 months old. They realized that he was not talking like other children his age. Matt had no single words and rarely even babbled. As Matt got older, he showed very little interest in playing with the toys that his parents had bought him, and when he did play with them, his play was quite unusual. He would line up blocks instead of building with them, and he would spin crayons on the kitchen table for hours at a time. Matt did have some vocalizations, but his parents noticed that the majority of the time, they were not intended for communicating with them or his siblings. The only time he did use purposeful vocalizations was when he wanted something to eat. He would grunt or squeal to let his parents know that he was hungry. Matt did not make eye contact with any of his family members. He would avert his gaze as soon as they began speaking to him. Matt also had some self-stimulatory behaviors such as rocking back and forth and flapping his hands when he experienced stress or was excited. When he was two and a half years of age, Matt's parents took him to a developmental pediatrician for an evaluation, and he received the diagnosis of autism. Matt is now 6 years old and continues to engage in self-stimulatory behaviors. He has several single words and is beginning to spontaneously put two words together with prompting from his ABA therapist. He is beginning to maintain a sustained eye gaze with his family during social interactions.

Questions for Critical Thinking

1. What additional information would you want to know about Matt and his family?

2. What might you need to take into consideration when working with Matt's family?

Intellectual Disabilities (ID)

Intellectual disabilities (ID) were historically referred to as mental retardation. Students with ID are characterized by significant limitations in both intellectual functioning and adaptive behavior (American Association of Intellectual and Developmental Disabilities, 2013). Intellectual disabilities are the most common developmental disorders. Approximately 4.6 million individuals have some type of intellectual disability. It is one of the 13 disability categories identified in the **Individuals with Disabilities Education Act (IDEA)**. According to IDEA, intellectual disability is defined as "significantly subaverage general intellectual functioning, existing concurrently with deficits in adaptive behavior and manifested during the developmental period, that adversely affects a child's educational performance" (934 CFR, 300.8[c][6])

Intelligence functioning refers to one's general mental capacity. If a student scores below a 70 on an IQ test, he is considered to be intellectually disabled. **Adaptive behavior** refers to a variety of skills needed for individuals to function in everyday life. Examples of adaptive behaviors include social skills such as following rules, obeying laws, and practical skills such as eating, dressing, and managing money (the Arc, 2011; see Chapter 6). Intellectual disabilities are diagnosed through the use of **standardized tests of intelligence** (IQ tests) and **adaptive behavior rating scales** (the Arc, n.d.). There are several causes of IDs including genetic conditions, problems during pregnancy, problems at birth, problems after birth, and poverty and cultural deprivation (the Arc, 2011).

Table 8.2 explains the various levels of IDs and how they present during childhood and adulthood.

TABLE 8.2 ■ Levels of Intellectual Disability			
Level	IQ Range	Adaptive Skills School Age (6 to 20)	Support Required at Adult Age (21 Years and Older)
Mild	52–69	Some difficulty learning reading, writing, and math, but can learn up to about the sixth-grade level by late teens	Needs guidance and assistance in complex tasks (such as health care and legal decisions) and during times of unusual social or economic stress
		Problems making plans or managing money	Can usually achieve enough social and vocational skills for self-support
		Socially immature but can be expected to learn appropriate social skills	
Moderate	36–51	With difficulty, can progress to elementary school level in work	Cares for simple personal and household needs after extended guidance
		May learn to travel alone in familiar places	Needs supervision and guidance managing money, scheduling, and in all but simple daily tasks
		Social judgment and understanding significantly limited but can learn some	May achieve self-support by doing unskilled or semiskilled work under sheltered conditions
		May have successful friendships and sometimes romantic relationships	
Severe	35–20	Can talk or learn to communicate about simple, everyday events and learn simple health habits	Can develop some self-protection skills in a controlled environment
		Little understanding of written language, numbers, time, or money	Requires support for all daily tasks although may contribute partially to self-care under complete supervision
		Benefits from habit training	
		Usually successful relationships with family members and familiar others but sometimes maladaptive behaviors (including self-injury)	
Profound	19 or below	Limited understanding of speech or gesture; communicates mainly nonverbally	Usually needs nursing care
		Enjoys company of well-known family and caretakers, but sensory and physical impairments often limit social activities	May have limited participation in self-care

Source: Porter, R. (Ed.). (2015). *Merck manual consumer version.* Kenilworth, NJ: Merck Sharp & Dohme Corp., a subsidiary of Merck & Co, Inc. Available at http://www.merckmanuals.com/home/. Accessed April 15, 2015.

Research indicates that families of children with IDs experience more tension than families of typically developing children (Hauser-Cram et al., 1999). Children with IDs are three to four times more likely to have psychiatric disorders than those without IDs (Baker & Pfeiffer, 1994). Some studies indicate that the behavior problems resulting from these psychiatric disorders cause depressive symptoms in their families (Maes, Broekman, Dosen, & Nauts, 2003). Other studies suggest the families of this subgroup appear to adapt well and are resilient in the face of the parenting challenges presented to them (Gerstein, Crnic, Blacher, & Baker, 2009) as a result of their child's disability. In fact, since the end of the 20th century, increasingly more studies have focused on the positive aspects of parenting a child with an ID (Turnbull et al., 1993). Families of children with mild IDs have reported viewing their own parenting behavior as flawed and perceive themselves as less competent than other families. Some children whose intellectual disability is mild may appear similar to their siblings such that families' concern is lessened (Hannah & Midlarsky, 2005).

Families of children with intellectual disabilities have reported several concerns with their child during the primary school years. Those noted include the child's medical, developmental, and behavioral issues (Baroff & Olley, 1999). It is important that families of a child with a suspected intellectual disability have their child evaluated to determine his strengths and needs. There is no one doctor who diagnoses children with intellectual disabilities but rather a combination of medical professionals. General medical tests as well as tests in areas such as neurology, psychology, psychiatry, special education, hearing, speech and vision, and physical therapy are employed. A pediatrician or a child and adolescent psychiatrist often coordinates these tests (American Psychiatric Association, 2016).

During adolescence, families have indicated concern with what life will look like once their child with an intellectual disability completes school and transitions to postsecondary life, work, and possibly independent living. Adolescence is considered a critical phase in the lives of individuals with an intellectual disability. It can be problematic to both the individual with an intellectual disability and the parent alike because of the number of life changes the child might be experiencing. Some individuals with intellectual disabilities have reported a better awareness of their disabilities as they prepare for adulthood (Tod & Jones, 2005). It is relevant to mention that families of adolescents with intellectual disabilities are typically also going through life changes simultaneously, as many of them are transitioning into midlife (La Sorsa & Fordor, 1990).

Speech or Language Impairments

According to IDEA, a speech or language impairment is "a communication disorder, such as stuttering, impaired articulation, a language impairment, or voice impairment that adversely affects a child's educational performance" (34 *CFR,* Part 300.8[c][11]). Currently, students with speech and language impairments comprise the largest disability population served under IDEA. Reported prevalence in children 2 to 7 years of age ranges from 2.3 to 19% (McLaughlin, 2011). Students with speech or language impairments often have problems with academic performance, social interaction, cognitive functioning, and behavior (Kuder, 2013). Examples of speech or language impairments include expressive and receptive language delays, stuttering, and difficulties articulating sounds and words.

During the birth-to-5 period in a child's language development, the home environment plays a particularly significant role. Children from lower socioeconomic backgrounds have been noted to participate in fewer interactions with their families and acquire a smaller vocabulary than children from middle and higher socioeconomic families (Kuder, 2013). It is also known that children living in impoverished settings have less exposure to printed language–based materials such as books and magazines. Research supports the notion that children from lower socioeconomic families are at risk for reading difficulties (Snow, Burns, & Griffin, 1998). Table 8.3 depicts speech and language acquisition of typically developing children.

Much research is currently available on the various types of speech, language, and communication disorders. However, significantly less research is available on parental roles, responsibilities, and attitudes toward parenting this disability population.

TABLE 8.3 ■ Speech and Language Developmental Milestones	
Birth to 3 Months	**4 to 6 Months**
Reacts to loud noises	Follows sounds with his or her eyes
Calms down or smiles when spoken to	Responds to changes in the tone of your voice
Recognizes your voice and calms down if crying	Notices toys that make sounds
When feeding, starts or stops sucking in response to sound	Pays attention to music
Has a special way of crying for special needs	Babbles in a speech-like way and uses many different sounds, including sounds that begin with p, b, and m
Smiles when he or she sees you	Laughs
	Babbles when excited or happy
	Makes gurgling sounds when alone or when playing with you
7 Months to 1 Year	**1 to 2 Years**
Enjoys playing peek-a-boo and pat-a-cake	Know a few parts of the body and can point to them when asked
Turns and looks in the direction of sound	Follows simple commands ("Roll the ball") and understands simple questions ("Where's your shoe?")
Listens when spoken to	Enjoys simple stories, songs, and rhymes
Understands words for common items such as "cup," "shoe," or "juice"	Points to pictures, when named, in books
Responds to requests ("Come here")	Acquires new words on a regular basis
Babbles using long and short groups of sounds ("tata," "upup," "bibibi")	Uses some one- or two-word questions ("Where kitty?" or "Go bye-bye?")
Babbles to get and keep attention	Puts two words together ("More cookie?")
Communicates using gestures such as waving or holding up arms	Uses many different consonant sounds at the beginning of words
Imitates different speech sounds	
Has one or two words ("Hi," "dog," "Dada," or "Mama") by first birthday	
2 to 3 Years	**3 to 4 Years**
Has a word for almost everything	Hears you when you call from another room
Uses two- and three-word phrases to talk about and ask for things	Hears the television or radio at the same sound level as other family members
Uses k, g, f, t, d, and n sounds	Answers simple "Who?" "What?" "Where?" and "Why?" questions
Speaks in a way that is understood by family members and friends	Talks about activities at daycare, preschool, or friends' homes
Names objects to ask for them or to direct attention to them	Uses sentences with four or more words
	Speaks easily without having to repeat syllables or words

(Continued)

TABLE 8.3 ■ (Continued)	
4 to 5 Years	
Pays attention to a short story and answers simple questions about it	
Hears and understands most of what is said at home and in school	
Uses sentences that give many details	
Tells stories that stay on topic	
Communicates easily with other children	
Says most sounds correctly except for a few (l, s, r, v, z, ch, sh, and th)	
Uses rhyming words	
Names some letters and numbers	
Uses adult grammar	

Source: National Institute of Deafness and Other Communication Disorders. (2014). Available at http://www.nidcd.nih.gov/health/voice/pages/speechandlanguage.aspx, Adapted from *How Does Your Child Hear and Talk?*, by the American Speech-Language-Hearing Association. Rerinted with Permission.

CASE STUDY 2
LAUREN, A CHILD WITH SPECIFIC LANGUAGE IMPAIRMENT

Lauren is an 8-year-old girl in a general education third-grade classroom. She is an intelligent girl and is a hard worker. Recently, her teacher, Mrs. Auer, called her mother to discuss some behaviors that Lauren was demonstrating in class. Mrs. Auer told Lauren's mother the following: Lauren does not appear to be tuned in to what I am saying in class. She often misunderstands my directions. This results in her submitting incomplete assignments or completing the wrong assignments. She does not participate very often in class, and when she does, she easily gets lost in the conversation. Lauren also has poor reading skills. She is able to read the words but is not able to comprehend their meaning. In school, Lauren's strength is math computation, where she can accurately add, subtract, and multiply. When given a word problem (application), however, she is not able to arrive at the correct answer. Lauren does not have many friends and often plays alone, although she would prefer to play with others if given the opportunity.

Questions for Critical Thinking

1. What critical information would you want to know about Lauren and her family?

2. What would you need to take into consideration when working with Lauren's family?

Sensory Disabilities

Sensory disabilities are disabilities of the senses: vision and hearing. Blindness or visual impairment and/or deafness and being hard of hearing are sensory disabilities. Sensory disabilities can have an impact on a several areas of functioning (Kuder, 2013). Visual impairment including blindness is one of the 13 categories receiving special education under IDEA. Visual impairment including blindness means an impairment in vision that, even with correction, adversely affects a child's educational performance. The term includes both partial sight and blindness. (20USC 1401 [2004], 20 *CFR* 300.8[c][13])

The degree of a visual impairment can range from mild to severe. Individuals with visual impairments are typically divided into one of two groups: low vision and blind. Many children in the United States have vision loss. However, only a small percentage require special education services as a result of this condition. Therefore, visual impairment is considered a low-incidence disability. During the 2010–2011 school year, approximately 28,000 children received special education services for vision impairment (U.S. Department of Education, 2013).

The causes of vision impairment can be grouped into three categories: refractive errors, structural impairments, and cortical visual impairments (Heward, 2013). According to the National Eye Institute (n.d.), refractive errors occur when the shape of the eye prevents light from focusing directly on the retina. The length of the eyeball (longer or shorter) changes in the shape of the cornea, or aging of the lens can cause refractive errors. "Visual impairments are often caused by poor development of, malfunction of, or damage to one or more parts of the eye's optical or muscular systems" (Heward, 2013, p. 351). Common causes of structural impairments are cataracts and glaucoma. Cortical visual impairments (CVI) are one type of common visual impairment. CVIs are a decreased visual response due to a neurological problem affecting the visual part of the brain (American Association for Pediatric Ophthalmology and Strabismus, 2015).

Low Vision

Low vision is a complex area in the field of visual impairments (American Association for Pediatric Ophthalmology and Strabismus, 2015). Individuals with low vision can have varying degrees of sightedness ranging from moderate impairment to near-total blindness. Typically, a child is considered to have low vision if he can benefit from the use of optical aids (electronic magnifying glass or eyeglass-mounted telescopes) and environmental and instructional modifications in order to learn (Kuder, 2013). Computer software has also been developed to assist individuals with low vision by increasing the type size and read-text-aloud features. In some cases, low vision can impede a person's ability to carry out day-to-day tasks but still allows for some functionally useful sight. Low vision cannot be fully corrected by surgery, contact lenses, or glasses.

Parenting a child who is blind or visually impaired presents its own unique challenges. Fewer studies exist on parenting a child with a vision impairment. One study indicates that child safety was a primary concern. Families have also indicated a desire for their child's instruction to be expanded in the core curriculum (Rosenblum, Hong, & Harris, 2009) that contains more mainstream academics.

Having a child with a visual impairment can result in certain child-rearing stressors for families. These include but are not limited to parent–professional relationship, attitudes of others, difficulty finding appropriate educational programs, money issues, and negative sibling relationships. Alternately, families also reported the benefits associated with having a child with a visual impairment. Families reported:

"Was uneasy, yet over the years obtained a deeper knowledge."

"I learned to appreciate my children, family, and friends so much more."

"I am less intimidated by professionals such as doctors and administrators. Not afraid to question them."

"I am a more demanding person for child's rights."

"I feel stronger and more confident that I can be an advocate for what I believe in."

(Leyser & Heinze, 2001, para. 13)

Blindness

Blindness refers to a person whose visual acuity is 20/200 or less in the better eye with the use of corrective lenses. According to Kuder (2013), there are currently as many as 65 definitions of blindness in the professional literature. A child who learns through tactile or visual input is considered blind. Blind children are educated in a variety of educational settings. These can range from a regular classroom in the neighborhood school to a separate school for the blind. However, about 90% of blind or visually impaired children, including those with additional disabilities, are educated in neighborhood schools (Castellano, 2004).

Hearing

Trouble in a child's ability to hear is another potential disability that can impact his educational performance and require attention from medical professionals and educators alike. Hearing loss is one of the 13 disabilities under IDEA. According to IDEA,

> Deafness means a hearing loss that is so severe that the child is impaired in processing linguistic information through hearing, with or without amplification, [and] that adversely affects a child's educational performance (PL 108-446, 20 U.S.C. 1401 [2004], 20 *CFR* 300.8[c][3]).

> Hearing loss means a loss in hearing, whether permanent or fluctuating, that adversely affects a child's education performance but that is not included under the definition of deafness in this section (PL 108-446, 20 U.S.C. 1401 [2004], 20 CFR 300.8 [c][5]).

It is estimated that 1.4 out of 1,000 babies screened experience some type of hearing loss (Centers for Disease Control and Prevention, 2015c). There are two types of hearing loss: a conductive hearing impairment and a sensory hearing impairment. According to Heward (2013), a conductive hearing impairment "involves a problem with the conduction, or transmission, of sound vibrations in the ear" (p. 320). A sensory impairment, on the other hand, "is attributed to abnormality or failure of the auditory nerve pathway" (Heward, 2013, p. 320). The degree to which a child experiences hearing loss will determine if he is deaf or hard of hearing. Deaf children have a hearing loss of 70 to 90 decibels or greater. They require amplification to develop language. On the other hand, children who are hard of hearing have a hearing loss in the 20-to-70 decibel range. They benefit from amplification but are able to communicate primarily through speaking (Turnbull, Turnbull, Wehmeyer, & Shogren, 2012). Causes of hearing loss are either congenital or acquired. Genetic factors (heredity) account for more than 50% of all hearing loss, which means the hearing loss is present at birth. Acquired hearing loss is due to conditions such as ear infections, medications that are toxic to the ear, head injury, noise exposure, and disease (American Speech-Language-Hearing Association, 2015). Depending on the student's needs and the severity of hearing loss, students who are deaf or hard of hearing may be educated in their neighborhood schools or, if the impairment is severe, require a private school serving children who are deaf.

Parenting a child who is deaf or hard of hearing can put strain on the family. Research indicates that the impact of deafness on the family can vary significantly from family to family (Antonopoulou, Hadjikakou, Stampoltzis & Nicolaou, 2012). Parental strain is primarily due to hearing the diagnosis, learning new communication methods, making appropriate educational decisions, and increasing visits to medical professionals (Calderon & Greenberg, 1999). Behavior problems such as aggression, noncompliance, and inattention also make parenting challenging. Families might also experience child-rearing difficulties if they rely on skills learned from parenting a hearing child because they do not have a model to follow (Jamieson, Zaidman-Zait, & Poon, 2011). Families of deaf and hard-of-hearing children typically have a high need for information regarding appropriate treatment, educational, and communication options for their child as well as receiving social support and parent-to-parent networks (Most & Zaidman-Zait, 2003).

According to Friend (2011), one suggestion for teachers working with families of students who have hearing impairments is to not assume that you understand what the family is experiencing. It is also recommended that you work closely with the families to develop a better understanding of the child with a hearing impairment.

Learning Disabilities

Unlike a vision impairment or an intellectual **disability** that is easily identifiable in young children, learning disabilities are relatively "invisible" in nature. Typically speaking, children with learning disabilities have no physical characteristics or intellectual deficits that would cause a parent to be concerned before the child enters school. As such, families of children with learning disabilities differ from other families of exceptional students in that they often do not discover their child's impairment until their child reaches school age. Families may experience a sense of shock upon receiving the diagnosis of learning disability because it was not anticipated (Seligman & Darling, 2007). They have also reported feelings of guilt, a strained family life, and a lack of social support with respect to raising their child with a learning disability (Dyson & Win, 2010).

IDEA defines the term "specific learning disabilities" (SLD) as indicated in what follows:

(A) In General—The term "specific learning disability" means a disorder in 1 or more of the basic psychological processes involved in understanding or in using language, spoken or written, which disorder may manifest itself in an imperfect ability to listen, think, speak, read, write, spell, or to do mathematical calculations.

(B) *Disorders included*—Such term includes such conditions as perceptual disabilities, brain injury, minimal brain dysfunction, dyslexia, and developmental aphasia.

(C) *Disorders not included*—Such term does not include a learning problem that is primarily the result of visual, hearing, or motor disabilities, of mental retardation, of emotional disturbance, or of environmental, cultural, or economic disadvantage. (PL 108-466, Sec. 602[30])

Learning disabilities are the result of neurological differences in brain structure and function. In essence, learning disabilities result from a difference in the way a person's brain is "wired" (LDOnline, 2015, para. 1). They may also be the result of an insult to the brain before or after birth such as maternal illness, drug or alcohol use during pregnancy, and maternal malnutrition (Cortella, 2014). However, it is important to note that the etiology of learning disabilities is largely unknown. Common types of learning disabilities include dyslexia, dyscalculia, dysgraphia, auditory processing deficit or auditory processing disorder, visual processing deficit or visual processing disorder, and nonverbal learning disabilities.

According to research, parenting and its emotional context are key to a child's developmental outcome. This is particularly true in the case of parenting a child with a learning disability (Heiman, 2002). Reported academic failure is a primary concern of families of children with learning disabilities. Oftentimes, families spend a good deal of their energy and attention on remediating the academic difficulties experienced by their child. Some families have reported that homework completion with their child is particularly frustrating. Other families have indicated an overall positive experience within the family system. Challenging behaviors have also been reported in children with learning disabilities. As such, families of children with learning disabilities are reported to have indicated lower levels of well-being than families of typically developing children as well as increased levels of stress, depression, and anxiety (Neece, Green, & Baker, 2012). Parent training programs help families address such problems. However, a scarcity of research exists on their implementation and effectiveness.

Parent–youth communication during the adolescent period for individuals with learning disabilities has been found to be important. Families communicating openly with their teens and allowing them to express ideas and feelings has led to a decrease in teens' risky behavior and increased their self-esteem, well-being, and coping (Razzino et al., 2004; Riesch, Anderson, & Krueger, 2006). In addition, mothers of adolescents with SLDs appear to have significantly more openness in communication than do fathers of this population (Heiman, Zinck, & Heath, 2015).

Two types of learning disabilities families might encounter are dyslexia and dyscalculia. Dyslexia, the most common type of learning disability, refers to the condition of having a severe difficulty in learning to read (Turnbull et al., 2012). It is a language-based disability that impacts both oral and written language. Several signs indicate a child might have dyslexia. For example, a young child may talk later than other children or be slow to add new vocabulary words to his repertoire. An elementary student might exhibit letter reversals (*d* for *b*), word reversals (*tar* for *rat*), or be impulsive or have difficulty planning (International Dyslexia Association, 2016).

Dyscalculia refers to the inability to achieve in mathematics corresponding to one's chronological age, normal intelligence, and adequate instruction (Dyscalculia.org, 2016). Characteristics of this learning disability include difficulties with visual–spatial perception, processing and discrimination, pattern recognition, and counting, to name a few.

Students with learning disabilities represent a significant number of children who receive special education services while being educated in general education classrooms, otherwise known as inclusion. Currently, due to the large number of children diagnosed with one or more learning disabilities, it is safe to say that many families are coping with issues related to these disorders and are focused on how to improve their children's lives both in and out of school.

Attention Deficit Hyperactivity Disorder (ADHD)

Unlike other disabilities discussed in this chapter, ADHD is not a disability category under IDEA. Instead, it is included in the "other health impairment" category of the current legislation.

According to IDEA, other health impairment means

having limited strength, vitality, or alertness, including a heightened alertness to environmental stimuli, that results in limited alertness with respect to the educational environment, that—

(i) is due to chronic or acute health problems such as asthma, attention deficit disorder or attention deficit hyperactivity disorder, diabetes, epilepsy, a heart condition, hemophilia, lead poisoning, leukemia, nephritis, rheumatic fever, sickle cell anemia, and Tourette Syndrome; and

(ii) adversely affects a child's educational performance (20 USC 1401 [2004], 20 *CFR* 300.8 [c][9])

According to the National Institute of Mental Health (2015), ADHD is one of the most common childhood brain disorders. In 2014, as many as 5.1 million children in the United States were reported as having ADHD (National Resource Center on ADHD, n.d.). Inattention, hyperactivity, and impulsivity are the key behaviors associated with ADHD. Although many children will experience these behaviors, in order to be diagnosed with ADHD, the child must have the symptoms for at least 6 months to a greater degree than other children his age. Causes of ADHD are linked to genes, environmental factors such as cigarette smoking and alcohol use during pregnancy, and possibly exposure to high levels of lead. Diagnosing a child with ADHD takes a multifaceted approach, and no single test will determine this disorder. Most children with ADHD will experience symptoms of this disorder until adulthood.

Families of children with ADHD experience elevated levels of parental stress (Johnson & Mash, 2001), increased depressive symptoms (Faraone & Biederman 1997), anxiety disorders (Perrin & Last, 1996), and problems with family functioning. They might also be recipients of criticism about their child's behavior from those around them. They also report lower rates of parenting satisfaction, efficacy, and competence. Parenting plays an important role in improving the performance of children with ADHD. One study noted that families of children with ADHD are less permissive with their ADHD children and follow a more authoritarian parenting style. Family therapy (see Chapter 2), behavioral parent training, education programs in school, and teaching coping skills can improve the quality of life and relationships in these families (Moghaddam, Assareh, Heidaripoor, Rad, & Pishjoo, 2013). Behavioral parent training (BPT) has demonstrated strong outcomes for improving the behaviors of children with ADHD. In this therapeutic approach, families are trained to be the change agents and are charged with implementing strategies to facilitate child behavior change (Heath, Curtis, Fan, & McPherson, 2014).

According to Friend (2011), families of children with ADHD might be faced with the decision of whether to medicate their child to best control its adverse symptoms. Typically, stimulant drugs are used to treat this disorder. There are several factors that families should consider when making this decision, including considerations such as whether the benefits of taking medication outweigh the risks and the potential side effects of the medication. According to Children and Adults with Attention-Deficit/Hyperactivity Disorder (2013, para. 21), the following suggestions might help families when making this decision:

1. Start with a good evaluation by a trusted professional.
2. Consider how your child might benefit from medicine.
3. Get accurate information regarding side effects.
4. Don't feel rushed to make a decision.
5. Know that your decision is reversible.

The three leading classifications under other health impairment (OHI) are epilepsy, asthma, and diabetes (Project Ideal, 2013). With respect to education, it is important to note that only children whose health impairment negatively impacts their ability to learn are eligible to receive special education services. With respect to its impact on the family, this can look very different depending on the severity of the health impairment and its ability to be controlled in order for a child to learn. Epilepsy is a common neurological disorder that affects people of all ages. When a child seizes, his brain's electrical activity is periodically disturbed, causing some degree of temporary brain dysfunction. It requires educators and other school officials to be able to respond appropriately in the event a seizure occurs during school hours. Much like epilepsy, asthma affects individuals of all ages but commonly begins in childhood. This chronic lung disease inflames and narrows airways, resulting in wheezing, shortness of breath, coughing, and chest tightness. Diabetes is a disease that occurs when the body has a shortage of insulin, a decreased ability to use insulin, or both. It is a long-term condition that causes high blood sugar levels. Characteristics indicating diabetes might be present include frequent urination, excessive thirst, weight gain, and cuts and bruises that do not easily heal.

Emotional and Behavioral Disorders

IDEA refers to emotional and behavioral disorders as emotional disturbance. A child with an emotional disturbance exhibits one or more of the following characteristics over a marked period of time to a significant degree. These characteristics must also adversely affect his educational performance. They are

(i) [a] condition exhibiting one or more of the following characteristics over a long period of time and to a marked degree that adversely affects educational performance:
   (A) An inability to learn that cannot be explained by intellectual, sensory, or health factors
   (B) An inability to build or maintain satisfactory interpersonal relationships with peers and teachers
   (C) Inappropriate types of behavior or feelings under normal circumstances
   (D) A general pervasive mood of unhappiness or depression
   (E) A tendency to develop physical symptoms or fears associated with personal or school problems. The term includes schizophrenia.
(ii) Emotional disturbance includes schizophrenia. The term does not apply to children who are socially maladjusted, unless it is determined that they have an emotional disturbance under paragraph (i) of this section.

(PL 108,446,20 CFR 300.8[c][4])

CASE STUDY 3
CHARLIE, A CHILD WITH ATTENTION DEFICIT/ HYPERACTIVITY DISORDER (ADHD)

Charlie is a friendly and funny child who can entertain just about anyone. From the time that Charlie was a young child, his parents recognized that he behaved differently from other children. As a toddler, he would not sleep for more than a few hours at a time. His parents would often hear him giggling in his bed while playing with his toys late at night. He was always "on the go" and could rarely sit still during family mealtime. When Charlie entered kindergarten, his teachers were concerned about his lack of focus and his inability to attend to instruction and activities throughout the school day. He would not complete his assignments and oftentimes would misplace them. At first, his teachers thought that Charlie was unable to do the work. However, they later realized that this was not the case. Charlie's parents sought professional help, and when he was 6 years old he received a diagnosis of ADHD. Maintaining peer relationships was difficult for Charlie due to his high energy level and social deficits. As Charlie got older, his behaviors became more troublesome. His parents reported that his bedroom frequently looked as if a cyclone had gone through it, with papers, magazines, and old toys strewn carelessly throughout. He regularly demonstrated impulse control problems and had difficulty controlling his urges. To illustrate, one day Charlie spray painted his neighbor's cat black because he thought it would be fun. He would also climb onto his parents' roof when he wanted to be alone, not realizing the dangers associated with being in such an unprotected place.

Questions for Critical Thinking

1. What critical information would you want to know about Charlie and his family?

2. What would you need to take into consideration when working with Charlie's family?

Emotional and behavioral disorders are the fourth-largest disability group served under IDEA. Statistics indicate that as many as 10% of school-aged children have some kind of emotional and behavioral disorder. Causes may be due to biology, home and community environments, and school. Emotional and behavioral disorders comprise five disorders. They are anxiety disorder, mood disorder, oppositional defiant disorder, conduct disorder, and schizophrenia.

According to Modrcin and Robinson, the following can be noted about families and students with emotional and behavioral disorders:

1. A family does not anticipate the onset of a severe emotional disorder in one of its children.
2. These children present a unique set of developmental challenges to which families must adapt and adjust.
3. Families experience a loss as they begin to understand their child's disability.
4. Families of these children are faced with long-term support issues that extend and modify the parenting role beyond the expected years.
5. Families vary in response to stress.
6. Families will need a range of coping strategies and resources to manage the stress in their lives.

(1991, p. 284)

Families of students with emotional and behavioral disorders face specific challenges. For example, students with emotional and behavioral disorders have an increased chance of having at least one parent with an emotional and behavioral disorder. Families of students with emotional and behavioral disorders also tend to be single-parent families and have a lower SES and a lower-than-average education (Friend, 2011).

During the birth-to-age-5 period, families typically begin to notice the behavioral differences that their child exhibits. As the child matures, families begin to realize their changed role as families and how they differ from typical parenting (Modrcin & Robison, 1991). To illustrate, during the primary years, families might notice the differences that occur between their child's capabilities and those of their child's peer group. This disparity can be an isolating factor for families, as they may be left out of the shared job of parenting with their peers (Modrcin & Robison, 1991). Additionally, as the child gets older, the family will notice typical physical development. However, there will many times only be minimal changes to the child's cognitive and emotional abilities (Meyer, 1986). Parenting a child during his adolescence can be a taxing process. Families of adolescents with emotional and behavioral disorders may face increased parenting demands through the teen years.

Bipolar disorder and anxiety disorders are two prevalent emotional disorders seen in schools today. Bipolar disorder, formerly referred to as manic depression, typically begins in childhood and continues into adult life. It is characterized by excessive mood swings identified as "highs" or euphoria that can change suddenly into "lows" or sadness (Kids' Mental Health, 2009). Anxiety occurs when someone feels uneasy, distressed, or even frightened for no apparent reason. Examples of anxiety disorders include panic disorder and obsessive-compulsive disorder. When a child experiences panic disorder he might experience episodes of intense fear, whereas an individual with obsessive-compulsive disorder might demonstrate repeated action (e.g., hand washing or bathing) or have recurring thoughts that are impossible to stop. Families with emotional and behavioral disorders tend to be under considerable stress and benefit from quality special education services and home–school collaboration to best support their child with special needs.

THE BENEFITS OF HOME–SCHOOL COLLABORATION: TEACHERS AND FAMILIES WORKING TOGETHER

Research supports the notion that families and teachers working together as a team benefits the special needs child's overall educational experience throughout his school years (Houser, 2014). In fact, the benefits of home–school collaboration have been clearly documented over the years. Examples of the benefits of a home–school partnership include students earning higher grades, performing better on tests, attending school more regularly, having better behavior, and demonstrating better attitudes toward both themselves and adults (Canter, n.d.). Families of special-needs children value positive home–school relationships between themselves and their child's special education school personnel (Houser, 2014).

Positive steps can be taken to strengthen the home–school relationship between families and school personnel. Table 8.4 depicts ways that both teachers and families can develop positive communication to benefit children with special needs.

TABLE 8.4 ■ Positive Steps Toward Home–School Communication	
Teachers	**Families**
• Select a communication method (communication notebook, emails, or phone calls) that you can use with relative ease.	• Consistently communicate with your child's teacher through the selected communication method.
• Communicate on a consistent basis with your families. Checking in with them inconsistently does not provide families with an accurate picture of how their child is performing at school.	• Be patient. Realize that teachers have many daily demands and will get back to your emails or phone calls as soon as they are able to.
• Remember to communicate the child's successes as well as his difficulties.	• Support your child's teacher by being consistent with academic and behavioral expectations in the home environment.
• Do not be afraid to ask for parent input and advice about their child regarding academic performance and behavior.	• Keep your child's teacher aware of any changes in your child's behavior or medication, if possible.
• Be specific about how the child is doing at school. Avoid statements such as "Justin had a good day." Instead, make statements such as "Justin completed his classwork and made an attempt to talk with classmates. I was pleased with his work today."	• Get involved. When possible, volunteer to help in your child's classroom.
• Be compassionate. Realize that many families are stressed during the school day wondering how their child's school day is going.	

Source: From *Autism Parenting Magazine*, 2014. Reprinted with permission of Mary A. Houser, Ed.D. and Charlotte L. Fontenot, Ed.D.

Summary

Families of children with special needs encounter a variety of child-rearing experiences throughout their child's lifespan. Often times these will be directly related to the child's specific disability and will change as the child develops and matures. These challenges present themselves differently in the birth-to-5, primary, and secondary years. Families of children with special needs must adapt to the varying demands of their child's life cycle. Recent studies reflect more families reporting the positive aspects of parenting a child with special needs.

Depending on the child's disability, families will be required to learn new skills that support their child's growth. Examples of these may include learning a new communication system or strategies to support difficult behavior. Positive aspects reported include a changed perspective on life, increased tolerance of others, sensitivity to others, experiencing more family time, and opportunities to learn more about disability. One of the best ways to enhance the success of exceptional children is through improved home–school communication.

Additional Resources

Web-Based

American Speech-Language-Hearing Association: http://www.asha.org. A national association for audiologists, speech-language pathologists, speech, language, and hearing scientists, audiology and speech-language pathology support personnel, and students.

Autism Speaks: https://www.autismspeaks.org. A science and advocacy organization focusing on funding research for the causes, prevention, treatments, and cure for autism.

Council for Children with Behavioral Disorders: http://www.ccbd.net/home. An organization dedicated to providing support and treatment to children with behavioral needs.

Learning Disabilities Association of America: http://ldaamerica.org/educators/. An association that provides support to people with learning disabilities and their parents, teachers, and other professionals.

National Dissemination Center for Children with Disabilities: http://www.nichcy.org. A center for parent resources and information on disabilities.

Parent to Parent: USA. www.p2pusa.org/p2usa/sitepages/p2p-home.aspx. A national organization that provides emotional and informational support to families of children who have special needs.

The Arc: For People with Intellectual and Developmental Disabilities : http://www.thearc.org. The world's largest community-based organization of and for people with intellectual and developmental disabilities.

Print

American Psychiatric Association. (2013). *Diagnostic and statistical manual of mental disorders: DSM-5* Washington, DC: Author.

The standard classification of mental disorders used by mental health professionals in the United States

Dowling, C., & Nicoll, N. (2011). *A different kind of perfect: Writings by parents on raising a child with special needs*. Boston: Shambhala.

A compilation of parent writings that reflect the various stages of emotions they experience raising a child with special needs.

Park, J. H., Alber M.S.R., & Fleming, C. (2011). Collaborating with parents to implement behavioral interventions for children with challenging behaviors. *Teaching Exceptional Children, 43*(3), 22–30.

9

BIRTH THROUGH AGE 5

MELINA ALEXANDER
Weber State University

BRENDA EATON

"Do not train a child to learn by force or harshness; but direct them to it by what amuses their minds, so that you may be better able to discover with accuracy the peculiar bent of the genius of each."

—Plato

LEARNING OBJECTIVES

Specifically, after reading this chapter, you will:

1. Have an understanding of the systems and professionals that provide services to children from birth to 5 years of age.

2. Identify the potential needs of families of young children with disabilities.

3. Have an understanding of transition from one service system to the next and how to support a child and family through this process.

INTRODUCTION

There is not a set time for when a child's disability is discovered. This determination may happen any time during pregnancy, infancy, early childhood, or in some instances later during the child's school career. Families may learn they are having a child with a disability such as Down syndrome during a routine prenatal checkup, they may notice that their infant is not responding to sound and with medical assistance determine that their infant is deaf, they may notice their toddler is experiencing a regression in development and engaging in stereotypical patterns of behavior associated with autism, or they may find later that their child is lagging behind their preschool peers and has a developmental delay. Regardless of when a child's disability is identified, families discovering they have or are having a child with a disability are often thrown into turmoil. Typically families go through a process similar to those experiencing loss. They experience denial, anger, loss, then acceptance (McGill Smith, 2014). They are faced with many concerns about their child's future, not the least of which is education. The Individuals with Disabilities Education Improvement Act (IDEIA) allows for educational services for all children with disabilities ages birth through 22 (IDEA, 2004). For families of children ages birth to 3, this may mean their child receives early intervention. For families of children ages 3 to 5, this may mean their child receives specialized preschool programing. This chapter will help you understand the unique needs of families of children birth through age 5 who have been identified as having a disability.

CHILDREN FROM BIRTH TO AGE 3

For most families, there is no greater joy than the addition of a child. Upon discovering the addition of a new family member, families begin preparations. Families may begin buying furniture and clothes, prepare their home for the new arrival, and pore over resources to determine what they should expect once the child arrives. Families have expectations that their child will develop in the typical fashion and may even harbor hopes that their child will develop faster than most. It is not uncommon for families to compare their child's developmental milestones with those of their peers. They may become overly concerned if their child's development seems atypical. It is therefore important for professionals to relay accurate information about developmental expectations.

Development. Children develop rapidly in the first few years of life in all areas. In fact, we can see rapid development in the first 3 months of life. Newborns come with very little ability to do things on their own (Mayo Clinic, 2014). They communicate only through crying and are unable to physically support themselves. By the time an infant reaches 3 months of age, they are able to communicate through smiling and may even mimic facial expressions. Infants now lift and turn their heads, kick, and stretch and may even briefly grasp objects. At 3 months, families may detect that a baby can see or hear when they turn in response to a stimulus (Mayo Clinic, 2104).

At the end of the first year, children are moving from infant to toddler. Families look for patterns in child development across a wide range of areas, including physical development, communication, social and emotional development, and even cognitive development (Centers for Disease Control and Prevention, 2014a). Physically, a 1-year-old should sit without assistance, crawl, stand, and maybe even take a few steps. Typically, 1-year-olds communicate through gestures. They respond to requests and may even use a few words such as "mama" or "dada." Socially, 1-year-old children show reticence around new people. They cry when their parents leave and show a preference for certain activities and people. The 1-year-old shows cognitive development in many different ways. She may explore things, banging, throwing and dropping objects. He may find objects that are hidden, look for named items, and use items correctly, for example, drinking from a cup (Centers for Disease Control and Prevention, 2014a).

When children reach 3 years of age, there are many expectations for their development; families watch for how their child moves, learns, speaks, and plays (Centers for Disease Control and Prevention, 2014b). By their third birthday, children should be able to climb stairs, run, climb, and even pedal a tricycle. At this age, children can communicate well, most strangers can understand them, they use the name for most objects, use plural and singular forms of words, know the meaning of most prepositions, and use two to three sentences when communicating. Socially, the 3-year-old has friends and knows how to take turns. Emotionally, they show little anxiety separating from their parents and show affection toward friends but may get upset if there is a change to their routine (Centers for Disease Control and Prevention, 2014b). Cognitively, 3-year-olds can accomplish many tasks; they complete small puzzles, build towers of blocks, turn pages in a book, and understand that two is more than one. If families notice that their child is behind on more than one task in any area of development (see Table 9.1), they may be in need of additional educational services.

TABLE 9.1 ■ Typical Development and Warning Signs Children Ages Birth to 3				
Age	Physical Development	Social and Emotional Development	Intellectual Development	Language Development
Birth to 1 Month Typical Development	• Raises head briefly. • Reacts to sudden sound. • Closes eye to bright light.	• Smiles at parent.	• Becomes aware of physical sensations such as hunger. • Explores using his senses.	• Cries vigorously. • Respond to high-pitched tones by moving his limbs.
Birth to 1 Month Red Flags	• Doesn't feed or suck well • Seems stiff or floppy • Doesn't respond to loud sounds	• Doesn't focus with eyes		
3 Months Typical Development	• Back and neck firm when held sitting. • Grasps objects placed in hands. • Turns head round to have a look at objects. • Establishes eye contact.	• Reacts with pleasure to familiar routines. • Discriminates smile.	• Takes increasing interest in his surroundings. • Shows interest in playthings.	• Indicates needs with differentiated cries. • Beginning to vocalize. • Smile in response to speech.

Age	Physical Development	Social and Emotional Development	Intellectual Development	Language Development
3 Months Red Flags	• Can't support head • Can't grasp objects • Doesn't react to sound	• Doesn't smile • Ignores new faces • Upset by unfamiliar people and surroundings		
4-7 Months Typical Development	• Sits up with support. • Enjoys standing and jumping. • Pulls self up to sit and sits erect with supports. • Rolls over prone to supine.	• Responds to different tones of mother. • May show fear of strangers. • Takes stuff to mouth.	• Understand simple words such as up and down. • Makes appropriate gestures, such as raising his arms to be picked.	• Uses double syllable sounds such as mama and dada. • Laughs in play. • Screams with annoyance.
4-7 Months Red Flags	• Seems stiff or floppy • Can't hold head steady • Can't sit on their own	• Doesn't respond to smiles • Isn't affectionate with parents	• Doesn't reach for high objects	
7-12 Months Typical Development	• Stands alone for a second or two. • Walks holding one hand. • Pulls to stand and sits deliberately. • Holds spoon. • Points at objects.	• Cooperates with dressing. • Waves goodbye. • Understands simple commands. • Demonstrate affection. • Participate in nursery rhymes.	• Responds to simple instructions. • Uses trial-and-error to learn about objects.	• Babbles 2 or 3 words repeatedly. • Responds to simple instructions. • Understands several words.
7-12 Months Red Flags	• Doesn't crawl • Seems to drag one side when crawling • Can't stand with support	• Doesn't shake head no	• Doesn't try to find objects you've hidden • Doesn't point at objects	• Doesn't say any words
13-24 Months Typical Development	• Can walk alone. • Picks up toy without falling over. • Begins to jump with both feet. • Can build a tower of 3 or 4 cubes.	• Plays alone near familiar adult. • Drinks from a cup with both hands. • Feeds self with a spoon. • Attains bowel control.	• Enjoys simple picture books. • Explores environment. • Knows the names of parts of his body.	• Uses many intelligible words. • Repeats an adult's last word. • Jabbering established.
13-24 Months Red Flags	• Can't walk by 18 months • Loses skills previously had	• Doesn't imitate • Loses skills previously had	• Doesn't understand the use of everyday objects • Doesn't follow simple instructions • Loses skills previously had	• Doesn't speak at least 6 words by 18 months or two-word sentences by 24 months • Loses skills previously had

(Continued)

TABLE 9.1 ■ (Continued)				
Age	Physical Development	Social and Emotional Development	Intellectual Development	Language Development
24-36 Months Typical Development	• Can kick large ball. • Squats with ease. • Rises without using hands. • Able to run. • Walks up and down stairs 2 feet per step.	• Throws tantrum if frustrated. • Can put on shoes. • Completely spoon feeds and drinks from cup. • Dry by day.	• Joins 2-3 words in sentences. • Recognizes details in pictures. • Uses own name to refer to self.	• Talks to self continuously. • Speaks over two hundred words.
24-36 Months Red Flags	• Can't climb stairs with alternating feet	• Struggles with separation anxiety • Doesn't interact with people outside family • Doesn't play with other children	• Doesn't play make-believe	• Isn't able to complete a sentence • Difficult for strangers to understand

From: Child development Milestone Chart retrieved from http://www.child-development-guide.com/child-development-milestone.html?fb_comment_id=10150149833038075_17716979#f22daaeae12544 and Baby Center retrieved from http://www.babycenter.com/milestone-charts-birth-to-age-3

EARLY INTERVENTION

Early intervention services are programs provided to infants and toddlers with or at risk of developing disabilities. These programs are critical in producing positive outcomes for these children (Center on the Developing Child, 2010). The necessity of these programs was first identified in federal regulations in 1986. Congress enacted the initial program to address not only the needs of children identified with disabilities but also the needs of families of children with disabilities. This initial law has changed since 1986 and now recognizes the significant brain development that occurs during the first 3 years of life. In its current iteration it is included under Part C of the Individuals with Disabilities Education Act (IDEA Part C, 2004).

PART C OF THE IDEA

Part C of IDEA defines programs for children, ages birth to 3, with developmental delays or who have been diagnosed with disabilities or physical or mental conditions that have a high probability of resulting in such a delay. These services are called early intervention, and their purpose is to prepare children with the skills necessary to be successful in preschool and kindergarten (ed.gov, n.d.). In order to participate in Part C of IDEA, states must meet specific requirements. Among these requirements is the state assuring early intervention is available to all eligible infants and toddlers and their families. Part C of the IDEA requires "to the maximum extent appropriate to the needs of the child, early intervention services must be provided in natural environments, including the home and community settings in which children without disabilities participate" (34 CFR §303.12(b)). Services under Part C are therefore family oriented. Currently all states and eligible territories participate in Part C of IDEA.

In order for a child who is from 0 to 3 years old to receive services under Part C, a referral must be made (Center for Parent Information and Resources, 2012). Families do not need to wait for some external agency to make this referral. If they have concerns, families can contact a Part C program and request an evaluation. Families, however, are not solely responsible for recognizing the potential need for early intervention services; IDEA allows for extensive Child Find procedures for all children age birth to 21.

CHILD FIND   As discussed in Chapter 4, Child Find is mandated under IDEA. It is a requirement that local education agencies locate and evaluate children who are in need of special education services. School districts are required to locate and evaluate children in need of special education services across all ages, birth to 21, but Child Find can look different for children who are very young. Often families of young children in need of special education services have had no contact with their school districts. In addition, there may be children who do not visit a pediatrician's office; they therefore do not have access to screenings provided by medical personnel. It is up to local education agencies to offer Child Find programs at preschools, community agencies, clinics, shelters, and other programs with which families may come into contact.

Child Find programs geared at locating and evaluating young children in need of special education services include two parts. First, these programs should include a public awareness component. Local education agencies should work with other professionals such as physicians, social service workers, and community agencies, including local churches and community centers. These agencies should collaborate to raise awareness in the general public about the importance of early identification and early intervention for children with or at risk of developing disabilities. In addition, they should work together to provide families information on the availability of early intervention services offered in the community. Second, local education agencies should include a method for families to determine if their child may have or be at risk of developing a disability. This should include both information to develop knowledge and understanding on typical child development and a method for screening and for families to request evaluation if they so desire.

EVALUATION   Once a child with or at risk of having disabilities is located, a referral is made to the local education agency. This agency will then begin the evaluation process, and the lead agency (program provider) will assign a **service coordinator**. The service coordinator has 45 calendar days to coordinate an evaluation to make a determination of eligibility for early intervention services for the child and to get services in place. As stated in Chapter 4, in order for this evaluation to occur, the program must provide prior notice to families and must obtain parental consent. Evaluation for eligibility of Part C services includes assessment in five areas of the young child's development, including cognitive, physical, communication, social-emotional, and adaptive (Center for Parent Information and Resources, 2012). Information is gathered on the child's developmental history; this may require interviewing the family, reviewing medical, educational, or other records, and gathering information from other sources if necessary. Additionally, assessments may be given to determine the child's unique needs. This will help determine the early intervention programs best suited to meet the child's needs. In addition, the service coordinator may send someone in to observe the child and family in the home environment. For more information on these assessments, please refer to Chapter 6.

It is important to note that a specific diagnosis is not necessary to qualify for services. Early intervention is put in place for infants and toddlers with or at risk of developing developmental delays. Early intervention allows these children to learn skills that typically developing children learn in the first few years of life. This is done through the development of an individual family service plan (IFSP).

INDIVIDUAL FAMILY SERVICE PLAN (IFSP)

The IFSP is a family-based treatment plan that details early intervention services. The multidisciplinary team that develops the IFSP includes the parent(s) of the child, other family members if the parent requests, an advocate or person outside the family if the parent requests, the service coordinator, the person(s) who conducted the evaluations and assessments, and possibly, if appropriate, those who are proposed to provide the services to the child and family.

MEMBERS OF THE MULTIDISCIPLINARY TEAM

PARENTS AND FAMILY MEMBERS Of course parents are critical members of the IFSP team. Parents are pivotal team members, in fact, because the IFSP is being written for and about their infant or toddler. Parents have invaluable perspectives to offer on their child's growth and development, areas of strength and need, and overall medical and personal history. They can also contribute substantively to IFSP development by sharing with the other team members the priorities, resources, and concerns of the family unit. In addition, other family members such as siblings, grandparents, or others who have a close relationship or extended contact with the child can be invited to participate on the multidisciplinary team. The regulations clearly recognize the deep involvement and commitment that a child's family members can bring to supporting his or her well-being. Family members can and often do play a variety of roles in enhancing a child's development. It is critical that those working with families validate their concerns and ideas and anticipate their needs. For some parents, this may be their first experience working with special education professionals. They must be given clear explanations of the IFSP process and be made aware of the important role they play in the child's IFSP. Unlike the individualized education plan, for which teachers and other service providers carry the primary responsibility for implementing the plan, in the IFSP, families are expected to be active participants in the implementation of team-determined interventions.

OTHER PARTICIPANTS AT THE REQUEST OF THE PARENT Families of the child may also request that an advocate or another person from outside the family unit be included on the IFSP team. An advocate typically helps the family articulate their perspectives and concerns, while a person from outside the family might contribute professional or personal knowledge about the child's needs and strengths or the family's needs regarding supporting the child's development.

THE SERVICE COORDINATOR The early intervention provider or lead agency designates a service coordinator to help the parents and family members understand and navigate the early intervention process. This is obviously a key role; not surprisingly, the service coordinator has many specific duties and responsibilities, including coordinating all services across agency lines and serving as the single point of contact for carrying out the early intervention services and activities identified in the child's IFSP.

INDIVIDUALS INVOLVED IN EVALUATION AND ASSESSMENTS Individuals who have been directly involved in carrying out the evaluation and assessments of the child and family are also on the IFSP team. This may be one individual or several, with key contributions to explain the results of the evaluation and assessment process and to help the other team members identify the early intervention services appropriate to addressing the child's developmental needs.

PROVIDER(S) OF EARLY INTERVENTION SERVICES   If appropriate, the team may also include one or more providers of early intervention services. Again, this may be one or more individuals who can speak directly to the question of which early intervention services are needed and what measurable goals or outcomes are appropriate for the child.

CONTENT OF THE IFSP

An IFSP has two general purposes: to set outcomes and to define the early intervention program including family services. Unlike information included in an individualized education plan, described later in this chapter, an IFSP must include the specific content used for early intervention (Center for Parent Information and Resources, 2012). In addition, collaborating with family members in the development of the IFSP is critical. As the name implies, services and programming are developed for families.

EARLY INTERVENTION PROGRAMMING   Early intervention programs are put in place to assist identified infants and toddlers in development. They focus on five main areas of growth: physical, cognitive, communication, social-emotional, and self-help (Center for Parent Information and Resources, 2012). Depending on the child's and the family's needs, these programs may focus on one or more development areas and include additional services such as training for families in nutrition, using assistive technology, and implementing educational programs. Early intervention can also include speech language services, physical therapy, occupational therapy, counseling and psychological services, and medical and nursing services (Center for Parent Information and Resources, 2012).

LOCATION OF EARLY INTERVENTION SERVICES   Part C of the IDEA specifies that services are to take place in the natural environment, which is usually the family's home. In the home environment, the family is more open socially to bond with the service provider and to build a more personal relationship. This can help build the necessary system for the transfer of skills from the professionals to the family. Each service provider and multidisciplinary team member works on targeted developmental skills but also shares child progress reports with the other interventionists to assure that all team members are working towards the IFSP goals. It is expected that, as the family learns to collaborate with professionals, they take methods and strategies used during their child's intervention sessions and use them throughout the week to extend the program into the home and other environments. When the interventionist comes to the home, the family takes an active role in programming for their child by offering feedback that will allow the interventionist to better understand whether to either refine programming or move on to new skills. Family involvement leads to positive gains over time with interventions, and families may actually start to suggest new strategies and interventions themselves.

SERVICES AND PRACTICES IN EARLY INTERVENTION   The services provided in early intervention are as varied as the participating children. Many types of services are available, but the most common according to the National Early Intervention Longitudinal Study (Bailey, Scarborough, Hebbeler, Spiker, & Mallik, 2004) are speech/language therapy, special instruction, occupational and or physical therapy, and developmental monitoring. Each of these service providers is committed to provide the best possible interventions, and most specialty services subscribe to a set of recommended best practices.

The field of early intervention views the development of recommended practices as a way to provide continuity in service to children and families while ensuring a level of best practice. Over time, these best practices have come from a variety of sources and come in the form of guides, standards, and position statements. Within the field, descriptions of what adults should do with young children have been a staple of the literature at least since 1986 and are referred to as developmentally appropriate practices (DAP). Currently, the Division for Early Childhood *(DEC) Recommended Practices (2014)* consists of eight domains: leadership, assessment, environment, family, instruction, interaction, teaming and collaboration, and transition. Special notes on the family practices encompass three themes:

1. Family-centered practices: Practices that treat families with dignity and respect; are individualized, flexible, and responsive to each family's unique circumstances; provide family members complete and unbiased information to make informed decisions; and involve family members in acting on choices to strengthen child, parent, and family functioning.
2. Family capacity-building practices: Practices that include the participatory opportunities and experiences afforded to families to strengthen existing parenting knowledge and skills and promote the development of new parenting abilities that enhance parenting self-efficacy beliefs and practices.
3. Family and professional collaboration: Practices that build relationships between families and professionals who work together to achieve mutually agreed-upon outcomes and goals that promote family competencies and support the development of the child.

OUTCOMES OF EARLY INTERVENTION

As stated previously, early intervention has been a mandated component of special education for more than 30 years. It was originally implemented with infants and toddlers with or at risk of developing disabilities to minimize the potential for developmental delay and subsequent need for special education or institutionalization. In addition, it was set in place to help families meet the needs of their child. With such an extensive mandated program, it became necessary to evaluate early intervention (EI) programs to determine their success. In 1996, the National Early Intervention Longitudinal Study (NEILS) set out to provide this information. It aimed specifically to answer the following questions:

- Who are the children and families receiving EI services?
- What EI services do participating children and families receive?
- What are the costs of the EI services?
- What outcomes do participating children and families experience?
- How do outcomes relate to variations in child and family characteristics and services received?

(Bailey et al., 2004, p. 12)

The study provided detailed answers to these questions, and the full report can be accessed in the weblinks provided at the end of this chapter. For the purpose of this text, it is important that we look at family outcomes and the implications of these outcomes for professionals working with families.

FAMILIES' EXPERIENCES IN BEGINNING EARLY INTERVENTION As discussed previously, identifying infants and toddlers with need for early intervention services is a product of quality Child

Find programs. We know that for many families, this is their first introduction to special education programs. They may not be aware that such programs exist unless outside professionals step in. This may be the reason that the NEILS data (Bailey et al., 2004) indicate that the age of program implementation varies depending on disability, with children with readily recognized disabilities such as spina bifida receiving services much earlier than those with the more difficult-to-recognize developmental delays. The NEILS data did indicate that overall families viewed early intervention services easy to access, with 75% of families reporting that the information on the availability of early intervention services was readily available (Bailey et al., 2004). This information could indicate that families need more information on what to expect in their child's development and factors that could indicate a developmental delay (see Table 9.1).

FAMILY OUTCOMES   There is no doubt that early intervention can have a profound effect on families. According to the NEILS data (Bailey et al., 2004), at the end of early intervention services, when the child is approximately 36 months old, most families reported positive outcomes for their child, with 72% of families reporting that they were better off than before receiving services. At this time, most families, 99%, indicated that early intervention helped them become competent caregivers. However, this was not necessarily the case when it came to families addressing children's behavior issues; 35% of families indicated that they often did not know what to do when behavior issues occurred. In addition, 26% of families expressed little ability to participate in community activities, including school, church, or other social events. These findings could indicate that professionals working with families in the child's first 3 years should provide behavior management techniques and work with families to access community activities.

When families look back at the outcomes of early intervention when their child enters kindergarten, their perceptions remain consistent (Bailey et al., 2004; see Figure 9.1).

A slight drop from 91% to 89% occurred when families reported that they know how to work with professionals. In addition, families still felt that they had good support systems—89%. While showing some improvement, families still indicated difficulty in participating in community activities, with 67% indicating that they took part in activities such as church, school, and other social events. Managing child behavior still seemed to create concern for families, with 34% indicating that they did not know how to handle their child's misbehavior.

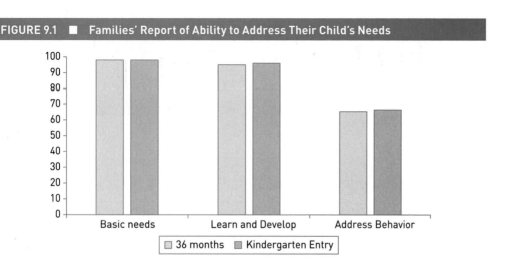

FIGURE 9.1 ■ Families' Report of Ability to Address Their Child's Needs

CASE STUDY 1

AISHA'S FAMILY

Jordan and Shaundra were eagerly anticipating the birth of their first child. Both in their twenties, Shaundra had just finished graduate school, and Jordan was scheduled to finish law school in the fall. While this baby was unexpected, both parents were excited about the prospect of becoming parents. Shaundra and Jordan had read all the materials on what to expect during pregnancy and were starting their reading on parenting.

Early in March they were scheduled for an ultrasound to determine if their child's development was on target. When the day of the ultrasound came, both parents were in the waiting room debating whether to have the technician tell them the sex of their baby. They were ushered to the ultrasound room and filled out the remaining paperwork, including a request for the technician to tell them whether they were having a boy or girl. The technician came into the room, explained the procedure and then plopped a gooey substance on Shaundra's belly. Shaundra shuttered, Jordan giggled, and both looked to the monitor at a display the technician began to decipher. The expectant parents and the technician chatted about the baby while the technician began to take routine measurements. Shaundra and Jordan noticed the technician started to look concerned and was not as chatty as at the beginning of the appointment. She told them to stay there for a minute and left the room. Shaundra and Jordan were confused and upset. They began talking about the possibility of there being complications.

When the technician came back in, she asked them to schedule further tests and told them that their doctor had requested for them to go straight to her office for a visit. At the physician's office, the doctor informed the parents that the ultrasound indicated that their child might have Down syndrome. The doctor stated that she would not know anything for certain until further tests were run. She asked Shaundra and Jordan if they wanted to run these tests and informed them that there was a small possibility of miscarriage associated with the tests. Both Shaundra and Jordan felt they had to know. They scheduled the tests, praying for a result that indicated their child did not have Down syndrome. When the tests came back, they found out their baby was a girl and that she did indeed have Down syndrome. Their doctor let them know of educational programs offered by their local education agency.

Questions for Critical Thinking

1. Consider yourself a representative of the local education agency. What could you do to assist Shaundra and Jordan in finding out about your educational programs geared for infants and toddlers?

2. What other information do you think would be important for you to provide the couple?

3. What information would you need to know from Shaundra and Jordan before proceeding with an IFSP meeting?

CHILDREN AGES 3 TO 5

The ages of 3 to 5 mark the progression into early childhood (ParentFurther, 2015). Children become more independent and are rapidly developing social-emotional skills. At this stage, many children attend preschool and make connections with adults and other children beyond their family.

A child's social development occurs not only with interactions but can also be noted in their play. Most preschool-aged children engage in a significant amount of fantasy or imaginative play. Play not only facilitates a child's social development but also plays a significant role in a child's cognitive development. Children at this stage will see an increase of vocabulary from about 300 words at age 3 to 2,500 words by age 5. A child can now name colors and understand simple counting and is developing a concept of time (ParentFurther, 2015).

CHILDREN AGES 3 TO 5 WITH DISABILITIES

Once a child begins interacting with others outside the family, atypical development may be noticed by family members or others. Local education agencies are still required to have Child Find services in place, and medical professionals can still refer a child for special education programming. If a family member or other professional recognizes that the preschool-aged child may have a delay in development, just like for children ages birth to 3, families may request an evaluation to determine eligibility for services. The process follows similar procedures to those listed earlier; prior notice is given to parents; then with permission, the assessment process takes place. The local education agency has 45 days to complete all testing and schedule meetings. Children determined eligible will receive services under Part B of the IDEA, and an individualized education plan (IEP) will be created that includes preschool services (see Table 9.2).

For children already receiving services, at the age of 3 years, the child will transition to the Preschool Special Education (PSE) Program, indicated in Part B of the IDEA. A minimum of 90 days prior to this move, a transition plan must be included in the IFSP. Parents

TABLE 9.2 ■ Differences Between IFSP and IEP	
IFSP	**IEP**
For children birth through ages 2 and their families	For children ages 3–21
Used for early intervention	Used for special education
Includes: <ul><li>the child's current level of development</li><li>outcomes desired for child and family</li><li>methods, timelines, and plan to measure progress</li><li>services and supports provided</li></ul>	Includes: <ul><li>the student's current level of educational performance</li><li>annual educational goals</li><li>description of progress monitoring</li><li>services and supports</li><li>description of least restrictive environment</li></ul>
Team members: <ul><li>Parent(s) of the child</li><li>Family members requested by parents</li><li>Advocates outside the family requested by parents</li><li>Service coordinator</li><li>Assessment/evaluation specialist</li></ul>	Team members: <ul><li>Parent(s) of the student</li><li>Family members requested by parents</li><li>Student when appropriate</li><li>Regular education teacher</li><li>Special education teacher</li><li>Representative of the local education agency</li><li>A person that can interpret assessment/evaluation results</li><li>Others service providers, for example speech language specialist, school counselor</li></ul>

Note: Adapted from IDEA part B and C and Pacer Center ACTION sheet (2011): What is the difference between an IFSP and an IEP.

need time to adjust to the differences between the two serving systems due to the fact that the family is moving from Part C, a family-focused, developmentally based program in the natural environment, to Part B, a child-focused system that assumes the primary educational responsibility and monitors current levels of educational performance for progress instead of development.

PRESCHOOL PROGRAMS

Preschool-aged children with disabilities are guaranteed a free appropriate public education (FAPE) under section 619 of Part B of the IDEA. This means children identified as having a developmental delay or any disability named in Part B of the IDEA are entitled to special education and related services in the least restrictive environment (LRE). Preschool programs will vary depending on the child's needs determined by the IEP team.

LOCATION OF PRESCHOOL PROGRAMMING As stated, preschool programs will be provided in the child's least restrictive environment. This means that the child may receive services in the school district's general education preschool program or in any of a continuum of placements, including the child's home. Where the child receives services is determined by the IEP team, which must include families. For an example of this continuum of services, see Figure 9.2.

CURRICULUM IN PRESCHOOL PROGRAMS Regardless of where a child receives preschool services, the program must include curriculum that is developmentally appropriate and culturally meaningful. This curriculum must be focused on the child's area of need, whether physical, cognitive, social-emotional, in communication, and/or in self-help. This means that teachers must understand the child's developing skills and knowledge and ways of facilitating the family's support of this development.

FIGURE 9.2 ■ An Example of a Continuum of Services for a Preschool-Aged Child

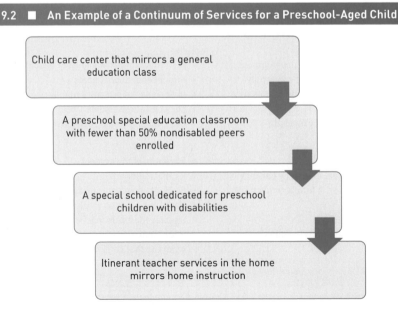

Child care center that mirrors a general education class

A preschool special education classroom with fewer than 50% nondisabled peers enrolled

A special school dedicated for preschool children with disabilities

Itinerant teacher services in the home mirrors home instruction

CHALLENGES IN PRESCHOOL PROGRAMING

The shift from the Part C early intervention (EI), which has a family-centered focus in the natural environment, to the Part B preschool special education, a student focus, in the regular and special education environment, often needs clarification for families with a child transitioning. Families that receive Part C EI are used to the service providers coming into the home one at a time to work with the child and family on identified areas of need. By the end of EI services, the family and the child are usually in a well-established routine. As families move into preschool special education they may find their child getting on a bus and going off to a center, school, or other location for special education preschool. For those families that are used to working directly with their child in the natural environment, feeling they know what is best for their child, and willing to advocate for it, the shift to the preschool model with a focus on functionality in the least restrictive educational environment can lead to confusion and frustration. This can lead to difficulties between the families and PSE staff. It is important for professionals working with families that they understand the difficulties these transitions can cause. Special education professionals must work to create open lines of communication that respect families' concerns and desires.

CASE STUDY 2
MATHIAS'S PARENTS

Mathias is 2 years old. He lives with his grandparents. Mathias's mother Candice is a single parent and did not list a father on Mathias's birth certificate. Mathias's grandparents never found out who his father was.

Mathias was born premature and drug addicted, but after an extended stay in the neonatal unit, he was pronounced able to go home. Mathias's mother had gone through a 4-week rehabilitation program while Mathias was in the hospital. She was able to take Mathias home at the end of his hospitalization but was under social service monitoring. Mathias continued to grow and develop normally, and his mother was working hard at keeping up with the program social workers had assigned her. When Mathias was 2, his mother was working part time in a convenience store, and her parents provided Mathias's care while she worked. Mathias's development appeared normal to his mother and grandparents. No concerns were raised by his pediatrician either at his 2-year checkup. Mathias's mother had a relapse a few months into his second year. She was arrested for distributing a controlled substance and was incarcerated. Mathias's grandparents were awarded temporary custody. A few weeks after Mathias moved into his grandparents' house, Mathias's grandparents began to notice that Mathias appeared to be regressing. He stopped talking, began to wet the bed, and stared off into space for hours while rocking back and forth. They attributed this behavior to his mother's incarceration and continued to try to care for him the best they knew how. By his third-year check-up, Mathias's grandparents had noticed little change in his behavior. They discussed their concerns with his pediatrician. The pediatrician referred Mathias for autism screening.

Questions for Critical Thinking

1. Consider yourself a representative of the local school district. What information would you need in order to assess Mathias for inclusion in your special education programming?

2. What procedures would you follow for this screening?

3. Provided that the IEP team determined eligibility for special education services, what would you do to support Mathias's grandparents in his educational process?

SUPPORTING FAMILIES WITH CHILDREN WITH DISABILITIES AGES BIRTH THROUGH 5

Families of young children with disabilities are learning how to navigate their child's educational experiences. Professionals that work with these families need to support them in gaining knowledge in a variety of areas.

KNOWING WHAT IS TYPICAL AND WHAT IS ATYPICAL   A child may be referred to *early intervention* (EI) or *preschool special education* (PSE) by a pediatrician who has done a developmental screening at a well visit that shows concerns and is providing information on services available to the family. Or perhaps a preschool identifies red flags and a suggestion is made to families highlighting the concern. Very often, families are caught off guard when concerns first arise, especially if they are not already asking questions of their child's pediatrician about typical development or milestone concerns. This leads to the reason some educational professionals are reticent to bring up this sensitive subject, as they do not feel comfortable or knowledgeable enough to discuss it in detail with families. It is important for educational professionals to understand typical development, when to discuss delays with families, and when to refer children for special education evaluation.

Many families with a child that has special needs may not be referred for services right away, or they may not be ready to accept that their child is "different" from peers. Friends, family members that have young children, or even their child's pediatrician may share a "wait and see" attitude; discussing the possibility of a disability is difficult. It is not uncommon for one parent to have a feeling something isn't right and for the other to dismiss these concerns, often due to a lack of understanding of typical development by all involved. Families often compare children to each other, which can be misleading, as every child develops at their own rate, in their own way. Families should be aware of typical child development and developmental milestones such as those outlined in Table 9.1.

KNOWING PARENT GROUPS IN THE AREA THAT CAN GIVE INFORMATION ABOUT SERVICES   Parent groups are often great resources for connecting families. These groups can help families navigate services. In addition, these groups can facilitate families coming together to deal with the common issues that arise when raising a child with a disability.

There are usually large national organizations that organize parent support groups and may have parent groups in the local area. The Autism Society of America, for example, is well known in the autism community for having parent support groups nationwide. The more common the disability, the more common it is to find a parent group in your local area. Grassroots parent groups may not be sophisticated enough to have a widely known presence but can provide families with much needed support. It is good to review the group's mission to understand its focus to determine if what the members believe and practice is beneficial to families. It is important that professionals working with children with disabilities research these organizations so they are comfortable referring parents to organizations in their area.

KNOWING HOW TO ADVOCATE FOR THE CHILD   As stated earlier, family involvement leads to positive gains over time for the child and family. When the family is working with their child, seeing progress provides an awareness of their child's capabilities. In this situation, many families become advocates for their child, letting professionals know that their child is capable of many great things when provided the appropriate opportunities and services.

Not every family, however, is comfortable advocating for their child. As discussed in Chapter 2, family system structures vary. Some families are able to support advocacy, but others may not feel comfortable in doing so. Many factors may play into this situation, including parents' education level, cultural differences, and socioeconomic pressures. In these situations, it is critical that families are encouraged to provide input on their child's education. Special education professionals must work to support the family's ideas while guiding the family through understanding best practices found in research. Family involvement is an important part of the educational process; professionals must respect families as critical players in their child's education.

Summary

The addition of a new child to a family is an exciting prospect. When families receive news of an addition, they greet the prospect with expectations that their child will grow and develop in a typical manner. In the first 5 years of life, children experience rapid growth in all aspects of development, including physical development, cognitive development, and social-emotional development. Not all children grow at the same pace, but there are milestones that each child is expected to reach by a specified time. There are times when families discover that their infant or child has or is at risk of developing a disability. When this happens, families seek services to help their children reach their full potential.

Services for infants and toddlers with or at risk of developing disabilities are provided under Part C of the IDEA. This includes early intervention services, provided by a number of different specialists, outlined in a individual family service plan. Early intervention services have been federally mandated for more than 30 years to promote a child's future success in school and provide families with the ability to care for and support their child's development. Overall, families have found these services to be beneficial, but special education professionals need to work with families of infants and toddlers with disabilities to support growth and success.

Special education services are also provided for older preschool-aged children with disabilities under Part B of the IDEA. These services include the development of an individualized education plan provided in the least restrictive environment. Families of pre-school-aged children are very important to the child's development. It is critical that special education professionals help families gain knowledge of typical and atypical development, parent support groups, and how to advocate for their child.

Additional Resources

Web-Based

Center for Parent Information and Resources, Parent participation in early intervention: http://www.parentcenterhub.org/repository/parent-participation-ei/

Early Childhood Technical Assistance Center: http://ectacenter.org/.

Early Learning: Preparing my child for school: http://www2.ed.gov/about/inits/ed/earlylearning/index.html.

First Signs, educating parents and professionals about autism and related disorders: http://www.firstsigns.org/.

Frank Porter Graham Child Development Institute, the University of North Carolina at Chapel Hill: http://fpg.unc.edu/projects/national-center-early-development-learning

National Early Intervention Longitudinal Study: https://www.sri.com/sites/default/files/publications/neils_finalreport_200702.pdf.

TRACE Tracking, Referral and Assessment Center for Excellence: http://www.tracecenter.info/

Zero to Three Early Experiences Matter: http://www.zerotothree.org/parenting-resources/.

Print

Küpper, L. (Ed.). (2014, September). Procedures for IFSP development, review, and evaluation (Module 5). Building the legacy for our youngest children with disabilities: A training curriculum on Part C of IDEA 2004. Washington, DC: National Dissemination Center for Children with Disabilities.

10

THE PRIMARY SCHOOL YEARS

MELISSA E. HUDSON
East Carolina University

"Growth is endless and our lives change and change us beyond anticipation."

—Clara Park (1982)

LEARNING OBJECTIVES

Specifically, after reading this chapter, you will be able to:

1. Identify ways to communicate effectively with families.

2. Describe strategies to help young children with disabilities transition successfully to elementary school.

3. Provide supports to help children with disabilities make friends.

4. Facilitate the development of communication skills for children with disabilities.

5. Access resources for teaching self-determination skills.

6. Describe how peer tutoring can be used to teach important skills to children with disabilities (e.g., social, self-determination, academic).

7. Understand the **individualized education program plan (IEP)**, the IEP process, and the collaborative team process.

For many families, beginning elementary school is an exciting time—the first step in a process that, if all goes as planned, will end with their child graduating from high school with a diploma, prepared to continue their journey into adulthood. In anticipation of the day, a new backpack filled with school supplies waits by the door for their kindergartener to carry to school. Tears may be shed, but these tears are likely tears of joy and anticipation for the good things to come.

For families of children with disabilities, the first day of school may evoke excitement as well, but other feelings are likely, too—feelings of fear and, possibly, disappointment (Smith, 2003). Feelings of fear may come from all of the unknowns surrounding the transition to elementary school. What will the new teacher be like? Will they take care of my child? Will my child be happy in the new school? The concerns of families may be even greater when their child has complex medical needs (e.g., tube feeding, seizures) due to the high level of care their child requires. Feelings of disappointment may come from the fact that their child's school experience will be different from the one their family imagined for them. This cycle (i.e., fear–disappointment–adjustment) will be repeated throughout their child's time in school. This chapter specifically addresses transitions commonly experienced in elementary school. While transitions can be stressful times, teachers and professionals can support families by preparing them for these events and can support children with disabilities by teaching them important communication, social, and **self-determination skills**.

COMMUNICATING WITH FAMILIES

Receiving information about their child's school day, classroom, and school events can help alleviate some of the apprehension family members feel at times of transition (Duncan & Brooks-Gunn,

2000). First and foremost, family members want to understand what happens during their child's school day. This information is particularly important when the child is unable to share about their day themselves, such as when a child has complex communication needs. Ongoing, informal, daily communication helps establish trust and build rapport between the family and the classroom teacher. Teachers can accomplish this with a simple school-to-home communication notebook that contains a brief summary of what happened during the child's day. Davern (2004) and Graham-Clay (2005) offer several strategies teachers can use to enhance the effectiveness of school-to-home notebooks. First, make it clear to families from the start what information will be communicated, by whom, and how often. Second, keep a balance between good and bad news in a message. Sometimes a face-to-face meeting is more appropriate if the topic is serious. Third, avoid educational jargon and acronyms that will likely be confusing and meaningless to families. Last, set a respectful tone by using titles to address the family members (e.g., Mr., Mrs., Ms., Dr.).

It is also important for family members to know what is happening in their child's classroom (e.g., upcoming events, new units of study, the arrival of a new classroom pet). Not only will this help families feel more a part of their child's school day, this information will enable families to make important connections from school to home with their child (e.g., "Oh, I see you got a new pet hamster in your classroom"). Classroom newsletters have traditionally been used to provide this information to families, but teachers can create classroom blogs that accomplish the same goal if family members use or have access to technology. If so, classroom blogs are quicker to produce and easier to update and maintain than paper newsletters (as well as much friendlier on the environment). Teachers can find free online blog platforms (e.g., Edublog, Weebly) to create their classroom blog and the steps for creating and maintaining a blog from the World Wide Web.

Whether it's a note, newsletter, or class blog, to make the most of a written communication with families, Graham-Clay (2005) recommends using everyday language with a readability level of sixth grade or less that is free of education jargon and proofing carefully for grammar and spelling errors before publishing or sending it home. In addition, a checklist (Nagro, 2015) called PROSE can be helpful to teachers in improving school-to-home written communication. The acronym PROSE stands for the different elements of print communication: (a) print, (b) readability, (c) organization, (d) structure, and (e) ease (see Figure 10.1). Apply the checklist to written communication to identify any areas that might be unclear to the reader.

Family members also need information about their child's school. Events scheduled throughout the year (e.g., back-to-school night, parent–teacher conferences) will be organized by the student's school. Teachers can help family members attend these events by making sure they know about the events and by encouraging them to attend. Families for whom English is not their native language will need information about these events translated into their primary language.

Likewise, teachers need tools for communicating with difficult parents. First, have a healthy respect for the different roles you both play in the education of the child. Being a parent is a hard job—especially for parents of children with disabilities. Parents are also an integral part of your job as a teacher and alienating them will not help you accomplish your job. Second, be proactive and positive in your interactions with parents to avoid problems from the start. For example, begin an IEP meeting by sharing a positive personal story about the child. This communicates to parents that you know and care about their child. Also, if parents receive frequent communications from school about problems involving their child, make sure to communicate with them at least as often about good things involving their child, no matter how small. Parents will appreciate your time and effort.

Third, when a parent is angry, consider that the anger may not be caused by the immediate situation but rather stem from the loss they perceive related to their child's disability (Kübler-Ross, 1969; Kübler-Ross & Kessler, 2005). While you may be able to do little in this situation

FIGURE 10.1 ■ **PROSE Checklist for Improving School-to-Home Written Communication**	
P	Print • All one font • Consistent font size throughout • Running text is medium font (e.g., 12-point font) • Sentence-case print rather than all capitals or italics • Selective use of highlighting or bold print to draw attention rather than to decorate
R	Readability • Reading level is ideally fifth grade but not higher than eighth grade • Multisyllabic words are limited so most words are one or two syllables • Sentences are 10 to 15 words long ideally but no more than 25 words • Longer sentences are broken into several shorter sentences • Prepositional phrases are limited to shorter sentence length
O	Organization • Predictable left-to-right, top-to-bottom layout • Headings guide the reader and are set apart from running text • Diagrams (lists, tables, charts, and graphs) are set apart from the running text • Diagrams (lists, tables, charts, and graphs) are simple (no more than 15 labels and 75 items) • Diagrams (lists, tables, charts, and graphs) are labeled and self-explanatory
S	Structure • Ideally one page or broken into sections • Page numbers are provided for documents longer than one page • Balance white space so text is not overly dense • Images and figures supplement the content rather than serve as decoration
E	Ease • Written in the active voice • Pronouns replaced by the original nouns so sentences have no more than one pronoun • Terms written out rather than using acronyms unless the acronym is widely known to parents • Real-world examples are included when possible

For more information about the PROSE Checklist, see the full article by Sarah Nagro (2015) in *Teaching Exceptional Children, 47*(5), 256–263.

except be supportive of the parent, keeping this in mind could help to not take the parent's anger personally. Fourth, when problem solving for a difficult child, ask parents how they manage similar situations at home. Pose leading questions to parents to get a picture of the child at home (e.g., What do you do at home when…?) and then relate this information to the school setting. For example, recently a special education teacher needed to stop a child from running away from her classroom. The teacher knew from completing an ABC chart (Alberto & Troutman, 2006) that just before the child ran away, she would spin in a tight circle. She asked the parent if the child ever ran away at home and, if so, what the parent did when this happened. Taking this approach kept the parent from feeling attacked (or blamed). In addition, the parent also provided information during the conversation that ultimately helped the teacher develop an effective plan to stop the child from running away. The teacher learned from the parent that the child loved to play in water. To stop the child from running from the classroom, the teacher used a water play area to redirect the child's attention when she started spinning.

In addition to these tools for dealing with difficult parents, teachers should always keep good documentation of their communications with parents and keep the appropriate professionals (e.g., building principal, director of special education) apprised of any interactions with difficult parents so they, too, may be proactive in dealing with potential problems.

Barriers to Effective Communication With Families

Effective communication is important for positive home–school relationships, but **barriers to communication** can hinder the communication efforts of teachers and others. Graham-Clay (2005) states that barriers to communication may exist on several levels, including societal, cultural, economic, technological, and school. On a societal level, family members are busy people who can easily feel unsupported and overwhelmed by daily demands (Taffel, 2001). Local schools can help address this barrier by providing workshops for families to address these needs (e.g., child development, stress management). On a cultural level, significant cultural differences between teachers and **families** can create communication challenges (Columbo, 2004). To avoid this, teachers should educate themselves about the cultures of their students' families and incorporate various cultures into their classrooms (e.g., providing diverse children's books, providing snacks from various cultures). Kasahara and Turnbull (2005) warn, though, that learning about culture is not enough—teachers need to understand the uniqueness of individual families within their cultural milieu to communicate effectively.

Economic and time constraints may also be significant barriers to communication (Finders & Lewis, 1994), to which flexibility and creativity are often effective remedies. Ask family members about their schedules at the beginning of the year so that convenient meeting times can be found. Also, to improve family participation, provide alternative places for meetings, such as a local community building or a family's home, as well as childcare and transportation for families who need it.

It is hard to imagine in this day and age, but a lack of technology access can also limit communication opportunities for many families (Ramirez, 2001). Ask families at the beginning of the year what technology they use, including Internet, voice mail, email, and computers, and plan communications accordingly.

Last, on a school level, it is important for educators to remember that nothing **breaks down communication** faster than a conversation or note full of educational jargon. To family members, educational jargon is meaningless. For this reason, all conversations and written communications to families need to be jargon free. In addition, the use of technical terms or acronyms should be avoided, as these are often hard for families to understand. When they are used, the technical

---

CASE STUDY 1
SOPHIA AND HER FAMILY

Sophia is a 6-year-old first-grade student with deafblindness. She lives with her mother, father, and sister. Her parents are native Spanish speakers, and Spanish is the primary language spoken at home.

Questions for Critical Thinking

1. What are some particular concerns Sophia's parents might have about Sophia beginning first grade due to her deafblindness?

2. What steps might need to be taken to ensure effective communication with Sophia's parents?

3. If you are not a native Spanish speaker, how might you go about translating the information that you need to communicate? What supports are available to help you in your school or community?

terms or acronyms should be thoroughly explained, and families should be encouraged to ask for clarification if they are unsure about the meaning.

TRANSITION TO ELEMENTARY SCHOOL

Few things are scarier than the unknown. It is important to prepare children with disabilities and their families for upcoming **transitions**, especially transitions that involve major changes to settings, routines, and expectations. These transitions will likely be stressful times for both children with disabilities and their families. One of the most effective ways to ease the stress for children and their families is to help them learn about the new school and all that comes with it (Duncan & Brooks-Gunn, 2000).

There are several approaches families may take to learn about their child's new school. Taking a look at the school's website can be helpful in obtaining general information about the school, such as when the school day begins and ends. For more specific information, a school visit can be scheduled to see the school building and meet their child's new teachers and school administrators. As the first day of school draws near, most schools offer an event (e.g., back-to-school night) for new and returning families to visit the school. Some common questions families ask about schools are:

1. What should I do before my child starts school?
2. What will my child's teacher expect of my child?
3. What can I do at home to help my child succeed in school?
4. How can I tell how well my child is doing in school?
5. How can I get the most out of parent–teacher conferences?

> For a discussion of these and other frequently asked questions families ask about schools, see *Questions Parents Ask about Schools* at: http://www2.ed.gov/parents/academic/help/questions/questions.pdf

Transitions can also be scary for children, and like their families, learning about their new school can also help them transition successfully. Several ideas for accomplishing this are described in this chapter, but keep in mind that these ideas should be adapted to meet the individual needs of the child with disabilities.

One way to facilitate transition to a new school is to involve the child and their teachers early in the individualized education program (IEP) planning process (Hains, Fowler, & Chandler, 1988; Martin et al., 2006; Morningstar et al., 2010). For example, at the IEP meeting prior to beginning elementary school, the sending teacher invites the receiving teacher to collaborate on the child's IEP goals and objectives. For children moving from kindergarten to elementary school, the meeting would include the current kindergarten teacher and the new elementary teacher. For children moving from elementary to middle school, the meeting would include the current elementary teacher and the new middle school teacher. This kind of collaboration allows important information sharing and sets a positive tone for the child's move.

Before the move, the child may spend a day (or more depending on the child's needs) at the new school. A paraeducator can accompany the child to the new school to provide support for the child as needed and also to learn about the new school environment along with the child. Information about the new school can then be shared with the sending teacher, who can emphasize aspects of the new school with the child throughout the remainder of the school year (e.g., "Luis, you will have a locker to put your things in next year.") A one-day visit may be too brief of a time period for some children to have a meaningful experience. For these children, more time can be planned for visiting the new school so that when the time comes, they know what to expect in their new school setting.

In addition to visiting the new school, many children can benefit from a book, movie, or DVD about their new school custom-made for them (Aronson, 1995; Ramirez, 2001). The idea is to use pictures or video taken at the new school that capture the child's day from beginning to end, just as they will experience it when they begin attending. If the child is transported to school on a school bus, the book/video might begin at the bus stop; if the child is dropped off at school, the book/video can start at the school's entrance. A new teacher and classroom are featured until the entire school day is presented. New teachers can share a little about themselves, their classrooms, and their feelings of excitement about meeting the child when school starts.

To create a book, pictures are placed on one page and text about the picture on the facing page, or a picture and text can be placed on each page. Text may need to be simplified depending on how the book is used (e.g., as a read-aloud or read independently by the child). The pages of the book can be laminated to increase durability and, when complete, put together in a three-ring binder. Families can read the book aloud to their child, or children who can read independently may prefer to read the book for themselves. If being used as a read-aloud, a second- to third-grade reading level is recommended for the text (see Browder, Trela, & Jimenez, 2007, for guidelines on adapting text). To create a movie or DVD from photographs, use a program readily available on most computers (e.g., Windows Movie Maker; Windows DVD Maker).

For children with visual impairments, a tactile book can be made about their new school as well. To be meaningful, objects or parts of objects that remind them of their visit to the new school should be included in the book. For example, a piece of chalk might be included for a teacher if the chalk reminds the child of the teacher. The objects serve the same purpose as photographs do for sighted children. For guidelines on creating a tactile book for a child with visual impairments, see Lewis and Tolla (2003) or visit the Texas School for the Blind website (http://www.tsbvi.edu/).

To optimize the interest of the child, consider how the child would most like the book (or movie or DVD) presented. For example, some children may be most interested in the new people they will meet or a friend that is also attending the new school. If that is the case, the presentation of the book or video should highlight the people at the school (e.g., teachers, peers). Other ideas include having a friend narrate the movie/DVD or act as a guide through the book. Other children may be more interested in the activities they are going to do at their new school. For these children, the presentation of the book or DVD can focus on the child's daily activities (e.g., first period is math, second period is science). Remember to include important administrators and support staff in the book or video, as well as familiar faces from their old school (e.g., friends, speech-language therapist). This will help the child transition smoothly from their old school to their new school.

Adjusting to a Longer School Day

Some children with disabilities will find adjusting to a longer school day challenging. In preschool, children likely attended a morning or afternoon program for part of the day. In elementary school, the school day will be 6 hours or more. Young children may find the new routines and activities exhausting. Families can help children adjust to the new school routine by setting a consistent bedtime that allows them to get enough rest. Teachers may need to consider adding in some downtime for very young children so that they can rest. These periods can be eliminated when they are no longer needed. For other children, it may be necessary to gradually build up to attending school for a full day. If families anticipate that the transition to elementary school will be particularly difficult on their child, they might consider arranging for their child to attend the new school during their kindergarten year on a regular basis to help them adjust to the longer school day.

Supporting Communication Skills

Times of transition highlight the need for good communication skills for all, including the child with disabilities. The ways children with disabilities communicate can vary greatly—some may use spoken words, others may use manual signs or facial grimaces; and still others may use a combination of gestures and vocalizations. For many children with disabilities, improving their communication skills will be a major focus at school and at home. An in-depth discussion of the needs of children with complex communication needs is beyond the scope of this chapter. Rather, the goal of this section is to highlight some strategies, assessments, and resources teachers and families can use to support a child's communication efforts.

While the way individuals communicate varies, the reasons they communicate do not. According to Light (1997), people communicate to accomplish four things: to express their needs and wants (e.g., "I'd like popcorn for a snack today, please"), engage in social closeness (e.g., best friends chat about a recent movie), share information (e.g., telling the school nurse you feel sick), and to fulfill the established conventions of social etiquette (e.g., "Hi. How are you?").

When some children enter elementary school, they use early communicative behaviors such as nonspeech vocalizations, motor behaviors, gestures, facial expressions, and eye gaze to communicate. For these children, the success of their communication efforts depends largely on the responsiveness of their communication partner (Beukelman & Mirenda, 2013). At school, communication partners may be teachers, therapists and other professionals, school staff, and peers. At home, communication partners may be family members, neighbors, or other people in the child's community. To be effective at supporting the child's early communicative behaviors, communication partners need to have a positive attitude, expect that the learner is communicating, and respond to subtle cues from a learner (Siegel-Causey & Bashinski, 1997).

Many of the communication efforts of early communicators are idiosyncratic, or specific to the child, and are only understood by those that know them well. For example, a mother might say that she just "knows" that her son wants a different toy when he taps the toy he is playing with on the floor. It is because of her experience with her son and not the tapping behavior specifically that she knows what he wants. People without such rich experiences with the child will not know what the child means or how to respond appropriately. When communication partners are unable to respond to the communication efforts of a child, this is known as a communication breakdown.

One strategy that can help communication partners avoid communication breakdowns with early communicators is through the use of a gesture dictionary. A gesture dictionary describes the child's gestures, along with their meanings, and makes suggestions for appropriate responses (Beukelman & Mirenda, 2013). The dictionary can be in the form of a poster that hangs on the wall in the classroom or as an alphabetized notebook that travels with the child. To make the gesture dictionary easier for communication partners to use, entries should be cross-referenced. For example, using the toy example, two entries would be created under "T" in the gesture dictionary—one for "tap" and one for "toys." Both entries would describe the meaning of the tapping behavior and how to respond (e.g., Tapping the toy he is playing with on the floor means he wants you to give him a different toy. Prompt him to sign "toy" and then give him a new toy).

Other children with complex communication needs are just beginning to use signals intentionally to gain attention and accept and reject things in their environment. These children will need many opportunities to practice using these signals during naturally occurring activities across their time at school and home. One way to do this is through the use of a scripted routine. A scripted routine is created around a typical activity in a child's day (e.g., going swimming, getting ready for bed) and includes five elements: a touch cue, a verbal cue, a pause, verbal feedback, and an action (Beukelman & Mirenda, 2013).

Scripted routines are created using the steps needed to complete the activity (i.e., task analysis). Touch cues give nonverbal information to the child about what is about to happen. Verbal cues are the words said while providing the touch cues. Pauses (i.e., 10–30 seconds) allow the child time to respond to the touch and verbal cues. Verbal feedback is the words said about what the child did and what will happen next. The action step is the step in the routine that was identified through a task analysis. Table 10.1 contains an example of a scripted routine created for a young child with blindness and intellectual disability who is preparing to ride a horse during a therapeutic horseback riding lesson. The child needs to wear a safety belt around their waist, so the scripted routine is built around accomplishing this task.

Other children with disabilities will have some understanding of symbols and they may communicate using objects, pictures, picture symbols (e.g., Boardmaker™ Picture Symbols; www.mayer-johnson.com), manual signs, spoken words, and/or written or brailed words. For these children, it is important that teachers and family members present information and provide communication supports in a form the child understands. For example, a child may need an object schedule for their daily routine instead of a written-word schedule printed on the board because they don't yet understand written words, but they do know that when they see a piece of a carpet square on their object schedule, it is time for morning circle.

TABLE 10.1 ■ Example of a Scripted Routine					
Steps	Touch Cue	Verbal Cue	Pause	Verbal Feedback	Action
1.	Rub seat belt under child's elbow. Release buckle so a sound is made.	*It's time to get ready to ride.*	Pause, observe.	*Okay, I see you smiling; You really like horseback riding.*	Continue to step 2.
2.	Rub belt under wrist.	*It's time to put on your belt.*	Pause, observe.	*I hear you laughing; I'll help you put the belt around.*	Continue to step 3.
3.	Pat his back where belt will go around.	*I'm going to put the belt on you now.*	Pause, observe.	*I see you looking at the belt; I am going to put the belt on now.*	Put belt around child and continue to step 4.
4.	Put pressure on belt where it is around child.	*Okay, the belt is around you, time to lean back.*	Pause, observe.	*Nice job! You leaned back in the seat.*	Make sure child is in the seat properly and continue to step 5.
5.	Tap the belt buckle to make noise and rub it under arm if possible.	*It's time to buckle that belt.*	Pause, observe.	*I see you nodding; I'm going to help you buckle the belt now.*	Buckle belt and continue to step 6.
6.	Tap child's hand.	*You are all ready to ride.*	Pause, observe.	*I see you smiling and looking toward the riding ring. Enjoy your ride!*	Lead horse to riding ring.

Source: Adapted from Lillian Reinisch's Scripted Routine for a therapeutic riding lesson.

Generally, children develop symbolic understanding following a continuum from least to most abstract: objects, color photographs, black-and-white photographs, miniature objects, black-and-white line drawings, logos, written words. This continuum is a guideline for symbolic development and is not set in stone. Additionally, children can understand more than one form at once and do not have to master one form before moving on to another. Other factors, such as motivation and opportunity, can influence what a child understands about a particular symbol as well. For example, even though many children are not able to read the word "McDonald's", they understand what the golden arches mean when they see the logo. In order to support comprehension, it is good practice to pair words with objects, pictures, and picture symbols (Abbott & Lucey, 2005; Detheridge & Detheridge, 2013). By pairing the written word with objects or pictures, children learn to assign meaning to the word (a more abstract form) from their experience with less abstract forms.

In order for effective instruction and communication supports to be given to children with **complex communication needs**, it is important that teachers and families understand how the child is currently communicating. Several communication assessments exist that can provide teachers and families with this information. One such assessment is the Communication Matrix (Rowland, 2004a, 2004b). The **Communication Matrix** is appropriate for individuals of all ages who are at the earliest stages of communication, including children with severe and multiple disabilities. The **Communication Matrix** is available in three ways: online (www.designtolearn. com), in a version for teachers and professionals (Rowland, 2004a), and in a parent-friendly version (Rowland, 2004b). The **Communication Matrix** involves two major aspects of communication: (1) the reasons people communicate (i.e., refuse, obtain, social, information) and (2) the behaviors people use to communicate (i.e., pre-intentional behavior, intentional behavior, unconventional

CASE STUDY 2
CHANDRA

Chandra is a 5-year-old kindergartener with CHARGE syndrome. Chandra can't wait to get to school each morning and smiles and vocalizes when she arrives. Her favorite place in the classroom is the play area, where she quickly finds her favorite toys on her own. Chandra explores the toys by putting them really close to her eyes and turning them over and over. Chandra also likes mealtime. She smiles and reaches toward her spoon when the food is something she likes (e.g., spaghetti, macaroni and cheese). Another thing Chandra likes to do is to play music on an iPad. Her teacher makes the room really dark so Chandra can see the strong visuals on the iPad that accompany the music Chandra makes. As you might have already guessed, Chandra is a happy girl who really likes people. Her teacher made a tactile cue for each of the important people in her life. When the teacher shows her a tactile cue for one of her "people," a big smile lights up her face. Chandra follows routines well with prompts and can use single words purposefully (e.g., saying "stop" to stop an activity). During circle-time activities, Chandra also uses pictures for choice making.

Questions for Critical Thinking

1. Chandra communicates with the people around her in several different ways. What are some of the ways she communicates?

2. What strategies from the chapter might you use to facilitate her current communication skills?

3. What strategies might you use to help her gain new communication skills?

communication, conventional communication, concrete symbols, abstract symbols, and language). Once the assessment is completed, the results are summarized in a one-page profile that shows the communication behaviors of the child at a glance. Teachers and families can each complete the Communication Matrix and compare differences in the ways a child communicates at home and at school. Table 10.2 contains information about the Communication Matrix (Rowland, 2004a, 2004b) and other communication assessments that can provide helpful information for addressing the communication needs of children with disabilities.

Supporting Friendships

Friendships are important for everyone, and as children with disabilities begin elementary school, they have more opportunities to make friends with children their own age; however, they may need

TABLE 10.2 ■ Communication Assessments for Children With Disabilities			
Communication Assessment	**Available From**	**Description**	**Cost**
All Kids Communicate	http://www.transitioncoalition.org/transition/tcfiles/files/docs/All_Kids_Communicate-_with_tabs1258861243.pdf/All_Kids_Communicate-_with_tabs.pdf	How to build and use a communication dictionary with nonsymbolic learners	Free online
Communication Matrix	https://www.communicationmatrix.org/ Matrix PDF (Parent and Professional versions) https://www.designtolearn.com/products/20	An assessment instrument designed for individuals of all ages who function at the earliest stages of communication and who use any form of communication	Free online Download-able PDF $5.00
Design to Learn: An Environmental Inventory	https://www.designtolearn.com/content/design-learn-inventory	Designed to track the opportunities to learn communication and object interaction skills provided in classroom activities for a specific child	$10.00 for 1; $93.00 for 10
Every Move Counts Clicks and Chats manual (Korsten, J. E., Foss, T. V., & Berry, L. M., 2007)	EMC Communication, Inc. 11944 W. 95th Street #281 Lenexa, KS 66214 http://www.everymovecounts.net/index.html	A sensory-based approach to communication and assistive technology for individuals with significant sensory motor differences, developmental differences, or autism	$90.00, plus $10.00 shipping and handling per manual
Tangible Symbol System	https://www.designtolearn.com/products/tangible_symbol_systems	Designed for people who are unable to understand the meaning of the abstract symbols used in formal language systems. The illustrated manual shows how to teach individuals to communicate using tangible symbols: objects or pictures that represent items, people, and events in their daily lives.	Manual: $50.00 DVD: $55.00

help from teachers and family members for this to happen. Children as young as 3 years are able to make friends, and usually friendships form around an activity both youngsters enjoy (Parker, Rubin, Earth, Wojslawowicz, & Buskirk, 2006). Children understand at an early age about friendship. When Heyne, Schleien, and McAvoy (1994) asked young children with disabilities participating in the Dowling Friendship Program who a friend is, their responses are insightful: a friend is someone who eats lunch with me, someone who plays with me, and someone who is nice to me. When these same children were asked what they like to do with friends, their responses included typical childhood activities (e.g., play with my toys, go swimming).

Friendships are enjoyable and give children with disabilities opportunities to build important social skills (Bukowski, Newcomb, & Hartup, 1996). Conversely, without friends, children with disabilities may experience feelings of anxiety, depression, and social withdrawal (Berndt, 2004). Children with disabilities are likely to have more trouble making friends than their peers without disabilities, especially children with developmental disabilities, challenging behaviors, or autism (Geisthardt, Brotherson, & Cook, 2002; Odom et al., 2006). In addition, friendships are not likely to develop just because children are in the same place at the same time (Geisthardt et al., 2002).

Fortunately, there are steps teachers and families can take to encourage the growth of friendships between children with and without disabilities. In a review of the literature on friendships and children with disabilities, Meyer and Ostrosky (2014) found teachers used both active and passive strategies for supporting and maintaining friendships. Passive strategies included letting children choose their own friends and providing time for free play (Hollingsworth & Buysse, 2009). Active strategies included facilitating two children's (a dyad) interactions or play (Hollingsworth & Buysse, 2009), commenting on children's play (Buysse, Goldman, & Skinner, 2003), discussing with children what it means to be friends (Hollingsworth & Buysse, 2009), modeling for children how to communicate and develop friendships (Buysse, 1993), and teaching social skills, such as how to share (Buysse, 1993; Hollingsworth & Buysse, 2009). Two strategies missing from the studies (but supported by research) are planning favorite activities to support a friendship (Hollingsworth & Buysse, 2009) and making contact with a child's family to help arrange out-of-school experiences with peers (Buysse et al., 2003). The use of these strategies offers effective ways for teachers to facilitate the friendships of young children with disabilities.

The time children with disabilities spend at home with their families can also be used for friendship building. In an exploratory study of 26 families with children with disabilities, Geisthardt et al. (2002) examined the friendships of children with disabilities, 3 to 10 years old, at home. From their work, four themes emerged around the topic of building friendships at home: contact with peers, attitudes influencing friendships, the family's focus on friendship, and the physical environment's influence on friendships. Findings from theme one (i.e., contact with peers) indicate that children with disabilities spent less time with peers without disabilities than their nondisabled siblings, and of the children with disabilities, children with behavioral problems and significant cognitive limitations spent the least amount of time with peers without disabilities.

Findings from theme two (i.e., attitudes influencing friendships) indicate that families believe that other children were more accepting of their child with disabilities when their child spent more time with them. On the other hand, families believe that the parents of children without disabilities were more hesitant to invite their child with disabilities over to play because the parents without children with disabilities perceived that the child with disabilities required a lot of assistance.

Findings from theme three (i.e., parents' focus on friendships) indicate that families took some steps to involve their child with other children (e.g., selecting homes in neighborhoods with lots of children, involving their child in community groups, arranging playdates) but rarely reported doing anything to increase their child's opportunities to interact with peers. Most families supervised their children while playing with peers as a safety precaution, intervening only when necessary.

Findings from theme four (i.e., physical environment influencing friendships) indicate that the play spaces in some homes were hard for children with disabilities to access (e.g., stairs); many children lived in close proximity to other children (i.e., subdivisions), but having other children around did not guarantee peer interactions; and children living in more isolated areas or off busy roads had limited peer contact.

Additionally, how a child with disabilities is perceived by their peers can affect friendships (Schaffner & Buswell, 1992). To set a positive tone, for instance, a child with disabilities can share his/her special interests or talents with peers. This helps peers view the child with disabilities as a competent individual. Another idea is to provide accommodations and/or adapt the environment so that the child with disabilities can be involved with other children in meaningful ways. Being perceived as competent by peers without disabilities is a critical factor for friendships (Siperstein & Leffert, 1997).

Since many friendships are built around a common interest or activity, teachers and families can encourage friendship between children with disabilities and their peers through recreation (Heyne, Schleien, & McAvoy, 2003).

What school staff can do:

- Include social and recreation skills in curricula.
- Assign friends to the same classroom.
- Provide opportunities for families to become acquainted.
- Include friendship and recreation goals in the IEP.
- Train school personnel on children's friendships.
- Offer disability awareness training to families and children without disabilities.
- Tell families when friendships develop.

What families can do:

- Make friendship development a family priority.
- Become acquainted with other families in their neighborhood.
- Schedule times together with other children.
- Invite children into their home and on outings.
- Discuss the needs of their child with other parents so they can become comfortable assuming responsibility for them.
- Discuss children's friendships at home.
- Encourage positive social interactions.
- Learn about community recreation resources their child might be interested in (e.g., YMCA, community centers).

Supporting Self-Determination Skills

Self-determination is an important lifelong process often associated with transition to adulthood and adult abilities; however, the foundation for **self-determination** begins early in childhood (Palmer, 2010). Research with elementary- and middle school–aged children with disabilities has demonstrated that young children can learn important self-determination skills associated with self-determined behavior (Palmer & Wehmeyer, 2003; Reid, Trout, and Schwartz, 2005). These skills include (but are not limited to): choice making, decision making, problem solving, goal setting and attainment, self-advocacy and leadership skills, self-awareness, and self-knowledge (Wehmeyer,

CASE STUDY 3

AHMAD

Ahmad is an 8-year-old third grader with physical disabilities, including cerebral palsy. Ahmad's physical disabilities require him to use a wheelchair and other adapted seating and modifications, including a prone stander (e.g., device that supports vertical stance) and walker during the school day. The cerebral palsy impacts Ahmad's spoken language as well, although he understands what is said to him. Ahmad has a small spoken vocabulary of words related to his environment, such as "eat," "drink," "done," "home," and he is beginning to verbalize "yes" and "no." Ahmad has seizures that are controlled with medications. He smiles and laughs when excited. Ahmad is very interested in participating in activities with his classmates, but his classmates struggle to include him.

Questions for Critical Thinking

1. What strategies might you use to help support the development of friendships between Ahmad and his classmates?

2. How might you approach Ahmad's parents about the topic of friendship?

2003). For young children, developing these skills is a place to start in moving toward self-determined behavior later in life (Palmer, 2010).

Many families of young children with disabilities may be unfamiliar with the construct of self-determination. It is important that teachers and families understand that self-determination may be different for each person and is focused on obtaining a level of independence for the individual that is rooted within the family's and culture's beliefs and values (Lahat, Helwig, Yang, Ran, & Liu, 2008).

Teachers and families alike can foster self-determination skills in young children. Table 10.3 describes developmentally appropriate expectations for elementary-aged children in three areas (i.e., How I Learn to Know Myself, Finding What I Would Like to Know, and Planning for the Future; Palmer, 2010). Each expectation is written from the perspective of the child and includes clear steps teachers and families can take to facilitate self-determination skills for children with disabilities. For example, when families and teachers teach an elementary-aged child when it is okay to talk, what to say, and with whom it is all right to talk, she learns to communicate her ideas and thoughts to others (i.e., self-advocacy). Self-advocacy is discussed in detail in Chapters 11 and 12.

A free online resource is available from the Beach Center entitled *A Parents' Guide to the Self-Determined Learning Model for Early Elementary Students* (Palmer & Wehmeyer, 2002). The guide includes an introduction to the Self-Determined Learning Model of Instruction (SDLMI) as well as a list of children's books about problem solving (Appendix A) and sample forms to teach self-determination skills (Appendix C).

Another free online resource guide, *Fostering Self-Determination Among Children and Youth with Disabilities—Ideas From Parents for Parents* (Weir, Crooney, Walter, Moss, & Carter, n.d.) was written by parents and includes practical ideas for teaching self-determination skills to children with disabilities. For example, three of the ideas shared to teach choice making were to model a choice-making process, provide opportunities for children to make choices throughout the day, and to use visuals (e.g., pictures, symbols) and words to encourage children to make choices.

TABLE 10.3 ■ Developmentally Appropriate Expectations for Elementary-Aged Children	
How I Learn to Know Myself	• I want to feel good about myself and know that this is important. • I need to know how to communicate to make my ideas and thoughts known with others. You may need to help me learn when it is okay to talk, what to say, and with whom it is all right to talk. • I want you to know that I might not be the same as others my age, depending on my disability. But I will continue to grow and change and need help to understand this. • I have friends because I "talk" to others, they "listen" to me, and I "listen" to them. We have shared ideas, experiences, and fun. • I know what is good (foods, sleep) and bad (drugs, smoking) for my body. When I get sick, I should know it and be able to ask someone for help.
Finding What I Would Like to Know	• School can help me learn lots of new things. Encourage me to pay attention and do my work. • I should try different group and individual activities to find out what I enjoy doing in my free time. • I need to be responsible for my actions and what I say. If I need help with my schoolwork or with someone in school, please help me work on this, but don't do it for me. • I need to start learning about many different jobs from my family, teachers, and others.
Planning for the Future	• I should be able to make simple decisions at school and at home. Help me do this until I learn to do this myself. • I may need help to become an active participant in my meetings (educational planning or person-centered planning). • I should understand about different kinds of jobs and what kinds of ways people prepare for them.

Source: From Palmer, S. B. (2010). Self-determination: A life-span perspective. Focus on exceptional children, 42(6), 1–18. Copyright Love Publishing Company, 2010

Keeping Children With Disabilities Safe From Abuse and Neglect

Due to their unique needs (e.g., cognitive impairments, communication skill deficits), children with disabilities are a particularly vulnerable group for abuse and neglect. In fact, according to Sobsey (2002), children with disabilities are at least twice as likely to be abused or neglected as children without disabilities. Parents and professionals in all 50 states and the District of Columbia have a responsibility to report suspected abuse to police or child protection agencies (U.S. Department of Health and Human Services, Administration for Children and Families, Administration on Children, Youth and Families, Children's Bureau, 2013), so it is important to be aware of the signs of abuse (see Table 10.4). Many of these signs are ambiguous in and of themselves, but taken together or when an overall pattern or impression emerges, action may be required (Thuppal & Sobsey, 2004).

The risk for abuse and/or neglect can be reduced by educating children with disabilities about their right to be free from abuse and neglect. Similarly, as mentioned early in this chapter, a way to communicate with others is paramount. When children have a way to communicate, they can tell others about their feelings as well as any instances of abuse or neglect they may experience.

Supporting Participation in General Education

Many children with disabilities will receive instruction in general education classrooms for part or all of the day. Careful planning is necessary for children with disabilities to participate successfully in general education (Browder, Spooner, & Jimenez, 2011; Wolfe & Hall, 2003). To plan for successful experiences in inclusive educational settings for students with disabilities, consider the following:

- Is the class activity accessible (i.e., physically, visually, auditorily, tactilely) for the student? If not, what changes are needed? See the American Printing House for the Blind (APH, http://www.aph.org/) for resources that promote accessibility.
- How is the classroom environment laid out? Are changes needed?

TABLE 10.4 ■ Common Signs of Child Abuse	
All Forms of Abuse	**Physical Abuse** (continued)
Direct observation (tangible acts)	Aggression
Withdrawal	Unreported fractures
Resistance to touch	Patterned injury
Fear of specific caregivers	Temporarily dispersed injuries
Poor self-esteem	**Sexual Abuse**
Victimization of others	Genital irritation
Disclosure	Aggression
Escape behavior	Resistance to touch
Hypervigilance	Noncompliance
Sleep disturbances	Gender-specific fear
Passivity	Promiscuity
Reenactment	Threats
Fear of specific environments	Sexual precocity
Self-abuse	Withdrawal
Stoical responses to discomfort	Inappropriate sexual behavior
Inappropriate behavior	Unexplained pregnancy
Behavior regression	Sexually transmitted disease
Physical Abuse	**Neglect**
Frequent injury	Low affect
Unexplained coma	Dehydration
Noncompliance	Indifference to other people
Unexplained injury	Unusual need for attention
Threats	Poor nutritional status
Grab marks	Stoical responses to discomfort
Atypical injury	Untreated illness or injuries

Source: Adapted from Thuppal, M., & Sobsey, D. (2004). Children with special health care needs. In F. P., Orelove, D. Sobsey, & R. K. Silberman, (Eds.), *Educating children with multiple disabilities: A collaborative approach* (4th ed., pp. 311–377). Baltimore, MD: Paul H. Brookes Publishing Co., Inc. Reprinted with permission.

- What is the general education teacher's instruction like? Is it a good match to the student's style of learning? Are multiple ways for the student to engage with instruction provided? What adaptations (i.e., accommodations or modifications) might be needed?
- Are general education learning materials presented in multiple ways? Do the materials need to be adapted? If so, what is needed, and who will make the adaptations?
- Does the student have multiple ways of showing what they know? Do the expectations for learning need to be adjusted?

- How could an intervener, paraeducator, or peer tutor support the student?
- Are goals focused on alternate achievement standards linked to academic content needed?

COLLABORATION WITH GENERAL EDUCATION TEACHERS Academic instruction is typically rich in the general education classroom, and it is hard to duplicate an equivalent experience in a separate special education classroom. For this reason, collaborating with general education teachers for academic instruction is a good idea. In their article "In Junior High You Take Earth Science," Siegel-Causey, McMorris, McGowen, and Sands-Buss (1998) described a four-step process for including a student with severe disabilities in general education classes. Although this article was written for a middle school student with disabilities, the same steps could be followed to plan inclusive opportunities for an elementary-aged child.

Step 1—Plan. First, establish the student's educational outcomes and annual goals. When prioritizing academic goals for students with disabilities, including the family's voice is important. One way to accomplish this is to have family members complete the Choosing Options and Accommodation for Children (COACH; Giangreco, Cloninger, & Iverson, 2011), educational planning tool. The COACH includes a multistep process for selecting and prioritizing learning outcomes for their child.

Step 2—Select classes. Second, the IEP team identifies several potential grade-level classes that have content likely to address the student's annual goals and teachers who use teaching styles that are a good match for the student (e.g., hands-on, tangible products, small groups).

Step 3—**Accommodations**. Next, the special education teacher works with each general education classroom teacher to develop accommodations based on the student's strengths, needs, preferences, and learning style. An annual goal matrix (see Figure 10.3) can be used to translate how the student's annual goals will be matched to the curricular objectives of the classroom instruction. The annual goal matrix describes opportunities to address each annual goal within each class. An "X" indicates the goal can be addressed, an "A" indicates that the goal can be addressed with some adaption, or a "-" indicates no opportunity to address the goal. In addition, the special education teacher and the general educator can problem solve ways to link the student's annual goals within a curricular unit. By going through this process with one curricular unit, strategies that can be used in other curricular units are identified.

Step 4—Collaboration. Last, the roles, duties, and communication strategies for each class are determined along with needed curricular adaptations and progress monitoring. The special education teacher usually takes the lead in accomplishing these activities, but this responsibility can be shared between general education and special education teachers. For monitoring

FIGURE 10.2 ■ The Annual Goal Matrix

	Circle Time	Physical Education	Science	Music/Art	ELA	SPED Classroom
Greet Others	X	X	X	X	X	X
Describe Events	X	X	X	X	X	X
Ask Questions of Others	X	X	X	X	X	X
Sustain Communication	X	X	X	X	X	X
Read Vocabulary	A	-	A	A	A	A
Follow Directions	X	X	X	X	X	X

Key: X = Goal can be addressed, A = Goal can be addressed with adaption, - = No opportunity progress, two areas are prioritized—achievements in meeting annual goals and level of classroom participation.

Regardless of where the child with disabilities receives instruction, they will be taught content linked to the general curriculum standards all children learn (i.e., the general curriculum). For children with significant cognitive disabilities who are assessed with an alternate assessment based on alternate achievement standards, this content will be reduced in complexity (e.g., extended standards).

Peer Tutoring

This chapter has discussed four important areas for children with disabilities during times of **transition**: (1) friendships, (2) communication skills, (3) self-determination skills, and (4) access to the general curriculum. While many strategies can be used to teach these skills to children with disabilities, there is one instructional strategy that has been successful in teaching all of these skills: **peer tutoring**. **Peer tutoring** is an instructional strategy in which one student teaches another student (Greenwood, Carta, & Hall, 1988) and the experience benefits both (Rohrbeck, Ginsburg-Block, Fantuzzo, & Miller, 2003). Peer tutoring typically involves children in the same grade but can also be used with children of different grade levels (i.e., cross-age tutoring), with older children assuming the role of tutor and younger children assuming the role of tutee (Barbetta & Miller, 1991). In **reciprocal or two-way tutoring**, children alternate between tutor and tutee roles (Eiserman, 1988), whereas in classwide peer tutoring (CWPT), children are taught by peers who are trained and supervised by the classroom teacher, a form of intraclass, reciprocal peer tutoring in which children alternate tutor and tutee roles during tutoring sessions (Greenwood, Maheady, & Delquadri, 2002).

Peer tutors have taught social skills and academic skills to children with disabilities in both the separate special education classroom and the general education classroom. Table 10.5 contains a description of the placement and school level as well as the content and skills taught by peers to children with disabilities. In each of these studies, peer tutors were trained and supported to deliver instruction to peers with disabilities. For more information on peer support interventions

TABLE 10.5 ■ Studies Using Peer Tutors Without Disabilities to Teach Elementary Students With Disabilities			
Placement	**School Level**	**Targeted Content/Skills**	**Reference**
Special Education Classroom	Elementary	Money skills, expressive language, and oral reading/comprehension skills	Kamps, Locke, Delquadri, & Hall, 1989
Special Education Classroom	Elementary	Sight word recognition	Kamps & Walker, 1990
General Education Classroom	Elementary	Expressive word naming and recognition of correct spellings	Wolery, Werts, Synder, & Caldwell, 1994
General Education Classroom	Elementary (CWPT)	Spelling	McDonnell, Thorson, Allen, & Mathot-Buckner, 2000
General Education Classroom	Elementary (4th grade)	Listening comprehension of adapted science lessons	Hudson, Browder, & Jimenez, 2014
General Education Classroom	Elementary (5th grade)	Listening comprehension of adapted literature (i.e., *The Watsons Go to Birmingham*, 1968)	Hudson & Browder, 2014

for individuals with disabilities, see Carter, Asmus, and Moss (2014); Carter, Cushing, and Kennedy (2009); and Hughes and Carter (2008).

THE INDIVIDUALIZED EDUCATION PLAN (IEP) PROCESS AND DOCUMENT

All school-aged students receiving special education supports and services have an individualized education plan (IEP document) to help them reach their full potential. Professionals follow specific steps for developing the IEP document called the IEP process. In this section, the process for developing an IEP will be discussed first, followed by the specific components included in the IEP document.

The IEP Process

The Individuals with Disabilities Education Act (IDEA, 2004) describes 10 steps to follow when developing the IEP document (see Steps in the IEP Process box).

STEPS IN THE IEP PROCESS

Step 1. Identify child who possibly needs special education and related services.

Step 2. Conduct comprehensive evaluation.

Step 3. Determine eligibility (see IDEA disability categories).

Step 4. Qualify child for special education supports and services.

Step 5. Schedule IEP meeting.

Step 6. Hold IEP meeting and write the IEP.

Step 7. Provide services.

Step 8. Measure progress and report to parents.

Step 9. Review IEP annually.

Step 10. Reevaluate child every 3 years.

A parent, local educational agency (LEA), or state educational agency (SEA) can recommend a child suspected of having a disability for the initial evaluation. Once the referral is made, a multidisciplinary team conducts a full and individualized evaluation in all areas of suspected disability to determine if a child is eligible to receive special education and/or related services. These areas can include general health, vision, hearing, speech and language skills, intellectual, academic, or prevocational/vocational skills. The initial educational evaluation must be completed within 60 days of the referral and before a child receives special education and/or related services. For each category of disability, the assessment results must demonstrate that there is an impact on the student's education caused by the disability and that the student can benefit from specially designed instruction. After all, not all children with a disability require special education services.

A child can qualify for special education supports and services under one or more of the 13 disability categories described in the IDEA (2004).

WHO QUALIFIES FOR SPECIAL EDUCATION SUPPORTS AND SERVICES?
IDEA 13 DISABILITY CATEGORIES

1. Autism
2. Deaf-blindness
3. Deafness
4. Emotional disturbance
5. Hearing impairment
6. Intellectual disability (ID)*
7. Multiple disabilities
8. Orthopedic impairment
9. Other health impairment
10. Specific learning disability
11. Speech or language impairment
12. Traumatic brain injury
13. Visual impairment

*ID has also been referred to as "mental retardation" (MR) in the past, and the term and its acronym may be used colloquially or in older documentation. It is not, however, a currently accepted practice to refer to individuals with intellectual disabilities as mentally retarded. For more information, see Rosa's Law (2010).

Additionally, the IDEA allows states and LEAs to use the term "**developmental disability**" to qualify children aged 3 to 9 years who experience delays in one or more areas of development (i.e., cognitive, physical, social or emotional, communication, or adaptive behavior) who, because of these delays, need special education supports and services.

The next steps in the process involve designing a plan (sometimes called program) that addresses the child's unique needs. This plan is described in very specific ways in the IEP document. The IEP document is a legally binding document that is reviewed annually in the IEP meeting. The first IEP must be in place within 30 days of the evaluation meeting in which the child was determined to be eligible for special education supports and services.

The last steps in the IEP process involve implementing the plan and measuring student progress. The IEP meeting is only one of the times a child's progress should be discuss by teachers, parents and other service providers throughout the year. Because the IEP is a working document, it can be modified and changed as needed.

THE INDIVIDUALIZED EDUCATION PROGRAM PLAN

All school-aged students receiving special education supports and services will have an individualized education program (IEP) plan. The involvement of families in the IEP process is crucial for a well-developed plan that meets the needs of students with disabilities. Although the forms used to create the IEP may look different from state to state, the Individuals with Disabilities Education Act (IDEA, 2004) requires that all IEPs contain the following information:

- Present levels of academic and functional performance (present levels)
- Annual goals

- Services and supports
- Participation with nondisabled children
- Modifications to state and districtwide assessments
- Location and duration of services
- Reporting child progress
- Transition services
- Age of majority

PRESENT LEVELS OF ACADEMIC ACHIEVEMENT AND FUNCTIONAL PERFORMANCE (PRESENT LEVELS)   This section of the IEP describes how the student is doing in school. This information comes from the results of current evaluations (e.g., classroom tests, individual tests given to decide eligibility or during reevaluation, observations from family members, teachers, related service providers). All the areas of development in which the student may need support should be assessed (e.g., academic skills, daily living or self-help skills, social skills, behavior, sensory skills, communication skills, mobility, vocational skills). Also, this section includes a description of how the student's disability affects his or her involvement and progress in the general curriculum (i.e., the knowledge and skills that all students are expected to learn while in school).

A well-written present levels document describes:

- the student's strengths and weaknesses;
- what helps the student learn;
- what limits or interferes with the student's learning;
- objective data from current evaluations of the student; and
- how the student's disability affects his or her ability to be involved and progress in the general education curriculum

It is very important that the student's present levels are written clearly and thoroughly, because this statement is the foundation for all of the IEP, including the annual goals.

ANNUAL GOALS   Annual goals describe what the student can reasonably be expected to accomplish in a year. For students who take the alternate assessment based on alternate achievement standards, annual goals will be broken down into smaller goals called short-term objectives or benchmarks. The student's present levels of academic achievement and functional performance are used to write the annual goals. Specifically, the present levels statement identifies what the student needs, and the goals (and objectives, if appropriate) are written to address those needs. Annual goals and objectives may target any area of need, including the general education curriculum, learning development, functional skills, social or behavioral needs, physical needs, or other educational needs such as communication. A well-written goal should be positive and describe a skill that can be seen and measured. It answers the questions:

1. **Who?** … will achieve?
2. What? … **skill or behavior?**
3. How? … **in what manner or at what level?**
4. Where? … **in what setting or under what conditions?**
5. **When?** … by what time? And ending data?

In addition to describing how the student's progress will be measured, the IEP must also describe when periodic reports on that progress will be provided to families. For many schools, periodic reports are report cards sent home quarterly, but local education agencies may decide to use another form or schedule. Regardless of the form, families should be able to see whether their student is making progress on the annual goals (and/or short-term objectives) described in the IEP.

SERVICES AND SUPPORTS   Under IDEA, special education supports and services are available to students who need them to reach their annual goals, be involved in and make progress in the general education curriculum, participate in extracurricular activities, and be educated with students without disabilities. The different types of services and supports include:

- Special education
- Related services
- Supplementary aids and services
- Accomodations and Modifications
- Program modifications or support for school staff

Each of these services and supports is defined and described in this section.

Special education is instruction designed to meet the individual needs of a student. An individualized curriculum is different from that of same-age peers who do not have disabilities (e.g., teaching a blind student to read and write using Braille), yet it is based on the same general education curriculum that all students learn. It is important to understand that a student's entire education is not captured in the IEP—only those areas in which a student needs special education support are included. That means that if a student does not need special education support to participate meaningfully in physical education, goals for physical education will not be included in the student's IEP. Also, it is important to remember that special education is not a place. It's a set of services that can be provided in many different places, depending on the needs of the student.

Related services offer additional help in areas such as speaking or moving. The IEP team reviews evaluation information to identify any related services needed by a student, and these related services are included in the IEP. Table 10.6 lists some related services that can be included on the IEP. Please note that this list is not exhaustive of all the related services that may be provided; related services may include other developmental, corrective, or supportive services (e.g., artistic and cultural programs, and art, music, and dance therapy) if they are needed by a student with a disability to benefit from special education.

Supplementary aids and services include other kinds of supports or services that a student needs to be educated with students without disabilities to the maximum extent appropriate. Some examples of supplementary aids and services are:

- adapted equipment (e.g., pencil grip, special seat)
- a one-on-one aide
- assistive technology (e.g., computer, special software, or an augmentative or alternative communication device/system)

TABLE 10.6 ■ Common Related Services		
Transportation	Physical therapy	Audiology
Psychological services	Counseling services	Occupational therapy
Early identification and assessment of disabilities	Rehabilitation counseling	Interpreting services
School health services and school nurse services	Recreation, including therapeutic recreation	Social work services in schools
Orientation and mobility services	Speech-language pathology	Parent counseling/training
Medical services for diagnostic or evaluation	Assistive technology services	

- training for staff, the student, and/or families
- adapted materials (e.g., adapted books, books on tape, large-print materials)
- peer tutors
- collaboration/consultation among staff, families, and/or other professionals (e.g., occupational therapist, behavior specialist, mobility specialist)

Accommodations and modifications help a student with disabilities access the general education curriculum and other learning materials and activities. Accommodations or modifications can be made to:

- scheduling (e.g., giving extra time to complete assignments or tests)
- setting (e.g., working in small groups, working one-on-one with the teacher)
- materials (e.g., providing audiotaped books, using large-print books)
- instruction (e.g., reducing the difficulty of assignments, reducing the reading level)
- student response (e.g., allowing answers to be given orally, using a computer for written work)

Program modifications or support for school staff include the supports available to the people who work with a student with disabilities. These supports are provided to help these people help the student:

- achieve his or her annual goals;
- be involved in a make progress in the general education curriculum;
- participate in extracurricular and other nonacademic activities; and
- be educated and participate with students who do not have disabilities.

PARTICIPATION WITH CHILDREN WITHOUT DISABILITIES   While IDEA does not require students with disabilities to be educated in the general education classroom, it does require them to be educated with their peers without disabilities *to the maximum extent appropriate* for each student. With this requirement in mind, the IEP must include an explanation of the extent, if any, to which the student will *not* participate with students without disabilities in the regular class and in extracurricular and nonacademic activities. This means that if a student with disabilities receives special education supports and services someplace other than the general education classroom, the IEP team must explain why in the IEP.

MODIFICATIONS TO STATE- OR DISTRICTWIDE ASSESSMENTS   In order for students with disabilities to show what they know on state- or districtwide assessments, appropriate accommodations may be needed by the student. These accommodations are described on the IEP and offered in the same areas as the instructional modifications discussed earlier (i.e., scheduling, setting, materials, and student response). The IEP team will also decide how a student with a disability will participate in state- or districtwide assessments: the student may (1) participate in the assessment with no testing accommodations or modifications, (2) participate in the assessment with testing accommodations or modifications, or (3) participate in an alternate assessment. Alternate assessments are based on alternate achievement standards and are taken by students with significant cognitive disabilities who cannot participate in the regular assessment with or without testing accommodations or modifications.

LOCATION AND DURATION OF SERVICES   Each of the services a student needs is described in the IEP. Along with a description of these services, the IEP must also include:

- how often a student will receive the service(s) (e.g., number of times per day or week);
- how long each session will last (e.g., number of minutes);

- where services will be provided (e.g., in the general education classroom); and
- when services will begin and end (e.g., starting and ending dates).

Sometimes students with disabilities need to receive special education supports and services after the school year has ended. This is called extended school year or ESY services. The IEP team will determine whether a student is eligible for ESY services based on the guidelines provided by the LEA.

> Additional information about the IEP and the IEP process can be found at *A Parent's Guide to Developing Your Child's IEP* (2009), available from the National Dissemination Center for Children with Disabilities website: http://www.parentcenterhub.org/repository/pa12/.
>
> The PDF is available in English and in Spanish.

WORKING TOGETHER—THE IEP TEAM AND THE COLLABORATIVE TEAM MODEL

Many individuals are involved in planning and implementing a student's IEP. At a minimum, the members include the student, family members, special education teacher, general education teacher, related services professionals, and a local education agency representative such as the school principal (see Figure 10.3). If needed, other members are included on the IEP team (e.g., school nurse, **assistive technology** specialist). Each of the team members has an important role to play. Figure 10.3 describes some of the individuals that might be included on an IEP team.

STUDENT   The student is the reason the team exists, and the team's energies should focus on the student's educational needs. As much as possible, the student should be involved in all team functions, including learning how to lead their IEP meeting (Hawbaker, 2007; Uphold & Hudson, 2012).

FIGURE 10.3 ■ Possible Members on a Student's IEP Team

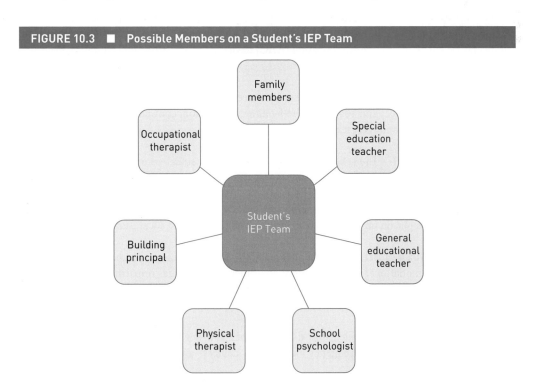

FAMILY MEMBERS   Family members are the most knowledgeable about the student with disabilities, and their input is crucial to developing appropriate goals for the student. Additionally, family members have the greatest stake in their student's future, making their input all the more valuable to the other team members.

SPECIAL EDUCATION TEACHER   The special education teacher develops and implements the IEP with input from the other team members. The special education teacher is an expert in effective instructional strategies. In addition, they will educate and supervise paraprofessionals who work with the student, plan inclusive educational opportunities with general education teacher(s) to address IEP goals, and serve as a liaison between family and school and an advocate for students with disabilities.

GENERAL EDUCATION TEACHER(S)   The general education teacher(s) shares their expertise in the general curriculum by describing typical learning expectations and activities for their grade and content area. They may also describe their class schedule, rules, and routines so that the other members of the IEP team get an idea of what is expected for a typical student at a particular grade level. The general education teacher and special education teacher will work together to plan inclusive educational opportunities that address IEP goals for the student with disabilities.

PHYSICAL THERAPIST (PT)   The physical therapist focuses on the student's physical functions, including: gross motor skills, handling, positioning, transfer techniques, range of motion, muscle strength, endurance, flexibility, mobility, and relaxation and stimulation.

OCCUPATIONAL THERAPIST (OT)   The occupational therapist focuses on the development and maintenance of functional skills, including: daily living skills, fine motor skills, sensory perception, range of motion, muscle tone, sensorimotor skills, posture, and oral-motor skills.

SPEECH-LANGUAGE PATHOLOGIST (SLP)   A speech-language pathologist provides services in receptive and expressive communication, articulation and fluency, voice quality and respiration, augmentative and alternative communication (AAC) devices, and assessing and facilitating mealtime skills.

ASSISTIVE TECHNOLOGY SPECIALIST   The assistive technology specialist focuses on the use of high- and low-technology devices and adaptations to facilitate instruction, communication, environmental management, mobility, and recreation.

SCHOOL PSYCHOLOGIST   The school psychologist focuses on social-emotional issues, assessment and evaluation, interpretation of testing information and counseling of students and families.

SCHOOL ADMINISTRATOR   This team member is usually a school principal or director of special education and is the person on the team who ensures compliance with local, state, and federal laws.

TEACHER OF STUDENTS WITH VISUAL IMPAIRMENTS   This team member provides direct instruction, accommodations, and adaptations to students with visual impairments. Additionally, they may teach tactile communication and use of optical devices as well as adapt general education classroom materials, consult with general educators, and provide orientation and mobility training.

AUDIOLOGIST   An audiologist identifies different types and degrees of hearing loss, consults on equipment (e.g., hearing aids, frequency modulation devices) and their use, and environmental modifications when needed.

SCHOOL NURSE   The school nurse is an important member for students who have medical needs. They administer medications, provide medical procedures when needed (e.g., catheterization, suctioning, tube feeding), develop safety and emergency protocols, and consult with other medical professionals.

COLLABORATIVE TEAM MODEL

It would be highly inefficient for a single teacher to gather and integrate all the information needed to plan, implement, and evaluate a student's IEP (Ryndak, Lehr, Ward, & DeBevoise, 2014). To meet the various needs of students with disabilities, therefore, team approaches have been developed (e.g., multidisciplinary, interdisciplinary, collaborative; Cloninger, 2004). For children with disabilities, the **collaborative team model** has been described as an exemplary practice for providing educational support (Giangreco, Cloninger, Dennis, & Edelman, 2000; Heller & Forney, 2009). Figure 10.4 contains a diagram of the collaborative team model. In this diagram, the child and their family are at the center, and the professionals who support their educational goals surround them.

In the **collaborative team model**, team members have expertise that is relevant to the needs of the child with disabilities. For planning and sharing information purposes, team members are grouped into core members and support members (Heller & Forney, 2009). Core members are the people who are involved in designing and implementing the student's education program. In Figure 10.4, these individuals are found in the second and third circles. For example, core team members for an elementary student with visual impairments could be the child, their family members, the special education teacher, the general education teacher, the teacher of students with visual impairments, an orientation and mobility specialist, and the classroom teaching assistant.

Other members of the team play a supportive role and offer their expertise when needed. These members are important to the team, but their roles do not directly support the child's day-to-day educational program. In Figure 10.4, these individuals would be in the outermost circle. Examples of possible support team members include the school psychologist, a social worker, vocational rehabilitation counselor, school nurse, and physicians (Heller & Forney, 2009).

In the collaborative team model, the roles of team members are dynamic, changing as the child's needs change. For example, if a child requires a feeding tube, the school nurse might move from being a support member on the child's team to a core member because her expertise will be needed on a regular basis. In addition to their areas of expertise, team members need specific

FIGURE 10.4   ■   Collaborative Team Model

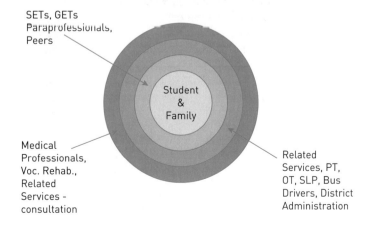

SETs, GETs Paraprofessionals, Peers

Medical Professionals, Voc. Rehab., Related Services - consultation

Student & Family

Related Services, PT, OT, SLP, Bus Drivers, District Administration knowledge related to the education of students with severe disabilities such as use of evidence-based interventions, methods for embedding evidence-based interventions and strategies, use of Universal Design for Learning principles, and use of accommodations and modifications (Ryndak et al., 2014).

Times of transition are likely periods when team members might need to shift their participation on the team to meet the changing needs of the student. For example, when a child with significant health-care needs begins first grade, the highest priority during the first few weeks is establishing safe routines for the delivery of the child's care. During this time, the school nurse, occupational therapist, and physical therapist might work with the classroom teacher and teaching assistants on positioning, handling, and daily living skills (e.g., feeding, toileting). While initially intense, once these procedures are in place, the interactions of the nurse, occupational therapist, and the physical therapist with the student may lesson, allowing time for the speech-language pathologist to work on a communication system with the student.

In the collaborative team model, some roles and responsibilities are shared by all team members. For example, all team members will help make decisions about the child's IEP, problem solve issues related to the child's educational program, share their specific knowledge and skills so that other team members understand the child's capabilities and needs, support the contributions of other team members, and support practices that facilitate the child's education and integration into the community (Cloninger, 2004; Heller & Forney, 2009).

To function successfully, collaborative teams are advised to establish and follow rules of operation from the onset (Ryndak et al., 2014). These rules might address (a) team member interactions, (b) development of team goals, (c) role assignments, (d) individual accountability, (e) measurement of effectiveness, (f) reflective evaluation of the team's functioning, (g) problem-solving process and action planning, and (h) receipt of mutual benefits from their collaboration (Jorgensen, McSheehan, & Sonnenmeier, 2010).

Summary

In the first part of this chapter, transitions occurring during elementary school for children with disabilities and their families are described. These times of transition will likely be stressful for both family members and their children with disabilities due to the changes these transitions bring. Educators can help by providing effective communication, both written and electronic, to families that includes information about their child's day, classroom, and school events. In addition, educators can teach children with disabilities important skills that facilitate successful transitions, including communication skills, self-determination skills, social skills (e.g., friendships with peers without disabilities), and skills to participate successfully in general education. The second half of the chapter describes two ways effective instruction and supports are obtained for children with disabilities. The child's individualized education program (IEP) plan is the written document that describes the present levels of academic achievement and functional performance (i.e., present levels). From these "present levels," annual goals are written to address the areas of need, and other needed supports and services are identified and provided. The IEP team is a diverse group of people that includes the child with disabilities and family members. The members of the IEP team are devoted to the success of the child with disabilities and work collaboratively to make this happen.

Additional Resources

Web-Based

Questions Parents Ask about Schools. A discussion of frequently asked questions families ask about schools: http://www2.ed.gov/parents/academic/help/questions/questions.pdf.

A Parents' Guide to the Self-Determined Learning Model for Early Elementary Students. A free online resource that includes an introduction to the Self-Determined Learning Model of Instruction (SDLMI) as well as a list of children's books about problem solving and sample forms for teaching self-determination skills: http://www.beachcenter.org/RESOURCE_LIBRARY/BEACH_RESOURCE_DETAIL_PAGE.ASPX?INT RESOURCEID=2505&TYPE=BOOK&JScript=1.

Fostering Self-Determination among Children and Youth with Disabilities—Ideas from Parents for Parents. A free online resource guide written by parents that includes practical ideas for teaching self-determination skills to children with disabilities: http://www.waisman.wisc.edu/naturalsupports/pdfs/FosteringSelfDetermination.pdf.

A Parent's Guide to Developing Your Child's IEP. Available in English and Spanish, this guide describes information about the IEP and the IEP process: http://www.parentcenterhub.org/repository/pa12/.

11

SECONDARY
SCHOOL YEARS

MELINA ALEXANDER
Weber State University

DESNA BERGOLD
DB Consulting

"Adolescence is a period of rapid changes. Between the ages of 12
and 17, for example, a parent ages as much as 20 years."

—Author Unknown

LEARNING OBJECTIVES

Specifically, after reading this chapter, you should be able to:

1. Describe the major features of adolescent development.
2. Relay the influence of adolescence on families and schooling.
3. Analyze the important transitions during the secondary school years.
4. Include families in educational planning and decision making.

The transition from primary to secondary school is an exciting and intimidating process for most students and their families. The school day may now entail working with a variety of teachers. These teachers are experts in their content areas and may place higher expectations on students. In addition, each of these teachers will have their own classroom rules and procedures. To add to this excitement, students are transitioning into adolescence. This developmental period brings on many changes in both appearance and behavior. About the time students have mastered these transitions, another daunting rite of passage occurs: moving to high school and graduation preparations. It is important that professionals working with students and their families not only understand adolescent students and the unique challenges for students with disabilities in secondary schools but also know how to support families through this exciting and sometimes difficult process.

ADOLESCENCE

Adolescence is a developmental stage that encompasses the years from puberty to adulthood. During adolescence, children experience many transitions, including physical, cognitive, emotional, and social (Steinberg & Silk, 2002), occurring and maturing throughout this developmental stage. During this time period, children should acquire the ability for abstract thought, including understanding abstract ideas, more satisfying relationships that are free from imposed inhibitions and worry, and a sense of purpose and place in the world. Adolescents may do this through questioning old values (Manheim, Zieve, Eltz, Slon, & Wang, 2013).

In addition to these progressions, according to Greydanus and Bashe (2003), there are seven key developmental tasks:

1. Learning to feel comfortable with their bodies.
2. Becoming emotionally independent from their parents.
3. Learning to think and express themselves conceptually.
4. Developing a personal set of values: ideals, priorities, concepts of right and wrong.

5. Forming meaningful relationships with members of both sexes.

6. Defining their sexual orientation, and deciding whether or not to become sexually active.

7. Working toward economic stability.

(Greydanus & Bashe, 2003, p. 6)

The purpose of all of these changes are to help form one's own identity and prepare for adulthood.

The adolescent years can be divided into three stages: early adolescence, generally 12 and 13; middle adolescence, 14 to 16; and late adolescence, 17 to 21 (Greydanus & Bashe, 2003). The age range of late adolescence has been stretched into the 20s as more teens have extended their education. Stages and ages are generalizations; not all teenagers enter or leave adolescence at the same time or rate (Stang & Story, 2005). Furthermore, an adolescent may be further along in some areas of development than others. This is a very confusing time for the child and the family.

EARLY ADOLESCENCE

In early adolescence, the child grows taller and starts to think and feel in more mature ways. This is a time of change throughout the body, with a growth spurt that usually accompanies puberty. This growth spurt includes changes in height, changes in weight, growth of body hair, changes in skin including oiliness, pimples, or acne, and changes in sex organs. Children are very sensitive to their changing bodies and often compare themselves to others or idealized adult images. There are also many changes in motor development, as brains need time to adjust to longer limbs and bigger bodies, so a child may be awkward or clumsy (Spano, 2004; WebMD, 2012).

Beginning to understand long-term effects and that issues are not clear-cut marks early adolescents' cognitive development. Most early adolescent children are only beginning to move away from concrete views into abstract thought (Stang & Story, 2005). While children at this stage are mostly focused on the here and now, they may show an interest in future career options (Spano, 2004). This is a time when children typically learn the fundamental skills needed to succeed in adulthood. They are able to think about their thinking and learning, a process called metacognition. Using metacognitive strategies, adolescents can retrieve and apply information to solve problems (Eccles, 1999). In addition, children at this stage may show a greater ability to work (Spano, 2004).

Emotional and social development at this time is marked by the early adolescent's desire to garner independence. The cognitive changes adolescents experience move them to an expanded view of their world (Eccles, 1999). This leads them to seek out peers with similar interests and develop a sense of peer community. Peer groups influence early adolescent children's sense of conformity and deviancy. Peers also provide measures of social competency (Brinthaupt & Lipka, 2012). Additionally, at this time, children feel the urge to be more independent from their families, and friends replace parents as sounding boards. Early adolescents begin exploring independence by showing families less attention and being rude to them. All of these changes may cause concern to families. Exacerbating these concerns is the adolescents' sense of invincibility or lack of awareness of mortality. Children at this age may therefore engage in risky behaviors.

Early adolescents are also developing their self-identity. Self-identity is linked to self-concept. Many things may contribute to a child's self-concept, including their perceived competence. Self-concept in early adolescence shifts with the child's burgeoning abilities in abstract thought (Brinthaupt & Lipka, 2012). While students in the primary years are very optimistic about their abilities, children in early adolescence often question their competence (Eccles, 1999). They may compare their performance to that of their peers and find they come up short. This is of particular relevance in the school setting because an adolescent's self-concept is correlated with their academic achievement (Manning, 2007).

MIDDLE ADOLESCENCE

Physical changes are still occurring during the middle adolescent years, particularly for boys. Male adolescents generally begin their growth spurt and may experience the growth of facial hair, increased perspiration, rapid increase in height and weight, deepening of the voice, and changes in skin (Spano, 2004). Girls, however, may have experienced the majority of changes associated with puberty by middle adolescence (Stang & Story, 2005). At this stage, teens are very concerned with their physical appearance and believe others are too. This leads to experiments with clothing, hair, and makeup. Teens begin to have concerns about their own attractiveness, and sexuality is a major preoccupation (Greydanus & Bashe, 2003).

Cognitively, the middle adolescent is progressing toward more abstract thought. This means the child will experience an expansion of their verbal abilities (Stang & Story, 2004). Middle adolescence is a time when the brain is continuing to create new pathways. Because of this and increased abilities in abstract thought, learning opportunities are heightened (Halpren, Heckman, & Larson, 2013). The middle adolescent will also have an increased interest in their future career choices (KidsGrowth.com, n.d., table 1). The advances in verbal abilities may encourage the child to express their educational desires, often leading to expressions of extreme distaste toward particular academic areas (Spano, 2004).

Middle adolescence marks a time of drastic emotional and social changes. Through relationships with adults that are not their parents, the middle adolescents are beginning to be exposed to new and unfamiliar situations and lifestyles, which may be frightening and influence their social and emotional development (KidsGrowth.com, n.d. table 1). This is due to the middle adolescent's need to seek out role models (Spano, 2004). In most instances, these individuals are not the middle adolescent's parents. These role models may affect teens choices on smoking and eating behaviors, charitable contributions, volunteering, and employability skills (Christiansen, Qureshi, Schaible, Park, & Gittelsohn, 2013; Ottoni-Wilhelm, Estell, & Perdue, 2014; Wiium, Breivik, & Wold, 2006).

These new role models influence family relationships during the middle adolescent years. This stage marks the most conflict between teens and their families (Greydanus & Bashe, 2003). Teens have a lowered opinion of their families and may withdraw (Spano, 2004). Adopting annoying habits are normal ways the middle adolescent tries to become independent. With their demand for independence, at this stage, most middle adolescents will hide their continued need for parental love and family acceptance (Greydanus & Bashe, 2003).

Peer groups and peer approval continue to be essential and are a primary focus of the middle adolescent. Good friends are important, and a loss of friendships can cause depression. They often confide more in friends than in family. In addition, the middle adolescent is experiencing an increased interest in emotional relationships with the opposite sex (Stang & Story, 2004). Many teens experiment by frequently changing relationships and may even experience fears regarding sexual identity (Spano, 2004). This may cause concern, because most teens still feel invincible, and experimentation with "risky" behavior may increase sharply (Centers for Disease Control, 2015).

Identity formation for the middle adolescent is more intense. The changes in physical, cognitive, and emotional and social development make establishing an identity outside of the family critical (LaVoie, 1976). This stage of development is referred to as Identity Versus Role Confusion in Erickson's stages of psychosocial development. According to Erikson, at this stage, teens are in a crisis-like search for an autonomous sense of self. Middle adolescents are often struggling to express their uniqueness while attempting to still fit in (Oswalt & Zupanick, n.d.).

LATE ADOLESCENCE

By late adolescence, physiological development is complete. However, growth, including an increase in height and muscle mass, may still continue for some young men (Spano, 2004). At this stage, the young adult has gained a better acceptance of their physical appearance, and concerns about body image take a back seat to concerns about romantic relationships (Greydanus & Bashe, 2003).

The late adolescent has achieved the capacity for abstract thought. Each has the ability to reason and problem solve (APA, 2002). Cognitively, late adolescents engage in what some theorists call postformal thinking. This includes being able to understand differing opinions, allowing for contradiction and integrating complexities into dialectics (Chang & Chiou, 2014). They have a greater ability to express their ideas and are often idealistic. The world of work may be becoming very real, and concerns about the future loom. Many young adults engage in long-term planning and goal setting, centered on future career choices.

The late adolescent has increased emotional and social stability. The peer group fades, and a few close friends may remain. As young adults, they may listen to their families' advice and even seek their opinion. They begin to realize their own mortality and worry about the future, although some may still feel invincible. Late adolescents have established a sense of identity and feel less threatened seeking advice or counseling.

ADOLESCENTS WITH DISABILITIES

"It seems funny and ironic…that most people spend an exorbitant amount of time trying to distinguish themselves as unique and different while all that [an individual with a disability] wants is to be just like everyone else" (Patton, Payne, & Beirne-Smith, 1986, p. 469).

Adolescents with disabilities are as individual and unique as those without disabilities. Making any broad generalizations runs counter to what is known about all individuals with and without disabilities. There are, however, two areas that are of particular concern to the individual with disabilities and their family: peer pressure and self-image.

Peer Pressure

During the adolescent years, peer influence increases (Giedd, 2012). Adolescents often look to their peers for behavioral choice making. Peer influences can inspire adolescents to engage in either prosocial or risky behaviors (Ali, Amialchuk, & Nikaj, 2014). Peer groups even influence students' educational outcomes. The term "peer pressure" generally refers to negative peer influence. Adolescents with disabilities may be particularly vulnerable to peer pressure. For example, one of the authors of this text worked with a child with neurofibromatosis, a disability which results in intellectual disabilities. This young adolescent, in order to have "friends," was persuaded to steal a car with them and "take the blame." When he got involved with professionals from the Department of Human Services, appropriate services were placed into this child's home to protect and support him. Behaviors seen in many adolescents with disabilities have been linked with succumbing to peer pressure, including low task orientation, the ability to stick with tasks until completion, and low positive affect (experiencing enjoyment or a positive mood; Giedd, 2012).

Adolescents with disabilities may also be taken advantage of by their peers. During adolescence, teens have a need to be liked and accepted by their peers. This is also true for adolescents with disabilities. This need for acceptance may leave students with disabilities vulnerable (Zeedyk, Rodriguez, Tipton, Baker, & Blacher, 2014). Nondisabled adolescents may use their disabled peers to engage in inappropriate or even illegal activities. Teens with disabilities that impair their social functioning have been encouraged to engage in behaviors that nondisabled peers would find embarrassing or even rude. Teens with disabilities that impair cognitive functioning have been used to transport drugs and weapons (Jaramillo, 2012).

Self-Image

A positive self-image is linked to positive outcomes. Developing a positive self-image is critical in psychological adjustment and for educational attainment (Preckel, Niepel, Schneider, & Brunner, 2013). Adolescents with disabilities may see themselves as different and therefore struggle to develop and maintain a positive self-image.

Self-image is often derived from interactions in social situations. Adolescents' social interactions primarily take place in a school setting. These interactions take place throughout the school day, where adolescents interact with a variety of individuals including teachers, peers, and friends (Prince & Nurius, 2014). Friendships during adolescence have a profound effect on self-image. Positive peer relationships have also been linked with feelings of inclusion, self-worth, and well-being (Oberle, Schonert-Reichl, & Thomson, 2010). Unfortunately, many children with disabilities have difficulties establishing meaningful friendships. It is important that adolescent students with disabilities be assisted in establishing and maintaining peer friendships. This may be done by providing adolescent students with disabilities social skills training or strategies to support students in fitting in with peer groups (Zambo, 2010).

FAMILIES OF ADOLESCENT STUDENTS WITH DISABILITIES

Families of an adolescent student are faced with unique challenges. Adolescence is marked by significant behavioral changes. During this stage, children are trying to establish their independence, distancing themselves from their families. In addition, they may engage in sensation-seeking behaviors, including those that involve risk (Giedd, 2012). All families struggle with the teenage child's change in behavior and battle for independence; for families of a child with a disability, this struggle may be more difficult. Often families of a child with special needs see their role as that of protector and advocate. The parents want to minimize their child's exposure to harm. They may feel that the only way to do this is through control. This need for control runs counter to the child's battle for independence (Peterson, 2004). Families are still very important to the adolescent, even though this may not be evident in the child's behavior. Multidisciplinary team members must understand these struggles and work to make both the child with special needs and the parent understand their value to the team decision-making process. It is important to note that significant rights have been afforded families *and* children with special needs, including participation in individualized educational program (IEP) planning (Mandlawitz, 2007). Children with special needs, who may have played a minor role in previous team meetings, should now be encouraged to be active in multidisciplinary team decision making, particularly decisions that address issues of educational choice. At the same time, families must be given a voice for their educational concerns as well (see Table 11.1)

Bullying

One area of particular concern for families of students with disabilities is that of bullying. Students with disabilities may have experienced bullying during the primary school years. However, the increased value of peer acceptance experienced by the adolescent makes bullying more acute. Adolescents with disabilities may be more vulnerable to bullying, with the likelihood of bullying being 10 times more than that of their nondisabled peers (National Collaborative

TABLE 11.1　■　Issues Faced by Families
Issues Faced by Families of Adolescents With Disabilities
Adjusting emotionally to possibility of life long disability
Addressing siblings' concerns and needs
Dealing with physical and emotional changes of puberty
Acknowledging the increasing need for peer interaction
Planning for post-high school education
Planning for career/vocational development
Teaching the adolescent how to self-advocate

on Workforce and Disability, 2011). Bullying is usually caused by an imbalance of power in relationships. Teens with disabilities may already be at a disadvantage in these situations because they typically assume secondary positions in relationships (Zeedyk et al., 2014). Discussions with families about bullying should occur during the IEP meetings throughout the adolescent years; in addition, bullying may need to be addressed in some manner in the IEP.

IEP Planning

Individualized education planning during the secondary years goes beyond simply planning academic courses. The issues faced by families of adolescents with special needs must also be addressed throughout the secondary school years. Team members work with families and children to determine additional areas of focus. IEPs in the secondary years should not only address the academic and social needs of the student with special needs but also develop into plans that address a student's goals for post–high school experiences.

THE MULTIDISCIPLINARY TEAM DURING THE SECONDARY SCHOOL YEARS

In the secondary school setting, the multidisciplinary team still participates in the student with special needs' assessment, instructional program planning, and even identification (Hendrickson, Ross, Mercer, & Walker, 1988). Secondary students with disabilities typically have received services for a number of years. Often, multidisciplinary teams at this level become overly comfortable with the meeting process. Families may be tired of these meetings, particularly when the focus is on the student's shortcomings. Multidisciplinary meetings should, therefore, provide focus not only on student needs but also student strengths and goals for the future.

There are also families in secondary settings for whom the IEP process is new. For families experiencing this process for the first time, these meetings can seem overwhelming. They are often unaware of the procedures and potential outcomes of such meetings. Families and the student with special needs may not be aware of the critical role that they play in the decision-making process. Families must be encouraged to participate. They should be made to feel they are invaluable members of the team. This may require that individual members of the multidisciplinary team, for example the special education teacher, brief the parent on the meeting procedures beforehand. Referrals to parent organizations or families experienced in the process may also be warranted. The meeting process may prove daunting even for experienced families. The developmental stage of the adolescent student with special needs influences the tone and process of these meetings, as do the major life events that occur during these years. Considerations should be made on a case-by-case basis. It is important that team members understand their roles in facilitating these meetings to ensure best outcomes for the student.

CASE STUDY 1
CARLOS (PART-DAY GENERAL EDUCATION)

Up until last winter, Carlos was receiving his education in general education. Carlos was on the honor roll with a 3.99 grade point average. In addition, Carlos was captain of the lacrosse team, a member of the soccer team, and president of the snowboarding club. Carlos was considering his options after graduation and was being scouted by a few major universities. Last winter, Carlos and a few of his friends from the snowboarding club were driving back from a day on the slopes when they encountered black ice and rolled their SUV. Most of his friends acquired only minor injuries, but Carlos was thrown from the car and sustained a brain injury. Carlos has been in rehabilitation for the last 6 months and is ready to return to school. Unfortunately, the school district has not been part of this rehabilitation effort. Carlos's mother wanted him back in school and asked the school what was available. The vice principal stated that Carlos was welcome back to school anytime and that if he needed a shortened day to accommodate physical and speech therapy, it could be arranged. Carlos's mother was concerned that he could not perform as he used to in his classes. She discussed this issue with a member of her church who also happened to be a professor of education at the local university. This person stated that she believed Carlos might qualify for special education services and gave her the number of a parent support group for traumatic brain injury (TBI). After Carlos's mother talked to the parent support group, she contacted the school's special education department.

Questions for Critical Thinking

1. What should the school have done to assist Carlos and his family during this trying time?

2. What are the possible options for Carlos, and how would you promote collaboration with the family in making this decision?

ROLES OF MEMBERS OF THE MULTIDISCIPLINARY TEAM

LEA Representative

The role of the LEA (local education agency) representative remains consistent. This individual must be qualified to provide (or supervise those who provide) the individualized education program. This means that they must know the general education curriculum. In addition, they must know what local education agency resources are available to assist the student with special needs in accessing the general education curriculum (IDEA, 2004). At the secondary level, the general education curriculum becomes more sophisticated. An LEA representative may not fully understand the curricular nuances of each content area. The representative must, therefore, become familiar with the expectations and demands of each curricular option offered by their local education agency.

General Education Teacher

The role of the general education teacher is to provide information about the general education curriculum. During the secondary school years, special consideration must be taken in selecting the general education teacher who will be on the multidisciplinary team. This member must have a potential role in the student's educational program. Selecting this member based solely on availability does a disservice to the team as a whole. The general education teacher must be able to articulate the unique demands of the general education classroom. The family may have insights into who this individual may be. For example, if the student would like to participate in general education art classes, a member of the art department may be the general education teacher selected to participate on this team.

Special Education Teacher

Unlike in the typical primary setting, students with special needs in the secondary setting may have interactions with more than one special education teacher. The special education teacher that is selected as a member of the multidisciplinary team may be the individual responsible for maintaining the student's educational records. This should be someone familiar with the student with special needs. This teacher must also be knowledgeable about the educational opportunities in the special education setting and provide information on these options to the team. This team member needs to report on student progress and may need to interpret and report assessment information in a manner that is understandable to all team members.

Other Service Providers

The members of this team vary depending on the student and parent needs. If sophisticated assessment and evaluation materials are required, an individual able to interpret these materials needs to be included, perhaps a medical professional or a psychologist. Other members may be an occupational or physical therapist or both, as well as a school counselor, a speech pathologist, and other service providers knowledgeable about the unique demands of the secondary school setting. Around 16 years of age, the student may need individuals who provide adult services or a vocational rehabilitation expert.

Families

As always, families are critical members of the multidisciplinary team. The family's role is to provide unique insight into their child's educational needs. It is important that they understand the importance of their contribution to the team, particularly during this time, when planning addresses needs associated with positive adult outcomes.

Student

The student's role as a member of the multidisciplinary team increases throughout the secondary school years. Students must play an active role in their educational planning.

> [Individuals with disabilities] who have a high quality of life obtain an understanding of their condition, take control and introduce an order and predictability in their lives. They learn what is possible, and set goals. They develop or elaborate a value set that helps them make sense of their disability. (Albrecht & Devlieger, 1999, p. 986)

Being an active member of the multidisciplinary team assists students in attaining a high quality of life.

ISSUES ADDRESSED BY MULTIDISCIPLINARY TEAMS DURING THE SECONDARY SCHOOL YEARS

Transition From Elementary to Secondary Schools

The transition from primary school to middle or junior high school usually takes place when students reach sixth or seventh grade. For all students, this move is difficult. As stated earlier, adolescents are grappling with the need for independence. Middle and junior high schools address this need with changes to the educational setting. In this new setting, students no longer interact with only one or two teachers; they now have daily interactions with seven or more educational professionals. With the inclusion of elective courses, students are also given choices in their educational content.

This change in educational setting can cause concern for families of students with special needs. Families often worry that choices made at this time will influence later educational outcomes. They may be concerned that their child will not adjust well to the change in setting. Families and children need information on educational choices. This should be given during the IEP that addresses the move from primary school. All educational options should be explained, including least-restrictive-environment settings and educational opportunities within each setting (see Figure 11.1).

The intent of least restrictive environment, as presented in the Individuals with Disabilities Education Act (IDEA), is to "ensure an appropriate education for all students with disabilities" (Fuchs & Fuchs, 1995 p. 22). Least restrictive environment is usually seen as a matter of inclusion. Inclusion, or educating students with their same-grade peers, is still a hotly debated subject. The term itself is inconsistently used throughout the field of special education (Hines, 2001). The whats, whys, and hows of inclusion are not uniform across states, districts, schools, programs, or even students within given programs. This is to be expected, and inclusion practices must be determined by IEP teams. Determining the appropriate placement for students with special needs in the middle or junior high school setting must take special

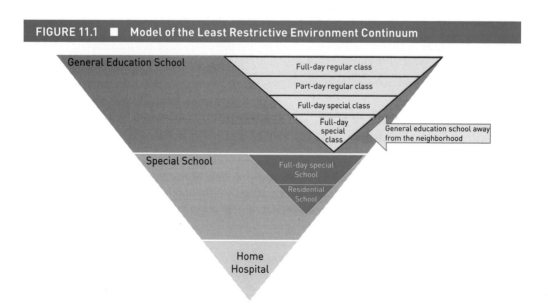

FIGURE 11.1 ■ Model of the Least Restrictive Environment Continuum

consideration of the family's wishes. Teams must look at long-term student goals and choose the educational environment that will best assist the student in achieving those goals. Providing detailed information on all considered educational options may mitigate parent concerns over placement.

CASE STUDY 2
EDDIE (RESIDENTIAL FUNCTIONAL SKILLS PROGRAM)

Eddie is a 13-year-old with Down syndrome. Eddie has received special education services since birth. Eddie and his family are members of a small rural community. His local primary school serves children living in a 50-mile radius. Throughout primary school, Eddie received his special education services in a full-inclusion model. He spent all day in the general education classroom with an assigned special education paraeducator. Socially, Eddie thrived in this school. He made many friends and was a member of his community's youth soccer team. Eddie transitioned into his neighborhood secondary (grades 6–12) school in the sixth grade. This school incorporated three primary schools. Because this school services rural communities spread throughout the county, transportation to the school can last up to 90 minutes each way. Eddie spent about 50 minutes on the bus to and from school each day. Some of the students in this new placement were unfamiliar with Eddie and would tease him. Eddie brought the issue to his parents' attention, and a multidisciplinary team meeting was held. The team came up with a plan to address the teasing, including Eddie receiving social skills training, weekly counseling sessions, and a schoolwide antibullying program. The teasing appeared to be reduced, but the demands of the general education curriculum were proving difficult for Eddie. Eddie's parents requested additional achievement and adaptive skills assessments be conducted. After testing, a multidisciplinary team meeting was held, and the district psychologist reported that although Eddie's adaptive skills seemed to be on target, his achievement test indicated that he was performing far below expectations. This, along with the previous teasing incidents, caused Eddie's parents to question his current placement. The LEA representative informed Eddie's parents that due to the rural nature of the district, few alternative programs were available. However, she did let Eddie's parents know of a multidistrict residential program available for students with functional skills and vocational training needs.

Questions for Critical Thinking

1. What could have been done before and during the IEP addressing the transition to middle school to foster a more collaborative decision-making process for Eddie and his family?

2. How should the family placement concerns be addressed?

Transition to High School

The move to high school marks another major change in the life of a student with special needs. For most, this means an increased focus on academic outcomes. Families are still concerned with least restrictive environment placement issues. Multidisciplinary teams must reevaluate educational placement and determine the student's best placement option. Families must also now take into consideration their student's post–high school goals. These goals help determine the educational focus.

Multidisciplinary teams must decide whether a student's focus should be academic (recommended for students planning on attending higher education) or vocational

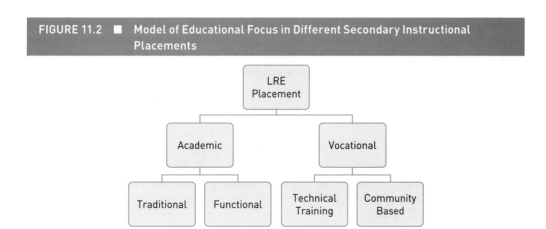

FIGURE 11.2 ■ Model of Educational Focus in Different Secondary Instructional Placements

(recommended for those seeking either assisted employment or a technical career such as welding, hair dressing, etc.; see Figure 11.3). For many students, their high school education may include a combination of both an academic and vocational focus. Many technical training programs require students have basic skills in English language arts or math. It may be necessary to include a member of the vocational training program as part of the multidisciplinary team.

Another important consideration for students entering high school is whether they will work towards receiving a regular high school diploma. Receiving a high school diploma is the goal for most students, as it marks a rite of passage. For some students with disabilities, receiving a regular high school diploma is unrealistic, placing demands that are too high for the student to achieve. For these students, there may be a graduation option of obtaining a certificate of completion. The requirements for certificates of completion vary by state, but across states these certificates recognize that a student has met the course requirements

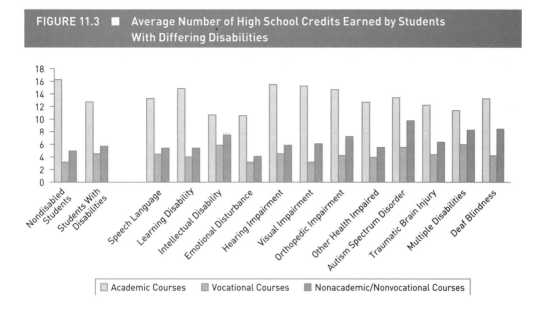

FIGURE 11.3 ■ Average Number of High School Credits Earned by Students With Differing Disabilities

needed to complete high school. However, receiving a certificate of completion may put a student at a disadvantage. For example, there are some post–high school education programs, such as university degree programs, that require a student to have a high school diploma upon admission. The decision to obtain a high school diploma or a certificate of completion should be made with considerable family input. Families have an interest in their student's post–high school options.

Needed Skills in Secondary Schools

Regardless of the educational placement or educational focus, in order to navigate the world of secondary schooling successfully, all students, including those with disabilities, need more sophisticated social and academic skills.

SOCIAL SKILLS   Social skills consist of behaviors, both verbal and nonverbal, that enable individuals to successfully participate in social situations (Steedly, Schwartz, Levin, & Luke, 2008). For individuals with special needs, navigating the social landscape may prove to be a particular challenge. In a recent study, fifth- and sixth-grade schoolchildren with special needs reported experiencing less social participation than students without special needs (Schwab, Gebhardt, Krammer, & Gasteiger-Klicpera, 2015). Difficulty with social skills becomes more pronounced during the secondary school years, where schooling becomes more impersonal. As stated earlier, adolescence is a time when peer relationships become paramount. Adolescents with disabilities often have difficulties in establishing relationships (Skär, 2003). This may be due, in part, to a student's lack of social skills. Youth with positive social skills show ease at establishing and maintaining relationships (Hair, Jager, & Garrett, 2002). Students with strong social skills are more apt to succeed in school and in employment (Bremer & Smith, 2004). Social skills are therefore of critical importance when considering future employment opportunities for a student with special needs. For most of us, social skills come naturally (National Association of School Psychologists, 2002). Students with special needs may need to receive social skills training in the areas of peer relationships, self-management, compliance, and assertion.

The prospect of including a social skills curriculum for a student with special needs can be a sensitive subject. Families may not be aware of their child's social deficits. Suggesting student training in this area may cause offense if not approached respectfully. Families should be made aware of the different options available for social skills training and consulted when determining the program that will best meet the student's immediate and long-term needs.

INSTRUCTIONAL STRATEGIES   Before beginning a social skills program, it is important to determine the reason(s) for the social skills deficit. Working with families is critical in these determinations. Families should be asked whether these same deficits are seen at home or in other social situations. Families can let program planners know if social skills deficits are due to their child's lack of knowledge or if there is an underlying cause for a child's inability to perform in social situations. When appropriate, siblings should be included in this process; there is often a different family dynamic among siblings.

Once the type of social skill deficit has been determined, a program can be chosen to best meet the child's needs. There are many different social skills programs available. The chosen program should address the specific needs of the child based on information gathered in collaboration with the family. Social skills programs should include both instruction in social skills and an opportunity for student practice (see Table 11.2).

Table 11.2 ■ Components of Social Skills Programs

Quality Social Skills Programs	
What	**How**
Focus on social and emotional learning strategies that encourage reflection and self-awareness.	• Encourage students to consider how individual actions and words have consequences. • Develop students' ability to take different perspectives and viewpoints. • Teach students to think through situations and/or challenges by rehearsing possible outcomes.
Create opportunities to practice effective social skills both individually and in groups.	• Model effective social skills in the classroom and at home through praise, positive reinforcement, and correction and redirection of inappropriate behaviors. • Discuss effective interactions with specific attention to the steps involved. • Role-play scenarios that build social skills.
Adjust instructional strategies to address social skills deficits.	• Arrange the physical environment effectively. • Clearly state instructional objectives and behavioral expectations throughout each lesson. • Simulate real-life challenges students may encounter at school, at home, and in the community to place social skills in their practical contexts.
Tailor social skills interventions to individual student needs.	• Refer to assessment and diagnostic results when deciding upon an intervention. • Investigate strategies designed to meet particular social skills deficits. • Make sure the duration and intensity of the intervention are appropriate for the student's needs.

Source: Steedly, Schwartz, Levin, & Luke, 2008, pp. 2–3.

ACADEMIC SKILLS The academic skills needed in the secondary school setting change dramatically from those necessary in primary school, regardless of the adolescent's school placement. Families may provide insight into the student's unique instructional needs. It is important that families understand the options available for their student and help determine which program will best suit current and future goals. After careful consideration, the multidisciplinary team will establish whether the middle or junior high school student's IEP should address regular class support, basic skills, functional life skills, or any combination of these instructional targets. In high school, families need to assist in determining the educational model that best suits their student's instructional needs for attaining both immediate and long-term goals. A vocational skills focus may be required to meet these goals.

REGULAR CLASS SUPPORT In a regular class support model, students receive content instruction in the general education classroom. At times, students on an IEP can be successful in general education courses without any support. Students with disabilities should be given the opportunity to achieve success in these courses without assistance from the special education team. The IEP team may decide that the student be monitored in these classes and provide support only when necessary. For classes where additional support is needed, different instructional structures may be used including tutoring support, learning strategies instruction, and compensatory support including identification of accommodations, which may include assistive technology and modifications, or some combination thereof.

INSTRUCTIONAL STRATEGIES Families and the team may agree that a student needs tutoring in the area of concern. There are various tutoring options available for students with special needs. One method of tutoring that has shown promise in producing higher student outcomes is peer tutoring (National Tutoring Association, 2010). In a peer-tutoring model, students work in pairs to practice academic tasks and help one another learn content. In successful models, students will switch roles from tutor to tutee (What Works Clearinghouse, 2012). Other tutoring options may include one-on-one instruction during an identified class period or after school tutoring programs.

Another effective option in increasing student outcomes is providing instruction in learning strategies. Learning strategies are approaches to learning that enable students to gain information and solve problems. There are different learning strategy programs available, including content-specific strategies in reading, writing, and math, strategies that address metacognitive skills in organization and evaluation, and strategies that address study skills. There are also strategies that address transition skills such as self-advocacy. The choice to include a learning strategy option for secondary students with special needs should be made in conjunction with the student and their family. These programs require additional instruction, and it may be necessary to include a class that provides this type of instruction.

Accommodations and modifications are included in regular class support to help the student with special needs participate in the general education curriculum. IDEA does not specify what these accommodations and modifications are. This decision should be made in conjunction with families as part of the educational programing processes.

An accommodation is anything that does not change the evaluation component of the curriculum. It allows students to access the same assignments and assessments as their nondisabled peers. Instructional accommodations may include allowing extra time on assignment completion, formatting an exam in Braille, providing a text-reader assistive device, or having a student take an exam in a quiet room. A modification adjusts the curriculum evaluation standard. It provides access to different evaluative measures than a student's nondisabled peers. Evaluative modifications include a test that has fewer items, assessing only part of the taught curriculum, or assignments addressing different functional topics. Modifications need to be written on a student's IEP (Families and Advocates Partnership for Education, 2001). Families may want to carefully consider including modification at the secondary level. For students planning on continuing their education post–high school, it is important to note that modifications provided in the K–12 setting may not transfer to post–high school educational institutions.

BASIC ACADEMIC SKILLS The basic academic skills focus is a remedial model. This model is commonly used in primary school for students with mild or moderate disabilities. Families may determine that this model should continue in the secondary setting. In the basic academic skills model, students receive intensive instructional remediation in specific content areas, generally reading, writing, or math. The assumption of this model is that students receiving targeted instructional interventions will ultimately increase their academic achievement in these curricular areas. This model does have the advantage of focusing on a student's particular area of need; however, it may minimize focus on a student's strengths. If a student has unsuccessfully achieved outcomes in this model in primary school, it may be due to an inability to generalize or transfer learning across instructional settings. For example, a student is able to read and comprehend a grade-level story when read with the resource teacher in the resource room. However, when asked to read a passage from the social studies text in the general education class, the student may be able to read the text but not comprehend what was read. This may be due to a variety of factors, including lack of assistance and prompts from the resource teacher, increased level of anxiety produced from reading in front of peers, or even an inability to understand expository text. Families should be included in discussions about continuing this model in the secondary setting, as their child may be better served in either a regular class support model or a functional skills model.

INSTRUCTIONAL STRATEGIES In the basic academic skills model, instruction is usually provided by a special education professional. This instruction should take place in a small-group setting, allowing teachers to provide the intensive support that is necessary for students requiring remediation. Research has shown that using direct explicit instruction promotes students' learning and retention (Hollingsworth & Ybarra, 2008). A critical component of direct explicit instruction is providing supports to instruction. This may mean a teacher will break the content into small, more accessible units of instruction. Instructional delivery also includes a teacher model and gives the students opportunity to practice with teacher support (Archer & Hughes, 2011). An underlying assumption in direct explicit instruction is that the students will be engaged throughout the lesson and that feedback will be provided on student performance throughout the lesson.

FUNCTIONAL LIFE SKILLS In the functional life skills model, a student's needs in areas of difficulty are identified and targeted for alternative instruction. This model emphasizes future social competence. Families and the team will need to consider what a student will need to function in future life settings. Functional life skills programs include instruction in foundational academics. Foundational academics incorporate basic arithmetic skills such as working with money, that is counting back change, telling time, and basic addition and subtraction skills. Foundational academics also includes basic English language arts skills such as beginning reading, sign/symbol identification, reading schedules and maps, and basic writing. Along with foundational academics, functional life skills programs may include acquisition of skills in community participation including recreation and leisure activities and personal care (Alwell & Cobb, 2006). In the high school setting, these programs may incorporate training in job skills consisting of on-the-job training with the assistance of a job coach. Social skills training is usually a critical component of any functional life skills program. This model does have advantages. It is tailored to a student's identified deficits. Social competence and the demands of daily living are addressed. This is a skill-acquisition model focusing on behaviors needed to successfully navigate adult living. The disadvantage to this model is that it has set adult outcome expectations. It may not allow students to achieve beyond this expectation. Families should be included in determining each of the functional skills categories needed by the student. In addition, any limits set on student adult outcomes should only be determined in careful consultation with the family.

INSTRUCTIONAL STRATEGIES The instructional strategies used in this model are individualized to the student. In general, functional academic skills are set at the student level and are taught using methods that address the student's concrete learning needs. In most cases, extended practice opportunities are necessary for the student to acquire the needed skills. The specific strategies needed for community participation also are based primarily on the student's needs. Families are consulted on the student's likes and dislikes, and content and strategies are chosen accordingly.

Job-training services are usually provided in specific programs. These may include specific vocational training or focus on social skills necessary to be successful in a job setting. Job training program availability varies across educational settings. Families should be made aware of programs available for students in their location and be informed of the instructional strategies that are used within these settings. This will allow families to make informed decisions about including a functional life skills program as part of their student's individualized education program.

VOCATIONAL TRAINING   The vocational training model frequently is conducted in partnership with other educational agencies. Vocational training includes instruction in knowledge and skills required for a specific job such as data entry, carpentry, or veterinary technician. Available programs vary across educational settings. If families express interest in vocational training, a representative of the identified program should be part of the multidisciplinary team.

CASE STUDY 3
TANZY (ALTERNATIVE HIGH SCHOOL)

Tanzy was referred for special education services in the third grade. Her general education teacher reported that she was unable to read and was beginning to struggle in mathematics. Following unsuccessful tier-three interventions in both reading and math, an evaluation was conducted, and the multidisciplinary team decided Tanzy should receive services under the category of learning disability. Tanzy showed some progress in her mathematics performance, and in junior high she received special education services in English language arts only. While in the eighth grade, Tanzy and her mother were involved in a convenience store robbery. Her mother was taken hostage by the robber but was released without physical injuries, and the criminal fled through the rear of the store. Tanzy has been receiving counseling since this event but still has some anxiety issues. At her parents' request, the multidisciplinary team determined that Tanzy should be placed in a small alternative setting to help minimize the effects of her anxiety. In this placement, Tanzy receives coursework in all of the content areas required for graduation. In addition, this school has a partnership with the local trade school. This trade school has programs in construction, service, health care, and manufacturing. Many students graduate from this alternative setting with a technical certificate. Tanzy's parents would like her to graduate with a certificate, and currently she is working on her CNA (certified nurse assistant). She is not enthusiastic about the courses required for this and is falling behind. In her transition individual education program (IEP), Tanzy expressed a desire to become a massage therapist.

Questions for Critical Thinking

1. How might Tanzy's anxiety affect her postschool options? What role should Tanzy and her family play in in addressing this concern during the transition IEP?

2. Tanzy and her family have different ideas about the trade school options. As a member of the multidisciplinary team, how could you assist Tanzy's family in coming up with a plan regarding trade school?

Transition Planning

It is well documented that postschool outcomes for students with disabilities are not on par with those of their nondisabled peers. Students with disabilities have dropout rates at about two times the rate of students without disabilities (Chapman, Laird, Ifill, & KewalRamani, 2011). Addressing post–high school outcomes for students with disabilities has been recommended since the early 1980s, with transition plan requirements being added to IDEA in 1990. All students with IEPs must have a transition plan in place by age 16. This means that transition planning considerations should take place before a student's 16th birthday. Families are critical in transition IEP development; in fact, the law specifies that the student be a part of this planning process. It is important to note that sometimes the student may be of the age of majority. If this is the case, the student must be informed of his right and provide consent for the inclusion of representatives outside the specified IEP team.

IDEA Requirements

IDEA has outlined specific requirements that must be on a transition IEP. According to IDEA [34 CFR 300.43 (a)] [20 U.S.C. 1401(34)]:

The term "transition services" means a coordinated set of activities for a child with a disability that:

- Is designed to be within a results-oriented process, that is focused on improving the academic and functional achievement of the child with a disability to facilitate the child's movement from school to postschool activities, including postsecondary education, vocational education, integrated employment (including supported employment), continuing and adult education, adult services, independent living, or community participation;
- Is based on the individual child's needs, taking into account the child's strengths, preferences, and interests; and
- Includes instruction, related services, community experiences, the development of employment and other postschool adult living objectives, and, if appropriate, acquisition of daily living skills and functional vocational evaluation.

The transition IEP must include measureable postsecondary goals. In addition, it must specify the needed services for completion of the IEP goal. This should also include a course of study.

Introduction to Adult Services

Transition IEP meetings when the student nears the age of majority need to include an introduction to available adult services. Individuals from the community responsible for these services may be invited to these meetings, but this invitation must meet the family's approval. These individuals may include representatives from employment agencies, including vocational rehabilitation and job services, representatives from adult social services, and individuals from educational institutions (see Table 11.3).

Table 11.3 ■ Agencies for Individuals With Disabilities
Employment
• Department of Vocational Rehabilitation (VR)
• Job Accommodation Network (JAN)
• ADA National Network
• Accessible Community Transportation in Our Nation (Project ACTION)
• Career One-Stop (website)
• Goodwill Industries International
• Job Access and ABILITY Jobs

(Continued)

Table 11.3 ■ (Continued)	
Employment *(continued)*	
	National Center on Workforce and Disability/Adult (NCWD)
	NISH
	Office of Disability Employment Policy
	EARN The Employer Assistance and Resource Network
	Social Security Administration (SSA)
	START-UP/USA
	Access Board
	Equal Employment Opportunity
Postsecondary Education	
	Association on Higher Education and Disability (AHEAD)
	Division of Adult Education and Literacy
	HEATH Resource Center
	Colleges, Career Colleges, Tech Colleges and Schools by State
	DO-IT
	Study.com
	PEP Net
Recreation	
	Department of the Interior
	Disabled Sports USA
	Mobility International USA (MIUSA)
	National Center on Accessibility
	National Center on Physical Activity and Disability (NCPAD)
	National Library Service for the Blind and Physically Handicapped (NLS/BPH)
	Learning Ally (formerly Recording for the Blind and Dyslexic)
	United States Adaptive Recreation Center
Independent Living	
	AbleData (website)
	Government Benefits (website)
	National Council on Independent Living (NCIL)
	National Rehabilitation Information Center (NARIC)
	Research and Training Center on Independent Living
	Social Security Administration (SSA)
Assistive Technology	
	Alliance for Technology Access (ATA)
	Assistivetech.net
	Family Center on Technology and Disability (FCTD)
	Parent

From the Center for Parent Information and Resources http://www.parentcenterhub.org/repository/foradults/

Prepare Child Ahead of Time for Transition

The most important person involved in the transition process is the student. Decisions made during these meetings can have a profound effect on endeavors later in life. Making goals for adult living can be an overwhelming process. Transition-age students with disabilities are going through all the difficult changes associated with adolescence, including establishing an independent identity. Students may experience fear or anxiety when making decisions, often experiencing conflict choosing post–high school options presented at a transition IEP meeting. It is important that teams work with families to prepare the student for this situation. Families working together to plan for these meetings will reduce the anxiety often associated with such an event and allow them time to discuss the options available post–high school and determine what might work best for the student.

PREPARATION ACTIVITIES   In preparing for future transition IEP meetings, families might want to consider giving their student opportunities to experience greater responsibility or independence. This can be done through a variety of activities both at home and in the community. In order to foster self-advocacy, families may want to give the student opportunities to negotiate and establish routines at home, for example, when a student moves from primary school to junior high school, families may consider letting the student negotiate for a later bed time. Students could be given the opportunity to belong to a school club or choose after-school activities. To foster responsibility, families might want to have their student open a bank account or schedule dentist appointments. To foster independence, families may want to consider encouraging their student to engage in activities away from the home that require the use of public transportation. Families should be encouraged to share the steps taken in the home setting with the multidisciplinary team. These activities may be mirrored in the school setting. Families and team members should work together to promote student success in the transition to adulthood.

Postsecondary Outcomes

Families should be aware of the different options available for their student after graduation. There are different outcome areas of concern, including employment, continued education, living, and leisure. Each of these should be discussed, and families should come to the transition IEP with questions regarding the options available for their student (see Table 11.4). Postschool outcomes are covered in depth in Chapter 12.

TABLE 11.4 ■ Issues Addressed in Transition Planning			
Postsecondary Outcomes			
Employment	**Education**	**Living**	**Leisure**
• Assisted employment • Independent employment • Vocation	• Vocational training • College or university	• Residential placement • Group home • Living with family • Independent living	• Clubs • Sports • Church • Fitness center • Extracurricular courses (arts)

POTENTIAL NEEDS OF THE FAMILY DURING THE SECONDARY YEARS

Families continue to be the most important part of an adolescent's life. Even though the child is now struggling for independence, they still need and appreciate their family support (Greydanus & Bashe, 2003). It is important to recognize and encourage the value of families in the educational process. There are family needs that are particular to the secondary school years, including the navigation of the transition process.

Family Involvement

Families are critical members of the multidisciplinary team. Their participation in individualized education programming is guaranteed by IDEA. Families need to feel comfortable in participating in these activities. Measures should be taken to ensure that they can actively participate in their student's education. This should happen during each transition phase of the student's secondary education experience. This includes not only the transition IEP but also for the transition from primary school to middle or junior high school, the transition from middle or junior high school to high school, when needed, the transition from high school to 18–22 programs, and graduation. Education professionals should assist families in preparing for these transitions. Meetings between families and teachers should be scheduled to outline expectations and demands. Also, families should be informed of the purpose of multidisciplinary meetings and informed of specific areas where their input will be necessary. They should be encouraged to provide information and opinions throughout any educational programming meeting, and they must be made aware of their rights and responsibilities during these meetings. It is the team's responsibility to empower the family to advocate for the child.

Student Involvement

Student involvement in educational decision making increases throughout the secondary years. This begins with planning the transition from primary school to middle or junior high school. Including a student as an active member of these teams addresses the student's developmental need for independence. Student participation in planning and decision making during these early transitions will help minimize the anxiety around these transitions. Additionally, having students as active participants in these plans promotes success in future placements. Students should be included in course planning. Allowing students the opportunity to select courses provides them with a sense of autonomy. Students need to be active participants in planning for their future. IDEA requires that students are active members of the transition planning team. A student best understands their likes and dislikes and their plans for their future post–high school. The multidisciplinary team may want to provide the student with interest surveys, career choice programs, or future-planning programs. These are available for students at a variety of academic levels. The student should be also be encouraged to evaluate their strengths and weaknesses. Teams may want to encourage the student to engage in goal-setting activities prior to the planning meeting. Some students may require training in self-advocacy. With these skills, a student can speak up for themselves and make decisions about their own life. These plans are, after all, determining what their adulthood may entail.

Summary

Adolescence is a time of rapid developmental changes. Adolescents experience physical, social, and emotional changes. Adolescents strive to express their independence, often challenging their childhood role in the family. Children at this age also experience educational changes. Major educational transitions occur during this time, including the move from elementary to secondary school and increased academic demands. In addition to the many changes and challenges adolescents and their families face, families of adolescents with disabilities experience added concerns. Families of students with disabilities often feel protective, particularly when they experience worry over their child's social dealings. Concerns over bullying and peer pressure, social issues that increase during adolescence, are prevalent in families of children with disabilities. These concerns as well as others are addressed by the multidisciplinary team during the secondary years.

In the secondary years, the multidisciplinary team has members representing groups similar to those seen in the primary years. As always, families are critical members of this team. However, the role of the student with disabilities increases at this time. Educational planning now focuses not only on K–12 outcomes but also on what the adolescent plans on doing after high school. The team must determine what educational placement will best help the student meet post–high school goals. An educational focus must also be determined. Depending on the student's and family's vision for post–high school living, the team may determine the student needs an academic or vocational focus. This focus may change as the student approaches high school. The team, before the adolescent's 16th birthday, is required to create a transition plan.

The transition plan meeting will review resources to determine the student's post–high school goals. It is therefore important at this meeting that community agencies important in the adolescent's postsecondary life be included as members of the team. The transition plan should address all areas of post–high school living, including employment, education, living, and leisure. With significant input from the family and the student, a plan will be created that will help the student reach post–high school goals.

Additional Resources

Web-Based

American Psychological Associations: http://www.apa.org/pi/families/resources/develop.pdf. A reference for professionals: Developing Adolescents.

Families and Advocates Partnership for Education: http://www.wrightslaw.com/info/sec504.accoms.mods.pdf. School accommodations and modifications.

Medline Plus the U.S. National Library of Medicine: http://www.nlm.nih.gov/medlineplus/ency/article/002003.htm. Adolescent development.

National Collaborative on Workforce and Disability: http://www.ncwd-youth.info/. A website providing information on employment for youth with disabilities.

U.S. Department of Education IDEA: http://idea.ed.gov/. A website providing resources related to IDEA implementation and regulations.

Wrights Law: http://www.wrightslaw.com/. A website providing information about special education law.

Print

Brinthaupt, T. M., & Lipka, R. P. (Eds.). (2012). *Understanding early adolescent self and identity: Applications and interventions.* New York: SUNY Press.

Eccles, J. S. (1999). The development of children ages 6–14. *The Future of Children When School Is Out, 19*(2), 30–44.

Greydanus, D. E., & Bashe, P. (2003). *Caring for your teenager.* New York, NY: Bantamum.

Hendrickson, J. M., Ross, J. R., Mercer, C. D., & Walker, P. (1988). The multidisciplinary team: Training educators to serve middle school students with special needs. *The Clearing House, 62*(2), 84–86.

Mandlawitz, M. (2007). *What every teacher should know about IDEA laws and regulations.* Boston: Pearson.

Spano, S. (2004). *Stages of adolescent development: Research facts and findings.* Ithaca, NY: ACT for Youth: Upstate Center of Excellence, Cornell University.

12

POSTSCHOOL

BRIAN FREEDMAN
University of Delaware

LAURA EISENMAN
University of Delaware

CATHY COWIN

SEAN ROY
Pacer Center

"Treat people as if they were what they ought to be and you help
them become what they are capable of becoming."

—Goethe

LEARNING OBJECTIVES

After reading this chapter, you will be able to:

1. Identify common challenges faced by students and families during the postschool transition process and strategies for a successful transition.
2. Describe the landscape of adult lives (employment, postsecondary education, and independent living) and available supports.
3. Recognize how to partner with families so that postschool connections can be made.

Educators may be tempted to think of graduation as the ultimate goal for their students, imagining their students crossing the finish line after the long educational race from preschool through high school. However, for most families of students who have disabilities, graduation is just the beginning of a much longer adventure, supporting their children as they travel into adulthood and through many more years of community membership. In fact, **the Individuals with Disabilities Education Act (IDEA)** recognizes this lifelong journey as one of the major reasons for providing special education services in the first place. The regulations for IDEA describe the primary purpose of special education services this way:

> ...to ensure that all children with disabilities have available to them a free appropriate public education that emphasizes special education and related services designed to meet their unique needs *and prepare them for further education, employment, and independent living.* (IDEA, 2006; emphasis added)

With this understanding, educators are considered to have a strong **measure of accountability for the postsecondary outcomes of the students with** disabilities that they serve. Why should educators be concerned about what happens *after* a student leaves school? Is it even possible for educators to have an impact on students' postschool situations? The purpose of this chapter is to share the experiences and challenges faced by students with disabilities and their families after they leave high school as well as share strategies for effectively partnering with families during this time.

POSTSCHOOL OUTCOMES

Concerns for the postschool outcomes of students with disabilities were raised by national longitudinal studies conducted in the 1990s and 2000s (see, for example, Blackorby & Wagner, 1996; Newman et al., 2011; Wagner, Newman, Cameto, & Levine, 2005). These studies documented that, although there was variability within and across disability categories, too few of these students experienced postschool success, and they had significantly poorer outcomes than their peers who did not have disabilities. Not only were students with disabilities graduating at far lower rates than their peers, they also were significantly less likely to be employed, enroll in further education, and live independently. Blackorby and Wagner (1996) noted that 3 to 5 years after leaving school, slightly more than half (57%) of students with disabilities were employed, yet 69% of their peers had found jobs. In regard to postsecondary education, the gap was even larger: only 27% of students with disabilities had experienced any further education, but 68% of their peers had. A similar gap was seen in the area of independent living. Three to 5 years after leaving school, approximately 37% of students with disabilities were living independently, while 60% of their peers were doing so. More recently, Wagner et al. (2005) and Newman et al. (2011) noted that students with disabilities' postschool situations have been improving in some areas, but overall they continue to lag behind their peers. While the percentages of students who graduate high school and enroll in postsecondary education have slowly increased, there is still room for significant improvement, and their rates of employment and independent living continue to be low.

PREDICTORS OF POSTSCHOOL SUCCESS

Research has demonstrated that the foundation for postschool success is strongly related to the educational opportunities and experiences students have before they leave school, including in the earliest years of their education (Haber et al., 2015). Educators can have a strong impact on the postschool outcomes of their students. Table 12.1 shows a variety of school-age factors that have been found to contribute to positive adult outcomes in each of the three major postschool domains. Perhaps not surprisingly, involving families and collaborating with community agencies during the school years are important predictors of adult success for children with disabilities. And, as discussed in the preceding chapter, beginning when students enter their secondary school years, the IDEA includes expectations for how schools will involve families, students, and adult service agencies in the transition planning process as part of IEP development and the delivery of transition services. Especially as students approach their final years of school, educators must work closely with families, students, and community agencies to understand the important legal transitions and role adjustments that will occur.

TABLE 12.1 ■ School-Age Predictors Associated With Positive Postschool Outcomes			
	Outcome Domains		
Predictors	Education	Employment	Independent Living
Inclusion in General Education	✔	✔	✔
Paid Employment/Work Experience	✔	✔	✔
Self-Care/Independent Living	✔	✔	✔
Student Support	✔	✔	✔
Career Awareness	✔	✔	
Goal-Setting	✔	✔	
Interagency Collaboration	✔	✔	
Occupational Courses	✔	✔	
Parent Expectations	✔	✔	
Self-Advocacy/Self-Determination	✔	✔	
Social Skills	✔	✔	
Transition Program	✔	✔	
Vocational Education	✔	✔	

Predictors	Outcome Domains		
	Education	Employment	Independent Living
Youth Autonomy/Decision-Making	✔	✔	
Community Experiences		✔	
Exit Exam Requirements/Diploma		✔	
Parent Involvement		✔	
Program of Study		✔	
Travel Skills		✔	
Work Study		✔	

Source: Adapted from National Technical Assistance Center on Transition (NTACT, n.d.). http://transitionta.org/sites/default/files/Pred_Outcomes_0.pdf

A checkmark indicates that research has shown a significant connection between a factor and a postschool outcome. An absence of a checkmark does not mean that there is not a relationship; rather, it indicates inconclusive or lack of research in that area.

AGE OF MAJORITY

In most states, when young people have their 18th birthday, they are considered to have reached the "age of majority"; they are no longer minors. Adult students are legally entitled to make their own decisions in many matters where their parents had previously been in charge. This includes being responsible for their educational services decisions if they are still in school. This shift in responsibility is recognized in IDEA 2004, which requires schools to inform families about the approaching change in legal status. Specifically:

- Beginning no later than one year before the child reaches the age of majority under State law, the IEP must include a statement that the child has been informed of the child's rights under Part B of the Act, if any, that will transfer to the child on reaching the age of majority under §300.520.

This means, for example, that an adult student will now receive the annual notice of IEP meetings and act as his or her own representative on the IEP team. Parents will be notified of the meeting and may be *invited* to attend by their adult child, but they are no longer the legal representative of the student on the IEP team. Even with this legal change, most students will continue to need their families' involvement and support, and families will continue to be critical members of transition teams. Educators can facilitate these new decision-making roles by teaching students self-determination skills and coaching families on the types of advocacy that will be helpful to their adult child (Wandry & Pleet, 2009).

Families may have additional questions about the implications of this change in their adult child's legal status and wonder whether guardianship should be considered. Many families struggle with the decision to pursue guardianship. While most families want their youth to live self-directed lives, a small percentage of individuals with disabilities are genuinely vulnerable and may need a family member to make certain decisions on their behalf. Families should be educated on and encouraged to consider different options for shifting or sharing decision-making authority. Full guardianship is the most restrictive approach, because it transfers a person's right to make their own decisions to another person. Obtaining guardianship involves a lengthy legal process that varies from state to state. Guardianship is typically irreversible. Due to the time, expense, and concerns about limiting their young adults' rights, families my not wish to pursue this option. Limited guardianship and power of attorney restrict the shifting of decision-making authority to specific areas of the person's life and power of attorney can be revocable.

In general, it is important to know that helping adults with disabilities make choices for themselves rarely requires an "all or nothing" approach. Some individuals may be able to make informed decisions in one area of their life but require support in another. Likewise, different levels of support can be applied. Supported decision making is a less restrictive approach for those individuals who do require assistance (Blanck & Martinis, 2015). This method involves trusted family, friends, and professionals who assist an individual to understand and express choices by considering the person's unique preferences, providing information in forms that are accessible to the person, and incorporating accommodations and other supports that the person may need to enact a decision. Students who have had opportunities to develop **self-determination skills** during their school years will be better situated to act as informed decision makers in the transition to adulthood.

ENTITLEMENT VERSUS ELIGIBILITY

Another important legal change that occurs as students exit school relates to their eligibility for special services. Throughout their education, students with disabilities are protected from discrimination by the Americans with Disabilities Act (ADA) and Section 504 of the Rehabilitation Act and, importantly, they are entitled to education and related services that are free and individualized to their specific strengths, needs, and interests through the IDEA. However, once students with disabilities leave secondary school and move into postsecondary life, IDEA no longer applies. As adults, they are no longer entitled to special services. Their civil rights to be protected from disability discrimination and receive reasonable accommodation (under the Americans with Disabilities Act and Section 504 of the Rehabilitation Act) do remain in place, but access to disability-related services will depend upon the state and locality in which they live. Typically, people with disabilities must apply for services through state, county, or regional government agencies such as vocational rehabilitation or developmental disabilities programs. These agencies will determine whether the nature of a person's disability makes them eligible for services based on each agency's particular regulations and funding. Just because a child with a disability was eligible for services under IDEA does not mean that the child will be eligible for services as an adult in the areas of employment, further education, or independent living. For example, a young adult with a significant learning disability would likely not be eligible to receive state-funded adult services that support independent living unless that person was deemed to have an intellectual disability. Even if the student had independent living–related goals on their IEP, they may not qualify as an adult for services that fund the development and maintenance of daily living skills.

UNDERSTANDING CONCERNS, KNOWING OPTIONS, AND CREATING PARTNERSHIPS

Each of the following sections of this chapter will address these issues in more detail. As students **transition** to adult roles, educators must be knowledgeable about the options for students' employment, further education, and independent living. They need to be aware of the kinds of questions and concerns that families may have about the next steps in the postschool journey and must be skilled at creating true partnerships with families in support of their children's transition into adulthood.

Employment

Common Questions From Families

- How can we strengthen my son's/daughter's IEP so skills needed for employment are attained?
- What are the community supports available to help support my youth in employment?
- I have heard the term "supported employment" but do not understand what it is. Does it apply to my youth?
- Should I encourage my youth to disclose his/her disability during a job interview?
- Are employers willing to hire people with disabilities?

CURRENT STATISTICS AND OPTIMISTIC TRENDS

The completion of high school brings about a transition toward employment, with students taking those critical next steps toward establishing a career. While some students will continue into postsecondary education, many students will seek employment immediately following high school. However, successfully finding and maintaining a paid job in an inclusive setting can be challenging for a person with a disability. In fact, the participation rate of people with disabilities in the labor force was estimated at about 20% in 2012 and 2013, compared with 70% of people without disabilities (U.S. Bureau of Labor Statistics, 2014).

Historically, many people with disabilities were denied the opportunity to become competitively employed despite being capable of success. However, there have been recent policy movements that have strongly encouraged and even mandated that all people with disabilities have the opportunity to work in a competitive environment. One such movement is called Employment First, through which advocates and policy makers have formally identified the importance of people with disabilities finding meaningful employment in an integrated setting (Wehman & Brooke, 2013). Federal **legislation** called the Workforce Innovation and Opportunity Act, passed in 2014, also ensures that all people with disabilities will be given the opportunity to seek competitive employment and requires that states devote more funding than ever before to transition-age youth. The transition to employment should start early, though, to ensure that the student has adequate time to develop an understanding of career options, an awareness of strengths and weaknesses, and the skills necessary to be successful. Collaboration among the student, families, school professionals, and adult service providers can ensure this can happen.

CAREER DEVELOPMENT

As a student nears the end of high school, they have likely begun a multistep process of career development, in which they participate in learning experiences designed to help them prepare for employment and other facets of adulthood. Students often begin the career development process in elementary school through the acquisition of work-related dispositions, interests, and habits. This should accelerate during ages 14 to 16 for students with disabilities, coinciding with the mandated inclusion of transition-related goals on their IEP related to the four stages of career development:

- *Career awareness*—learning about career roles and tasks
- *Career exploration*—comparing strengths and weaknesses to a variety of different careers. This process may include job shadowing or volunteer work.

- *Career preparation*—identifying an initial career path and taking steps toward that—for example, beginning an internship or apprenticeship in employment is being pursued post–high school, or AP courses or entrance exams for a postsecondary education program
- *Career assimilation*—shifting fully out of the high school setting and into the postsecondary setting

Through the IEP process, employment goals and appropriate career development activities are identified. One commonly used model for engaging in career development is the Life Centered Education (LCE) Model (Council for Exceptional Children, 2015).

As the student prepares to enter the adult world, multiple federally funded state agencies are available to offer potential support. State vocational rehabilitation (VR) programs offer support and services for people with physical and cognitive disabilities who are interested in finding gainful employment. Each state has a different system for how support is offered through VR, and there may be varying degrees of collaboration between a student's school and their VR case manager. In working with VR, all students will develop an individual plan for employment (IPE) that establishes the student's career goals and the activities necessary to achieve these goals. The IPE is critical, as this plan is used to determine the types of support that VR will offer in pursuit of the activities and goals determined by the student and team.

Students with intellectual/developmental disabilities may also have access to employment support services through additional state agencies. For these students, resources from multiple state agencies can often be used in conjunction to provide more extensive supports to help a person find and maintain their job. Typically, the earlier students are connected to these services, the better the outcome (NTACT, n.d.). However, many families may not fully understand the importance of connecting early on with these agencies, and their support may be needed in order to submit eligibility applications. Furthermore, many families may be so consumed with external stressors that they may have difficulty devoting the necessary time and energy to making these connections to adult agencies independently. School officials can therefore facilitate this process of students and families connecting to these adult agencies (Pleet & Wandry, 2009).

EMPLOYMENT SETTINGS

There are many types of settings in which people with disabilities find employment. The job responsibilities and work environment will depend on the student's goals, interests, strengths, and weaknesses, as well as their level of support need and the services available in their region. The job search process frequently begins in high school and may often be supported by the student's assigned adult service agency case manager(s) if the student has been declared eligible for those services. The following are options for students with disabilities:

- *Day programs and sheltered workshops*—activity centers exclusively for people with disabilities. These typically include recreational activities, makeshift work, prevocational activities, and skill training. Sheltered workshops have come under recent scrutiny and even shut down, as many suggest that they have similar qualities to institutions. While some claim that sheltered workshops serve as a stepping stone for people with disabilities to move into competitive, community-based employment, the research does not back this claim (Cimera, Wehman, West, & Burgess, 2012).
- *Job placement*—Rehabilitation counselors or community-based service providers support people with disabilities through VR in preparing a resume, identifying and applying for jobs, interviewing effectively, and advocating for necessary accommodations. VR counselors or other service staff can then remain involved for a specific period of time, providing job coaching or supporting the creation of natural supports that allow the person to function independently.

- *Internships*—opportunities for genuine work experiences in a business setting for a limited period of time. Internships might be supported by school staff, VR counselors, or others. They provide an opportunity for a person with a disability to learn about different types of jobs and job tasks in that employment setting, the workplace social skills that are necessary for success, and opportunities for networking. These types of early work experiences are one of the strongest predictors of success, particularly for students with significant disabilities (Carter, Austin, & Trainor, 2011).
- *Self-Employment*—Some people with disabilities elect to create their own business, either due to a unique passion or skill or in order to create their preferred employment setting. Vocational rehabilitation agencies typically offer support in creating a business plan and engaging in job tasks that may be too difficult for the individual to handle because of their disability.
- *Supported employment*—This service is typically accessed by people with the most significant support needs with the goal of finding competitive employment. Support is offered for the person to engage in job exploration activities, apply for open positions, and then for on-the-job support on an ongoing basis. Supported employment services usually constitute a joint effort between vocational rehabilitation and developmental disabilities services so that support can be offered beyond the usual timeline allowed by VR.
- *Customized employment*—a process often encompassed within supported employment in which a person and employer agree on a job description that matches the person's strengths and interests, as well as the needs of the employer. The job responsibilities often differ from a standard job description.

The process of identifying career goals and prospective employment opportunities should be led by the student. Students will likely require support to consider their career options and the various positions available in different fields. Some students may have had previous discussions with their families about their career and employment options. Families offer valuable ideas to the discussion about employment options and job prospects. Students may also differ in opinions from their families about the career they hope to pursue. School staff have an important role in facilitating a balance between empowering the student to lead the process of deciding next steps while ensuring that the family's ideas, opinions, and support are nurtured and included.

RIGHTS, ACCOMMODATIONS, AND SELF-DISCLOSURE

People with disabilities are offered civil rights protections through the Americans with Disabilities Act (ADA), which ensures equal opportunities in multiple aspects of a person's life, including employment (U.S. Equal Employment Opportunity Commission, 2009). The ADA prevents discrimination against "qualified individuals," defined as a person who can perform the essential functions of a job, with or without reasonable **accommodations**. A reasonable accommodation is a modification or adjustment to a job or work environment that allows a person to perform a job or participate in that organization as all other employees are able to do. It might include creating a physically accessible workspace or documents that offer typed instructions that are otherwise offered verbally. ADA does not automatically require an employer to hire a person with a disability or provide any accommodation requested, but rather it is designed to create a more equal playing field through which people with disabilities can be hired and maintain their jobs. In order to receive employment accommodations, a person must disclose how they are impacted by a disability. This process, though, requires potentially complicated decisions, and many students will benefit from support in making this decision.

Multiple variables factor into a person's decision about whether or not to disclose their disability and request accommodations. People with visible disabilities may be more inclined to disclose early on versus someone with a hidden disability, like attention deficit/hyperactivity disorder. Negative past experiences with being identified as disabled may influence disclosure decisions, as well as concerns that others may perceive the person as less capable or competent or that accommodations will be costly or time consuming. Unfortunately, some employers continue to hold negative attitudes about hiring and retaining people with disabilities or have unclear procedures for disclosing and requesting accommodations (Erickson, von Schrader, Bruyere, & VanLooy, 2014). One study discussed the disclosure process with focus groups of people with disabilities (Jans, Kaye, & Jones, 2012). Participants had differing opinions about the timing of disclosure (e.g., before/at interview, before/at start of work), although most agreed that disclosure at some point was important. Overall recommendations that were offered for interviewing for jobs and disclosing information included focusing on abilities, exhibiting enthusiasm and self-confidence, inquiring about the job tasks and work environment early in order to consider potential accommodation needs, and preparing ahead of time about how to handle inappropriate questions.

FEDERAL BENEFITS

Some people with disabilities are eligible to receive federal income support because their disability significantly impacts their ability to maintain full-time employment. This benefit involves a program called Supplemental Security Income (SSI). Eligible students and families go through an application process in which they need to show proof of their disability and financial need. When a student receives SSI, they should not be discouraged from seeking employment either in addition to their SSI or in replacement of their SSI. However, some students and families may be fearful of losing their benefits, as they depend on this income. Students and families should be made aware that (a) students can work while they receive SSI; (b) SSI recipients may be able to receive additional benefits for paying for items that are necessary for work; and (c) some students may be able to keep Medicaid, federal health insurance that is received along with SSI, even while they are working (Brooke, Revell, McDonough, & Green, 2013). Benefits counseling is highly recommended for students who are applying for and receiving SSI so that informed decisions can be made about employment.

COMMON QUESTIONS FROM FAMILIES REGARDING SPECIFIC ISSUES RELATED TO EMPLOYMENT

How Can I Help Build Needed Work Skills and Soft Skills So My Son Can Be Successful in Employment?

Employment is a key aspect of a young person's transition to adulthood, and families can play a crucial role in making sure youth have the work skills and soft skills needed to be successful at work. It is important to note that young people with disabilities may function at different levels but should be expected to acquire these skills to the extent they are able.

The term "work skills" refers to abilities in reading, writing, and math, as well as employment-specific skills like communicating, working with others, making decisions, and becoming a lifelong learner (Center for Literacy, Education, and Employment, n.d.). The National Collaborative on Workforce and Disability for Youth (NCWD-Youth) authored an info brief titled *Helping Youth Build Work Skills for Job Success: Tips for Parents and Families* (NCWD-Youth, 2012). The brief offers ideas for parents on how they can help youth build work skills through home-based activities. Those ideas include:

- Helping youth identify his or her learning style to find the most effective way they learn and communicate.
- Plan family activities that help youth develop their powers of observation.
- Have youth practice sending thank-you notes for appropriate occasions.
- Bring a job application home, or find one online, and help your youth fill it out.
- Ask your youth to read a book or newspaper article, and then ask them to summarize the key points of what they read.
- Ask your youth to identify a task with multiple steps, such as making a meal, and have them guide you through it.
- Encourage your youth to participate in school- or community-based activities that promote leadership.
- Keep your weekly grocery receipts and ask your youth to make a chart to track spending.
- Help your youth find opportunities to practice working with money.
- Consider what assistive technology is available to help with reading, communicating, and math.
- Make sure your youth's IEP includes goals and activities related to building key work skills.
- Many youth, including youth with disabilities, struggle with displaying appropriate "soft skills" in employment situations. A lack of soft skills can lead to poor work performance, conflict with coworkers, and even losing the job altogether. Soft skills are the nontechnical interpersonal and communication skills we use every day to be successful at work and in the community. They include having a positive attitude, taking directions from others, working well as part of a team, communicating so that others can understand, and being at work on time.

For many adults, building soft skills was something that happened naturally. They may have been acquired through parental expectations such as chores, respectful communication, or an emphasis on work ethic. Many youth with disabilities will gain these skills the exact same way. Here are some ideas on how families can help youth build soft skills that lead to success in employment:

- Find opportunities for youth to practice respectful communications with adults. This may include shaking hands, maintaining eye contact, and answering questions when asked.
- Have a discussion with your youth about the need for employees to take work direction. Point out that employment may mean having to do things you don't want to do but that need to be done if they are part of the job.
- Schedule monthly family meals where everyone dresses in clothes considered "work casual" (slacks, dresses, shirts with buttons, dress shoes, etc.). This helps youth understand that there are times when dressing a certain way is a requirement.
- Assign your youth a chore where they have to take responsibility for getting something done every day or week. This may include unloading the dishwasher, getting themselves up for school, or taking out the trash. Hold the youth accountable for remembering to do their jobs.
- Ask your youth to plan, shop for, and make a family meal once a month. If a youth is not able to do this independently, then work as part of a team to make decisions and prepare the meal.
- Make sure your youth's IEP includes goals and activities related to identified need areas. This could include social functioning or reading social cues, hygiene, clear communication, or completing tasks with accuracy.

My youth has a job goal that I don't think is realistic. How can I help him/her explore something more attainable without compromising the dreams he/she has for herself/himself?

It is not uncommon for youth with or without disabilities to dream of having an extraordinary job. There is nothing wrong with young people wanting to be pro athletes, music stars, or video game designers, but it is problematic if this is the only career interest or if skills are not present that would make attaining that goal reasonable. Parents can find themselves in a tricky situation—not wanting to dash their youth's dreams but wanting to make sure youth are preparing for an employment goal that can be met.

Youth often gravitate toward these grand career interests because they don't have experiences that allow them to recognize the wide array of employment options available. In other cases, youth may be very interested in a certain area (such as sports or video games) and have picked jobs (pro athlete or video game designer) because that is what they have seen. Families can still respect their youth's goals while helping them explore attainable job options within the fields they find interesting. Here are some strategies:

- Help your youth research the actual number of jobs that are available in a given field. For example, there are approximately 450 players on pro basketball rosters at a given time. Discuss that a minute percentage of players actually make it to the pros. Then help them explore other jobs related to basketball, pro sports, sports marketing, athletic training, or working in a sports stadium, just in case they don't become a pro athlete.
- Many states have detailed web sites that offer state-specific labor market statistics and information on career fields and relevant education. Use this information to help your youth explore aspects of the job they are interested in. For example, a youth may see that being a microbiologist requires advanced degrees in college but that a laboratory assistant only needs an AA degree.
- If all else fails, parents can encourage their youth to secure a different job as a means to gain income while the youth is working on their desired career goal. In time, the youth may become interested in other careers or continue to work toward their dream job, which is OK too.

How Can I Use My Own Networks to Find Work Experience Opportunities for My Youth?

Networking is often described as a powerful tool for getting a job. The common saying is that "who you know" is more important than "what you know." Unfortunately, youth may not have the social connections to take advantage of the power of networking. Families can assist by accessing their own personal networks to find potential career exploration activities, work experience opportunities, or job leads for youth.

Some may see their "network" as a formal group made up of professional contacts. This is only partly true. A person's personal network can also include family, friends, coworkers, neighbors, members of a church, or owners of businesses you frequent. Families are encouraged to use these valuable contacts to cultivate possible work opportunities for their youth. Once potential network partners are identified, they should then be connected to the student's support team and included as part of the student's career plan. Examples might include:

- Asking a neighbor who works at the airport to speak with a youth about the range of jobs found there.
- Asking members of your book club if anybody knows a veterinarian that your daughter can conduct an informational interview with.
- Asking your brother, who works in retail, if he is aware of any job openings at his stores.
- Checking your church bulletin for possible volunteer opportunities to add to a resume.
- Having discussions with other parents to see if anybody has contacts at a manufacturing plant for a youth who wants to know more about welding.

STRATEGIES FOR PARTNERING WITH FAMILIES

Consider the following methods for partnering with families in supporting a student in finding postschool employment:

- Have honest discussions with the parents/student about the student's strengths, challenges, how current skills transfer to potential careers, and future supports.
- Listen to the family's input on the student's strengths and future job prospects, as they may have awareness of strengths and experiences that are unknown to school staff or ideas for jobs that had not been considered.
- Encourage family/students to provide additional information to the team (school/agency) that will help promote better employment outcomes, such as connections in the business community or other networking opportunities.
- Incorporate the additional information shared by parents/students into the IEP.
- Facilitate the relationship among the student, families, and state agencies (e.g., vocational rehabilitation). Be open to supporting families who may be reluctant or take longer to connect.
- Adhere to confidentiality requirements (e.g., explaining release of information forms) in order to promote trust with families. Ensure parent/student is fully informed about what information will be released to agencies.
- If needed, help facilitate completion of applications for state agency support. That may include helping the parent/student answer questions and obtain paperwork.
- Help the parent/student understand all options available for employment support, for example, by offering a workshop or provider fair in which different agencies present.

CASE STUDY 1
PARTNERING TO SUPPORT SUCCESS IN EMPLOYMENT

Ben is preparing to graduate from high school with a diploma. He has multiple learning disabilities (dyslexia and dysgraphia) that were first identified in elementary school. Ben has worked very hard to maintain a C average, and he describes school as "really hard." He really enjoys baseball but had to leave his high school varsity team in order to focus on his studies. Ben still has dreams of playing professionally. He also has an intuitive understanding of how to put things together, from cars to electronics. Ben is popular and is considered the kind of person that can get along well with various groups of people. Ben is looking forward to finishing high school and expresses no interest in going to college.

Ben's family is considered middle class. His mother is an administrative assistant in a law office, and his father has a manufacturing job at a factory in a neighboring town. Ben also has an older brother who is excelling at the state university. Over the course of his schooling, Ben's parents have had both positive and negative experiences with his IEP teams.

Ben's school team has conducted career assessments with Ben and helped him see how his strengths might be applied to a variety of jobs. The school also helped him set up an internship at an auto body shop this past year. This was a positive experience for him, although Ben remains unclear about his future career goals. When Ben's family was asked about their thoughts on Ben's future employment and career, they pointed out that he had successfully earned money the past several summers by mowing neighbors' lawns and doing yard work and that he had

(Continued)

CASE STUDY 1 (Continued)

developed a strong customer base. Ben acknowledged that he really enjoys this work but did not think that he could find a "regular" job doing that. Ben's school team also learns from his family that they are strongly connected to the Lutheran church and that Ben is well liked there. Ben's family understands that school has been challenging for him, although they are still hoping he will go to college in order to maximize his future opportunities. The school team does not dismiss this suggestion and instead facilitates a discussion with Ben and his family about the options for Ben pursuing postsecondary education or training. They discover that Ben is unaware of postsecondary training options in the fields that he is interested in, although he remains unsure of whether he wants to continue education and training beyond high school.

Over the past few years, his school team has helped Ben take charge of his IEP process. He is able to communicate his strengths and weaknesses well. Ben's family is also supportive of him playing a lead role in the decision-making process, although they are also nervous about him making decisions for himself that are not informed. Ben's school team helps him get connected to vocational rehabilitation (VR). Before doing so, they ensure that Ben and his family are educated on the types of supports that VR can offer, and they discuss the role that Ben and his parents will play in working with VR. The school team participates in the initial meetings with VR in order to contribute information about Ben's goals, school experiences, and previous career exploration activities. Together, Ben's new team creates his individual plan for employment (IPE). Prior to the meeting, Ben's family helped him think about how he wanted to advocate for himself, including by requesting help developing a resume, identifying internships, and continuing with the assistive technology that has helped him in school. Ben's parents also share with VR that they are hopeful that Ben will at some point pursue postsecondary education. The newly expanded team creates a plan that includes a variety of options for Ben to pursue.

Questions to Consider

1. How did Ben's school team create a partnership with his family?

2. What information was provided by the family that the team did not otherwise have?

3. How did the school team promote Ben's self-determination while respecting and valuing input from his family?

4. What supports might Ben and his family need as he pursues his plan?

POSTSECONDARY EDUCATION

Common Questions From Families

- How can we strengthen my son/daughter's IEP so skills needed for postsecondary education are attained?
- What are the main ways college differs from high school?
- What can my son or daughter expect from the college in terms of academic accommodations?
- What other supports can students with disabilities access through the college?
- What assistive technology is available to help my youth be a success in college?
- What will the college disability services office require in terms of documentation of the disability?
- Can my child with an intellectual disability go to college?
- What are the options for my child with a disability to pay for postsecondary education?

POSTSECONDARY EDUCATION OPTIONS

Families and students with disabilities may not see college as an option because of struggles they experienced in school or their beliefs about what "college" is and who it is for. The reality is that postsecondary education comes in many forms to fulfill the many different educational needs of adults across the lifespan. For example:

- Four-year colleges or universities that typically require students to meet particular academic standards for admission and offer bachelor's and graduate degrees
- Community colleges that may have open admissions policies and offer shorter-term technical certificates and 2-year associate's and other degrees
- Disability-specific degree-granting institutions (e.g., Landmark College) or certificate programs housed within institutions of higher education
- Career (vocational) technical schools that provide training and certification in specific trades
- Adult education programs that support attainment of literacy and other basic academic skills (e.g., GED programs)
- Lifelong learning programs that engage people in courses related to their personal interests

Not everyone needs or wants to go to college. Many people, with or without disabilities, move directly from high school into employment. However, there is no reason that people with disabilities should not have the same opportunities as their peers to continue their learning after high school as they pursue their academic, career, and social-recreational goals. Increasing numbers of youth with disabilities of all types are choosing to enroll in postsecondary education (Newman et al., 2011). In fact, when the Higher Education Opportunity Act was reauthorized in 2008, it created new opportunities for students with intellectual disabilities—a group that has had extremely limited postsecondary education options. The act created model demonstration programs in universities and community colleges for students whether or not they had a high school diploma. The act also created access to federal financial aid for students with intellectual disabilities enrolled in federally approved comprehensive transition and postsecondary (CTP) programs in institutions of higher education (Federal Student Aid, 2015). The main point is that postsecondary education is not a one-size-fits-all situation. Supporting students with disabilities to access postsecondary education requires helping families and students think about how to create a good match with the person's educational goals and the types of supports the person will need in college or other adult education settings.

FROM ENTITLEMENT TO ELIGIBILITY

As mentioned in the beginning of this chapter, an important part of planning for the transition to new adult roles is to be aware that the IDEA no longer applies once a student exits high school. The emphasis in postsecondary education will be on equal access and reasonable accommodation under the ADA and Section 504 of the Rehabilitation Act. One major consequence of this critical legal transition is that students are now responsible to *self-identify* as a person with a disability if they want to receive accommodations. Once accepted into a postsecondary education institution, students must actively seek out the institution's disability services office and request services. Many students are reluctant or uncomfortable with this process due to fear of being viewed negatively because of their disability. Unfortunately, too many wait until they are struggling or even failing before meeting with someone in the disability office (Getzel & Webb, 2012). Other students who were not previously identified as disabled or who may not be sure what kinds of accommodations they need also may be unsure about presenting themselves to the disability office. In general, it is better to arrange an initial meeting as early as possible to discuss students' concerns and possible accommodation or service needs.

Another important consequence of the legal transition is that *eligibility* for disability support services must be established with the institution (AHEAD, 2012). Just because a student had an IEP in high school does not mean he or she will be automatically eligible for disability services in college. Conversely, a student who was not eligible for special education during high school could be determined eligible for accommodations in college. In some institutions, students must make a case for their eligibility for disability services by providing a current diagnostic evaluation report (usually not more than 3 years old) from a licensed, appropriately credentialed professional. This is especially important for students with less visible disabilities such as learning disabilities or attention disorders. A recent *comprehensive* psychological-educational evaluation from a school psychologist completed within the last 3 years of high school may be acceptable. If an institution requires a current diagnostic evaluation, the student is responsible for assembling the necessary documentation, even if that means getting a new evaluation at his/her own expense, and then working with the disability office to determine eligibility for accommodations.

ACCOMMODATIONS

In line with these changes, which **accommodations** will be deemed reasonable must be negotiated based on the nature of the impairment, the demands of the specific academic setting, and the standards of the education program. There are no IEPs in college! When meeting with the disability office, the student must be prepared to act in a self-determined manner. They need to be able to describe the nature of their disability and express their educational goals, strengths, and weaknesses. They need to be able to explain what accommodations have worked for them and why and be ready to do some problem solving about their support needs in postsecondary environments, including options for **assistive technology** (AT). As needed, educators should support students in thinking about how AT may have been helpful for them in high school, refer students for AT evaluations, and encourage students and families to explore what is available. Common examples of accommodations available in postsecondary education institutions include:

- exam accommodations (e.g., quiet setting, extra time)
- alternate-format books and materials
- notetakers, readers, and scribes
- assistive technology and software
- interpreter services/Communication Access Realtime Translation (CART)
- reduced course load
- faculty notifications and consultation
- accessible classroom locations
- accessible on-campus transportation

It is important to be aware that personal devices (e.g., hearing aids, communication systems) and personal assistants (e.g., aides for daily living activities) are not the responsibility of the institution. Some institutions may offer—for free or for a fee — additional support services that go beyond what is required under ADA. Examples of these include:

- individual or small-group tutoring
- academic coaching
- life skills coaching
- disability-focused social support groups

SOCIAL LIFE AND CAMPUS PARTICIPATION

Families and students also need to consider that social life is often a big part of the postsecondary education picture, especially in 4-year and residential college settings. Students and families need to think about the type of social environment a student prefers, the impact of disability-related factors such as fatigue or stress, and how to stay connected to support systems (e.g., family and friends). Likewise, on-campus living can offer a supportive, transitional experience to independent living. It can also raise a host of new challenges related to self-management and social interactions. Students and families need to consider transportation and location, need for personal assistants, single room versus roommates, and managing community living.

Families may be surprised to learn that privacy regulations restrict their access to information about their children's activities and performance in postsecondary education. Under the Family Educational Rights and Privacy Acts (FERPA), adult students must give formal consent for other people, including family members, to access their educational information. Therefore, families and adult students should discuss the support or advocacy roles family members will play during the college years and consider what kinds of communication systems and information access should be put into place to support those activities.

FINANCIAL FACTORS

Finances also will be an important consideration. Who will pay for tuition, books and supplies, room and board, transportation, and daily living needs? Similar to other students, students with disabilities will need to use personal and family resources such as savings, loans, federal financial aid, and scholarships to help pay for postsecondary education expenses. However, students with disabilities may have access to other sources of financial support (Health Resource Center, 2014). For example, state vocational rehabilitation agencies will sometimes pay for certain postsecondary education expenses if a student's program of study is part of a career plan developed with the agency. Students with disabilities who are eligible for other government benefits such as SSI should consult with their local social security office to determine how to maintain their benefits when receiving scholarships or participating in work-study arrangements that may affect their monthly income and total assets.

Common Questions From Families Regarding Specific Issues Related to Postsecondary Education

As a Parent, How Can I Best Support My Child to Be Successful Academically and Socially in College?

College is traditionally a time when students explore living independently, gain lifelong friends and social networks, and take responsibility for their education and career choices. In the past, college students were seen as independent of their parents, but that perception is changing. We now understand that youth are often interdependent—learning how to live on their own while still being connected to their families.

Parents of youth with disabilities are often used to playing the role of advocate and coordinator while their student is in high school. Once the student reaches postsecondary education, the role of family changes from coordinator to support person and mentor. Colleges generally want their main relationship to be with the student, and this is preferable since it helps build independence and self-determination skills. However, parents can still support their youth's academic success and social connections in college. Here are some ideas.

- Many colleges have parent/family programs designed to inform parents about how college works and how they play a role in student success. Check to see if the college your student is choosing has one of these programs. Visit the Association of Higher Education Parent/Family Program Professionals (www.aheppp.org) for more information.
- Encourage your youth to disclose their disability to the college's disability support office before they begin their coursework so the appropriate academic accommodations can be secured. Many youth with disabilities choose not to do this, thinking they can get by on their own. Academic performance can be severely impacted if the right accommodations are not in place.
- If your youth is still in high school, and you anticipate possible issues with social functioning, consider asking the IEP team how that can be addressed. Supports like social coaching can be effective and may be offered by community-based employment agencies.
- Check in often with your youth to make sure academic and social issues aren't present. Many families may be hesitant to do this, but an open line of communication can allow parents to identify problems before they get out of hand.
- Strongly encourage your student to get involved in campus clubs, intermural sports, or arts activities. College is often a place where it is easy to find somebody who shares similar interests. However, connections cannot be made if the student becomes isolated from his or her peers.

Will the College Notify Me If My Son or Daughter Experiences Academic Problems or Mental Health Issues?

As a general rule, college students are their own legal guardians and considered adults in the eyes of a college. Therefore, it is not common practice for colleges to notify parents about academic problems or emerging mental health issues. Some families may find this frustrating, maybe because they have always had a role in monitoring academic performance or because they have valid concerns about their youth's mental health. There are good reasons to protect students' privacy and workable strategies parents can use to help support students' academics and mental wellness.

As mentioned earlier, the Family Educational Rights Act (FERPA) of 1974 protects the rights of students and limits who has access to educational records. For parents of college students, this law limits what colleges can share about academic performance. However, FERPA is often misinterpreted as meaning that colleges cannot share any personal or academic information with parents under any circumstances. This is not true. For example, FERPA allows parents to have access to education records if the student signs a release form or if the student is still claimed as a dependent on the parent's taxes. FERPA should be seen as a good opportunity for parents to work together with their college student to establish communication and accountability around academic performance.

Parents who have youth with mental health issues should seek to establish a plan of action before the student enrolls in a given college. To begin with, this means helping the student understand the value in disclosing the disability and choosing a college that has the appropriate counseling supports in place. The Jed Foundation (2015; www.jedfoundation.org) suggests the following strategies for parents to protect a student's mental health in college:

- Keep the lines of communication open with your child so they feel comfortable letting you know if they are having issues.
- Understand under what circumstances a college will notify you regarding a mental health issue. This should be done prior to enrolling a student.
- Understand what mental health services are available at the college, especially if the student has an existing disorder.
- Be honest on the college medical history form about your youth's current or past mental health issues.

- Identify if your youth is eligible for support through the college's disability services office.
- Transfer care and records to the college counseling center or local mental health provider.

STRATEGIES FOR PARTNERING WITH FAMILIES

- Understand the family's perspective, values, and expectations related to postsecondary education in order to incorporate these into team discussions.
- Provide support for parents/student in the application process for colleges, federal financial aid, and other available forms of financial support.
- Connect the parent/student with outside agencies (such as vocational rehabilitation) that may provide support for postsecondary education.
- Provide the student with a summary of performance (SOP) as required by federal law. The IEP, psychoeducational evaluation, academic achievements, and accommodations will help the student when applying for college and disclosing a disability.
- Work with the student and family to help them learn how to explain the impact of the student's disability in academic settings and the kinds of accommodations that are helpful.

CASE STUDY 2

PARTNERING TO SUPPORT SUCCESS IN POSTSECONDARY EDUCATION

Zoe wanted to attend the local community college to pursue her goal of becoming a dental assistant. Because this was Zoe's last IEP meeting before high school graduation, Ms. Kelly, the special education team leader, made a point to carefully review and discuss the transition plan components of the IEP. Zoe had done a fine job during the early part of the IEP meeting of explaining her academic strengths and why she needed certain accommodations for reading and writing tasks. Zoe's mother, Mrs. Hernandez, had confirmed that the family had completed the free application for federal student aid (FAFSA) and that Zoe had completed the college application during the school's recent College Night event. Ms. Kelly reminded Zoe and Mrs. Hernandez to save copies of the educational evaluation report that had been completed the previous year by the school psychologist. Zoe might need to give a copy to the college as a way to document her learning disability. Mrs. Hernandez looked puzzled at this and asked whether the IEP would be better to show them. Plus, she was not sure they had a copy. Ms. Kelly promised to give them a copy before they left along with a summary of performance and explained that the IEP would no longer be in effect. The college would make its own determination of Zoe's eligibility for disability accommodations under the Americans with Disabilities Act (ADA). She explained that many colleges make that determination based on professional disability evaluations and the student's own explanation of her accommodation needs. She encouraged Zoe and Mrs. Hernandez to contact the disability services office at the community college to confirm what documentation they would prefer. She recommended that they also request a meeting with a disability services counselor at the college to learn more about the steps Zoe would need to take for requesting accommodations. This reminded Ms. Kelly that she also wanted to refer Zoe for an assistive technology consultation so that she could explore some alternative technologies that might be useful for her in college. The school had supplied Zoe with a laptop that had many accessibility features, but the laptop would remain at the

(Continued)

school. It would be important for the family to explore whether they should invest in a similar laptop for use in college or consider some other options, like a "smart" pen.

Questions to Consider

1. What partnership opportunities did Ms. Kelly and the school help create?

2. What other opportunities could have been discussed as part of the IEP process?

3. How might other teachers partner with the family to support Zoe's success in college?

INDEPENDENT AND INTERDEPENDENT LIVING

Common Questions From Families

- What supports are available in school to help them prepare for independent living?
- What are the common housing options for people with disabilities?
- What is the role of Social Security benefits programs in my youth's ability to live independently?
- How can my adult child participate as part of the community?
- My child will not be able to drive. What community supports are available to help provide transportation after he graduates?

People with disabilities can live successful lives of their choosing and be participating members of their communities. Depending on how they are impacted by disability, some students may need to learn particular skills in order to promote their independence and perhaps require support in conducting daily living skills. Direct instruction is often necessary to teach students self-determination skills, how to self-advocate, and to improve daily living skills, and while some of these skills might be learned during high school, for many students with disabilities, the learning will continue beyond high school and with their families and postschool support team.

DEVELOPMENT OF LIFE SKILLS

Life skill instruction in high school needs to be individualized according to the student's IEP and is not typically a part of the academic curriculum (Test, Richter, & Walker, 2012). Test et al. (2009) examined the literature and identified several life skills that could be taught using evidence-based practices. As seen in Table 12.2, Life skills instruction includes not only practical skills of daily living such as banking, home maintenance, and cooking, but also "soft" skills such as self-advocacy and negotiation, which are critical across postschool settings and significantly improve a student's likelihood for success. Life skills can be taught in a variety of environments, including the classroom or through computer-based instruction or community-based instruction (Test, Richter, & Walker, 2012). Professionals or family members may be hesitant to allow the person to pursue a particular skill or test it out (e.g., taking a public bus). However, if the skill is important *for* the student and *to* the student, members of the support team should consider allowing the student to pursue attaining the skill with individualized instruction and supports. In some cases, the student may be able to learn a skill that others thought would be too difficult. Even if the skill is not attained as planned or to the desired level, the experience represents a very important learning opportunity for the student and team to evaluate the types of instruction and supports the student will need in the future and to consider alternative skill sets that would be useful for the student. Given the nature of these skills, they represent another opportunity to partner with family members so that the student can be developing these skills across environments. Lesson plans and more information about evidence-based practices are available for free to the public from the National Technical Assistance Center on Transition (see http://transitionta.org/evidencepractices).

SUPPORT FROM STATE AND FEDERAL GOVERNMENT

As the end of high school approaches, students and families should be supported in getting connected to state services that can support people with disabilities during adulthood. Students with more significant disabilities may have access to services available through their state developmental disabilities (DD) services agency or their state aging and disability (AD) agency. The type of support a student receives could vary greatly from state to state. As part of this connection to adult services, students may be declared eligible to receive Medicaid, a federal program that provides supports for health care and other aspects of daily living. If the student was previously eligible for Medicaid as a child, they must be reevaluated for eligibility as an adult, usually when they turn 18 years of age. The connection to these services should be made as early as possible in order to facilitate a smooth transition as the student departs high school and leaves the IDEA system. As mentioned previously, the adult service system is quite different than IDEA, as the student, with the support of family, is expected to apply for services (and is not necessarily sought after by the agency), identify their own goals and support needs, and advocate for themselves when they desire change in services. In general, states do not have the same level of obligation for ensuring that comprehensive services are provided.

People with disabilities who have Medicaid often receive therapeutic and support services in their own home and community. Historically, these individuals have been institutionalized, isolated from society and segregated in order to receive necessary services. However, recent changes to the Home & Community-Based Services (HCBS) regulations, the rules which determine how Medicaid services are delivered, create new assurances that people with disabilities receiving Medicaid will have greater access to community-based services and activities of their choosing (Centers for Medicare & Medicaid Services, 2014). Adult services provided through Medicaid funding are now required to be guided by a person-centered plan, through which the person is supported in identifying desired outcomes and supports needed to achieve those outcomes. Furthermore, the HCBS regulations are designed to ensure that Medicaid-funded community-based residential services (services provided to a person in their home instead of an institution) occur in a community setting that does not isolate the person and is a setting that offers privacy, dignity, and respect to the individual. Medicaid also funds institutional residential services, but less restrictive environments with individualized supports that meet the needs of the person should be considered first. The choice of residential options is important for young adults who desire to move out of their family home or for families who are having difficulty providing needed supports in the home.

TYPES OF RESIDENCES

Upon completion of high school, many young adults begin to think about and make preparations to leave their family's home, living either independently or in a shared or supported living situation. The decision about whether a young adult with a disability moves out is again a very personal one made by the young adult and their family and is usually based on multiple factors. For some, the decision to move out may be a natural next step because the young adult and family feel ready, or perhaps the student is going away to college. For others, the young adult and family may believe that the individual does not have the skills to live independently or the appropriate support may not be available. For individuals with more significant support needs, like intellectual and developmental disabilities, there are a variety of housing options available (Larson, Salmi, Smith, Anderson, & Hewitt, 2013):

- *Congregant settings*—a residence that is owned, rented or managed by an adult services provider for the purpose of providing housing for people with significant cognitive disabilities. These residences typically offer instruction, supervision, and other forms of support. These settings include intermediate care facilities (ICF) and group homes.
- *Host family/foster care*—a home that is owned or rented by an individual or family who provide support and care for an unrelated person with a significant disability.
- *Own home*—a home owned or rented by one or more people with disabilities where instruction, supervision, personal assistance, and other support is provided as needed. "Supported living" can be offered in these settings and refers to services and supports that are provided by a provider who comes into the person's home.
- *Family Home*—a home owned or rented by a family member in which the person with the disability resides and in which the individual receives paid care, instruction, supervision, or other support from persons other than family members and/or from family members who are paid.

In 2011, according to a national study, the vast majority of adults with intellectual and developmental disabilities lived at home (57.8%), while a smaller percentage lived in congregate settings (26.5%), and even fewer adults lived in their own home (11.6%) or with a host family (4.1%) (Larson, Salmi, Smith, Anderson, & Hewitt, 2013).

The type of residence a person lives in does seem to be correlated with other facets of their life. Individuals who live in their own home tend to experience greater independence and self-determination and have greater participation in their community. Ticha, Hewitt, Nord, and Larson (2013) found that individuals with intellectual and developmental disabilities who owned or rented their own home (versus living with their family or in a group home) were more self-determined in decision making, including decisions about how their funds were spent. Kim and Dymond (2012) found that individuals with significant disabilities receiving supported living supports were more independent in domestic and safety skills and participated more meaningfully in their communities than individuals in group homes. In this study, however, most individuals—regardless of living situation—participated only minimally in their communities, suggesting the importance of equipping students with skills and connections they need to fully participate in their communities as adults.

SOCIAL RELATIONSHIPS AND COMMUNITY PARTICIPATION

The development of connections to the community, including social relationships and recreational activities, is critical for maintaining a strong quality of life (Amado, Stancliffe, McCarron, & McCallion, 2013). Developing personal and social relationships has also been characterized as the most important transition goal (Halpern, 1994). For some young adults with disabilities, this may come naturally due to well-developed relationships in high school or a continuation of involvement in activities from high school to postschool. However, for many others, it will require some focus on developing the relationships and daily activities that will allow the person to benefit the most and remain connected to their community.

During their postschool years, many students with disabilities report that they remained connected to their high school peers (Newman et al., 2001). These interactions were both face to face and through electronic communication and remained fairly steady from 1 to 8 years post–high school. The level of interaction ranged according to type of disability, as more than 80% of young adults with learning disabilities and speech impairments reported seeing friends weekly, whereas about 50% of students with intellectual disabilities reported seeing friends on a weekly basis. Community participation was much more limited across groups, though, as 50% of all young adults with disabilities reported engaging in at least one community activity (e.g., volunteer activity, community group) during the year.

Families often provide significant social support for students with disabilities during school and are a source for connecting with the community through family outings or family membership (e.g., in religious organizations). Many adults continue to rely on family members' support postschool, which would also seem natural given the high rate at which many people with disabilities, particularly adults with intellectual and developmental disabilities, continue to live with their families (Larson, Salmi, Smith, Anderson, & Hewitt, 2013). However, people with intellectual and psychiatric disabilities may have less support available over time, as their parents age, siblings move away, and they are less likely to have spouses, partners, and children (Widmer, Kempf-Constantin, Robert-Tissot, Lanzi, & Carminati, 2008). In fact, family and paid staff often represent the majority of social networks for people with intellectual and developmental disabilities (Amado, Stancliffe, McCarron, & McCallion, 2013). This can be quite limiting over the course of time, and without more proactive action, young adults with intellectual disabilities may have few people with whom to engage in reciprocal and meaningful social relationships.

Social networks can serve as important tools for developing and maintaining social relationships and social support beyond high school. Social networks represent the numerous relationships that form connections within groups and between different groups. These connections are important for people with disabilities in order to form an effective support system, connect with those who share similar interests, identify potential mentors; and facilitate connections to additional outlets for social and recreational activities (Eisenman & Celestin, 2012).

Steps should be taken before the completion of high school to examine and develop a student's social network in order to maximize opportunities in the community for social interaction and participation. Students should be encouraged to participate in extracurricular activities during school, as this will help provide the basis for relationships that can perhaps continue postschool. Given the nature of community participation, activities should not be limited to the school setting, and IEP goals and activities should include the child's school team as well as families and perhaps other community members. The planning process should start with an examination of those activities that the student enjoys and wants to continue postschool. The process should also include identification of existing and desired relationships and a discussion of whether those peers are connected to activities that the young adult would like to join (Eisenman & Celestin, 2012). This process lends itself well to both the IEP as well as the person-centered planning process that was mentioned earlier as the driver of adult services. Therefore, finding opportunities to have the information shared across these two processes might represent an important model for the student and members of the multidisciplinary team in order to further promote a steady transition process into postschool life.

In order for individuals with disabilities to access various activities (e.g., employment, community participation), transportation will need to be considered. There are multiple transportation options, and each requires some planning and consideration of the individual's strengths, weaknesses, personal choice, and knowledge of the local transportation system to determine whether it should be accessed. Newman et al. (2011) reported that 78% of young adults with disabilities postschool had either a driver's license or learner's permit. Many adults with disabilities utilize the public transportation system (e.g., bus, train). While these are technically required to be accessible to all people according to the Americans with Disabilities Act, some buses do not maintain their accessible equipment and many train stations are still inaccessible (National Council on Disability, 2005). People with disabilities who cannot utilize a fixed-route transportation system with accommodations (e.g., due to their physical or cognitive disability or lack of access to accessible fixed-route systems) can apply to use the paratransit bus system. Paratransit buses are specifically designed for people with disabilities and offer door-to-door service at least within ¾ of a mile from a fixed-route bus stop. Unfortunately, the paratransit bus system has its own challenges. Riders frequently report trip denials or significantly late arrivals, which impact their ability to participate in daily activities (e.g., employment, doctor's appointments).

Transportation training is important for ensuring that the person is able to access the preferred method of transportation and access their postschool activities. This might include an adapted driver's education class, individualized instruction and practice on how to use a fixed-route bus or train system, or developing independence in scheduling and riding a paratransit bus. This is another activity that is beneficial to begin while the student is still in high school in order to promote a more seamless transition postschool, and the nature of the activity suggests an important partnership with family and future adult service providers.

Common Questions From Families Regarding Specific Issues Related to Independent and Interdependent Living

How Can I Help My Child Increase Their Self-Advocacy Skills?

One of the true measures of an independent adult is the ability to understand what your strengths and needs are and to be able to communicate those needs to others so you can get what you need. This self-advocacy is a vital part of the transition process for youth with disabilities. Not all youth have the skills to speak up for themselves effectively. Here are some tips for parents to help build self-advocacy skills in youth:

- *Help youth understand their disability*—Many youth with disabilities are unaware of what their disability is and how it impacts them in key areas. This can lead to youth struggling for reasons they don't understand or failing to seek useful accommodations and supports. Parents can work with the IEP team to help youth understand what their disability is and how it impacts them in learning, working, independent living, and social situations.
- *Have students lead their IEP meetings*—Regular meetings of a student's IEP team tend to be adult dominated and not youth friendly. This is unfortunate, because the meeting is for the student to help plan for education success and, ultimately, transition to the community. Parents and educators can gradually get youth more involved in their own IEP meetings, eventually having youth lead them as they near graduation.
- *Practice communicating needs*—Asking for help takes a set of skills not all youth have. It's also not something everyone is comfortable doing. Youth should be given safe opportunities to practice communicating their needs to others, for example, with trusted teachers or internship supervisors or in IEP meetings.

What Can I Do to Make Sure My Youth Has Social and Recreational Opportunities Once She Graduates?

Families of youth with disabilities want what is best for their youth transitioning to adulthood. To many families, having friends and being connected to a community are equally as important as having their youth find employment. Unfortunately, many youth with disabilities experience isolation and a disconnectedness to the outside world once they leave high school. Families can ensure that their youth have social connections and recreational opportunities, but it is important to start early. Here are some ideas for what families can do:

- Many of us forge social connections and friendships through employment. Families should support youth in finding work not only because of the income it brings but also for the structure and social benefits employment can provide.
- Many communities have social recreational opportunities operated out of community education or a community-based organization. Some may be specific to people with disabilities, and some may be for the general public. Offerings may include classes on a topic of interest, dances, sports leagues, or community outings.
- Some youth who have difficulty establishing social connections benefit from friendship clubs created for people with disabilities. These clubs or organizations are often established by parents as a way for disconnected young adults to socialize with one another. Consult your local parent training and information center or advocacy organization for more information.
- For youth who are still in high school, identifying possible social and recreational opportunities is an excellent activity for the IEP. Ask youth to research options in their community and report back during the IEP meeting. Schedule visits or interviews with the ones that look promising as subsequent activities.
- Volunteering and service learning in the community is another way for youth to make social connections. Consider participating with your youth in a food drive, home-building project, or community cleanup. This may instill an obligation to serve and give opportunities to meet a variety of people.

My Youth Has Complicated Health Care Needs. What Unique Transition Considerations Should I be Aware of?

Youth with special health care needs may have a unique set of challenges as they envision independent lives for themselves. Postschool transition will often impact three major areas: transition from pediatric health care to adult providers, transition from high school to postsecondary education or employment, and transition from home to more independence in the community (PACER, 2015).

Many families find it particularly difficult to help their youth move from the pediatric to the adult health care system. There tends to be a comfort level built up over years of seeing the same doctor, and finding a new specialist in the adult system that knows the disability can be a challenge. Parents are encouraged to start this transition process early and to address such aspects as their youth's ability to manage their own health care, health care financing (insurance, the Affordable Care Act, Social Security programs), transferring care, and understanding how adult care will differ from the pediatric world.

Youth with special health care needs may have access to transition planning options in high school, either by virtue of qualifying for special education or by having an individualized accommodation plan (i.e., a "504 plan"). This structured process is the perfect time for youth to work on understanding the impact of their health condition on learning, working, and living in the community and how to build skills needed to function in those areas. Possible areas of focus on the IEP for a youth with special health care needs might include communication skills (including disclosing the disability if necessary), assistive technology, researching transportation options, building work skills and soft skills, understanding possible supports in postsecondary education, medication management (can be a goal on the IEP), and financial literacy.

Youth with unique health challenges may also have special considerations when planning on living independently in the community. A key area may be accessing needed services and supports so they can live on their own. Related to that is the issue of accessible housing if necessary and planning for where to live and setting up needed support systems. In addition, youth sometimes require home health staff or personal care attendants (PCA), which comes with a responsibility for managing those services. Transportation can be a significant challenge, especially for people that require assistance in rural areas. Finally, parents should help youth plan to make their own decisions once they turn 18 or explore options to support them in doing so.

How Can I Make an Informed Decision About Whether to Pursue Guardianship for My Son or Daughter?

Many families seek guardianship over their son or daughter with a significant disability without fully researching alternatives. This has led to many people with disabilities losing the ability to make decisions about their own lives. Guardianship should only be sought if a person is deemed incapacitated, unable to make important decisions for themselves, and perceived to be a personal or financial risk to themselves (Vining, 2012). The main question for families to consider is what the issue is that the disability raises and what can be done to address that specific issue. Many times, guardianship is an overly restrictive response to a problem that could be handled through different supports or planning.

However, there are times when the impact of the disability is such that a person cannot make their own financial, medical, or independent living choices. Parents are encouraged to consider all alternatives and only choose guardianship when other options are inappropriate. For example, there is a growing movement toward "supported decision making," mentioned earlier in the chapter, in which people with disabilities rely on trusted families and friends to help them understand situations and choices so they can make their own decisions.

Families must become aware of their state's laws and available options, as these may vary from state to state. Common alternatives to guardianship include: power of attorney, trusts, representative payee, conservatorship, living wills, and county case management.

STRATEGIES FOR PARTNERING WITH FAMILIES

- Listen to parents/student expectations, concerns, and fears about their child living independently.
- Link the parent and student to the appropriate person/organization who can answer questions about such matters as Social Security, special needs trusts, independent living supports, guardianship, and so forth.
- Help the parent to process their concerns and decisions that need to be made. Be mindful not to interject opinion. Respect the values of families.
- Encourage parents to allow their child to make decisions and to have opportunities to act independently.
- Help parents complete necessary paperwork to apply for supports through state and government agencies. The support will ensure follow-through and, in the long run, will reduce paper workload of educators.
- Take time to understand how the family's cultural background may impact decisions that are made regarding future decisions about independent living.
- Learn from the family how they are already connected to the community in order to understand ways in which the student might be able to leverage the family's social network and involve the student in the community.

CASE STUDY 3
PARTNERING TO SUPPORT SUCCESS IN THE COMMUNITY

Russell is 17 years old and in 12th grade. He has a mild intellectual disability and has been diagnosed with attention deficit/hyperactivity disorder (ADHD) and oppositional defiant disorder (ODD). He has exhibited behavior issues in the past at school but has improved greatly due to the structured environment of his classes. His teachers report that he consistently participates and follows class routines well. He demonstrates a strong work ethic and works hard in completing assignments. He is earning credits to receive a high school diploma and is on target to graduate in one year. He could remain in school until age 21 but would prefer to focus on receiving his diploma and exiting from school to work. He does not have his driver's license but has received travel training for public transportation through the school program.

While his behaviors have improved at school, his mother reports that many times he is verbally aggressive at home. She stated that he is often in disagreement with her suggestions but is more willing to take direction from other trusted adults, such as his teachers at school or family friends. His mother has also stated that she is very concerned about how he will manage living on his own and holding a job. She believes that he will be able to work with computers, as she sees how knowledgeable he is about them.

Russell lives with his mother. His father is not involved in his life. The family is struggling financially, although they do have a stable living situation. Transportation is an issue, as the family car is not dependable. Russell's mother has disclosed that she often feels overwhelmed by her financial situation, being a single parent and supporting Russell.

Russell's educational team at school has given his mother information about services through the developmental disabilities services agency, vocational rehabilitation and guardianship. They have told her she must complete applications, and they need to be completed as quickly as possible. His mother contacts the school often with questions and concerns but has not followed through with the paperwork. She says she is panicking and doesn't know what to do. Typically she is unable to attend meetings because of poor transportation.

The educational team recognizes that Russell's mother will need more one-on-one help with completing applications and connecting to agencies. The designated point person for Russell's mother listens empathetically to her concerns, addressing each one with factual information when appropriate. She makes sure that Russell's mother understands that the educators are partners in wanting Russell to successfully transition from the school environment into the community. She provides a checklist that is individualized for Russell that breaks down the steps that his mother must take.

Because Russell has an intellectual disability, the first step is to complete an application for the developmental disabilities services state agency. Russell's mother is connected to a person from the agency who assists in the application process. A trusted member of the school team facilitates the meeting and ensures that required school documentation is available. The meeting is set up close to where the family lives so that transportation is not an issue. The developmental disabilities agency staff explains to Russell's mother that if Russell qualifies, he would receive a case manager who would help oversee his services. This would include respite care, which would offer a break for Russell's mother. Russell would also receive supported employment services that include one-on-one assistance to help find employment and learn job-specific tasks.

Another concern that Russell's mother has is about his ability to live independently. Residential services through the agency are explained to her, and she feels much calmer. Guardianship and alternatives to guardianship, such as power of attorney, are also explained. She is given infor-

(Continued)

CASE STUDY 3 (Continued)

mation and told about an upcoming workshop in which a lawyer will be explaining the process in more detail.

The educational team finds that as Russell's mother's concerns are addressed and she becomes better informed, they receive fewer phone calls from her and, when they do, her questions are direct and without the degree of panic. At the time for his annual IEP meeting, the team is able to create a document that is rich with detail about the transition plan. The plan is not only compliant with federal regulations but also meaningful to Russell and his mother.

Questions to Consider

1. How did Russell's support team ensure that his mother would feel like a valued member of the team?

2. What elements of this case reflect important strategies for partnering with families?

3. Which members of the school team would be able to partner with the family as future decisions are made with Russell and his mom?

Summary

While the postschool transition process can feel like an ending to school professionals, it marks an important beginning for students and families. As students and family members prepare for potential employment, postsecondary education, and independent/ interdependent living, school professionals play a critical role in providing support for next steps. Through empowerment, partnership, creation of opportunities, and connection to community resources, the school team can facilitate a successful transition into adulthood.

Additional Resources

Web-Based

Disability Rights Education & Defense Fund: A Comparison of ADA, IDEA, and Section 504: http:// dredf.org/advocacy/comparison.html. A comparison among the Americans with Disabilities Act of 1990 (ADA), the Individuals with Disabilities Education Act (IDEA), and Section 504 of the Rehabilitation Act of 1973 in regards to each law's purpose, who is protected, how the laws affect education, funding for services as well as procedural safeguards and due process.

Employment & Disability Institute: https://www .edi.cornell.edu/. The Employment and Disability Institute (EDI) is a leading resource on employment and disability information for businesses, lawmakers, federal and state agencies, educational institutions, unions, and service providers. The institute provides research, technical assistance, training, scholarly reports, and training publications to support the contributions of people with disabilities and ensure their full inclusion in their communities.

Home and Community Based Services Advocacy: http://hcbsadvocacy.org/. Information about the Home and Community-Based Services (HCBS) regulations and requirements for several Medicaid authorities under which states may provide home- and community-based long-term services and supports. The regulations enhance the quality of HCBS and provide additional protections to individuals that receive services under these Medicaid authorities.

Institute on Community Integration. http://www.ici .umn.edu/. The Institute on Community Integration is based at the Minnesota University Center for Excellence in Developmental Disabilities (UCEDD) and is part of a national network of similar programs in major universities and teaching hospitals across the country. Through collaborative research, training, and information sharing, the institute improves policies and practices to ensure that all children, youth, and adults with disabilities are valued by and contribute to their communities of choice.

LDonline—the Law After High School. http://www .ldonline.org/article/The_Law_After_High_School. Question-and-answer format to provide information about the rights a person with disabilities may have under the Rehabilitation Act, ADA, and IDEA.

National Collaborative on Workforce and Disability for Youth (NCWD/Youth): http://www.ncwd- youth.info/. NCWD/Youth assists state and local workforce development systems to better serve all youth, including youth with disabilities and other disconnected youth. NCWD/Youth offers a range of technical assistance services to state and local workforce investment boards, youth councils, and other workforce development system youth programs.

National Longitudinal Transition Study–2 (NLTS2): http://www.nlts2.org. The National Longitudinal Transition Study–2 (NLTS2) includes information on 11,270 youth nationwide who were ages 13 through 16 at the start of the 10-year study. Information collected from parents, youth, and schools provides a national picture of the experiences and achievements of young people as they transition into early adulthood.

National Resource Center for Supported Decision-Making: http://supporteddecisionmaking.org/. Supported decision making (SDM) is an effective, less restrictive alternative to guardianship that uses trusted friends, family members, and advocates to give people with disabilities the help they need and want to understand the situations they face and the choices they must make so they can make their own decisions. Website provides information about legal cases, evidence-based outcome measures, advocacy for changes in law, policy, and practice to increase self-determination and demonstrate SDM to be a valid, less-restrictive alternative to guardianship.

National Technical Assistance Center on Transition (NTACT): http://transitionta.org. A national technical assistance and dissemination center funded by the U.S. Department of Education to provide technical assistance and disseminate information to state education agencies, local education authorities, schools, and other stakeholders to implement evidence-based practices leading to improved academic and functional achievement for students with disabilities, preparing them for postsecondary education and the workforce; as well as implement policies, procedures, and practices to facilitate and increase participation of students with disabilities in programs and initiatives designed to ensure college and career readiness and to achieve 100% compliance with IDEA, Part B Indicator 13 (I-13).

U.S. Department of Labor, Office of Disability Employment Policy (ODEP): http://www.dol.gov/odep/. The Office of Disability Employment Policy (ODEP) is a sub–cabinet-level policy agency in the Department of Labor. ODEP's mission is to develop and influence policies and practices that increase the number and quality of employment opportunities for people with disabilities.

PACER 2013 Minnesota Secondary Transition Toolkit for Families: A Guide to Preparing Your Child with a Disability for Life Beyond High School: http://www.pacer.org/publications/MDE-Toolkit-2013.pdf. This toolkit was created to make transition planning easier and offers easy-to-understand information about the purpose of transition planning, the goal and importance of age-appropriate assessments, and the required rules that are used by schools. It also includes information on the community partners that can provide youth with supports as adults. Topics include health care and health maintenance, benefits planning, postsecondary education and accommodations, recreation, social resources, transportation, and housing.

PACER Health Information Project: www.pacer.org/health. PACER's Family-to-Family Health Information Center (F2F HIC) provides a central source for families of children and young adults with special health care needs and disabilities to obtain support, advocacy, and information about the health care system. PACER promotes family-centered care and family and professional collaboration at all levels of health care. The F2F HIC also has a strong commitment to promote and support the needs of families from racially, culturally, and linguistically diverse communities.

PACER National Parent Center on Transition and Employment: http://www.pacer.org/transition/. Founded in 2014, PACER's National Parent Center on Transition and Employment builds on PACER's decades of experience providing high-quality assistance and support to parents, youth, and professionals on transition topics. This innovative project ensures that the needs of the family remain at the forefront and helps youth with disabilities find success in postsecondary education, employment, and life in the community.

Think College Differences Between High School and College: http://www.thinkcollege.net/topics/highschool-college-differences. Outlines the legal and procedural differences between the K–12 experience and the educational supports provided by the Individuals with Disabilities Education Act (IDEA) and how educational supports are provided in postsecondary education by the Americans with Disabilities Act and Section 504 of the Rehabilitation Act of 1973.

Print

Brown, J. T. (2012). *The parent's guide to college for students on the autism spectrum*. Shawnee Mission, KS: AAPC Pub.

Getzel, E. E., & Wehman, P. (2005). *Going to college: Expanding opportunities for people with disabilities*. Baltimore, MD: Paul H. Brookes.

Grigal, M., & Hart, D. (2010). *Think college! Postsecondary education options for students with intellectual disabilities*. Baltimore, MD: Paul H. Brookes.

Heath Resource Center. (2014). *Planning ahead: Financial aid for students with disabilities, 2014–15 edition*. National Youth Transitions Center, The George Washington University. Available at https://heath.gwu.edu/files/downloads/2014_2015_heath_financial_aid_publication.pdf

Varrassi, V. (2015). *Transition to college and career: Experienced-based strategies to improve readiness of students with disabilities*. Palm Beach Gardens, FL: LRP Publications.

EPILOGUE

To undertake writing a textbook is a monumental job that consists of research, experience and the author's perspective on practice and their profession. Each invited author has done just that—adding their research, experience, and their perspective for this textbook. We have chosen authors that have a multitude of experiences, are part of diverse family systems, and/or are in a family with a family member with a disability. We also have chosen authors with expertise in areas of the profession and lifespan stages that impact families with a family member with a disability.

As editors and authors of this textbook we made personal decisions on how to organize the book and what should be included. These decisions reflect our view that life in any family system is in constant change and thus, each family member is in constant varying levels of support and need; they are able to contribute differently at different stages of life and have diverse needs at these varying life stages.

Thus, the themes of this textbook are that (a) no families are alike—they all come with unique strengths and needs, as well as how they will approach disability; (b) professionals working with families must approach families from a strength based approach; (c) families will be able to contribute different strengths and needs at different lifespan times; and (d) professionals working with families need to understand the family—its system, culture, strengths and needs, diversity and human development.

Fundamental to the core of the work professionals will take on is based on Family Systems Theory, understanding the whole family to include the extended family and their relationship to their family member with a disability. The fundamental need of a trusting relationship between professionals and the family is incorpoacross this theory.

In editing and writing sections of this textbook, it has reaffirmed our passion for working with families. They are the most important team member of the multidisciplinary team and serve to shape the work that we do as professionals. They keep us interested, learning, passionate about our work. They reaffirm our belief that all families come with strengths and it is our job to support and empower families to support their family member, whether it is with helping their child academically, helping their child seek postsecondary goals, and/or helping their child develop social skills that will lead to meaningful relationships.

This textbook addresses the importance of interdisciplinary work—teamwork and collabora If done right, we all benefit, and the most important person that benefits is the child. Take care of yourself, so that you can take care of the families you serve!

GLOSSARY

Accommodations: Changes that are made to provide equal access to learning and equal opportunity to demonstrate what is known; changes do not fundamentally alter expectations or standards in instructional level, content, or performance criteria.

Achievement tests: Achievement tests are designed to measure the knowledge and skills students learned in school or to determine the academic progress they have made over a period of time. Achievement tests are "backward-looking" in that they measure how well students have learned what they were expected to learn.

The Achieving a Better Life Experience (ABLE) Act: Signed into law on December 19, 2014, by President Obama, ABLE amends the federal tax code to allow tax-exempt savings accounts for disability-related expenses. ABLE accounts will enable people with autism and their families to save for housing, education, transportation, medical, and other expenses if related to their disability.

Adaptability or flexibility: Represents the extent to which a family can amend its organization, rules, and/or boundaries.

Adaptations: Accommodations and/or modifications that allow access to the general education curriculum for all students.

Adaptive Behavior Scales: According to the American Association on Intellectual and Developmental Disabilities (AAIDD, 2015), ABSs provide precise diagnostic information around the cutoff point where an individual is deemed to have "significant limitations" in adaptive behavior. The presence of such limitations is one of the measures of intellectual disability. Parents, teachers, and other caregivers who know the behaviors of the child or adolescent being rated typically complete adaptive behavior scales, such as semi-structured interview forms and rating scales. Such informant-based adaptive behavior scales offer a number of benefits to users, including providing summaries of observations of behaviors across varied settings, such as homes, schools, and community settings.

Adaptive equipment: Devices that are used to assist with completing activities of daily living.

Advocacy: The act of supporting, pleading for, or making recommendations to influence political, economic, or social decision making for a particular cause.

Age of majority: In the eyes of the law, when a person reaches the age of 18 years, he/she is presumed capable of making their own decisions, including educational decisions, in most states.

Age score/chronological age score: The number of years a person has lived, used especially in psychometrics as a standard against which certain variables, such as behavior and intelligence, are measured. Age equivalent scores are almost always given in years and months.

Alternate assessment: A generic term for a family of methods used to assess the academic performance of students with significant disabilities or limited proficiency with English. Alternate assessments are an important component of each state's assessment system and, as such, are required to meet the federal regulations outlined in Title I of the Elementary and Secondary Education Act.

Alternate Assessment based on Alternate Achievement Standards (AA-AAS): The achievement test based on adapted academic standards to measure progress in the general curriculum taken by students for whom the typical standardized achievement test is not appropriate, even with accommodations.

Annual goal matrix: A table that translates how the student's annual goals will be matched to the curricular objectives of the classroom instruction.

Annual goal: Statement that describes what a child with a disability can reasonably be expected to accomplish within a 12-month period in the child's education program.

Assistive technology (AT): An umbrella term that includes assistive, adaptive, and rehabilitative devices for people with disabilities.

Augmentative and alternative communication (AAC): Various methods of communication that can help people who are unable to use verbal speech to communicate. "Augmentative" refers to augmenting the communication a person already uses, and "alternative" refers to finding another mode of communication altogether for an individual.

Barriers to communication: Things that hinder the communication efforts of teachers and others.

Basal: Denoting a standard or reference state of a function as a basis for comparison. A basal is the "starting point." It represents the level of mastery of a task below which the student would correctly answer all items on a test. All of the items prior to the basal are not given to the student. These items are considered already correct. For example, on an IQ test, the examiner may start with Question 14 because of the age of the child. That is the basal.

Behavior rating scales: An assessment instrument designed to obtain the perceptions or judgments of a subject's behavior in a standardized format. Raters may be the subject (self-rating) or others with the opportunity to observe and describe aspects of the subject's behavior (i.e., parents, teachers, etc.). Behavior rating scales are often used as screening devices to obtain information on and help to identify individuals who may benefit from a more detailed assessment or who may be at risk for developing more serious problem and who may benefit from early interventions. Behavior rating scales are also used to monitor progress in treatment programs. Behavior rating scales should never be utilized as the sole source of information for the purposes of diagnosis or classification of a specific educational or psychological problem.

Blended family: A blended family is formed when remarriages occur or when children living in a household share one or no parents. The presence of a step-parent, stepsibling, or half-sibling designates a family as blended.

Boundaries: Rules about interactions, ranging from rigid to enmeshed. Rigid—isolation, not sharing aspects of one's life with other family members. Enmeshed—family members involved in all aspects of each other's lives; little respect for privacy. Healthy—balanced, organized, in middle of continuum.

Ceiling: The ceiling is the "ending point." It represents the level of mastery of a task above which the student would incorrectly answer all future items on a test. A ceiling is a testing term referring to the highest level of items a person can answer correctly before reaching the test's discontinuation criteria. Once the basal is determined, the examiner will administer the test until the student reaches a ceiling.

Children: The term "children," as used in tables on living arrangements of children under 18, are all persons under 18 years, excluding people who maintain households, families, or subfamilies as a reference person or spouse.

Circular communication: One conversation often leads to another conversation within and without subsystems.

Climate: The physical and emotional environment of the family.

Cohesion: Feeling connected, bonded, and close to one another.

Collaborative team model/process: A group of equal individuals who voluntarily work together in a spirit of willingness and mutual reward to problem solve and accomplish one or more common and mutually agreed-upon goals by contributing their own knowledge and skills and participating in shared decision making while focusing on the efficiency of the whole team.

Communication breakdown: Occurs when communication is incomprehensible to one party or entirely absent between two people.

Communication matrix: A free assessment tool developed by Charity Rowland (2013) to pinpoint exactly how an individual is communicating and to provide a framework for determining logical communication goals. The communication matrix is appropriate for individuals of all ages who are at the earliest stages of communication.

Communication partners: Any teacher, family member, or support person that communicates with students with complex communication needs.

Communication skills: The ability to convey information to another effectively and efficiently. Communication skills include verbal, nonverbal, and written communication.

Communication system: A combination of AAC devices used by individuals with complex communication needs.

Complex communication needs: The result of significant speech, language, and/or cognitive impairments when the individual can no longer communicate in conventional ways.

Complex medical needs (also called significant health-care needs): A child who has one or more of the following: (a) a diagnosable, enduring, life-threatening condition; (b) a medical condition that has resulted in substantial physical impairments; (c) medically caused impediments to the performance of daily, age-appropriate activities at home, school, or community; and/or (d) a need for medically prescribed services.

Confidence interval: A statistical approach that creates a band of acceptable passing rates based on size of the group tested, average test scores and the range of scores, among other factors. Confidence intervals constitute a range of statistical values within which a result is expected to fall with a specific probability. If a school misses the annual measurable objective (AMO), but it falls inside the range of the confidence interval, the school makes adequate yearly progress (AYP). For example, in a school of 1,000 students, 45 percent of students scored at the proficient and advanced level, and the state applied a 95 percent confidence interval. The confidence interval calculation indicated that the actual percentage of students scoring proficient or advanced was between 42 and 48 percent. In this example, if the AMO was 47 percent, the school would have made AYP, even though the actual percentage of students scoring proficient or advanced was below the AMO.

Correlation: The state or relation of being correlated; *specifically*: a relation existing between phenomena or things or between mathematical or statistical variables which tend to vary, be associated, or occur together in a way not expected on the basis of chance alone. Degree and type of relationship between any two or more quantities (variables) in which they vary together over a period; for example, variation in the level of expenditure or savings with variation in the level of income. A positive correlation exists where the high values of one variable are associated with the high values of the other variable(s). A 'negative correlation' means association of high values of one with the low values of the other(s). Correlation can vary from +1 to -1. Values close to +1 indicate a high-degree of positive correlation, and values close to -1 indicate a high degree of negative correlation. Values close to zero indicate poor correlation of either kind, and 0 indicates no correlation at all. While correlation is useful in discovering possible connections between variables, it does not prove or disprove any cause-and-effect (causal) relationships between them.

Criterion-referenced tests: Criterion-referenced tests are designed to measure student performance against a fixed set of predetermined criteria or learning standards—i.e., concise, written descriptions of what students are expected to know and be able to do at a specific stage of their education. In elementary and secondary education, criterion-referenced tests are used to evaluate whether students have learned a specific body of knowledge or acquired a specific skill set—for example, the curriculum taught in a course, academic program, or content area.

Cross-age tutoring: Peer tutoring with children of different grade/age levels, where older children assume the role of tutor and younger children assume the role of tutee.

Curriculum Based Assessment: A method to measure student progress in academic areas including math, reading, writing, and spelling. The child is tested briefly (1 to 5 minutes) each week. Scores are recorded on a graph and compared to the expected performance on the content for that year. The graph allows the teacher and parents to see quickly how the child's performance compares to expectations.

Demeanor: The way a person behaves.

Developmental disability: A term under IDEA that allows states and local educational agencies to qualify children aged 3 to 9 years who experience delays in one or more areas of development (i.e., cognitive, physical, social or emotional, communication, or adaptive behavior) who, because of these delays, need special education supports and services.

Developmental Disabilities Assistance and Bill of Rights Act (DD Act): Enacted in 2000, it assures that individuals with developmental disabilities and their families participate in the design of and have access to community services, individualized supports, and other types of assistance and programs that promote self-determination, independence, productivity, and integration and inclusion in all facets of community life.

Differential parenting: The degree to which parents treat each child in the family differently.

Disabilities: One of 13 disability categories defined under IDEA. See IDEA for a full description.

Early communicative behaviors: Intentional or unintentional behaviors used by beginning communicators that include primarily nonsymbolic modes of communication such as gestures, vocalization, facial expressions, and body language.

Early intervention: A system of coordinated services for children ages birth through 3. These services promote the child's age-appropriate growth and development and support families.

Ecological Assessment: An ecological assessment is a comprehensive process in which data is collected about how a child functions in different environments or settings. Sometimes, students eligible for special education perform or behave well in some environments but have difficulty in others. For example, at school, a student may be calm during class time but is always upset in the cafeteria. Other children even have school phobia, which is an irrational, persistent fear of going to school. These children seem fine at home but consistently become anxious, depressed, or scared every time they have to go to school.

Error analysis: Error analysis involves the analysis of error patterns to identify difficulties that students may have with facts, concepts, strategies and procedures. Identifying the type of error allows the teacher to address learner needs more efficiently.

Evidence-based interventions/practices: Instructional strategies, interventions, or teaching programs that have resulted in consistent positive results when experimentally tested.

Extended standards: Alternate learning expectations that are directly aligned to the grade-level expectations for all students.

Family: A family is a group of two people or more (one of whom is the householder) related by birth, marriage, or adoption and residing together; all such people (including related subfamily members) are considered members of one family. Beginning with the 1980 Current Population Survey, unrelated subfamilies (referred to in the past as secondary families) are no longer included in the count of families, nor are the members of unrelated subfamilies included in the count of family members. The number of families is equal to the number of family households. However, the count of family members differs from the count of family household members because family household members include any nonrelatives living in the household.

Family household: A family household is a household maintained by a householder who is in a family (as defined earlier), and includes any unrelated people (unrelated subfamily members and/or secondary individuals) who may be residing there. The number of family households is equal to the number of families. The count of family household members differs from the count of family members, however, in that the family household members include all people living in the household, whereas family members include only the householder and his/her relatives. See the definition of family.

Family Medical Leave Act (FMLA): United States federal law requiring covered employers to provide eligible employees unpaid, job-protected leave for qualified medical and family reasons.

Family systems theory: States that a family is a unit in which members of the family impact one another in bidirectional ways, striving to maintain equilibrium.

Functional behavioral assessment: Functional behavioral assessment (FBA) is a variation on procedures originally developed to ascertain the purpose or reason for behaviors displayed by individuals with severe cognitive or communication disabilities (e.g., individuals with intellectual disabilities or autism). Because these individuals were unable to fully explain why they were displaying certain inappropriate behaviors, methods were developed to determine why they demonstrated such actions. These investigatory procedures, derived primarily from the orientation and methods of applied behavior analysis.

The term "functional behavioral assessment" comes from what is called a "functional assessment" or "functional analysis" in the field of applied behavior analysis. This is the process of determining the cause (or "function") of behavior before developing an intervention.

General curriculum: The academic content all students are expected to learn in school.

General curriculum access: The opportunity to learn grade-level academic content (i.e., reading, math, science, and social studies) and the instructional support to demonstrate what has been learned.

General curriculum standards: Define the academic knowledge students are expected to learn in school.

Gesture dictionary: A compilation of descriptions of an individual's gestures, along with their meanings and suggestions for appropriate responses from communication partners.

Grade Score: If the purpose is to compare the student's scores with those of peers in the same grade, grade-based scores should be used.

Home–school communication: Communications between home and school that are typically child centered.

Household: A household consists of all the people who occupy a housing unit. A house, an apartment or other group of rooms, or a single room is regarded as a housing unit when it is occupied or intended for occupancy as separate living quarters—that is, when the occupants do not live with any other persons in the structure and there is direct access from the outside or through a common hall. A household includes the related family members and all the unrelated people, if any, such as lodgers, foster children, wards, or employees who share the housing unit. A person living alone in a housing unit or a group of unrelated people sharing a housing unit such as partners or roomers is also counted as a household. The count of households excludes group quarters.

Householder: The householder refers to the person (or one of the people) in whose name the housing unit is owned or rented (maintained) or, if there is no such person, any adult member, excluding roomers, boarders, or paid employees. If the house is owned or rented jointly by a married couple, the householder may be either the husband or the wife. The person designated as the householder is the "reference person" to whom the relationship of all other household members, if any, is recorded. The number of householders is equal to the number of households. Also, the number of family householders is equal to the number of families.

Idiosyncratic: Communication behaviors that are specific to an individual and that would likely not be understood by individuals who didn't know the person well.

Individuals with Disabilities Education Act (IDEA): Legislation that ensures students with a disability are provided with free appropriate public education (FAPE) that is tailored to their individual needs.

Individualized Education Program/Plan (IEP): A document that is developed for each public school child who is eligible for special education supports and services. The IEP is created through a team effort reviewed periodically. In the United States, this program is known as an individualized education program.

Individual Family Service Plan (IFSP): A family plan for special services for young children from ages birth through 3 with developmental delays.

Intelligence tests: Intelligence tests are designed to measure a variety of mental functions, such as reasoning, comprehension, and judgment.

The goal of intelligence tests is to obtain an idea of the person's intellectual potential. The tests center around a set of stimuli designed to yield a score based on the test maker's model of what makes up intelligence. Intelligence tests are often given as a part of a battery of tests. There are many different types of intelligence tests and they all do not measure the same abilities. Although the tests often have aspects that are related with each other, one should not expect that scores from one intelligence test, that measures a single factor, will be similar to scores on another intelligence test that measures a variety of factors. Also, when determining whether or not to use an intelligence test, a person should make sure that the test has been adequately developed and has solid research to show its reliability and validity. Additionally, psychometric testing requires a clinically trained examiner. Therefore, the test should only be administered and interpreted by a trained professional.

When taking an intelligence test, a person can expect to do a variety of tasks. These tasks may include having to answer questions that are asked verbally, doing mathematical problems, and doing a variety of tasks that require eye-hand coordination. Some tasks may be timed and require the person to work as quickly as possible. Typically, most questions and tasks start out easy and progressively get more difficult. It is unusual for anyone to know the answer to all of the questions or be able to complete all of the tasks. If a person is unsure of an answer, guessing is usually allowed.

Interval scale: The standard survey rating scale is an interval scale. When you are asked to rate your satisfaction with a piece of software on a 7 point scale, from Dissatisfied to Satisfied, you are using an interval scale. It is an interval scale because it is assumed to have equidistant points between each of the scale elements. This means that we can interpret differences in the distance along the scale. We contrast this to an ordinal scale where we can only talk about differences in order, not differences in the degree of order. Interval scales are also scales which are defined by metrics such as logarithms. In these cases, the distances are not equal but they are strictly definable based on the metric used. Interval scale data would use parametric statistical techniques.

Legislation: Law enacted by a legislative body at the national, state, or local level.

The Lifespan Respite Care Act: Authorized in 2006 under Title XXIX of the Public Health Service Act, it established a program to provide coordinated systems of accessible, community-based respite care services for family caregivers of children and adults of all ages and special needs.

Marital status: The marital status classification identifies four major categories: never married, married, widowed, and divorced. These terms refer to the marital status at the time of the enumeration.

The category "married" is further divided into "married, spouse present," "separated," and "other married, spouse absent." A person was classified as "married, spouse present" if the husband or wife was reported as a member of the household, even though he or she may have been temporarily absent on business or on vacation, visiting, in a hospital, and so forth, at the time of the enumeration. People reported as separated included those with legal separations, those living apart with intentions of obtaining a divorce, and other people permanently or temporarily separated because of marital discord. The group "other married, spouse absent" includes

married people living apart because either the husband or wife was employed and living at a considerable distance from home, was serving away from home in the armed forces, had moved to another area, or had a different place of residence for any other reason except separation as defined above.

Single, when used as a marital status category, is the sum of never-married, widowed, and divorced people. "Single," when used in the context of "single-parent family/household," means only one parent is present in the home. The parent may be never married, widowed, divorced, or married, spouse absent.

Married couple: A married couple, as defined for census purposes, is a husband and wife enumerated as members of the same household. The married couple may or may not have children living with them. The expression "husband-wife" or "married-couple" before the term "household," "family," or "subfamily" indicates that the household, family, or subfamily is maintained by a husband and wife. The number of married couples equals the count of married-couple families plus related and unrelated married-couple subfamilies.

Measures of central tendency: A single value that attempts to describe a set of data by identifying the central position within that set of data. As such, measures of central tendency are sometimes called measures of central location. They are also classed as summary statistics. The mean (often called the average) is most likely the measure of central tendency that you are most familiar with, but there are others, such as the median and the mode.

The mean, median, and mode are all valid measures of central tendency, but under different conditions, some measures of central tendency become more appropriate to use than others.

Measures of variability: A mathematical determination of how much the performance of the group as a whole deviates from the mean or median. The most frequently used measure of variability is the standard deviation.

Median: The middle score in a distribution or set of ranked scores; the point (score) that divides a group into two equal parts; the 50th percentile. Half the scores are below the median, and half are above it.

Mode: The score or value that occurs most often in a distribution.

Modifications: Changes made to provide students meaningful and productive learning experiences based on individual needs and abilities; changes do fundamentally alter expectations or standards in instructional level, content, or performance criteria.

Multigenerational households: Family households consisting of three or more generations. These households include (1) a householder, a parent or parent-in-law of the householder, and an own child of the householder, (2) a householder, an own child of the householder, and a grandchild of the householder, or (3) a householder, a parent or parent-in-law of the householder, an own child of the householder, and a grandchild of the householder.

Nominal scale: Value is named; naming category (i.e., male, female). The lowest measurement level you can use, from a statistical point of view, is a nominal scale. A nominal scale, as the name implies, is simply some placing of data into categories, without any order or structure. A physical example of a nominal scale is the terms we use for colors. The underlying spectrum is ordered but the names are nominal. In research activities a YES/NO scale is nominal. It has no order and there is no distance between YES and NO. The statistics which can be used with nominal scales are in the non-parametric group. The most likely ones would be:

- mode
- crosstabulation—with chi-square

There are also highly sophisticated modelling techniques available for nominal data.

Normal curve equivalent: The normal curve equivalent, or NCE, is a way of measuring where a student falls along the normal curve. The numbers on the NCE line run from 0 to 100, similar to percentile ranks, which indicate an individual student's rank, or how many students out of a hundred had a lower score. NCE scores have a major advantage over percentile rank scores in that they can be averaged. That is an important characteristic when studying overall school performance, and in particular, in measuring school-wide gains and losses in student achievement.

Normal distribution of scores: Also known as the bell-shaped curve because of its distinctive appearance in that scores are distributed symmetrically about the middle, such that there are an equal number of scores above as below the mean, with more scores concentrated near the middle than at the extremes. The normal distribution is a theoretical distribution defined by specific mathematical properties that many human traits and psychological characteristics appear to closely approximate (e.g., height, weight, intelligence, etc.). See also: Distribution, Median, Mode, and Standard Deviation. Some features of the normal distribution are:

1. The mean, median, and mode are identical in value.
2. The scores are distributed symmetrically about the mean (50.0% above the mean and 50.0% below the mean).
3. 68.26% of the scores are within 1 standard deviation of the mean (34.13% above the mean and 34.13% below the mean).
4. 95.44% of the scores are within 2 standard deviations of the mean (47.72% above the mean and 47.72% below the mean).
5. 99.72% of the scores are within 3 standard deviations of the mean (49.86% above the mean and 49.86% below the mean).

Norm-referenced test: Standardized tests designed to compare the scores of children to scores achieved by children the same age who have taken the same test. Most standardized achievement tests are norm-referenced.

Occupational therapy/therapist: Treatment that helps people who have physical or intellectual disabilities learn to do the activities of daily life.

The Older Americans Act (OAA): Originally enacted in 1965, this act supports a range of home- and community-based services. Services include meals on wheels, nutrition programs, in-home services, transportation, legal services, elder abuse prevention, and caregiver support services.

Own children: Sons and daughters, including stepchildren and adopted children, of the householder. Similarly, "own" children in a subfamily are sons and daughters of the married couple or parent in the subfamily. (All children shown as members of related subfamilies are own children of the person(s) maintaining the subfamily.) For each type of family unit identified, the count of "own children under 18 years old" is limited to never-married children; however, "own children under 25" and "own children of any age," as the terms are used here, include all children regardless of marital status. The counts include never-married children living away from home in college dormitories.

Peer tutoring: Teaming pairs of same-age students to practice academic skills.

Physical therapy/therapist: Therapy to preserve, enhance, or restore movement and physical function caused by disability, injury, or disease.

Policy statement: Statement of policy that is implemented as a procedure or protocol by a government, party, business, or individual.

Portfolio assessment: Portfolio assessment is an evaluation tool used to document student learning through a series of student-developed artifacts. Considered a form of authentic assessment, it offers an alternative or an addition to traditional methods of grading and high-stakes exams. Portfolio assessment gives both teachers and students a controlled space to document, review, and analyze content learning. In short, portfolios are a collection of student work that allows assessment by providing evidence of effort and accomplishments in relation to specific instructional goals (Jardine, 1996). At its best, portfolio assessment demands the following: clarity of goals, explicit criteria for evaluation, work samples tied to those goals, student participation in selection of entries, teacher and student involvement in the assessment process, and self-reflections that demonstrate students' metacognitive ability, that is, their understanding of what worked for them in the learning process, what did not, and why. These elements enhance the learning experience and the self-understanding of the student as learner.

There are a variety of portfolio types, each designed to help assess either the process or the products of learning: showcase portfolios, process portfolios, evaluation portfolios, and online or e-portfolios.

Present levels of academic and functional performance ("present levels"): A section on the IEP that summarizes an individual's academic and functional skills. The summary should include the student's strengths and weaknesses, what helps the student learn, what limits or interferes with the student's learning, objective data from current evaluations of the student, and how the individual's disability affects his or her ability to be involved and progress in the general education curriculum.

Range: The range is the simplest measure of variability to calculate, and one you have probably encountered many times in your life. The range is simply the highest score minus the lowest score. Example: What is the range of the following group of numbers: 10, 2, 5, 6, 7, 3, 4? The highest number is 10, and the lowest number is 2, so 10 - 2 = 8. The range is 8.

Ratio: A ratio scale is the top level of measurement and is not often available in social research. The factor which clearly defines a ratio scale is that it has a true zero point. The simplest example of a ratio scale is the measurement of length (disregarding any philosophical points about defining how we can identify zero length).

The best way to contrast interval and ratio scales is to look at temperature. The Centigrade scale has a zero point but it is an arbitrary one. The Farenheit scale has its equivalent point at -32°.

Raw Score: The first unadjusted score obtained in scoring a test. A raw score is usually determined by tallying the number of questions answered correctly or by the sum or combination of the item scores (i.e., points). However, a raw score could also refer to any number directly obtained by the test administration (e.g., raw score derived by formula-scoring, amount of time required to perform a task, the number of errors, etc.). In individually administered tests, raw scores could also include points credited for items below the basal. Raw scores typically have little meaning by themselves. Interpretation of raw scores requires additional information such as the number of items on the test, the difficulty of the test items, norm-referenced information (e.g., percentile ranks, grade equivalents, stanines, etc.), and/or criterion-referenced information (e.g., cut -scores).

Reciprocal/two-way tutoring: Students alternate tutor/tutee roles during peer tutoring.

Reference person: The reference person is the person to whom the relationship of other people in the household is recorded. The household reference person is the person listed as the householder (see definition of "Householder").

The subfamily reference person is either the single parent or the husband/wife in a married-couple situation.

Referral: A process asking the school district to evaluate a student to determine if the student qualifies to receive special education supports and services.

Related children: Own children and all other children under 18 years old in the household who are related to the householder by birth, marriage, or adoption. The count of related children in families was formerly restricted to never-married children. However, beginning with data for 1968, the Bureau of the Census includes never-married children under the category of related children. This change added approximately 20,000 children to the category of related children in March 1968.

Related services: Supportive services that are needed by a child with a disability to benefit from special education services.

Reliability: The consistency of a measure. In educational testing, reliability refers to the confidence that the test score will be the same across repeated administrations of the test. There is a close relation between the construct of reliability and the construct of validity. Many sources discuss how a test can have reliability without validity and that a test cannot have validity without reliability. In the theoretical sense, these statements are true but not in any practical sense. A test is designed to be reliable and valid, consistent, and accurate. Practical conceptualizations of reliability cannot be discussed separately from examples with validity.

Response to Intervention: Response to Intervention (RTI) is a multi-tier approach to the early identification and support of students with learning and behavior needs. The RTI process begins with high-quality instruction and universal screening of all children in the general education classroom. Struggling learners are provided with interventions at increasing levels of intensity to accelerate their rate of learning. These services may be provided by a variety of personnel, including general education teachers, special educators, and specialists. Progress is closely monitored to assess both the learning rate and level of performance of individual students. Educational decisions about the intensity and duration of interventions are based on individual student response to instruction. RTI is designed for use when making decisions in both general education and special education, creating a well-integrated system of instruction and intervention guided by child outcome data.

Rubric: A document that a teacher uses that articulates the expectations for an assignment by listing the criteria, or what counts, and describing levels of quality from excellent to poor.

Scripted routines: Structured opportunities for beginning communicators to practice using attention-getting, acceptance, and rejection signals in context of naturally occurring activities.

Self-determination skills: The skills needed to make one's own choices, learn to effectively solve problems, and take control and responsibility for one's life.

Self-determined learning model of instruction (SDLMI): An instructional model that teaches students to engage in self-regulated and self-directed learning.

Self-reliance: Relying on one's own resources, efforts, and abilities.

Significant health-care needs: see *Complex medical needs*

Social competence: A person's social, emotional, and cognitive skills and behaviors that are need for successful social adjustment.

Special education eligibility: To be eligible for special education services, a child must have a disability (as defined by IDEA) and must need special education services and related services.

Special education supports and services: Specially designed and/or supplemental instruction provided by a special education teacher.

Speech language pathologist: A highly trained professional who evaluates and treats children and adults who have difficulty with speech or language.

Standard deviation: A measure of the variability of a distribution of scores. The more the scores cluster around the mean, the smaller the standard deviation. In a normal distribution, 68% of the scores fall within one standard deviation above and one standard deviation below the mean.

Standard error of measurement: Is associated with the test scores for a specified group of test takers. The standard error of measurement (SEM) is the standard deviation of errors of measurement that are associated with test scores from a particular group of examinees. When used to calculate confidence bands around obtained test scores, it can be helpful expressing the unreliability of individual test scores in an understandable way. Score bands can also be used to interpret intraindividual and interindividual score differences. Interpreters should be wary of over-interpretation when using approximations for correctly calculated score bands. It is recommended that SEMs at various score levels be used calculating score bands rather than a single SEM value.

Standard score: A score that has been transformed to fit a normal curve, with a mean and standard deviation that remain the same across ages. Standard scores have a mean of 100 and a standard deviation of 15.

Stanine: Stanines are bands of standard scores that have a mean of 5 and a standard deviation of 2. Stanines range from 1 to 9. Despite their relative ease of interpretation, stanines have several disadvantages. A change in just a few raw score points can move a student from one stanine to another. Also, because stanines are a general way of interpreting test performance, caution is necessary when making classification and placement decisions.

Step-family: A step-family is a married-couple family household with at least one child under age 18 who is a stepchild (i.e., a son or daughter through marriage, but not by birth) of the householder. This definition undercounts the true number of step-families in instances in which the parent of the natural-born or biological child is the householder and that parents spouse is not the child's parent, as biological or step-parentage is not ascertained in the CPS for both parents.

Subfamily: A subfamily is a married couple with or without children or a single parent with one or more own never-married children under 18 years old. A subfamily does not maintain its own household but lives in the home of someone else.

Task analysis: Breaks down complex tasks into a sequence of smaller steps or actions, and is used to teach learners a skill that is too challenging to teach all at once.

Temperament: The usual attitude, mood, behavior, and reacting characteristics of a person.

Transition: A change from one thing to the next, such as the transition from preschool to elementary school.

Transition plan: The section of the IEP that lists goals for a student's successful transition into a postschool environment.

Universal design for learning: An educational framework that guides the development of flexible learning environments that can accommodate individual learning differences.

Unmarried couple: An unmarried couple is composed of two unrelated adults of the opposite sex (one of whom is the householder) who share a housing unit with or without the presence of children under 15 years old. Unmarried-couple households contain only two adults.

Unrelated individuals: People of any age who are not members of families or subfamilies.

Validity: The extent to which a test measures the skills it sets out to measure and the extent to which inferences and actions made on the basis of test scores are appropriate and accurate.

Vocational interest inventories: A career tool for self-assessment that aids in career planning to assesses the likes of particular objects, activities, and personalities using the theory that individuals with the same career tend to have the same interests.

Work Sampling System: The Work Sampling System, an authentic performance assessment, is based on teachers' observations of children at work in the classroom learning, solving problems, interacting, and creating products.

Designed for students in preschool through 5th grade, the Work Sampling System includes three interrelated elements:

- Developmental guidelines and checklists
- Portfolios
- Summary reports

The system is based on seven domains or categories, each with performance indicators: Personal and Social Development (focusing on self identity, the self as a learner, and social development); Language and Literacy (based on the theory that students learn to read and write the way they learn to speak, naturally and slowly); Mathematical Thinking (focusing on children s approaches to mathematical thinking and problem solving); Scientific Thinking (emphasizing the processes of scientific investigation, because process skills are embedded in and fundamental to all science instruction and content); Social Studies (understanding from personal experience and by learning about the experiences of others); The Arts (focusing on how using and appreciating the arts enables children to demonstrate what they know and to expand their thinking); and, Physical Development (developing fine and gross motor skills and a growing competence to understand and manage personal health and safety).

The Work Sampling System is a continuous assessment format, which helps teachers, families and students gain perspective on the student's development and skills over an eight-year period, from ages three to 11. It allows schools to create mixed-age groupings in classrooms if desired, and allows for longitudinal study over time to examine how a child has developed. The continuous use also allows parents and families to become extremely familiar with the assessment system and its benefits.

Zilbach's stages of the life cycle: Represents three phases: (1) gestational or courtship phase (forming and nesting), which includes coupling and arrival of the first dependent, which is usually a child but may be an elder relative or parent; (2) middle phase, which includes family separation processes during which children go to school, leave home, become independent; (3) last phases, which include adult children becoming fully independent and death of parents.

REFERENCES

Chapter 1: Defining the Family

Boberiene, L. (2013). Inside the Beltway: Can policy facilitate human capital development? The critical role of student and family engagement in schools. *American Journal of Orthopsychiatry, 83(2–3)*, 346–351.

Child Welfare Information Gateway. (2011). *Working with lesbian, gay, bisexual, and transgender (LGBT) families in adoption.* Washington, DC: U.S. Department of Health and Human Services, Children's Bureau.

Fields, J. (2001). *Living arrangements of children: Fall 1996.* US Census Bureau.

Kreider, R., & Lofquist, D. (2014). Adopted children and stepchildren: 2010. *Current population reports,* P20-572. Washington, DC: U.S. Census Bureau.

Laughlin, L. (2014). A Child's Day: living arrangements, nativity, and family transitions: 2011 (selected indicators of child well-being). *Suitland: US Department of Commerce, Economics and Statistics Administration, US Census Bureau.*

Newman, Lynn. (2005). *National longitudinal transition study 2: Family involvement in the educational development of youth with disabilities—a special topic report of findings from the National Longitudinal Transition Study-2 (NLTS2).* Menlo Park, CA: SRI International.

Noel, A., Stark, P., & Redford, J. (2015). Parent and family involvement in education. From the National Household Education Surveys Program of 2012 (NCES 2013-028. REV). Washington, DC: National Center for Education Statistics, Institute of Education Sciences, U.S. Department of Education. Retrieved from: http://nces.ed.gov/pubsearch

U.S. Census Bureau. (2013). American community survey and Puerto Rico community survey: 2013 subject definitions. Retrieved from: www2.census.gov/programs-surveys/acs/tech_docs/subject_definitions/2013_ACSSubjectDefinitions.pdf

U.S. Census Bureau. (2014). America's families and living arrangements: 2014: Children (C table series): Table C9 Children by presence and type of parent(s), race, and Hispanic origin: 2014. Retrieved from: www.census.gov/hhes/families/data/cps2014C.html

U.S. Census Bureau. (n.d.). Current population survey (CPS)—definitions. Retrieved from: http://www.census.gov/programs-surveys/cps/technical-documentation/subject-definitions.html

U.S. Department of Education. (2004). Individuals with Disabilities Education Act 2004. Retrieved from: http://idea.ed.gov

U.S. Department of Education. (n.d.). Family Educational Rights and Privacy Act: 34 CFR Part 99. Retrieved from: http://www.ecfr.gov/cgi-bin/text-idx?rgn=div5&node=34:1.1.1.1.33

U.S. Department of Housing and Urban Development Office of Public and Indian Housing. (2013). *Guidance on housing individuals and families experiencing homelessness through the Public Housing and Housing Choice Voucher Programs.* Notice PIH 2013-15. Washington, DC: US Government Printing Office.

Vespa, J., Lewis, J., & Kreider, R. (2013). America's families and living arrangements: August 2012. In Population Characteristics, pp. 20–570. Washington, DC: U.S. Census Bureau.

Vespa, J., Lewis, J. M., & Kreider, R. M. (2014). America's families and living arrangements: 2012. Washington, DC: US Government Printing Office.

Chapter 2: Family Systems Theory

Almagor, M., & Ben-Porath, D. D. (2013). Functional dialectic system (FDS) treatment: Integrating family systems theory with dialectic thinking. *Journal of Psychotherapy Integration, 23,* 397–405.

Berg-Cross, L. (2000). *Basic concepts in family therapy: An introductory text* (2nd ed.). New York, NY: Haworth Press.

Bronfenbrenner, U. (1977). Toward an experimental ecology of human development. *American Psychologist,* 513–531.

Children's Bureau. (2012). Adoption and foster care analysis report. Retrieved from: http://www.acf.hhs.gov/programs/cb/focusareas/foster-care

De Luccie, M. F. (1995). Mothers as gatekeepers: A model of maternal mediators of father involvement. *The Journal of Genetic Psychology, 156,* 115–131.

Engfer, A. (1988). The interrelatedness of marriage and the mother-child relationship. In R. A. Hinde & J. S. Hinde (Eds.), *Relationships within families: Mutual influences* (pp. 104–118). Oxford: Oxford University Press.

Goldberg, W. A., & Easterbrooks, M. (1984). Role of marital quality in toddler development. *Developmental Psychology, 20,* 504–514.

Goldenberg, H., & Goldenberg, I. (2000). *Family therapy: An overview* (5th ed.). Belmont, CA: Thomson Higher Education.

Kail, R. V. (2015). *Children and their development* (7th ed.). Boston, MA: Pearson.

Karraker, M. W., & Grochowski, J. R. (2012). *Families with futures: Family studies into the 21st century* (2nd ed.). New York, NY: Routledge.

King, V., Boyd, L. M., & Thorsen, M. L. (2015). Adolescents' perceptions of family belonging in stepfamilies. *Journal of Marriage and Family, 77,* 761–774. doi:10.1111/jomf.12181

Kwok, S. Y. C. L., Cheng, L., Chow, B. W. Y., & Ling, C. C. Y. (2015). The spillover effect of parenting on marital satisfaction among Chinese mothers. *Journal of Child and Family Studies, 24,* 772–783.

Laszloffy, T. (2002). Rethinking family development theory: Teaching with the systemic family development (SFD) model. *Family Relations, 51,* 206–214.

Lewis, E., Dozier, M., Ackerman, J., & Sepulveda Kozakowski, S. (2007). The effects of placement instability on adopted children's inhibitory control abilities and oppositional behavior. *Developmental Psychology, 43,* 1415–1427.

Margalit, M., & Heiman, T. (1986). Learning disabled boys' anxiety, parental anxiety and family climate. *Journal of Clinical Child Psychology, 15*, 248–253.

Minuchin, S. (1974). *Families & family therapy*. Cambridge, MA. Harvard University Press.

National Council on Disability. (2008). *Youth with disabilities in the foster care system: Barriers to success and proposed policy solutions*. Retrieved from: http://www.ncd.gov/publications/2008/02262008#_edn97

O'Gorman, S. (2012). Attachment theory, family systems theory and the child presenting with significant behavioral concerns. *Journal of Systemic Therapies, 31*, 1–16.

Robinson, M., & Neece, C. L. (2015). Marital satisfaction, parental stress and child behavior problems among young children with developmental delays. *Journal of Mental Health Research in Intellectual Disabilities, 8*, 23–46.

Santisteban, D. A., Muir-Malcolm, J. A., Mitrani, V. B., & Szapocznik, J. (2002). Integrating the study of ethnic culture and family psychology intervention science. In H. A. Liddle, D. A. Santisteban, R. F. Levant, & J. H. Bray (Eds.), *Family psychology: Science-based interventions* (pp. 331–351). Washington, DC: American Psychological Association.

Zilbach, J. (2003). The family life cycle: A framework for understanding family development. In G. P. Shovelar & L. D. Schwoeri (Eds.), *Textbook of family and couples therapy: Clinical applications*, (pp. 303-316). Washington, DC: American Psychiatric Publishing, Inc.

Chapter 3: Families of Children at Risk for Disability

Abedi, J. (2009). English language learners with disabilities: Classification, assessment, and accommodation issues. *Journal of Applied Testing Technology, 10*(2).

Alwan, A., & Modell, B. (1997). *Community control of genetic and congenital disorders*. EMRO Technical Publications Series, No 24. Alexandria, Egypt: World Health Organization.

Artiles, A. J., & Ortiz, A. A. (2002). *English language learners with special education needs: Identification, assessment, and instruction*. Washington, DC: Center for Applied Linguistics.

August, D., & Hakuta, K. (Eds.). (1997). *Improving schooling for language-minority children: A research agenda*. Washington, DC: National Academies Press.

Bailey, D. B., Skinner, D., & Warren, S. E. (2005). Newborn screening for developmental disabilities: Reframing presumptive benefit. *American Journal of Public Health, 95*(11), 1889–1893.

Baldwin, L., Omdal, S. N., & Pereles, D. (2015). Beyond stereotypes: Understanding, recognizing, and working with twice-exceptional learners. *Teaching Exceptional Children, 47*(4), 216–225.

Barnes, C., Mercer, G., & Shakespeare, T. (1999). *Exploring disability: A sociological introduction*. Malden, MA: Polity Press.

Baum, S. M., Schader, R. M., & Hébert, T. P. (2014). Through a different lens: Reflecting on a strengths-based, talent-focused approach for twice-exceptional learners. *Gifted Child Quarterly, 58*(4), 311–327.

Beaty, Lee A., (1995). Effects of paternal absence on male adolescents' peer relations and self-image. *Adolescence,* Winter, 873–880.

Bendersky, M., Bennett, D., & Lewis, M. (2006). Aggression at age 5 as a function of prenatal exposure to cocaine, gender, and environmental risk. *Journal of Pediatric Psychology, 31*(1), 71–84.

Benjamin, A. E., Wallace, S., Villa, V., & McCarthy, K. (2000). *Disability and access to health and support services among California's immigrant populations* (final report). Los Angeles: UCLA, Center for Health Research.

Besnoy, K. D., Swoszowski, N. C., Newman, J. L., Floyd, A., Jones, P., & Byrne, C. (2015). The advocacy experiences of parents of elementary age, twice-exceptional children. *Gifted Child Quarterly, 59*(2), 108–123.

Blencowe, H., Cousens, S., Chou, D., Oestergaard, M., Say, L., Moller, A. B., Kinney, M., & Lawn, J. (2013). Born too soon: the global epidemiology of 15 million preterm births. *Reproductive health, 10*(1), 1.

Boyd, D., & Bee, H. (2006). *Lifespan development* (4th ed.). Upper Saddle River, NJ: Pearson.

Bradsher, J. E. (1993). *Disability among racial and ethnic groups. Disability Statistics Abstract #10*. San Francisco: Institute for Health and Aging, University of California San Francisco. Retrieved from: http://dsc.ucsf.edu/abs/ab10.html

Brookover, W. B., & Erickson, E. L. (1969). *Society, schools, and learning*. Boston: Allyn and Bacon.

Calame, A., Fawer, C. L., Claeys, V., Arrazola, L., Ducret, S., & Jaunin, L. (1986). Neurodevelopmental outcome and school performance of very-low-birth-weight infants at 8 years of age. *European Journal of Pediatrics, 145*, 461–466.

Campos, J. & Keatinge, B. (1984). *The Carpenteria preschool program: Title VII second year evaluation report*. Washington, DC: Department of Education.

Carnoy, M. (1994). *Faded dreams: The politics and economics of race in America*. New York: Cambridge University Press.

Castellano, J. (2004). Empowering and serving Hispanic students in gifted education. In D. Booth & J. C. Stanley (Eds.), *In the eyes of the beholder: Critical issues for diversity in gifted education* (pp. 1–14). Waco, TX: Prufrock.

Castles, A., Adams, E. K., Melvin, C. L., Kelsch, C., Boulton, M. L. (1999). Effects of smoking during pregnancy. Five meta-analyses. *American Journal of Preventive Medicine, 16*, 208–215.

Centers for Disease Control and Prevention (CDC. (2012). CDC grand rounds: prescription drug overdoses—a US epidemic. *MMWR. Morbidity and mortality weekly report, 61*(1), 10.

Cummins, J. (1983a). *Heritage language education: A literature review*. Toronto: Ministry of Education.

Duttweiler, P. C., National Dropout Prevention Center, C. S., & National Educational Service, B. I. (1995). *Effective strategies for educating students in at-risk situations*. Clemson, SC: Clemson University.

Eklund, K., Tanner, N., Stoll, K., & Anway, L. (2015). Identifying emotional and behavioral risk among gifted and nongifted children: A multi-gate, multi-informant approach. *School Psychology Quarterly, 30*(2), 197-211.

Ellis, W. E., & Wolfe, D. A. (2009). Understanding the association between maltreatment history and adolescent risk behavior by examining popularity motivations and peer group control. *Journal of Youth and Adolescence, 38*(9), 1253-1263.

Ernst, C. C., et al. (1999). Intervention with high-risk alcohol and drug-abusing mothers: II. Three-year findings from the Seattle model of paraprofessional advocacy. *Journal of Community Psychology, 27*(1), 19-38.

Ernst, M., Moolchan, E. T., & Robinson, M. L. (2001). Behavioral and neural consequences of prenatal exposure to nicotine. *Journal of American Academy of Child & Adolescent Psychiatry, 40*(6), 630-641.

Ethnologue. (2009). Languages of the world. Retrieved from: http://www .ethnologue.com/ ethno_docs/ distribution.asp?by=country

Evans, G. W., & Kantrowitz, E. (2001). Socioeconomic status and health: The potential role of environmental risk exposure. *Annual Review of Public Health, 23*, 303-331.

Fernald, A., Marchman, V. A., & Weisleder, A. (2013). SES differences in language processing skill and vocabulary are evident at 18 months. *Developmental Science, 16*(2), 234-248.

Follesø, R., & Hanssen, J. K. (2010). Narrative approaches as a supplementary source of knowledge on marginalized groups. *Qualitative Sociology Review, 6*(1), 126-136.

Garmezy, N. (1994). Reflections and commentary on risk, resilience and development. In R. J. Haggerty, L. Sherrod, N. Garmezy, & M. Rutter (Eds.), *Stress, risk, and resilience in children and adolescents: Processes, mechanisms, and interventions* (pp. 1-19). New York: Cambridge University Press.

Garvey, E. (2012, September 1). Health matters blog. Retrieved May 2015 from: http://www.bmhvt.org/ healthmatters/pros-and-cons-of-genetic-screening-during-pregnancy

Gay, Lesbian and Straight Education Network (GLSEN). (2012). *The 2011 national school climate survey: Key findings on the experiences of lesbian, gay, bisexual and transgender youth in our nation's schools. Executive summary.* Gay, Lesbian and Straight Education Network (GLSEN): http:// eric.ed.gov/?id=ED535177 (accessed May 17, 2015).

Gersten, R., Baker, S. K., Shanahan, T., Linan-Thompson, S., Collins, P., & Scarcella, R. (2007). *Effective literacy and language instruction for English learners in the elementary grades: An IES practice guide.* Washington, DC: U.S. Department of Education, Institute for Education Sciences.

Gersten, R., Compton, D., Connor, C. M., Dimino, J., Santoro, L., Linan-Thompson, S., & Tilly, W. D. (2008). *Assisting students struggling with reading: Response to intervention and multi-tier intervention for reading in the primary grades. A practice guide* (NCEE 2009- 4045). Washington, DC: U.S. Department of Education, Institute of Education Sciences, National Center for Education Evaluation and Regional Assistance. Retrieved from: http:// ies.ed.gov/ncee/wwc/publications/ practiceguides

Gonzalez, L. M., Eades, M. P., & Supple, A. J. (2014). School community engaging with immigrant youth: Incorporating personal/social development and ethnic identity development. *School Community Journal, 24*(1), 99-117.

Gosine, K. K., & Islam, F. (2014). "It's like we're one big family": Marginalized young people, community, and the implications for urban schooling. *School Community Journal, 24*(2), 33-61.

Grunau, R. V. E. (1986). Educational achievement. In H. G. Dunn (Ed.), *Sequelae of low birthweight. The Vancouver study* (pp. 179-204). Philadelphia: Lippincott.

Hack, M., Taylor, H. G., Klein, N., Eiben, R., Schatschneider, C., & Mercuri-Minich, N. (1994). School-age outcomes in children with birth weights under 750 g. *The New England Journal of Medicine, 331*, 753-759.

Hart, B., & Risley, T. (1995). *Meaningful differences in the everyday experience of young American children.* Baltimore, MD: Paul Brookes.

Henderson, A. T., & Mapp, K. L. (2002) *A new wave of evidence: The impact of school, family, and community connections on student achievement.* Austin, TX: Southwest Educational Development Laboratory.

Henfield, M. S., Washington, A. R., & Byrd, J. A. (2014). Addressing academic and opportunity gaps impacting gifted black males: Implications for school counselors. *Gifted Child Today, 37*(3), 147-154.

Hidden Curriculum Definition. (2013, December 3). Retrieved May 10, 2015, from: http://edglossary.org/ hidden-curriculum/

Huffman, L., Mehlinger, S., & Kerivan, A. (2000). *Risk factors for academic and behavioral problems at the beginning of school* (Paper 1). Stanford, CA: Stanford University, School of Medicine.

Hughes, C., Newkirk, R., & Stenhjem, P. H. (2010). Addressing the challenge of disenfranchisement of youth: poverty and racism in the schools. *Reclaiming Children & Youth, 19*(1), 22-26.

Individuals with Disability Education Act Amendments of 2004 [IDEA]. (2004).

Jacobsen, L. K., Slotkin, T. A., Mencl, W. E., Frost, S. J., & Pugh, K. R. (2007). Gender-specific effects of prenatal and adolescent exposure to tobacco smoke on auditory and visual attention. *Neuropsychopharmacology, 32*, 2453-2464.

Johnstone, K. (2009). *Addressing under-representation of student populations in gifted programs: Best practices for student selection, service delivery models, and support structures* (Title I/LAP and Consolidated Program Review). Olympia, WA: Washington State Office of Superintendent of Public Instruction.

Jolly, J. L., & Hughes, C. E. (2015). The educational experience for students with gifts and talents. *Teaching Exceptional Children, 47*(4), 187-189.

Jones, K. L., & Smith, D. W. (1973). Recognition of the fetal alcohol syndrome in early infancy. *Lancet, i*, 999-1001.

Kyburg, R. M., Hertberg-Davis, H. H., & Callahan, C. M. (2007). Advanced Placement and International Baccalaureate programs: Optimal learning environments for gifted minorities. *Journal of Advanced Academics.*

Ladson-Billings, G. J. (2002). I ain't writin' nuttin': Permissions to fail and demands to succeed in urban classrooms. In L. Delpit & J. K. Dowdy, *Skin that We Speak* (pp. 109–120). New York: The New Press.

Lagerstrom, M., Bremme, K., Eneroth, P., & Magnusson, D. (1991). School performance and IQ test scores at age 13 as related to birth weight and gestational age. *Scandinavian Journal of Psychiatry, 32*, 316–324.

Lee, C.-T., et al. (2008). A mechanism for the inhibition of neural progenitor cell proliferation by cocaine. *PLoS Medicine, 5*(6), e117.

Linares, T. J., et al. (2006). Mental health outcomes of cocaine-exposed children at 6 years of age. *Journal of Pediatric Psychology, 31*(1), 85–97.

Lindsay, S., King, G., Klassen, A. F., Esses, V., & Stachel, M. (2012). Working with immigrant families raising a child with a disability: Challenges and recommendations for healthcare and community service providers. *Disability and Rehabilitation, 34*(23), 2007–2017.

Lippman, A. (1991). Prenatal genetic testing and screening: constructing needs and reinforcing inequities. *American Journal of Law & Medicine, 17*(1–2), 15–50.

Majd, K., Marksamer, J., & Reyes, C. (2009, October 16). Hidden injustice—lesbian, gay, bisexual and transgender youth in juvenile courts. In *Models for change*. Retrieved May 10, 2015, from www.modelsforchange.net/ publications/237

Media Centre. (2011, June 17). Retrieved May 9, 2015, from: http://www.unicef .org/eapro/media_16363.html

Miller, M. (2006). Where they are: Working with marginalized students. *Educational Leadership*, (5), 50.

Minnes, S., Lang, A., & Singer, L. (2001). Prenatal tobacco, marijuana, stimulant, and opiate exposure: Outcomes and practice implications. *Addiction Science & Clinical Practice, 6*(1), 57–70.

Montgomery, C. N. (2015). *Home care CEO: A parent's guide to managing in-home pediatric nursing.* Toledo, OH: Black & Blue Publishing.

Morrow, R. A., & Torres, C. A. (1995). *Social theory and education: A critique of theories of social and cultural reproduction.* Albany: SUNY Press.

Nagy, W. E. (1989). *Teaching vocabulary to improve reading comprehension.* Newark, DE: International Reading Association.

National Clearinghouse on English Language Learners. (2010). *NCELA state Title III information systems.* Retrieved from: http://www.ncela .us/t3sis

Neumeister, K. S., Yssel, N., & Burney, V. H. (2013). The influence of primary caregivers in fostering success in twice-exceptional children. *Gifted Child Quarterly, 57*(4), 263–274.

Noguera, P. A. (2003). The trouble with black boys: The role and influence of environmental and cultural factors on the academic performance of African-American males. *Urban Education, 38*(4), 431–459.

Olds, D. L., et al. (2004). Effects of nurse home-visiting on maternal life course and child development: Age 6 follow-up results of randomized trial. *Pediatrics, 114*, 1550–1559.

Olszewski-Kubilius, P., & Clarenbach, J. (2014). Closing the opportunity gap: Program factors contributing to academic success in culturally different youth. *Gifted Child Today, 37*(2), 103–110.

Parish, S. L., Rose, R. A., Swaine, J. G., Dababnah, S., & Mayra, E. T. (2012). Financial well-being of single, working-age mothers of children with developmental disabilities. *American Journal on Intellectual and Developmental Disabilities, 117*(5), 400–412.

Parker, S. E., Mai, C. T., Canfield, M. A., Rickard, R., Wang, Y., Meyer, R. E., Anderson, P., Mason, C. A., Collins, J. S., Kirby, R. S., Correa, A., National Center on Birth Defects and Developmental Disabilities. (2010). *Updated National Birth Prevalence estimates for selected birth defects in the United States, 2004–2006.* Atlanta, GA: Centers for Disease Control and Prevention.

Passel, J., & Cohn, D. (2008, February). U.S. population projections: 2005–2050. Washington, DC: Pew Hispanic Center. Retrieved from: http:// pewhispanic.org/files/reports/85.pdf

Paster, V. (1985). Psychosocial development and coping of black male adolescents: Clinical implications. *Beginning: The Social and Affective Development of Black Children*, (15), 2216–2229.

Pears, K. C., Kim, H. K., Fisher, P. A., & Yoerger, K. (2013). Early school engagement and late elementary outcomes for maltreated children in foster care. *Developmental Psychology, 49*(12), 2201–2211.

Pereira, N., & Oliverira, L. C. (2015). Meeting the linguistic needs of high potential English language learners. *Teaching Exceptional Children, 47*(4), 208–215.

Perrin, J. M., Bloom, S. R., & Gortmaker, S. L. (2011). The increase of childhood chronic conditions in the United States. *Journal of American Medical Association, 297*(24), 2755–2759.

Peterson, C. A., Mayer, L. M., Summers, J. A., & Luze, G. J. (2010). Meeting needs of young children at risk for or having a disability. *Early Childhood Education Journal, 37*(6), 509–517.

Pinkerton, J., & Dolan, P. (2007). Family support, social capital, resilience and adolescent coping. *Child & Family Social Work, 12*(3), 219–228.

Rauch, S. A., & Lanphear, B. P. (2012). Prevention of disability in children: Elevating the role of environment. *Future Child, 22*(1), 193–217.

Riley, E. P., & McGee, C. L. (2005). Fetal alcohol spectrum disorders: An overview with emphasis on changes in brain and behavior. *Experimental Biology and Medicine, 230*(6), 357–365.

Ritchotte, J. J., Rubenstein, L., & Murry, F. (2015). Reversing the underachievement of gifted middle school students. *Gifted Child Today, 38*(2), 103–113.

Rosier, P., & Holm, W. (1980). *The Rock Point experience: A longitudinal study of a Navajo school.* Washington, DC: Center for Applied Linguistics.

Roy, A. L., & Raver, C. C. (2014). Are all risks equal? Early experiences of poverty-related risk and children's functioning. *Journal of Family Psychology, 28*(3), 391–400. doi:10.1037/a0036683

Scarborough, H. S., & Dobrich, W. (1990). Development of children with early language delay. *Journal of Speech & Hearing Research, 33*, 70–83.

Singer, L. T., et al. (2004). Cognitive outcomes of preschool children with prenatal cocaine exposure. *Journal of the American Medical Association, 291*(20), 2448–2456.

Snapp, S. D., Hoenig, J. M., Fields, A., & Russell, S. T. (2015). Messy, butch, and queer: LGBTQ youth and the school-to-prison pipeline. *Journal of Adolescent Research, 30*(1), 57–82.

Sticht, T. G. (2012). Getting it right from the start: The case for early parenthood education. *Education Digest, 77*(9), 11–17.

Stone, S., & Zibulsky, J. (2015). Maltreatment, academic difficulty, and systems-involved youth: Current evidence and opportunities. *Psychology in the Schools, 52*(1), 22–39.

Stratton, K., Howe, C., & Battaglia, F. (Eds.). (1996). *Fetal alcohol syndrome: Diagnosis, epidemiology, prevention and treatment.* Washington, DC: National Academies Press.

Tanner, J. M. (1990). *Fetus into man: Physical growth from conception to maturity.* Cambridge, MA. Harvard University Press.

Taylor, L., & Adelman, H. S. (2000). Toward ending the marginalization and fragmentation of mental health in schools. *Journal of School Health, 70*(5), 210.

Toomey, R. B., & Russell, S. T. (2013). Gay–straight alliances, social justice involvement, and school victimization of lesbian, gay, bisexual, and queer youth: Implications for school well-being and plans to vote. *Youth & Society, 45*(4), 500–522.

U.S. Department of Health & Human Services, Administration for Children and Families, Administration on Children, Youth and Families, Children's Bureau. (2016). Child maltreatment 2014. Retrieved from: http://www.acf.hhs.gov/programs/cb/research-data-technology/statistics-research/child-maltreatment

Vaughn, S., Mathes, P. G., Linan-Thompson, S., & Francis, D. (2005). Teaching English language learners at risk for reading disabilities to read: Putting research into practice. *Learning Disabilities Research & Practice, 20*(1), 58–67.

Venn, J. J. (2004). *Assessing students with special needs* (3rd ed.). Upper Saddle River, NJ: Pearson.

Viezel, K. D., Freer, B. D., Lowell, A., & Castillo, J. A. (2015). Cognitive abilities of maltreated children. *Psychology in the Schools, 52*(1), 92–106.

Werner, E. E. (1992). The children of Kauai: Resiliency and recovery in adolescence and adulthood. *Journal of Adolescent Health, 13*(4), 262–268.

Wilkerson, D., Johnson, G., & Johnson, R. (2008). Children of neglect with attachment and time perception deficits: Strategies and interventions. *Education, 129*(2), 343–352.

Yeo, Frederick L. (1997). *Inner-city schools, multiculturalism, and teacher education: A professional journey.* New York and London: Garland Publishing.

Yoshitaka, I. (2014). Reflection on learnings from engaging and working with high-risk, marginalized youth. *Relational Child & Youth Care Practice, 27*(4), 24–35.

Young, J., Ne'eman, A., & Geiser, S. (n.d.). National Council on Disability. Retrieved May 3, 2015, from: http://www.ncd.gov/publications/2011/March92011

Yull, D., Blitz, L. V., Thompson, T., & Murray, C. (2014). Can we talk? Using community-based participatory action research to build family and school partnerships with families of color. *School Community Journal, 24*(2), 9–32.

Chapter 4: Laws That Support Families

Americans with Disabilities Act Amendment Act. 42 U.S.C. § 12101 *et seq.* (2008).

Bartlett, L. D., Etscheidt, S., & Weinstein, G. R. (2007). *Special education law and practice in public schools.* Upper Saddle River, NJ: Pearson Merrill Prentice Hall.

Board of Education of the Hendrick Hudson Central School District v. Rowley 458 U. S. 176 (1982).

Boyle, J. R., & Weishaar, M. (2001). *Special education law with cases.* Boston: Allyn and Bacon.

Brown v. Board of Education of Topeka Kansas, 347 U.S. 483. (1954)

Cambron-McCabe, N. H., McCarthy, M. M., & Thomas, S. B. (2007). *Legal rights of teachers and students.* Boston: Pearson.

Daniel R. R. v. State Board of Education, 874 F. 2d 1036 (Fifth Circuit 1989)

Fact Sheet on the EEOC's Final Regulations Implementing the ADAAA. (n.d.). Retrieved from: http://www1.eeoc.gov//laws/regulations/adaaa_fact_sheet.cfm?renderforprint=1

Family Education Rights and Privacy Act of 1974, 20 U.S.C. §1232g (1974)

Hardman, M. L., & Dawson, S. (2008). Impact of federal legislation and public policy on curriculum & instruction in the general classroom. *Preventing School Failure, 52*(2), 3–11.

Huefner, D. S. (2006). *Getting comfortable with special education law: A framework for working with children with disabilities* (2nd ed.). Norward, MA: Christopher-Gordon Publishers, Inc.

Huefner, D. S., & Herr, C. M. (2012). *Navigating special education law and policy.* Verona, WI: Attainment Company, Inc.

Individuals with Disabilities Education Improvement Act 2004. 20 U.S.C. § 1400 *et seq.*

Individuals with Disabilities Education Act 2004 Regulations. 34 CFR § 300 *et seq.*

Latham, P. S., Latham, P. H., & Mandlawitz, M. R. (2008). *Special education law.* Boston: Pearson.

McLaughlin, M. J. (2009*). What every principal needs to know about special education* (2nd ed.). Thousand Oaks, CA: Corwin Press.

Mills v. Board of Education of the District of Columbia, 384 F. Supp.866 (U.S. District Court, District of Columbia 1972)

Elementary and Secondary Education Act of 1965. 20 U.S.C. § 6301 *et seq.*

Osborne, A. G., & Russo, C. J. (2014). *Special education and the law: A guide for practitioners* (3rd ed.). Thousand Oaks, CA: Corwin Press.

Parents in Action on Special Education (PASE) v. Joseph P. Hannon, 506 F. Supp.831 (N.D. Illinois, 1980)

The Pennsylvania Association for Retarded Children (PARC) v. the Commonwealth of Pennsylvania, 334 F. Supp.1257 (U.S. District Court, E.D. Pennsylvania, 1972)

Pierangelo, R., & Giuliani, G. (2007a). *100 frequently asked questions about the special education process.* Thousand Oaks, CA: Corwin Press.

Pierangelo, R., & Giuliani, G. (2007b). *Special education eligibility.* Thousand Oaks, CA: Corwin Press.

Reichman, N., Corman, H., & Noonan, K. (2008). Impact of child disability on the family. *Maternal & Child Health Journal, 12*(6), 679–683.

Roncker v. Walter, 700. 2d 1058 (Sixth Circuit 1983)

Sacramento City Unified School District v. Rachel H., 14 F.3d 1398 (Ninth Circuit), cert. denied, 129 L. Ed. 2d 813 (1994)

Section 504 of the Rehabilitation Act of 1973, 29 U.S.C. §794 (2006)

Timothy W. v. Rochester School District, 875 F.2d 954 (First Circuit, 1989)

Wright, P. W., & Wright, P. D. (2012). *Special education law* (2nd ed.). Hartfield, VA: Harbor House Law Press, Inc.

Yell, M. L. (2012). *The law and special education* (3rd ed.). Boston: Pearson.

Yell, M. L., Katsiyannas, A., & Shriner, J. G. (2006). The No Child Left Behind Act, adequate yearly progress, and students with disabilities. *Teaching Exceptional Children, 38*(4), 32–39.

Ziegler, D. (2015). *What every educator needs to know about coming changes to special education policy.* Paper presented at the Annual Convention of Council for Exceptional Children, San Diego, CA.

Chapter 5: The Professionals and Their Roles

Aguilar, E. (2011). Twenty tips for developing positive relationships with parents. Retrieved from: http://www.edutopia.org/blog/20-tips-developing-positive-relationships-parents-elena-aguilar

American Speech-Language-Hearing Association. (2007). Scope of practice in speech-language pathology. Retrieved from: http://www.asha.org/policy/

Anderson, C. M., & Martin, M. M. (1995). Communication motives of assertive and responsive communicators. *Communication Research Reports, 12*(2), 86–91. doi:10.1080/08824099509362055

Bishop, S.C., Lau. M., Shapiro, S., Carlson, L., Anderson, N.D., Carmody, J., Segal, Z.V., Abbey, S., Speca, M., & Velting, D. (2004). Mindfulness: A proposed operational definition. *Clinical Psychology Science and Practice, 11*(3), 230–241. doi:10.1093/clipsy.bph077

Bodner, T. E., & Langer, E. J. (2001). *Individual differences in mindfulness: The Mindfulness/Mindlessness Scale.* Poster presented at the 13th annual American Psychological Society Convention, Toronto, Ontario, Canada.

Brown, K. W. & Ryan, R.M. (2003). *The benefits of being present: Mindfulness and its role in psychological well-being. Journal of Personality and Social Psychology, 84*(4), 822–848. doi:10.1037/0022-3514.84.4.822

Burgoon, J. K., Berger, C. R., & Waldron, V. R. (2000). Mindfulness and interpersonal communication. *Journal of Social Services, 56*(1), 105–127.

Clarocco, N. J., Sommer, K. L., & Baumeister, R. F. (2001). Ostracism and ego depletion: The strains of silence. *Personality and Social Psychology Bulletin, 27*(9), 1156–1163. doi:10.1177/0146167201279008

Deering, C. G. (1993). Working with people: Giving and taking criticism. *American Journal of Nursing, 93*(12), 56–61.

Elliott, S. E. & Gresham, F. M. (1993). Social skills intervention for children. *Behavior Modification, 17*(3), 287–313. doi:10.1177/01454455930173004

Ellis, D., & Hughes, K. (2002). *Partnerships by design: Cultivating effective and meaningful school–family–community partnerships: Creating communities of excellence.* Portland, OR: Northwest Regional Educational Laboratory.

Elmes , M. B., & Gemmill, G. (1990). The psychodynamics of mindfulness and dissent in small groups. *Small Group Research, 21*, 28–44.

Epstein, J. L. (2001). *School, family, and community partnerships: Preparing educators and improving schools.* Westview Press, 5500 Central Avenue, Boulder, CO 80301.

Epstein, J. (1995). School/family/community partnerships: Caring for the children we share. *Phi Delta Kappan*, 701–712.

Feinberg, E., Beyer, J., & Moses, P. (2002). *Beyond mediation: Strategies for appropriate early dispute resolution in special education.* Unpublished manuscript. Eugene, OR: National Center on Alternative Dispute Resolution (CADRE).

Filley, A. C. (1975). *Interpersonal conflict resolution.* Glenview, IL: Scott Foresman.

Gartin, B. C., & Murdick, N. L. (2005). IDEA 2004: The IEP. *Remedial and Special Education, 26*(6), 327–331. doi: 10.1177/07419325050260060301

Graham-Clay, S. (2005). Communicating with parents: Strategies for teachers. *School Community Journal, 16*(1), 117–129.

Herr, M., & Crandall, D. (n.d.). Physical therapy in school settings [PDF document]. Retrieved from: http://www.apta.org/uploadedFiles/APTAorg/Advocacy/Federal/Legislative_Issues/IDEA_ESEA/PhysicalTherapyintheSchoolSystem.pdf#search=%22physical therapy in schools%22

Heward, W. L. (2013). *Exceptional children: An introduction to special education.* Upper Saddle River, NJ: Pearson Education.

Howe, F., & Simmons, B. J. (1993). Parent teacher alliances. *Educational Issues, 4*(1), 5–22.

Howe, F., & Simmons, B. J. (2000). Connecting with parents. *Virginia Journal of Education, 93*(9), 7–10.

Johnson, D. W. (1974). Communication and the inducement of cooperative behavior in conflicts: A critical review. *Speech Monographs, 41*(1), 64–78. doi: 10.1080/03637757409384402

Johnson, L. J., Pugach, M. C., & Hawkins, A. (2004). School–family collaboration: A partnership. *Focus on Exceptional Children, 36*(5), 1–12.

Kelley, M. F. (1996). Collaboration in early childhood education. *Journal of Educational and Psychological Consultation, 7*(3), 275–282.

King, G., Strachan, D., Tucker, M., Duwyn, B., Desserud, S., & Shillington, M. (2009). The application of a transdisciplinary model for early intervention services. *Infants and Young Children, 22*, 211–223.

Kolb, S. M., & Griffith, A. C. (2009). I'll repeat myself, *again?!*: Empowering students through assertive communication strategies. *TEACHING Exceptional Children, 41*(3), 33.

Langer, E. J. (1989). *Mindfulness*. Boston: Addison-Wesley.

Lumsden, E. (2005). Joined-up thinking in practice: An exploration of professional exploration, in T. Waller (Ed.), *An introduction to early childhood* (pp. 39–54). London: Paul Chapman Publishing.

McNeal, R. B. (1999). Parental involvement as social capital: Differential effectiveness on science achievement, truancy, and dropping out. *Social Forces, 78*(1), 117–144.

Menlove, R. R., Hudson, P. J., & Suter, D. (2001). A field of IEP dreams: Increasing general education teacher participation in the IEP development process. *Teaching Exceptional Children, 33*(5), 28–33.

National Association of Social Workers, Center of Workforce Studies and Social Work Practice. (2010). *Social workers in schools: Occupational profile*. Retrieved from: http://workforce.socialworkers.org/studies/profiles/School%20Social%20Work.pdf

Orlich, D. C., Harder, R. J., Callahan, R. C., & Gibson, H. W. (1998). *Teaching strategies: A guide to better instruction* (5th ed.). Boston: Houghton Mifflin Co.

Palts, K., & Harro-Loit, H. (2015). Parent–teacher communication patterns concerning activity and positive-negative attitudes. *Trames: A Journal of the Humanities & Social Sciences, 2*, 139–154. doi:10.3176/tr.2015.2.03

Reeder, D. L., Arnold, S. H., Jeffries, L. M., & McEwen, I. R. (2011). The role of occupational therapists and physical therapists in elementary school system early intervening services and response to intervention: A case report. *Physical and Occupational Therapy in Pediatrics, 31*(1), 44–57. doi:10.3109/01942638.2010.497180

Rodriguez, R. J., & Elbaum, B. (2014). The role of student–teacher ratio in parents' perspective of schools' engagement efforts. *The Journal of Educational Research, 107*(1), 69–80. doi:10.1080/00220671.2012.753856

Simmons, B. J. (2002). Facilitative conferences: Parents and teachers working together. *The Clearing House, 76*(2), 88–93. doi:10.1080/00098650209604956

Sugai, G., Horner, R. H., Dunlap, G., Hieneman, M., Lewis, T. J., Nelson, C. M., ... & Ruef, M. (2000). Applying positive behavior support and functional behavioral assessment in schools. *Journal of Positive Behavior Interventions, 2*(3), 131–143. doi:10.1177/109830070000200302

Sui-Chu, E. H., & Williams, J. D. (1996). Effects of parental involvement on eighth-grade achievement. *Sociology of Education, 69*, 126–141.

U.S. Department of Education, National Center for Education Statistics. (2016). Digest of education statistics, 2014. Retrieved from https://nces.ed.gov/fastfacts/display.asp?id=64

Watkins, M. W., Crosby, E. G., & Pearson, J. L. (2001). Role of the school psychologist: Perceptions of school staff. *School Psychology International, 22*, 64–73. doi:10.1177/01430343010221005

Wherry, J. H. (2005). Working with parents: New teachers' greatest challenge. *Principal, 85*(2), 6.

Ziring, P. R., Brazdziunas, D., Cooley, W. C., Kastner, T. A., Kummer, M. E., de Pijem, L. G., ... & Sandler, A. D. (1999). The pediatrician's role in development and implementation of an individual education plan (IEP) and or an individual family service plan (IFSP). *Pediatrics, 104*(1), 124–127.

Chapter 6: Assessment to Research-Based Intervention: Providing Families Support

American Association on Intellectual and Developmental Disabilities. (2013). Resources for intellectual and developmental disability professionals. Retrieved September 12, 2016, from: http://aaidd.org/

American Psychiatric Association. (2013). *Diagnostic and statistical manual of mental disorders* (5th ed.). Washington, DC: Author

Autism Behavior Checklist. (n.d.). Retrieved July 13, 2016, from: http://drjenna.net/wp-content/uploads/2013/07/abc_checklist1-3.pdf

Autism Diagnostic Observation Schedule™ (ADOS™) | WPS. (n.d.). Retrieved July 13, 2016, from: http://wpspublish.com/store/p/2647/autism-diagnostic-observation-schedule-ados

Basterra, M., Trumbull, E., & Solano-Flores, G. (2011). *Cultural validity in assessment: Addressing linguistic and cultural diversity*. Florence, KY: Routledge, Taylor & Francis Group.

Bateman, B. D. (2011). Individual education programs for students with disabilities. In J. M. Kauffman & D. P. Hallahan (Eds.), *Handbook of special education* (pp. 91–106). New York: Routledge.

Bintz, W., & Harste, J. (1994). Where are we going with alternative assessments and is it really worth our time? *Contemporary Education, 66*, 7–12.

Brigham, F. J., & Crockett, J. B. (2013). Using assessments to determine placement in the least restrictive environment for students with disabilities. In J. W. Lloyd, T. J. Landrum, B. G. Cook, & M. Tankersley (Eds.), *Research-based approaches for assessment* (pp. 70–83). Upper Saddle River, NJ: Pearson.

Brolin, D. E., & Loyd, R. J. (2004). *Career development and transition services. A functional life skills approach* (4th ed.). Upper Saddle River, NJ: Merrill/Prentice Hall.

Bryan, T. (1997). Assessing the personal and social status of students with learning disabilities. *Learning Disabilities Research and Practice, 12*, 63–76.

Childhood Autism Rating Scale—Second Edition (CARS 2). (n.d.). Retrieved July 13, 2016, from: http://prasadpsycho.com/childhood-autism-rating-scale-second-edition-cars-2

Childre, A., & Chambers, C. R. (2005). Family perceptions of student-centered planning and IEP meetings. *Education and Training in Developmental Disabilities*, 217–233.

Davies, D. (1993). Benefits and barriers to parent involvement: From Portugal to Boston to Liverpool. *Families and Schools in a Pluralistic Society*, 205–216.

The Early Childhood Technical Assistance Center (2016). Improving Systems, Practices and Outcomes for Young Children with Disabilities and their Families. Retrieved September 12, 2016, from: http://ectacenter.org/

Fletcher, J., Coulter, W. A., Reschly, D. J., & Vaughn, S. (2004). Alternative approaches to the definition and identification of learning disabilities: Some questions and answers. *Annals of Dyslexia*, 54(2), 304–331.

Goh, D. S. (2004). *Assessment accommodations for diverse learners.* Boston: Pearson.

Goldstein, S., & Naglieri, J. A. (2011). *Encyclopedia of child behavior and development.* Springer.

Hall, L. J. (2008). Early childhood assessment. In J. A. McLoughlin & R. B. Lewis (Eds.), *Assessing students with special needs* (7th ed., pp. 502–531). Columbus, OH: Pearson Merrill Prentice Hall.

Hanson, M. J., & Lynch, E. W. (1995a). *Early intervention: Implementing child and family services for infants and toddlers who are at risk or disabled* (2nd ed.). Austin, TX: PRO-ED.

Hanson, M. J., & Lynch, E. W. (1995b). *Survival guide for interviewers.* Austin, TX: PRO-ED. Harcourt Brace Educational Measurement. (1996). Stanford-Diagnostic Mathematical Test—4th edition. San Antonio, TX: Harcourt Brace.

Harry, B. (1992). An ethnographic study of cross-cultural communication with Puerto Rican-American families in the special education system. *American Educational Research Journal*, 29(3), 471–494.

Harry, B. (2008). Collaboration with culturally and linguistically diverse families: Ideal vs. reality. *Exceptional Children*, 61, 364–377.

Hughes, C. A., & Ruhl, K. L. (1987). The nature and extent of special educator contacts with students' families. *Teacher Education and Special Education*, 10(4), 180–184.

Jardine, A. S. (1996). Key points of the authentic assessment portfolio. *Intervention in School and Clinic*, 31(4), 252–253.

Kalyanpur, M., & Harry, B. (1999). *Culture in special education: Building reciprocal family–professional relationships.* Baltimore, MD: Brookes.

Khattri N., & Sweet, D. (1996). Assessment reform: Promises and challenges. In M. B. Kane & R. Mitchell (Eds.), *Implementing performance assessment: Promises, problems, and challenges* (p. 1–21). Mahwah, NJ: Erlbaum.

Kritikos, E. P. (2010). *Special education assessment: Issues and strategies affecting today's classrooms.* Upper Saddle River, NJ: Merrill.

Linder, T. (1990). *Transdisciplinary play-based assessment.* Baltimore, MD: Brookes.

Lloyd, J. W., Landrum, T. J., Cook, B. G., & Tankersley, M. (2013). *Research-based approaches for assessment.* Boston, MA: Pearson.

Lord, C., Luyster, R.K., S., Gotham, K., & Guthrie, W. (2012). Autism Diagnostic Observation Schedule, Second Edition (ADOS-2) Manual (Part II): Toddler Module, Torrance, CA: Western Psychological Services.

Lord, C., Rutter, M., DiLavore, P. C., Risi, S., Gotham, K., & Bishop, S.I. (2012). Autism Diagnsotic Observation Schedule, Second Edition (ADOS-2) Manual (Part I): Modules 1-4. Torrance, CA: Western Pscyhologial Services.

Mayes, S. D. (1991). Play assessment of preschool hyperactivity. *Play Diagnosis and Assessment*, 249–282.

McCormick, L., & Noonan, M. J. (2002). Ecological assessment and planning. In M. Ostrosky & E. Horn (Eds.), *Assessment: Gathering meaningful information.* Monograph Series No. 4 (pp. 47–60). Longmont, CO: Sopris West.

McLoughlin, J. A., & Lewis, R. B. (2008). *Assessing students with special needs* (7th ed.). Upper Saddle River, NJ: Pearson.

Messick, S. (1995). Validity of psychological assessment: Validation of inferences from persons' responses and performances as scientific inquiry into score meaning. *American Psychologist, 50,* 741–749.

Meyer, J. A., & Mann, M. B. (2006). Teachers' perceptions of the benefits of home visits for early elementary children. *Early Childhood Education Journal*, 34(1), 93–97.

Miranda-Linné, F. M. & Melin, L. J. (2002). A factor analytic study of the autism behavior checklist. Journal of Autism and Developmental Disorders, 32(3), 281–188.

Moya, S. S., & O'Malley, J. M. (1994). A portfolio assessment model for ESL. *The Journal of Educational Issues of Language Minority Students, 13,* 13–36.

National Joint Committee on Learning Disabilities. (1994). *Collective perspectives on issues affecting learning disabilities.* Austin, TX: PRO-ED.

Nitko, J. J., & Brookhart, S. M. (2004). *Educational assessment of students.* Upper Saddle River, NJ: Merrill-Prentice Hall.

O'Neill, R. E., Horner, R. H., Albin, R. W., Sprague, J., Storey, J., & Newton, J. S. (1997). *Functional assessment and program development for problem behavior: A practical handbook.* Pacific Grove, CA: Brooks/Cole.

Orelove, F. P., Sobsey, D., & Silberman, R. K. (2004). *Educating children with multiple disabilities: A collaborative approach.* Brookes Publishing Company. PO Box 10624, Baltimore, MD 21285.

Pierangelo, R., & Giuliani, G. A. (2012). *Early childhood assessment: Assessment in special education, a practical approach* (4th ed.). Boston: Pearson.

Salvia, J., Ysseldyke, J. E., & Bolt, S. (2007). *Assessment in special and inclusive education.* Wadsworth.

Salvia, J., Ysseldyke, J. E., & Bolt, S. (2010). *Assessment in special and inclusive education* (11th Ed.). Boston, MA: Wadsworth Cengage Learning.

Schopler, E., Van Bourgondien, M., Wellman, J., & Love, S. (2010). Childhood autism rating scale—Second edition (CARS2): Manual. *Los Angeles: Western Psychological Services.*

Sileo, T. W., Sileo, A. P., & Prater, M. A. (1996). Parent and professional partnerships in special education:

Multicultural considerations. *Intervention in School and Clinic, 31,* 145S–153.

Sitlington, P. L., Neubert, D. A., & Leconte, P. J. (1997). Transition assessment: The position of the Division on Career Development and Transition. *Career Development for Exceptional Individuals, 20*(1), 69–79.

Spinelli, C. G. (2012). *Classroom assessment for students in general and special education* (3rd ed.). Boston: Pearson.

Stanford-Diagnostic Mathematical Test—4th edition. San Antonio, TX: Harcourt Brace.

Turnbull, A. P. (1995). *Exceptional lives: Special education in today's schools.* Old Tappan, NJ: Merrill/Prentice Hall.

Turnbull, A. P., & Ruef, M. (1996). What do students with disabilities tell us about the importance of family involvement in the transition from school to adult life? *Exceptional Children, 63*(3), 249–260.

Urie, Bronfenbrener. (n.d.). AZquotes. com. Retrieved September 12, 2016 from AZquotes.com website: http://www.azquotes.com/quote/917541

Wehman, P. (2006). Life beyond the classroom: Transition strategies for young people with disabilities (4th ed.). Baltimore, MD: Paul H. Brookes.

Ysseldyke, S. (1998). *Assessment.* Boston: Houghton Mifflin.

Chapter 7: Siblings of Children With Disabilities

Aksoy, A. B., & Yildirim, G. B. (2008). A study of the relationships and acknowledgement of non-disabled children with disabled siblings. *Educational Sciences: Theory & Practice, 8*(3), 769–779.

American Psychological Association (2015). *The Lifespan Respite Care Act (P.L. 109-442).* Retrieved from: http://www.apa.org/about/gr/issues/aging/respite-care-facts.aspx

Burbidge, J., & Minnes, P. (2014). Relationship quality in adult siblings with and without developmental disabilities. *Family Relations, 63,* 148–162.

Burton, S. L., & Parks, A. L. (1994). Self-esteem, locus of control, and career aspirations of college-age siblings of individuals with disabilities. *Social Work Research, 18*(3), 178–185.

Chambers, C. R. (2007). Siblings of individuals with disabilities who enter careers in the disability field. *Teacher Education and Special Education, 30*(3), 115–127.

Coyle, C. C., Kramer, J., & Mutchlert, J. E. (2014). Aging together: Sibling careers of adults with intellectual and developmental disabilities. *Journal of Policy & Practice in Intellectual Disabilities, 11*(4), 302–312.

Cuzzocrea, F., Larcan, R., Costa, S., & Gazzano, C. (2014). Parents' competence and social skills in siblings of disabled children. *Social Behavior and Personality, 42*(1), 45–58.

Family Medical Leave Act of 1993, 29 U.S.C. Sections 2601–2654, 2006.

Giallo, R., & Gavidia-Payne, S. (2006). Child, parent and family factors as predictors of adjustment for siblings of children with a disability. *Journal of Intellectual Disability Research, 50*(12), 937–948.

Giallo, R., Gavidia-Payne, S., Minett, B., & Kapoor, A. (2012). Sibling voices: The self-reported mental health of siblings of children with a disability. *Clinical Psychologist, 16,* 36–43.

Granat, T., Nordgren, I., Rein, G., & Sonnander, K. (2012). Group intervention for siblings of children with disabilities: A pilot study in a clinical setting. *Disability and Rehabilitation, 34*(1), 69–75.

Hames, A. (2008). Siblings' understanding of learning disability: A longitudinal study. *Journal of Applied Research in Intellectual Disabilities, 21,* 491–501.

Hannon, M. D. (2012). Supporting siblings of children with disabilities in the school setting: Implications and considerations for school counselors. *Journal of School Counseling, 10*(13). Retrieved from: http://www.jsc.montana.edu/articles/v10n13.pdf

Heller, T., & Arnold, C. K. (2010). Siblings of adults with developmental disabilities: Psychosocial outcomes, relationships, and future planning. *Journal of Policy and Practice in Intellectual Disabilities, 7*(1), 16–25.

Hodepp, R. M., & Urbano, R. C. (2007). Adult siblings of individuals with Down syndrome versus with autism: Findings from a large-scale U.S. survey. *Journal of Intellectual Disability Research, 51*(12), 1018–1029.

Howlin, P., Moss, P., Savage, S., Bolton, P., & Rutter, M. (2015). Outcomes in adult life among siblings of individuals with autism. *Journal of Autism & Developmental Disorder, 45*(3), 707–718.

Koch, C., & Mayes, R. (2012). The balancing act: Meeting the needs of all children including an adolescent with disabilities. *Journal of Applied Research in Intellectual Disabilities, 25,* 464–475.

Kramer, J., Hall, A., & Heller, T. (2013). Reciprocity and social capital in sibling relationships of people with disabilities. *Intellectual and Developmental Disabilities, 51*(6), 482–495.

Marks, S. U., Matson, A., & Barraza, L. (2005). The impact of siblings with disabilities on their brothers and sisters pursuing a career in special education. *Research and Practice for Persons With Severe Disabilities (RPSD), 30*(4), 205–218.

Mazaheri, M. M., Rae-Seebach, R. D., Preston, H. E., Schmidt, M., Kountz-Edwards, S., Field, N., ... Packman, W. (2013). The impact of PraderWilli syndrome on the family's quality of life and caregiving, and the unaffected siblings' psychosocial adjustment. *Journal of Intellectual Disability Research, 57*(9), 861–873.

National Council on Aging. (2016). *S. 192, Older Americans Act Reauthorization Act of 2016.* Retrieved from: https://www.ncoa.org/public-policy-action/older-americans-act/senate/s-192/

National Down Syndrome Society. (2012). *Achieving a Better Life Experience (ABLE) Act.* Retrieved from: http://www.ndss.org/Advocacy/Legislative-Agenda/Creating-an-Economic-Future-for-Individuals-with-Down-Syndrome/Achieving-a-Better-of-Life-Experience-ABLE-Act/

O'Neill, L. P., & Murray, L. E. (2016). Anxiety and depression symptomatology in adult siblings of individuals with different developmental disability diagnoses.

Research in Developmental Disabilities, 51, 116–125.

Orsmond, G. I., & Seltzer, M. M. (2007). Siblings of individuals with autism or Down syndrome: Effects on adult lives. *Journal of Intellectual Disability Research, 51*(9), 682–696.

Pollard, C. A., Barry, C. M., Freedman, B. H., & Kotchick, B. A. (2013). Relationship quality as a moderator of anxiety in siblings of children diagnosed with autism spectrum disorders or Down syndrome. *Journal of Child and Family Studies, 22,* 647–657.

Roper, S. O., Allred, D. W., Mandleco, B., Freeborn, D., & Dyches, T. (2014). Caregiver burden and sibling relationships in families raising children with disabilities and typically developing children. *Families, Systems, and Health, 32*(2), 241–246.

Ross, P., & Cuskelly, M. (2006). Adjustment, sibling problems and coping strategies of brothers and sisters of children with autistic spectrum disorder. *Journal of Intellectual & Developmental Disability, 31*(2), 77–86.

Saxena, M., & Adamsons, K. (2013). Siblings of individuals with disabilities: Reframing the literature through a bioecological lens. *Journal of Family Theory and Review, 5,* 300–316.

Sibling Leadership Network. (2013a). *Adult siblings of individuals with intellectual and developmental disabilities.* Retrieved from: http://siblingleadership.org/research/

Sibling Leadership Network. (2013b). *Young siblings of individuals with intellectual and developmental disabilities.* Retrieved from: http://siblingleadership.org/research/

Steel, R., Vandevelde, S., Poppe, L., & Moyson, T. (2013). How to support siblings of children with intellectual disabilities? A brief outline of a longitudinal, multi-perspective study on siblings with intellectual disabilities. *Journal of Communications Research, 5*(1), 81–85.

Tanis, E. S., Rizzolo, M. C., Hemp, R., & Braddock, D. (2013). *The state of the states in developmental disabilities policy brief: Siblings of individuals with intellectual/developmental disabilities.* Boulder, CO: State of the States Project and Sibling Leadership Network.

Taylor, J. L., & Hodepp, R. M. (2012). Doing nothing: Adults with disabilities with no daily activities and their siblings. *American Journal on Intellectual and Developmental Disabilities, 117*(1), 67–79.

Taylor, J. L., & Shivers, C. M. (2011). Predictors of helping profession choice and volunteerism among siblings of adults with mild intellectual deficits. *American Journal on Intellectual & Developmental Disabilities, 116*(4), 263–277.

Tozer, R., Atkin, K., & Wenham, A. (2013). Continuity, commitment and context: Adult siblings of people with autism plus learning disability. *Health and Social Care in the Community, 21*(5), 480–488.

Tsao, L., Davenport, R., & Schmiege, C. (2012). Supporting siblings of children with autism spectrum disorders. *Early Childhood Education Journal, 40,* 47–54.

U.S. Census Bureau. (2012). *Americans with disabilities: 2010 household economic studies.* Retrieved from: http://www.census.gov/prod/2012pubs/p70-131.pdf

U.S. Department of Health and Human Services, Administration for Community Living. (2015). *Administration on Aging: National Family Caregiver Support Program.* Retrieved from: http://www.aoa.acl.gov/AoA_Programs/HCLTC/Caregiver/

U.S. Department of Health and Human Services, Administration for Community Living. (2016). *Administration on Aging: Older Americans Act Reauthorization Act of 2016.* Retrieved from: http://www.aoa.acl.gov/AoA_programs/OAA/Reauthorization/2016/docs/2016-OAA-FAQs.pdf

Wolfe, B., Song, J., Greenberg, J. S., & Mailick, M. R. (2014). Ripple effects of developmental disabilities and mental illness on nondisabled adult siblings. *Social Science & Medicine, 108,* 1–9.

Chapter 8: Specific Disabilities Across the Lifespan

American Academy of Pediatrics. (2014). Heath issues: Developmental disabilities. Retrieved on March 28, 2015, from: http://www.healthychildren.org/English/health-issues/conditions/developmental/Pages/Congenital-Abnormalities.aspx

American Association on Intellectual and Developmental Disabilities. (2013). Frequently asked questions on intellectual disabilities. Retrieved March 10, 2015, from: http://www.aaidd.org/intelectual-disability/definition/faqs-on-intellectual-disability#.vq

American Association for Pediatric Ophthalmology and Strabismus. (2015). Cortical visual impairments. Retrieved March 14, 2015, from: https://www.http://www.aapos.org/terms/conditions/40.

American Psychiatric Association (2016). *What is Intellectual Disability?* Retrieved on September 8, 2016, from: http://www.psychiatry.org/patients-families/intellectual-disability/what -is-intellectual-disability

American Speech-Language-Hearing Association. (1997–2015). Hearing loss: Beyond early childhood: Causes. Retrieved on April 18, 2015, from: http://www.asha.org/Practice-Portal/Clinical-Topics/Hearing-Loss/

Antonopoulou, K., Hadjikakou, K., Stampoltzis, A., & Nicolaou, N. (2012). Parenting styles of mothers with deaf or hard-of-hearing children and hearing siblings. *Journal of Deaf Studies and Deaf Education, 17*(3), 306–318.

The Arc. (n.d.). Intellectual disabilities: Diagnosis of an intellectual disability. Retrieved on April 16, 2015, from: http://www.thearc.org/learn-about/intellectual-disability/diagnosis

The Arc. (2011). Resources: Introduction to intellectual disabilities. Retrieved March 11, 2015, from: http://www.tjearc.org/page.aspx?pid=2448

Autism Speaks. (2015). What we have learned about autism prevalence. Retrieved March 13, 2015, from: http://www. autismspeaks.org/site-wide prevalence

Baker, B., Blacher, J., & Pfeiffer, S. (1993 June). Family involvement in residential treatment of children with psychiatric disorder and mental retardation. *Hospital Community Psychiatry, 44(6)*, 561–6.

Baroff, G. S., & Olley, J. G. (1999). *Mental retardation: Nature, cause, and management* (3rd ed.). Philadelphia: Taylor & Francis.

Boutot, E. A., & Myles, B. S. (2011). *Autism spectrum disorders: Foundations, characteristics, and effective strategies*. Boston: Pearson.

Brainy Quotes. (2001–2016). Erik Erikson Quotes. Retrieved September 8, 2016, from: http:www.brainyquote .com/quotes/authors/e/erik_erikson .html

Calderon, R., & Greenberg, M. T. (1999). Stress and coping in hearing mothers of children with hearing loss: Factors affecting mother and child adjustment. *American Annals of the Deaf, 144*, 7–18.

Camarena, P. M., & Sarigiani, P. A. (2009). Postsecondary educational aspirations of high-functioning adolescents with autism spectrum disorders and their parents. *Focus on Autism and Other Developmental Disabilities, 24(2)*, 115–128.

Canter, A. (n.d.). Parents and teachers: Strategies for working together. *National Association of School Psychologists*. Retrieved on April 17, 2015, from: http://www .nasponline.org/communications/ spawareness/Parents%20and%20 Teachers.pdf

Castellano, C. (2004, Spring/Sum). Future reflections: A brief look at the education of blind children. Retrieved March 7, 2015, from: https://www .infbiorg/fr/fr13/fro04ss07.htm

Centers for Disease Control and Prevention. (2015a). Autism spectrum disorders. Retrieved on April 17, 2015, from: http://www .cdc.gov/ncbddd/autism/signs.html

Centers for Disease Control and Prevention. (2015b). Developmental disabilities: Facts about developmental disabilities. Retrieved March 8, 2015, from: http://www .cdc.gov/ncbddd/developmental disabilities/facts.html

Centers for Disease Control and Prevention. (2015c). Hearing loss in children. Retrieved April 16, 2015, from: http://www.cdc.gov/ncbddd/ hearingloss/data.html

Centers for Disease Control and Prevention. (2014). Fetal alcohol syndrome disorders (FASD): Basics. Retrieved March 8, 2015, from: http://www.cdc.gov/ncbddd/fasd/ index

Children and Adults with Attention-Deficit/Hyperactivity Disorder. (2013). ADHD and the decision to medicate. Retrieved on April 16, 2015, from: http://www.chadd.org/Membership/ Attention-Magazine/View-Articles/ ADHD-and-the-Decision-to-Medicate.aspx

Cortella, C. (2014). *The state of learning disabilities: Facts, trends, and emerging issues*. Retrieved on April 16, 2015, from: http://www.ncld.org/wp-content/uploads/2014/11/2014-State-of-LD.pdf

Croen, L. A., Grether, J. K., Yoshida, C. K., Oduouli, R., & Van de Water, J. (2005). Maternal autoimmune disorders, asthma and allergies, and childhood autism spectrum disorders. A case control study. *Archives of Pediatrics and Adolescent Medicine, 159*, 151–157.

Dunlap, G., Kern, L., & Worchester, J. (2001). ABA and academic instruction. *Focus on Autism and Other Developmental Disabilities, 16(2)*, 129–136.

Dyson, L. Win. (2010). Unanticipated effects of children with learning disabilities on their families. *Learning Disabilities Quarterly, 33(1)*, 23–55.

Dyscalculia.org. (2016). What is dyscalculia? Retrieved on June 9, 2016, from: http://www.dyscalculia. org/dyscalculia

Estes, A., Munson, J., Dawson, G., Koehler, E., Zhou, X. H., & Abbott, R. (2009). Parenting stress and psychological functioning among mothers of preschool children with autism and developmental delay. *Autism, 13(4)*, 375–387.

Faraone, S. V., & Biederman, J. (1997). Do attention deficit hyperactivity disorder and major depression share familial risk factors? *Journal of Nervous and Mental Disease, 185*, 531–541.

Friend, M. (2011). *Special education: Contemporary perspectives for school professionals* (3rd ed.) Upper Saddle River, NJ: Pearson.

Gerstein, E. D., Crnic, K. A., Blacher, J., & Baker, B. L. (2009). Resilience and the course of daily parenting stress in families of young children with intellectual disabilities. *Journal of Intellectual Disabilities, 53(12)*, 981–997.

Hannah, M., & Midlarsky, E. (2005). Helping siblings of children with mental retardation. *American Journal on Mental Retardation, 110*, 87–99.

Hauser-Cram, P., Warfield, M. E., Shonkoff, J. P., Krauss, M. W., Upshur, C. C., & Sayer, A. (1999). Families' influences on adaptive development of young children with Down syndrome. *Child Development, 70*, 979–989.

Heath, C., Curtis, D., Fan, W., & McPherson, R. (2014). The association between parenting stress, parenting self-efficacy, and the clinical significance of child ADHD symptom change following behavior therapy. *Child Psychiatry and Human Development, 46*, 118–129.

Heiman, T. (2002). Parents of children with disabilities: Resilience, coping, and future expectations. *Journal of Developmental and Physical Disabilities, 14*, 159–171.

Heiman, T., Zinck, L., & Heath, N. (2015). Parents and youth with learning disabilities: Perceptions of relationships and communication. *Journal of Learning Disabilities, 41(6)*, 524–534.

Heward, W. L. (2013). *Exceptional children: An introduction to special education* (10th ed.). Boston: Pearson.

Houser, M. (2014). Teacher–parent communication and students with autism spectrum disorders. *Autism Parenting, 12*, 34–32.

Hume, K. (2014). Introduction to special education issue: Autism, adolescence, and high school. *Remedial and Special Education, 35(2)*, 67.

Humphrey, N., & Lewis, S. (2008). "Make me normal": The views and experiences of pupils on the autistic spectrum in mainstream secondary schools. *Autism, 12(1)*, 23–46.

Humphrey, N., & Symes, W. (2010). Perceptions of social support and experience of bullying among pupils with autism spectrum disorders in mainstream secondary schools.

European Journal of Special Needs Education, 25(1), 77–91.

International Dyslexia Association. (2016). Common signs of dyslexia. Retrieved on June 9, 2016, from: https: www.readingrockets.org/ article/common-signs-dyslexia-0

Jamieson, J. R., Zaidman-Zait, A., & Poon, B. (2011). Family support needs as perceived by parents of preadolescents and adolescents who are deaf or hard of hearing. *Deafness & Education International, 13*, 110–130. doi:10.1179/1557069 X11Y.0000000005

Johnson, C., & Mash, E. J. (2001). Families of children with attention-deficit/hyperactivity disorder. *Journal of Abnormal Child Psychology, 28*, 569–583.

Johnson, K. P., Giannotti, F., & Cortesi, F. (2009). Sleep patterns in autism spectrum disorders. *Child and Adolescent Psychiatric Clinics in North America, 18*(4), 917–928.

Kids' Mental Health. (2009). Children's behavioral and emotional disorders. Retrieved on June 9, 2016, from: http://www.kidsmentalhealth.org/ childrens-behavioral-and-emotional-disorders/

Kuder, S. J. (2013). *Teaching students with language and communication disabilities* (4th ed.). Boston: Pearson.

La Sorsa V. A., & Fodor, I. G. (1990). Adolescent daughter/midlife mother dyad. *Psychology of Women Quarterly, 14*, 593–606.

LDOnline. (2015). LD Basics: What is a learning disability? Retrieved March 10, 2015, from: http//:www .ldonline.org/ldbasics/whatisld

Leyser, Y., & Heinze, T. (2001). Perspectives of parents of children who are visually impaired: Implications for the field. *RE:view, 33*, 37.

Maes, B., Broekman, T. G., Dosen, A., & Nauts, J. (2003). Caregiving burden of families looking after persons with intellectual disability and behavioural or psychiatric problems. *Journal of Intellectual Disability Research, 46*, 447–455.

McLaughlin, R. (2011). Speech and language delay in children. *American Family Physician, 85*(10), 1183–1188.

The Merck Manual. (2015). Levels of intellectual disability. Retrieved on April 17, 2015, from: http://

www.merckmanuals.com/home/ children-s-health-issues/learning-and-developmental-disorders/ intellectual-disability

Meyer, D. J. (1986). Fathers of handicapped children. In Fewell, R. R., & Vadasy, P. F. (Eds.), *Families Handicapped Children* (pp. 35–73). Austin, TX: ProEd.

Mirenda, P. (2003). "He's not really a reader..." Perspectives on supporting literacy development in individuals with autism. *Topics in Language Disorders, 23*, 271–282.

Modrcin, M., & Robison, M. (1991). Parents of children with emotional disorders: Issues for consideration and practice. *Community Mental Health Journal, 27*(4), 281–292.

Moghaddam, M., Assareh, M., Heidaripoor, A., Rad, R., & Pishjoo, M. (2013). The study comparing parenting style of children with ADHD and normal children. *Archives of Psychiatry and Psychotherapy, 15*, 45–49.

Most, T., & Zaidman-Zait, A. (2003). The needs of parents of children with cochlear implants. *The Volta Review, 103*(2), 99–116.

National Dissemination Center for Children with Disabilities. (2012). *Categories of disability under IDEA*. Retrieved on April 17, 2015, from: http://www.parentcenterhub.org/ wp-content/uploads/repo_items/ gr3.pdf

National Eye Institute. (n.d.). Refractive errors. Retrieved on March 15, 2015, from: https://www.nei.nih.gov/ health/errors

National Institute of Mental Health. (2015). What is attention deficit hyperactivity disorder? Retrieved March 9, 2015, from: http://www .nimh.nih.gov/health/publications/ attention-deficit-hyperactivity-disorder/index.shtml?rf=71264

National Institute on Deafness and Other Communication Disorders. (2014). speech and language developmental milestones. Retrieved on April 17, 2015, from: http://www.nidcd.nih .gov/health/voice/pages/ speechandlanguage.aspx

National Resource Center on ADHD. (n.d.). About ADHD. Retrieved on April 16, 2015, from: http://www .help4adhd.org/en/about/statistics

Neece, C. L., Green, S. A., & Baker, B. L. (2012). Parenting stress and children with behavior problems: A transactional relationship across time. *American Journal on Intellectual and Developmental Disabilities, 117*(1), 48–66.

Newacheck, P. W., & Kim, S. E. (2005). A national profile of health care utilization and expenditures from children with special health needs. *Archive of Pediatric and Adolescent Medicine, 159*, 10–17.

Peele, P. B., Lave, J. R., & Kelleher, K. J. (2002). Exclusions and limitations in children's behavioral health care coverage. *Psychiatric Services, 53*, 591–594.

Perrin, S., & Last, C. G. (1996). Relationship between ADHD and anxiety in boys: Results from a family study. *Journal of the American Academy of Child and Adolescent Psychiatry, 35*, 988–996.

Phetrasuwan, S., & Miles, M. S. (2009). Parenting stress in mothers of children with autism spectrum disorders. *Journal for Specialists in Pediatric Nursing, 14*(3), 157–165.

Project Ideal. (2013). Other health impairments. Retrieved on June 9, 2016, from: http://www. projectidealonline.org/v/health-impairments/

Razzino, B. E., Ribirdy, S. C., Grant, K., Ferrari, J. R., Bowden, B. S. & Zeisz, J. (2004). Gender-related processes and drug use: Self-expression with parents, peer group selection, and achievement motivation. *Adolescence, 39*, 167–177.

Riesch, S. K., Anderson, L. S., & Krueger, H. A. (2006). Parent–child communication processes: Preventing children's health-risk behavior. *Journal for Specialist in Pediatric Nursing, 11*, 41–56.

Rosenblum, P. L., Hong, A., & Harris, B. (2009). Experiences of parents with visual impairments who are raising children. *Journal of Visual Impairment and Blindness, 103*(2), 81–93.

Seligman, M., & Darling, R. B. (2007). *Ordinary families, special children: A systems approach to childhood disability*. New York: The Guildford Press.

Snow, C. E. Burns, M. S. & Griffin, P. (1998). *Preventing reading difficulties in young children.* Washington, DC: National Academies Press.

Taunt, H. M., & Hastings, R. P. (2002). Positive impact of children with developmental disabilities: Challenges and roles for school counselors. *Professional School Counseling, 10,* 52–75.

Thomas, K. C., Morrissey, J. P., & McLaurin, C. (2007). Use of autism-related services by families and children. *Journal of Autism and Developmental Disorders, 37,* 818–829.

Tod, S., & Jones, S. (2005). Looking at the future and seeing the past: The challenge of the middle years of parenting a child with intellectual disabilities. *Journal of Intellectual Disability Research, 49*(6), 389–404.

Turnbull, A. P., Patterson, J. M., Behr, S. K., Murphy, D. L., Marquis, J. Q., & Blue-Banning, M. J. (1993). *Cognitive coping, families and disabilities.* Baltimore, MD: Paul H. Brookes.

Turnbull, A., Turnbull, R., Wehmeyer, M., & Shogren, K. (2012). *Exceptional lives: Special education in today's schools* (7th ed.). Boston: Pearson.

U.S. Department of Education, National Center for Education Statistics. (2013). *Digest of education statistics, 2012* (NCES 2014-015), Table 48. Washington, DC: National Center for Education Statistics, Institute of Education Sciences, U.S. Department of Education.

Whitehurst, T. (2012). Raising a child with foetal alcohol syndrome: Hearing the parent voice. *British Journal of Learning Disabilities, 40*(3), 187–193.

Chapter 9: Birth Through Age 5

Baby Center (2016). Developmental milestones: What to expect from birth to age 3. Retrieved from: http://www.babycenter.com/milestone-charts-birth-to-age-3.

Bailey, D., Scarborough, A., Hebbeler, K., Spiker, D., & Mallik, S. (2004). *National early intervention longitudinal study: Family outcomes at the end of early intervention.* Menlo Park, CA: SRI International.

Center for Parent Information and Resources. (2012). Module 1: Basics of early intervention. Retrieved from: http://www.parentcenterhub.org/repository/partc-module1/#section1

Center on the Developing Child at Harvard University. (2010). The foundations of lifelong health are built in early childhood. Retrieved from: http://developingchild.harvard.edu/library/reports_and_working _papers/foundations-of-lifelong-health/

Centers for Disease Control and Prevention. (2014a). Important milestones: Your child by one year. Retrieved from: http://www.cdc.gov/ncbddd/actearly/milestones/milestones-1yr.html

Centers for Disease Control and Prevention, (2014b). Important milestones: Your child by three years. Retrieved from: http://www.cdc.gov/ncbddd/actearly/milestones/milestones-3yr.html

Division for Early Childhood. (2014). DEC recommended practices in early intervention/early childhood special education 2014. Retrieved from: http://www.dec-sped.org/recommendedpractices

ed.gov. (n.d.). IDEA 2004: Building the legacy, Part C (birth–2 years old). Retrieved from: http://idea.ed.gov/part-c/search/new

Individuals With Disabilities Education Act, 20 U.S.C. § 1400 (2004).

Individuals With Disabilities Education Act Part C, 20 U.S.C. §303.13(b)(3) of the Part C regulations (2004).

Mayo Clinic. (2014). Infant development: Birth to 3 months. Retrieved from: http://www.mayoclinic.org/healthy-lifestyle/infant-and-toddler-health/in-depth/infant-development/art-20048012

McGill Smith, P. (2014). You are not alone. Retrieved from: http://www.parentcenterhub.org/repository/notalone/

Pacer Center. (2011). *What is the difference between an IFSP and an IEP?* Retrieved from: http://www.pacer.org/parent/php/PHP-c59.pdf

ParentFurther. (2015). Ages 3–5 developmental overview. Retrieved from: http://www.parentfurther.com/content/ages-3-5-developmental-overview

Chapter 10: The Primary School Years

Abbott, C., & Lucey, H. (2005). Symbol communication in special schools in England: The current position and some key issues. *British Journal of Special Education, 32,* 196–201.

Alberto, P. A., & Troutman, A. C. (2006). *Applied behavior analysis for teachers* (7th ed.). Upper Saddle River, NJ: Merrill/Prentice Hall.

Aronson, M. M. (1995). *Building communication partnerships with parents.* Westminster, CA: Teacher Created Materials, Inc.

Barbetta, P. M., & Miller, A. (1991). Tugmate: A cross-age tutoring program to teach sight vocabulary. *Education & Treatment of Children, 14,* 19–37.

Beukelman, D. R., & Mirenda, P. (2013). Supporting participation and communication for beginning communicators. In D. R. Beukelman & P. Mirenda (Eds.), *Augmentative & alternative communication. Supporting children & adults with complex communication needs* (4th ed., pp. 225–254). Baltimore, MD: Paul H. Brookes.

Brendt, T. J. (2004). Children's friendships: Shifts over a half-century in perspectives on their development and their effects. *Merrill-Palmer Quarterly, 50,* 206–233.

Browder, D. M., Trela, K., & Jimenez, B. (2007). Training teachers to follow a task analysis to engage middle school students with moderate and severe developmental disabilities in grade-appropriate literature. *Focus on Autism and Other Developmental Disabilities, 22,* 206–219.

Browder, D. M., Spooner, M., & Jimenez, B. (2011). Standards-based individualized education plans and progress monitoring. In D. M. Browder & F. Spooner (Eds.), *Teaching students with moderate and severe disabilities* (pp. 42–91). New York, NY: Guilford Press.

Bukowski, W. M., Newcomb, A. F., & Hartup, W. W. (1996). Friendship and its significance in childhood and adolescence: Introduction and comment. In W. F. Bukowski, A. F. Newcomb, & W. W. Hartup (Eds.),

The company they keep: Friendship in childhood and adolescence (pp. 1–15). New York, NY: Cambridge University Press.

Buysse, V. (1993). Friendships of preschoolers with disabilities in community-based child care settings. *Journal of Early Intervention, 17,* 380–395.

Buysse, V., Goldman, B. D., & Skinner, M. L. (2003). Friendship formation in inclusive early childhood classrooms: What is the teacher's role? *Early Childhood Research Quarterly, 18,* 485–501.

Carter, E. W., Asmus, J. M., & Moss, C. K. (2014). Peer support interventions to support inclusive schools. In J. McLeskey, N. L. Waldron, F. Spooner, & B. Algozzine (Eds.), *Handbook of research and practice for effective inclusive schools* (pp. 377–394). New York, NY: Routledge.

Carter, E. W., Cushing, L. S., & Kennedy, C. H. (2009). *Peer support strategies for improving all students' social lives and learning.* Baltimore, MD: Paul H. Brookes.

Cloninger, C. J. (2004). Designing collaborative educational services. In F. P. Orelove, D. Sobsey, & R. K. Silberman (Eds.), *Educating children with multiple disabilities: A collaborative approach* (4th ed., pp. 1–29). Baltimore, MD: Paul H. Brookes.

Colombo, M. W. (2004). Family literacy nights...and other home–school connections. *Educational Leadership, 61,* 48–51.

Davern, L. (2004). School-to-home notebooks: What parents have to say. *Teaching Exceptional Children, 36*(5), 22–27.

Detheridge, T., & Detheridge, M. (2013). *Literacy through symbols: Improving access for children and adults* (2nd ed.). New York, NY: Routledge.

Duncan, G. J., & Brooks-Gunn, J. (2000). Family poverty, welfare reform, and child development. *Child Development, 71,* 188–196.

Eiserman, W. D. (1988). Three types of peer tutoring: Effects on the attitudes of students with learning disabilities and their regular class peers. *Journal of Learning Disabilities, 21,* 249–252.

Finders, M., & Lewis, C. (1994). Why some parents don't come to school. *Educational Leadership, 51,* 40–42.

Geisthardt, C. L., Brotherson, J. J., & Cook, C. C. (2002). Friendships of children with disabilities in the home environment. *Education and Training in Mental Retardation and Developmental Disabilities, 37,* 235–252.

Giangreco, M. F., Cloninger, C. J., Dennis, R. E., & Edelman, S. W. (2000). Problem-solving methods to facilitate inclusive education. In R. A. Villa & J. S. Thousand (Eds.), *Restructuring for caring and effective education; Piecing the puzzle together* (2nd ed., pp. 293–359). Baltimore, MD: Paul H. Brookes.

Giangreco, M. F., Cloninger, C. J., & Iverson, V. S. (2011). *Choosing outcomes & accommodations for children. A guide to educational planning for students with disabilities* (3rd ed.). Baltimore, MD: Paul. H. Brookes.

Graham-Clay, S. (2005). Communicating with parents: Strategies for teachers. *The School Community Journal, 15*(1), 117–129.

Greenwood, C. R., Carta, J. J., & Hall, R. V. (1988). The use of peer tutoring strategies in classroom management and educational instruction. *School Psychology Review, 17,* 258–275.

Greenwood, C. R., Maheady, L., & Delquadri, J. C. (2002). Class-wide peer tutoring. In G. Stoner, M. R. Shinn, & H. Walker (Eds.), *Interventions for achievement and behavior problems* (2nd ed.; pp. 611–649). Washington, DC: National Association of School Psychologists.

Hains, A. H., Fowler, S. A., & Chandler, L. K. (1988). Planning school transitions: Family and professional collaboration. *Journal of the Division for Early Childhood, 12,* 108–115.

Hawbaker, B. W. (2007). Student-led IEP meetings: Planning and implementation strategies. *Teaching Exceptional Children Plus, 3*(5) Article 4. Retrieved from: http://escholarship.bc.edu/education/tecplus/vol3/iss5/art4

Heller, K. W., & Forney, P. (2009). Understanding disabilities and effective teaming. In K. W. Heller, P. E. Forney, P. A. Alberto, S. J. Best, & M. N. Schwartzman (Eds.), *Understanding physical, health, and multiple disabilities* (2nd ed., pp. 2–17). Upper Saddle River, NJ: Pearson.

Heyne, L. A., Schleien, S. J., & McAvoy, L. H. (1994). *Making friends: Using recreation activities to promote friendship between children with and without disabilities.* (Contract No. H029F90067; H133B80048). Retrieved from the U.S. Department of Education, Office of Educational Research and Improvement, Educational Resources Information Center (ERIC) website: http://files.eric.ed.gov/fulltext/ED379857.pdf

Heyne, L. A., Schleien, S. J., & McAvoy, L. H. (2003). *Ideas for encouraging children's friendships through recreation.* In V. Gaylord, L. Lieberman, B. Abery, & G. Lais (Eds.), *Impact: Feature Issue on Social Inclusion Through Recreation for Persons with Disabilities, 16*(2). Minneapolis MN: University of Minnesota, Institute on Community Integration. Retrieved from the *Impact* Newsletter website: https://ici.umn.edu/products/impact/193/over13.html

Hollingsworth, J. L., & Buysse, V. (2009). Establishing friendships in early childhood inclusive settings: What roles do parents and teachers play? *Journal of Early Intervention, 31,* 287–307.

Hudson, M. E., & Browder, D. M. (2014). Improving listening comprehension responses for students with moderate intellectual disability during literacy class. *Research and Practice for Persons with Severe Disabilities, 39,* 11–29.

Hudson, M. E., Browder, D. M., & Jimenez, B. A. (2014). Effects of a peer-delivered system of least prompts intervention with adapted science read-alouds on listening comprehension for students with moderate intellectual disability. *Education and Training in Autism and Developmental Disabilities, 49,* 60–77.

Hughes, C., & Carter, E. W. (2008). *Peer buddy programs for successful* secondary school inclusion. Baltimore, MD: Paul H. Brookes.

Individuals with Disabilities Education Act, 20 U.S.C. § 1400 (2004).

Jorgensen, C. M., McSheehan, M., & Sonnenmeier, R. M. (2010). *The beyond access model: Promoting membership, participation, and learning for students with disabilities in the general education classroom.* Baltimore, MD: Paul H. Brookes.

Kamps, D., Locke, P., Delquadri, J., & Hall, V. (1989). Increasing academic skills of students with autism using fifth grade peers as tutors. *Education & Treatment of Children, 12*, 38–51.

Kamps, D., & Walker, D. (1990). A comparison of instructional arrangements for children with autism served in a public school. *Education & Treatment of Children, 13*, 197–216.

Kasahara, M., & Turnbull, A. P. (2005). Meaning of family–professional partnerships: Japanese mother's perspectives. *Exceptional Children, 71*, 249–265.

Kübler-Ross, E. (1969). *On death and dying.* New York, NY: Scribner.

Kübler-Ross, E., & Kessler, D. (2005). *On grief and grieving: Finding the meaning of grief through the five stages of loss.* New York, NY: Scribner.

Lahat, A., Helwig, C. C., Yang, S., Ran, D., & Liu E. (2008). Mainland Chinese adolescents' judgments and reasoning about self-determination and nurturance rights. *Social Development, 18*, 690–710.

Lewis, S., & Tolla, J. (2003). Creating and using tactile experience books for young children with visual impairments. *Teaching Exceptional Children, 35*(3), 22–28.

Light, J. (1997). "Communication is the essence of human life": Reflections on communicative competence. *Augmentative and Alternative Communication, 13*, 61–70.

Martin, J. E., Van Dycke, J. L., Christensen, W. R., Greene, B. A., Gardner, J. E., & Lovett, D. L. (2006). Increasing student participation in their transition IEP meetings: Establishing the self-directed IEP as an evidenced-based practice. *Exceptional Children, 72*, 299–316.

McDonnell, J., Mathot-Buckner, C., Thorson, N., & Fister, S. (2001). Supporting the inclusion of students with moderate and severe disabilities in junior high school general education classes: The effects of classwide peer tutoring, multi-element curriculum, and accommodations. *Education & Treatment of Children, 24*, 141–160.

McDonnell, J., Thorson, N., Allen, C., & Mathot-Buckner, C. (2000). The effects of partner learning during spelling for students with severe disabilities and their peers. *Journal of Behavioral Education, 10*, 107–121.

Meyer, L. E., & Ostrosky, M. M. (2014). Measuring the friendships of young children with disabilities: A review of the literature. *Topics in Early Childhood Special Education, 34*, 186–196. doi: 10.1177/0271121413513038

Morningstar, M. E., Frey, B. B., Noonan, P. M., Ng, J., Clavenna-Deane, B., Graves, P., & Williams-Diehm, K. (2010). A preliminary investigation of the relationship of transition preparation and self-determination for students with disabilities in postsecondary educational settings. *Career Development for Exceptional Individuals, 33*, 80–94.

Nagro, S. A. (2015). PROSE checklist. Strategies for improving school-to-home written communication. *Teaching Exceptional Children, 47*(5), 256–263.

Odom, S. L., Zercher, C., Li, S., Marquart, J. M., Sandall, S., & Brown, W. H. (2006). Social acceptance and rejection of preschool children with disabilities: A mixed-method analysis. *Journal of Educational Psychology, 98*, 807–823.

Palmer, S. B. (2010). Self-determination: A life span perspective. *Focus on Exceptional Children, 42*(6), 1–16.

Palmer, S. B., & Wehmeyer, M. L. (2003). Promoting self-determination in early elementary school. Teaching self-regulated problem-solving and goal setting skills. *Remedial and Special Education, 24*, 115–126.

Palmer, S. B., & Wehmeyer, M. L. (2002). *Parent's guide to the self-determined learning model of instruction for early elementary students.* Lawrence, KS: Beach Center on Disability.

Park, C. (1982). *The siege: The first eight years of an autistic child with an epilogue, fifteen years later.* Boston, MA: Atlantic-Little Brown.

Parker, J. G., Rubin, K. H., Earth, S., Wojslawowicz, J. C., & Buskirk, A. A. (2006). Peer relationships, child development, and adjustment: A developmental psychopathology perspective. In D. Cicchetti (Ed.), *Developmental psychopathology: Vol. 3: Risk, disorder, and adaptation* (pp. 419–493). New York, NY: Wiley.

Ramirez, F. (2001). Technology and parent involvement. *Clearing House, 75*(1), 30–31.

Reid, R., Trout, A. L., & Schwarz, M. (2005). Self-regulation interventions for children with attention deficit/ hyperactivity disorder. *Exceptional Children, 71*, 361–377.

Rohrbeck, C. A., Ginsburg-Block, M. D., Fantuzzo, J. W., & Miller, T. R. (2003). Peer-assisted learning interventions with elementary school students: A meta-analytic review. *Journal of Educational Psychology, 95*, 240–257.

Rosa's Law, Pub. L. No. 111-256, § 1, 124 Stat. 2643 (2010).

Rowland, C. (2004a). *Communication matrix. A communication skill assessment for individuals at the earliest stages of communication development.* Portland, OR: Oregon Health Sciences University, Center on Self-Determination.

Rowland, C. (2004b). *Communication matrix especially for parents.* Portland, OR: Oregon Health Sciences University, Center on Self-Determination.

Ryndak, D., Lehr, D., Ward, T., & DeBevoise, H. (2014). Collaboration and teaming in effective inclusive schools. In J. McLeskey, N. L. Waldron, F. Spooner, & B. Algozzine (Eds.), *Handbook of research and practice for effective inclusive schools* (pp. 395–409). New York: NY: Routledge.

Schaffner, C. B., & Buswell, B. E. (1992). *Connecting students: A guide to thoughtful friendship facilitation for educators and families.* Colorado Springs, CO: PEAK Parent Center.

Siegel-Causey, E., & Bashinski, S. M. (1997). Enhancing initial communication and responsiveness of learners with multiple disabilities: A tri-focus framework for partners. *Focus on Autism and Other Developmental Disabilities, 12,* 105–120.

Siegel-Causey, E., McMorris, C., McGowen, S., & Sands-Buss, S. (1998). In junior high you take earth science. Including a student with severe disabilities into an academic class. *Teaching Exceptional Children, 31,* 66–72.

Siperstein, G. N., & Leffert, J. S. (1997). A comparison of socially accepted and rejected children with mental retardation. *American Journal on Mental Retardation, 101,* 339–351.

Smith, P. M. (2003). You are not alone. For parents when they learn their child has a disability. *News Digest, 20* (3rd ed.). Retrieved from the National Information Center for Children and Youth with Disabilities website: www.nichcy.org

Sobsey, D. (2002). Exceptionality, education, & maltreatment. *Exceptionality, 10*(1), 29–46.

Taffel, R. (2001). *Getting through to difficult kids and parents.* New York, NY: The Guildford Press.

Thuppal, M., & Sobsey, D. (2004). Children with special health care needs. In F. P. Orelove, D. Sobsey, & R. K. Silberman (Eds.), *Educating children with multiple disabilities: A collaborative approach* (4th ed., pp. 311–377). Baltimore, MD: Paul H. Brookes.

Uphold, N., & Hudson, M. (2012). Student-focused planning. In D. W. Test (Ed.), *Evidence-based instructional strategies for transition* (pp. 55–77). Baltimore, MD: Paul H. Brookes.

U.S. Department of Health and Human Services, Administration for Children and Families, Administration on Children, Youth and Families, Children's Bureau. (2013). *Child maltreatment 2012.* Available from: http://www.acf.hhs.gov/programs/cb/research-data-technology/statistics-research/child-maltreatment

Wehmeyer, M. L. (2003). A functional theory of self-determination: Definition and categorization. In M. L. Wehmeyer, B. J. Abery, D. E. Mithaug, & R. J. Stancliffe

(Eds.), *Theory in self-determination: Foundations for educational practice* (pp. 174–181). Springfield, IL: Thomas.

Weir, K., Crooney, M., Walter, M., Moss, C., & Carter, E. (n.d.). *Fostering self-determination among children and youth with disabilities—ideas from parents for parents.* Retrieved from the Waisman Center's University Center for Excellence in Developmental Disabilities website: http://www.waisman.wisc.edu/naturalsupports/pdfs/FosteringSelfDetermination.pdf

Wolery, M., Werts, M. G., Snyder, E. D., & Caldwell, N. K. (1994). Efficacy of constant time delay implemented by peer tutors in general education classrooms. *Journal of Behavioral Education, 4,* 415–436.

Wolfe, P. S., & Hall, T. E. (2003). Making inclusion a reality for students with severe disabilities. *Teaching Exceptional Children, 35*(4), 56–60.

Chapter 11: Secondary School Years

Albrecht, G. L., & Devlieger, P. J. (1999). The disability paradox: High quality of life against all odds. *Social Science & Medicine, 48,* 977–988.

Ali, M. M., Amialchuk, A., & Nikaj, S. (2014). Alcohol consumption and social network ties among adolescents: Evidence from Add Health. *Addictive Behaviors, 39*(5), 918–922.

Alwell, M., & Cobb, B. (2006). *Teaching functional life skills to youth with disabilities.* National Secondary Transition Technical Assistance Center. Retrieved from: http://www.nsttac.org/sites/default/files/assets/pdf/pdf/life_skills_executive_summary.pdf

American Psychological Association. (2002). *A reference for professionals: Developing adolescents.* Retrieved from: http://www.apa.org/pi/families/resources/develop.pdf. Read, 5, 2015

Archer, A. L., & Hughes, C. A. (2011). *Explicit instruction: Effective and efficient teaching.* New York, NY: Guilford Press.

Bremer, C. D., & Smith, J. (2004). *Teaching social skills.* Information

brief: Addressing trends and developments in secondary education, 3 (5), National Center on Secondary Education and Transition. www.ncset.org

Brinthaupt, T. M., & Lipka, R. P. (Eds.). (2012). *Understanding early adolescent self and identity: Applications and interventions.* New York: SUNY Press.

Centers for Disease Control. (2015). *Teens (ages 12–19)—risk behaviors.* Retrieved from: http://www.cdc.gov/parents/teens/risk_behaviors.html

Chapman, C., Laird, J., Ifill, N., & KewalRamani, A. (2011). Trends in high school dropout and completion rates in the United States: 1972–2009. *Compendium Report.* NCES 2012-006. Washington D.C: National Center for Education Statistics.

Chang, Y.Y.C., & Chiou, W. B. (2014). Diversity beliefs and postformal thinking in late adolescence: A cognitive basis of multicultural literacy. *Asia Pacific Education Review 15*(4), 585–592.

Christiansen, K.M.H., Qureshi, F., Schaible, A., Park, S., & Gittelsohn, J. (2013). Environmental factors that impact the eating behaviors of low-income African American adolescents in Baltimore city. *Journal of Nutrition Education & Behavior, 45*(6), 652–661.

Eccles, J. S. (1999). The development of children ages 6–14. *The Future of Children When School Is Out, 19*(2), 30–44.

Families and Advocates Partnership for Education. (2001). *School accommodations and modifications.* Retrieved from: http://www.wrightslaw.com/info/sec504.accoms.mods.pdf

Fuchs, D., & Fuchs, L. (1995). Sometimes separate is better. *Educational Leadership, 52*(4), 22–26.

Giedd, J. N. (2012). The digital revolution and adolescent brain evolution. *Journal of Adolescent Health, 51,* 101–105.

Greydanus, D. E., & Bashe, P. (2003). *Caring for your teenager.* New York: Bantamum.

Hair, E. C., Jager, J., & Garrett, S. B. (2002, July). *Helping teens develop healthy social skills and relationships: What research shows about navigating adolescence.* Retrieved from:

http://www.hhs.gov/ash/oah/oah-initiatives/ta/paf_training2_healthysocialskills.pdf

Halpern, R., Heckman, P. E., & Larson, R. W. (2013). *Realizing the potential of learning in middle adolescence.* The Sally and Dick Roberts Coyote Foundation. Retrieved from: http://www.erikson.edu/wp-content/uploads/Realizing-the-Potential-of-Learning-in-Middle-Adolescence.pdf

Hendrickson, J. M., Ross, J. R., Mercer, C. D., & Walker, P. (1988). The multidisciplinary team: Training educators to serve middle school students with special needs. *The Clearing House, 62*(2), 84–86.

Heward, W. L. (2013). *Exceptional children: An introduction to special education* (10th ed.). Boston: Pearson.

Hines, R. A. (2001). *Inclusion in middle schools.* Champaign, IL: ERIC Clearinghouse on Elementary and Early Childhood Education.

Hollingsworth, J. R., & Ybarra, S. E. (2008). *Explicit direct instruction (EDI): The power of the well-crafted, well-taught lesson.* Thousand Oaks, CA: Corwin Press.

Individuals With Disabilities Education Act, 20 U.S.C. § 1400 (2004).

Jaramillo, M. (2012). *Our mother's tears: A book about gangs.* USA: Trafford Publishing.

KidsGrowth.com. (n.d.) Stages of adolescent development. Retrieved from: http://www.kidsgrowth.com/resources/articledetail.cfm?id=1140

LaVoie, J. C. (1976). Ego identity formation in middle adolescence. *Journal of Youth and Adolescence, 5*(4), 371–385.

Mandlawitz, M. (2007). *What every teacher should know about IDEA laws and regulations.* Boston: Pearson.

Manheim, J. K., Zievo, D., Eltz, D. R., Slon, S., & Wang, N. (2013). *Adolescent development.* Medline Plus. Retrieved from: http://www.nlm.nih.gov/medlineplus/ency/article/002003.htm

Manning, M. A. (2007). Self-concept and self-esteem in adolescents. *Principal Leadership (Middle School Ed.), 7*(6), 11–15.

National Association of School Psychologists. (2002). Social skills: Promoting positive behavior, academic success, and school safety. Retrieved from: http://www.nasponline.org/resources/factsheets/socialskills_fs.aspx

National Collaborative on Workforce and Disability. (2011). Bullying and disability harassment in the workplace: What youth should know. Information brief, 11. Retrieved from: http://www.ncwd-youth.info/information-brief-29

National Tutoring Association. (2010). *Peer tutoring factsheet.* Retrieved from: https://peers.aristotlecircle.com/uploads/NTA_Peer_Tutoring_Factsheet_020107.pdf

Oberle, E., Schonert-Reichl, K. A., & Thomson, K. C. (2010). Understanding the link between social and emotional well-being and peer relations in early adolescence: Gender-specific predictors of peer acceptance. *Journal of Youth and Adolescence, 39*(11), 1330–1342.

Oswalt, A., & Zupanick, C. E. (n.d.). Erik Erikson and self-identity. Retrieved from: http://www.sevencounties.org/poc/view_doc.php?type=doc&id=41163&cn=1310

Ottoni-Wilhelm, M., Estell, D. B., & Perdue, N. H. (2014). Role-modeling and conversations about giving in the socialization of adolescent charitable giving and volunteering. *Journal of Adolescence, 37*(1), 53–66.

Patton, J. R., Payne, J. S., & Berne-Smith, M. (1986). *Mental retardation.* Columbus, OH., Merrill.

Peterson, K. (2004). *Supporting dynamic development of youth with disabilities during transition: A guide for families.* Information Brief. Volume 3 Issue 2. Mineapolis. MN: National Center on Secondary Education and Transition.

Preckel, F., Niepel, C., Schneider, M., & Brunner, M. (2013). Self-concept in adolescence: A longitudinal study on reciprocal effects of self-perceptions in academic and social domains. *Journal of Adolescence, 36*(6), 1165–1175.

Prince, D., & Nurius, P. S. (2014). The role of positive academic self-concept in promoting school success. *Children and Youth Services Review, 43*, 145–152.

Schwab, S., Gebhardt, M., & Krammer, B. (2015). Self-rated social inclusion to social behavior. An empirical study of students with and without special education needs in secondary schools. *European Journal of Special Needs Education, 30*(1), 1–14.

Skär, L. (2003). Peer and adult relationships of adolescents with disabilities. *Journal of Adolescence, 26*(6), 635–649.

Spano, S. (2004). *Stages of adolescent development: Research facts and findings.* Ithaca, NY: ACT for Youth: Upstate Center of Excellence, Cornell University.

Stang, J., & Story, M. (2005). *Guidelines for adolescent nutrition services.* Minneapolis: University of Minnesota School of Public Health.

Steedly, K. M., Schwartz, A., Levin, M., & Luke, S. D. (2008). Social skills and academic achievement. *Evidence for Education, 3*(2), 1–8.

WebMD. (2012). Physical development, ages 11 to 14 years guide. Retrieved from: http://www.webmd.com/children/tc/physical-development-ages-11-to-14-years-topic-overview

What Works Clearinghouse. (2012). *Peer-assisted learning strategies.* Retrieved from: http://ies.ed.gov/ncee/wwc/pdf/intervention_reports/wwc_pals_013112.pdf.

Wiium, N., Breivik, K., & Wold, B. (2006). The relationship between smoker role models, and intentions to smoke among adolescents. *Journal of Youth and Adolescence, 35*(4), 549–560.

Zambo, D. M. (2010). Strategies to enhance the social identities and social networks of adolescent students with disabilities. *Teaching Exceptional Children, 43*(2), 28–35.

Zeedyk, S. M., Rodriguez, G., Tipton, L. A., Baker, B. L., & Blacher, J. (2014). Bullying of youth with autism spectrum disorder, intellectual disability, or typical development: Victim and parent perspectives. *Research in Autism Spectrum Disorders, 8*(9), 1173–1183.

Chapter 12: Postschool

AHEAD. (2012). *Supporting accommodation requests: Guidance on documentation practices.* Available at: http://www.ahead

.org/uploads/docs/resources/ Final_AHEAD_Supporting%20 Accommodation%20Requests%20 with%20Q&A%2009_12.pdf

Amado, A., Stancliffe, R., McCarron, M., & McCallion, P. (2013). Social inclusion and community participation of individuals with intellectual/developmental disabilities. *Intellectual and Developmental Disabilities, 51*(5), 360–375.

Blackorby, J., & Wagner, M. (1996). Longitudinal postschool outcomes of youth with disabilities: Findings from the National Longitudinal Transition Study. *Exceptional Children, 62,* 399–413.

Blanck, P., & Martinis, J. (2015). The right to make choices: The National Resource Center for Supported Decision-Making. *Inclusion, 3,* 24–33.

Brooke, V., Revell, W. G., McDonough, J., & Green, H. (2013). Transition planning and community resources. In P. Wehman, *Life Beyond the Classroom* (pp. 143–171). Baltimore, MD: Paul H. Brookes Publishing.

Carter, E. W., Austin, D., & Trainor, A. A. (2011). Factors associated with early career work experiences of adolescents with severe disabilities. *Intellectual and Developmental Disabilities, 49*(4), 233–347.

Center for Literacy, Education and Employment. (n.d.). Equipped for the Future Content Standards. Retrieved May 19, 2015, from: http:// eff.clee.utk.edu/fundamentals/ eff_standards.htm

Centers for Medicare & Medicaid Services. (2014). *Home and community based services fact sheet.* Retrieved May 16, 2015, from Home and Community-Based Services: http://www.medicaid.gov/medicaid-chip-program-information/by-topics/ long-term-services-and-supports/ home-and-community-based-services/downloads/final-rule-fact-sheet.pdf

Cimera, R. E., Wehman, P., West, M., & Burgess, S. (2012). Do sheltered workshops enhance employment outcomes for adults with autism spectrum disorder? *Autism, 16*(1), 87–94.

Council for Exceptional Children. (2015). Life centered education. Available

from: https://www.cec.sped.org/ Publications/LCE-Transition-Curriculum/Benefits-of-Using-LC

Eisenman, L., & Celestin, S. (2012). Social skills, supports, and networks in adolescent transition education. In M. L. Wehmeyer & K. W. Webb, *Handbook of adolescent transition education for youth with disabilities* (pp. 223–232). New York: Routledge.

Erickson, W. A., von Schrader, S., Bruyere, S. M., & VanLooy, S. A. (2014). The employment environment: Employer perspectives, policies, and practices regarding the employment of persons with disabilities. *Rehabilitation Counseling Bulletin, 57*(4), 195–208.

Federal Student Aid. (2015). Students with intellectual disabilities. Available at: https://studentaid. ed.gov/eligibility/intellectual-disabilities#ctp-programs

Getzel, E., & Webb, K. (2012). Transition to postsecondary education. In M. Wehmeyer & K. Webb (Eds.), *Handbook of adolescent transition education for youth with disabilities* (pp. 295–311). New York: Routledge.

Haber, M., Mazzotti, V., Mustian, A., Rowe, D., Bartholomew, A., Test, D., & Fowler, C. (2015). What works, when, for whom, and with whom: A meta-analytic review of predictors of postsecondary success for students with disabilities. *Review of Educational Research.* First published online April 22, 2015. doi:10.3102/0034654315583135

Halpern, A. (1994). The transition of youth with disabilities to adult life: A position statement of the Division on Career Development and Transition. *Career Development for Exceptional Individuals, 17*(2), 115–124.

Heath Resource Center. (2014). *Planning ahead: Financial aid for students with disabilities, 2014–15 edition.* National Youth Transitions Center, The George Washington University. Available at: https://heath.gwu.edu/ files/downloads/2014_2015_heath_ financial_aid_ publication.pdf

Individual with Disabilities Education Act, 34 C.F.R. § 300.1 (2006).

Jans, L. H., Kaye, H. S., & Jones, E. C. (2012). Getting hired: Successfully employed people with disabilities

offer advice on disclosure, interviewing, and job search. *Journal of Occupational Rehabilitation, 22*(2), 155–165.

Jed Foundation. (2015). *Protecting your child's mental health: What parents can do.* Retrieved May 19, 2015, from: https://www.jedfoundation .org/assets/Programs/Program_ downloads/parentsguide.pdf

Kim, R. K., & Dymond, S. K. (2012). A national study of community living: Impact of type of residence and hours of in-home support. *Research & Practice for Persons with Severe Disabilities, 37*(2), 116–129.

Larson, S. A., Salmi, P., Smith, D., Anderson, L., & Hewitt, A. S. (2013). *Residential services for persons with intellectual or developmental disabilities: Status and trends through 2011.* Minneapolis, MN: University of Minnesota, Research and Training Center on Community Living, Institute on Community Integration.

National Collaborative on Workforce and Disability for Youth. (2012). Helping youth build work skills for job success: Tips for parents and families. Washington, DC. Available from: http://www.ncwd-youth.info/ information-brief-34

National Council on Disability. (2005). *The current state of transportation for people with disabilities in the United States.* Washington, DC: National Council on Disability.

Newman, L., Wagner, M., Knokey, A., Marder, C., Nagle, K., Shaver, D., et al. (2011). *The post high school outcomes of young adults with disabilities up to 8 years after high school. A Report from the National Longitudinal Transition Study–2 (NLTS–2) (NCSER 2011-3005).* Menlo Park, CA: SRI International.

NTACT. (n.d.). Predictors by Outcome Area. National Technical Assistance Center on Transition. Available at: http://transitionta.org/sites/default/ files/Pred_Outcomes_0.pdf

PACER Center's Family-to-Family Health Information Center. (2015). Transition planning information for physicians to share with families. Retrieved May 20, 2015, from: http:// www.pacer.org/health/For-Medical-Professionals/trans-planning-info .asp

Pleet, A. M. & Wandry, D. L. (2009). Introduction to the role of families in secondary transition. In D.L. Wandry & A.M. Pleet, *Engaging and Empowering Families in Secondary Transition: A Practitioner's Guide* (pp. 1–20). Arlington, Virginia: Council for Exceptional Children.

Test, D. W., Fowler, C. H., Richter, S. M., White, J., Mazzotti, V., Walker, A. R.... Kortering, L. (2009). Evidence-based practices in secondary transition. *Career Development for Exceptional Individuals, 32,* 115–128.

Test, D. W., Richter, S., & Walker, A. R. (2012). Life skills and community-based instruction. In M. L. Wehmeyer & K. W. Webb, *Handbook of adolescent transition education for youth with disabilities* (pp. 121–138). New York: Routledge.

Ticha, R., Hewitt, A., Nord, D., & Larson, S. (2013). System and individual outcomes and their predictors in services and supports for people with IDD. *Intellectual and Developmental Disabilities, 51*(5), 298–315.

U.S. Bureau of Labor Statistics. (2014, June 11). Economic news release. Retrieved May 17, 2015, from Bureau of Labor Statistics U.S. Department of Labor: http://www.bls.gov/news.release/disabl.a.htm

U.S. Equal Employment Opportunity Commission. (2009, February 4). Americans with Disabilities Act questions and answers. Retrieved May 16, 2015, from Americans with Disabilities Act: http://www.ada.gov/q&aeng02.htm

Vining, A. (2012). *Alternatives to guardianship for adults.* Everett, WA: Northwest Justice Project.

Wagner, M., Newman, L., Cameto, R., & Levine, P. (2005). *Changes over time in the early postschool outcomes of youth with disabilities. A report of findings from the National Longitudinal Transition Study (NLTS) and the National Longitudinal Transition Study–2 (NLTS2).* Menlo Park, CA: SRI International. Available at: www.nlts2.org/reports/2005_06/nlts2_report_2005_06_complete.pdf

Wandry, D., & Pleet, A. (2009). *Engaging and empowering families in secondary transition: A practitioner's guide.* Arlington, VA: Council for Exceptional Children.

Wehman, P., & Brooke, V. (2013). Securing meaningful work in the community: Vocational internships, placements, and careers. In P. Wehman, *Life Beyond the Classroom* (pp. 309–338). Baltimore, MD: Paul H. Brookes.

Widmer, E. D., Kempf-Constantin, N., Robert-Tissot, C., Lanzi, F., & Carminati, G. G. (2008). How central and connected am I in my family? Family-based social capital of individuals with intellectual disability. *Research in Developmental Disabilities: A Multidisciplinary Journal, 29*(2), 176–187.

INDEX